TAIWAN

TAIWAN

Nation-State or Province?

FIFTH EDITION

JOHN F. COPPER
Rhodes College

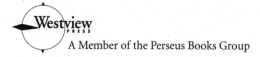

Westview
PRESS
A Member of the Perseus Books Group

Library of Congress Cataloging-in-Publication Data
Copper, John Franklin.
Taiwan : nation-state or province? / John F. Copper. — 5th ed.
p. cm.
Includes bibliographical references and index.
ISBN 978-0-8133-4422-5 (alk. paper)
1. Taiwan. 2. Taiwan—International status. I. Title.
DS799.C67 2009
951.24'9—dc22
2008034596
10 9 8 7 6 5 4 3 2 1

To My Loving Wife

CONTENTS

PREFACE

According to a recent edition of the US Central Intelligence Agency's often-cited *World Factbook* there are 268 "entities" in the world, of which 192 are "independent states" and 63 are "dependencies and areas of special sovereignty." Taiwan alone is in the category of "other." The reason it is in this category is because whether Taiwan is a sovereign nation-state or a province of China is in question.

Much else about Taiwan is either unique or uncertain, or both.

In the past Taiwan was called a "pariah nation"—an authoritarian country diplomatically isolated. But even before it lost that opprobrium Taiwan became widely hailed as a "model country" for its economic (rapid growth with equity) and political (quick but peaceful democratization) "miracles."

Taiwan ranks very high in almost all of the criteria used to measure globalization—trade, foreign investment, travel in and out, etc. Yet it is the world's most isolated nation (if it is a nation) by other criteria—ranking last in memberships in international organizations and second to the last in the number of foreign embassies it hosts. Taiwan is the only important "national entity" not a member of the United Nations.

Taiwan has one of the best militaries in the world. It is often listed as a country that is capable of building nuclear and chemical/biological weapons. Some say it has already. Yet Taiwan's existence is tenuous; it would likely survive but a few days or weeks if the United States were to decline to guarantee its security.

Leaders in Beijing say Taiwan is China's territory. In 2005, China's parliament wrote a law declaring it will use nonpeaceful measures against Taiwan if it declares independence—even though the current government of China has never exercised control over Taiwan, and its leaders say they will not kill their own people in war.

America's Taiwan policy is likewise contradictory. When establishing diplomatic ties with Beijing in 1979, the Carter administration agreed that Taiwan is a part of

China. Yet only a few months later Congress passed a law (the only one of its kind) setting the parameters of US-Taiwan relations that treated Taiwan as a sovereign state.

So is Taiwan a US protectorate? If America abandons Taiwan, it loses its credibility and its allies in Asia. It may as well retreat into isolationism. If Taiwan were to allow the military forces of another country a presence on the island or proclaim its legal independence, China would likely use its military to prevent either.

Thus most analysts label the Taiwan Strait the world's number one "flashpoint." The world's only superpower and its only rising power, both with nuclear weapons targeted at the other, seem poised to fight over Taiwan—the only nonnegotiable issue between them.

In 1996, they almost did. Taiwan says that being a democracy it should decide its future. It held its first-ever direct presidential election to underscore this. Seeing this as a sign of secession, China conducted intimidating missile tests near Taiwan's shores. In reaction the United States sent the biggest military force to the area since the Vietnam War. For a while a U.S.-China conflict appeared imminent.

When asked about independence or unification with China, the vast majority of Taiwan's citizens favors the status quo. This arguably isn't relevant, even though Taiwan is a democracy, and it should matter. Similarly it does not help solve the matter of Taiwan's status, now or in the future.

Two other puzzling facts about Taiwan: It is more linked to China economically than most members of the European Community are to each other. Taiwan's economic health literally depends on China, and most people in Taiwan know this. Political links, however, are almost nonexistent. Will economics or politics decide Taiwan's future? No one seems to know.

In the following pages the author will examine the background, details, and problems associated with this "other" place. This means looking at its geography, history, society, economy, political system, and its foreign and defense policy with an eye on the issue of Taiwan having nation-state status or not.

The Chinese terms used in this book have been mostly rendered into English script using the Wade-Giles system long used in Taiwan, though with an individual's name, the author uses the spelling that that person prefers. The term "Beijing" is used for the capital of China; "Peking" is used for that same place when it was written that way in the past. In some instances, for convenience, the spelling used in China is included in parentheses for names or places.

JOHN F. COPPER

ACRONYMS

ADB	Asian Development Bank
APEC	Asia Pacific Economic Cooperation
ASEAN	Association of Southeast Asian Nations
BCC	Broadcasting Corporation of China
CAL	China Airlines
CNA	Central News Agency
DPP	Democratic Progressive Party
EPZ	export processing zones
GATT	General Agreement on Tariffs and Trade
GNP	gross national product
GSP	Generalized System of Preferences
JCRR	Joint Commission on Rural Reconstruction
KMT	Nationalist Party or Kuomintang
NIC	newly industrializing country
NP	New Party
PFP	People First Party
PLA	People's Liberation Army
TMD	theater missile defense
TRA	Taiwan Relations Act
TSU	Taiwan Solidarity Union
WTO	World Trade Organization

Taiwan

1

THE LAND AND THE PEOPLE

LOCATED IN THE WESTERN PACIFIC just east of the south-central coast of China, the island of Taiwan comprises most of the land area of the nation known officially as the Republic of China—also called Nationalist China, Free China, the Republic of China on Taiwan, the Republic of Taiwan—but most often referred to as just Taiwan. Taipei is its capital. In the West, Taiwan was formerly known as Formosa. The term Formosa has fallen into disuse, though it has been revived at times by advocates of Taiwan's independence looking for a non-Chinese term for the island. Some Aborigines call for using the word "Kaitagelan" or some other native word for the island and/or the nation. Chinese leaders in Beijing regard Taiwan not as a nation but rather as territory belonging to the People's Republic of China and refer to the island of Taiwan, the Pescadores, and some other islands close to Taiwan as "Taiwan Province." In the past, the government of Taiwan likewise espoused a one-China policy and claimed sovereignty over all of China, or both China and Taiwan, saying that the government in Beijing was illegal and illegitimate. Subsequently, government officials in Taiwan proclaimed both Beijing and Taipei possessed sovereignty and spoke of unification at some unspecified time in the future. Others, especially the opposition Democratic Progressive Party (DPP), said that Taiwan was not a part of China and should be legally independent. Chen Shui-bian, a member of the DPP, became president in 2000 and promptly vowed not to declare independence; but his subsequent statements and actions indicated legal separation from China was his intention. The DPP was soundly defeated in a legislative election in early 2008 and then, two months later, lost the presidency to the

Nationalist Party or Kuomintang (KMT). Thence, formally splitting from China seemed to be a losing issue. Nonetheless, Taiwan's status, being part of China (however defined), or not, still divides the country's leaders and its population. The political parties and the various ethnic groups espouse different and often clashing views on independence, self-determination, one China versus two, one China and one Taiwan, "Greater China," unification, and so on. The United States, in whose hands Taiwan's fate ostensibly rests, and most other nations treat Taiwan as *de facto* independent, but *de jure* part of China—a seeming contradiction.

Physical Setting

More than a dozen smaller islands surround the island of Taiwan and the various islets considered geologically linked to it. Also under the Republic of China's governance are the Pescadore (P'eng-hu) Islands, sixty-four in all—twenty of which are inhabited; Orchid Island (Lan Tao); Green Island (Lu Tao); some smaller islands off Taiwan's eastern coast; the Offshore Islands (the Quemoy and Matsu groups and some other small islands near them); and some islands in the South China Sea. All the territory under Taipei's control is also claimed by the People's Republic of China, which regards it as "Taiwan Province"—except for the Offshore Islands, which it regards as a part of Fukien (spelled Fujian in China) Province, and the islands in the South China Sea.[1]

Approximately 230 miles long and 85 miles wide at the center, the surface area of the island of Taiwan is 13,814 square miles, about the size of Holland or the US states of Massachusetts, Rhode Island, and Connecticut combined. The Pescadores add another 49 square miles, Quemoy about 68 square miles, and Matsu 10 square miles. If Taiwan and the other territory under the jurisdiction of the Republic of China were regarded as a province of China, it would be the People's Republic of China's second smallest province (the smallest before Hainan Island was made a province in 1988). Taiwan has less than 1/260th of China's land area. Yet if Taiwan were seen as a nation, it would rank above average in population (number 49 of 221 countries) and just below average in land area (number 136 of 232).[2]

The Pescadore Islands lay twenty-five miles off Taiwan's west coast, slightly south of the island's center. The Quemoy group (six islands, two of them controlled by the People's Republic of China) is located within shouting distance (at the closest point) of Fukien Province of the People's Republic of China, west of central Taiwan. This island group is situated strategically near the port of Amoy. The Matsu group is located northwest of Taiwan and, like the Quemoy group, is close to the Mainland. It is near the Chinese port of Fuchou. Both the Quemoy and Matsu island groups are geologically part of China.

The Republic of China also lays territorial claim to some of the Pratas (Tungsha) Islands and Spratly (Nansha) Islands, located in the South China Sea, and maintains military forces on islands in both groups. These island groups are small but strategically located adjacent to sea-lanes in the South China Sea. In addition, ownership may provide the basis for claims on ocean territory and undersea minerals, including oil, around the islands. These claims involve Taipei in a territorial dispute with the People's Republic of China, Vietnam, the Philippines, Malaysia, Brunei, and Indonesia.[3] Taipei's position vis-à-vis the People's Republic of China has differed, however, from its disputes with the other claimants. The dispute was not about whether the islands were Chinese territory, but rather about which government has legal jurisdiction. Recently, this has changed. In fact, Taipei has made claim to at least part of the Spratly Islands based on Japanese jurisdiction over the islands when Taiwan was part of the Japanese Empire and the islands were considered part of Kaohsiung "prefecture."[4]

Taipei has claimed ownership of the Senkaku Islands, or Tiaoyutai (meaning "fishing stage" in Chinese) Islands—eight tiny, uninhabited islets just over one hundred miles northwest of Keelung. This claim was made in 1971 after the US government agreed to return the Ryukyu Islands, which included the Senkakus, to Japan. The issue grew more intense after UN reports suggested the presence of undersea oil, possibly very large deposits, in the vicinity. Taipei based its claim on the fact that Taiwanese fishermen had been using the islands for some years as a stopping-off place to gather bird eggs and dry their nets. Also, since the islands are geologically part of China's continental shelf, and since Taipei claimed sovereignty over all of China at this time, it also made an argument based on geography.[5] Beijing likewise laid claim to the islands.

The United States turned over the islands to Japan without paying much attention to either Taipei's or Beijing's claims. The Japanese government assumed sovereignty over the islands at this time, rejecting both Beijing's and Taipei's positions. The territorial issue remained essentially dormant until 1989, when the Japanese navy chased some Taiwan's fishermen away from the islands. The next year, Japan built a lighthouse on one of the islands. Subsequently, citizens from Taiwan organized a protest and put an Olympic torch on one of the islands in the chain. In 1992, China's legislature passed a territorial sea law that declared the islands to be part of the People's Republic of China. In 1996, groups from Hong Kong and Taiwan went to the islands to support Chinese sovereignty over the islands, and one protester was killed. This incident focused global attention on the dispute. China and Japan continue aggressively to make claim to the islands. Taiwan does not.

In the past, advocates of Taiwan's independence proposed the abandonment of Taiwan's claim to Quemoy and Matsu so that Taiwan would be more distinctly separate from China and thus legally independent, but they found the public did not support this view. There has been talk that Taiwan may give up its claim to islands in the South China Sea, but this has not provoked much controversy. Taipei may quietly drop its claim to the Senkaku Islands since China and Japan have sounder claims. It seems less likely to drop its claims to islands in the South China Sea or the Offshore Islands.

The island of Taiwan is positioned between 21°459 and 25°509 north latitude, which in the Western Hemisphere would be just north of Cuba. The northern part of Taiwan shares the same latitude as southern Florida. The Tropic of Cancer bisects the island just below its center. Taiwan is bordered on the east by the Pacific Ocean, on the west by the Taiwan (Formosa) Strait (95 miles from China at its closest point), on the northwest by the East China Sea, and on the southwest by the South China Sea. To the north, less than 80 miles away, lie the Ryukyu Islands, Japan's southernmost territory—the closest land area to Taiwan. The island of Kyushu (the southernmost of Japan's main islands), however, is 700 miles away, and Tokyo is 1,274 miles away. Less than 100 miles to Taiwan's south, separated by the Bashi Channel, lie the Philippine Islands, though the island of Luzon is 230 miles from Taiwan. East of Taiwan is the great expanse of the Pacific Ocean and finally Mexico. Of the major cities in the region, Hong Kong is the closest to Taiwan—483 miles away. Next in proximity is Guangzhou, which is 564 miles from Taipei. Manila is 705 miles from Taiwan, Seoul is 885, and Beijing is 1,677 miles away.

Taiwan and the Pescadores lie on the edge of the East Asian continental shelf. Thus, to the west of Taiwan, the water (in the Taiwan Strait) is relatively shallow, its depth averaging 300 feet. The ocean waters off Taiwan's east coast, in contrast, are deep; in fact, thirty miles offshore in the Pacific Ocean, the seabed drops precipitously to a depth of 13,000 feet.

Some geologists say that Taiwan was originally part of the Asian mainland. The depth of the water in the Taiwan Strait, the configuration of Taiwan's coastlines, and the age of rocks and their formations on Taiwan's periphery all indicate that the time of Taiwan's birth was not the same as that of the Ryukyu Islands to the north or the Philippines to the south. The soil, plants, and animal life do not suggest great differences between Taiwan and China.[6] Yet others contend that because Taiwan has volcanic soil and is part of the long chain of islands extending south from the Alaskan Aleutian Islands, the island's origins are similar to those of Japan, the Philippines, and other islands off the eastern Asia coast that were created by volcanic activity in the Pacific Ocean. The frequency of earthquakes—an average of 160 per year—also makes Taiwan resemble Japan more than South China.[7] This evidence suggests either a more distant time connection, or none at all, to the Asian mainland.[8]

Mountains cover approximately two-thirds of Taiwan's surface. The highest and most rugged are found in the eastern part of the island. In some areas, mountains or mountain cliffs extend right up to Taiwan's eastern shore. Fifty peaks tower near or above 10,000 feet; Yu Shan (Jade Mountain), reaching 13,114 feet above sea level, is the highest. When Taiwan was part of the Japanese empire, Yu Shan was labeled Japan's highest mountain.

Because the Central Mountain Range, which traverses Taiwan from north to south as if it were a spine, lies close to the island's eastern shoreline, there are few natural harbors there. Suao Bay is an exception. Keelung harbor, which serves Taipei, is located on the north coast. In contrast, the west coast has good ports— including Kaohsiung, Tainan, and Taichung—and is home to most of Taiwan's population and all of its large cities.

Foothills surround the Central Mountain Range and account for nearly 50 percent of Taiwan's surface area. Around the foothills are sloping tablelands, many terraced for rice cultivation. Below the tablelands stretch plains and then basins. The plains constitute Taiwan's most productive farming areas. On the west coast there are tidal basins and, in some areas, swamps. Elsewhere there are spits and sandbars. On the east side of the island, the mountains turn into foothills and plains much more quickly than in the west, leaving less flatland to be farmed.[9] Although China is not lacking in mountains and foothills, most of its population resides in areas that are relatively flat.

The point of origin for Taiwan's rivers is the mountainous central part of the island. Most of the island's rivers, however, are short and the flows are rapid. Only one, the Choushui, is longer than one hundred miles. Because its rivers are not big or even flowing, Taiwan relies very little on river transport. The Tamsui River, less than ninety miles long, flows past Taipei and into the Taiwan Strait; it is considered Taiwan's only navigable river.[10] Unlike China, where water control has been a major concern for centuries and floods have caused untold human suffering and loss of life, Taiwan's rivers do not pose a serious flood menace. They seldom overflow, except during typhoons, and farmers do not depend on them to a great extent for irrigation.

In many respects, Taiwan's geography and topography resemble Japan's (where a feudal system of government evolved) more than China's (where the need to control water by building and maintaining levees and dikes gave rise to a bureaucratic political system). Taiwan, however, is not as compartmentalized as are the Japanese islands. Comparing Taiwan's geography with China's evokes quite contentious views. On the one hand, Taiwan is not very much like most of China: It is an island; its soil is volcanic; its rivers are smaller; its rainfall patterns are very different. On the other hand, China is a very large nation, and differences in terrain and geography from east to west and north to south are as great as or greater than differences between Taiwan and southeastern China.

Climate, Soil, and Natural Resources

Taiwan's climate is subtropical; the very southern tip of the island is tropical. Summers are hot, humid, and long, extending from April or May to September or October. Winters are short and mild, lasting from December to February. During the winter, snow falls in the mountains and occasionally even at some lower elevations in the northern part of the island. Taiwan's climate and weather patterns change considerably, however, with variations in elevation and shifts in the prevailing winds.

The average daytime high temperature on the island is 70 degrees Fahrenheit (21 degrees Centigrade). Although the temperature rises or falls by about 1.5 degrees Fahrenheit for every degree of latitude in the winter, little variation occurs in the summer: Keelung's mean July temperature of over 81 degrees compares with 83 degrees at the island's southernmost tip. The fact that Taipei lies in a basin makes the hot summers there similar to those of cities much farther south, such as Jakarta and Bangkok.[11]

Temperature fluctuations during any of the seasons are minimized by the proximity of the ocean; this is only somewhat less true in the central part of the island compared with the coastal areas. The Japan Current, which flows from Southeast Asia past Taiwan and on north, also moderates Taiwan's weather.

Taiwan has abundant rainfall year-round; the mean annual precipitation is 102 inches. The east coast usually receives more rain than the west and the mountains more than the lowlands. Some of the mountains on the windward side of the island (the east) often see rainfall exceeding five inches within a twenty-four-hour period. One odd feature about Taiwan's rain patterns is that the dry season at one end of the island coincides with the rainy season at the other. In the north, the heaviest rains fall between October and March; in the south, it is between April and September.[12]

Agriculture is not much of a gamble in Taiwan compared to other places in the world (including China) owing to the ample and predictable rainfall and because water for irrigation, when needed, can be obtained from small streams, lakes, and reservoirs. The plentiful rain supply also provides Taiwan with hydroelectric power, which in the early post–World War II period was cheap and facilitated the island's industrialization.

The patterns of precipitation in the Pescadores resemble those of the southwest coastal part of Taiwan, except that rainfall is not so much influenced by the mountains on Taiwan. Rainfall on the Offshore Islands (Quemoy and Matsu) is like the coastal areas of Fukien Province in China. The islands Taiwan claims in the South China Sea have rainfall patterns like the other islands there and the adjacent Southeast Asian countries.

Located near the Asian land mass but in the world's largest ocean, Taiwan's winds are monsoonal—or periodic—and seasonal, yet Taiwan experiences none of the strong continental winds, cyclones, and tornadoes common in parts of China. However, typhoons plague the island, particularly in the late summer and early fall, as they do the Philippines, Vietnam and other places to the south, the Ryukyu Islands and the main Japanese islands to the north (though they are seldom so strong further north), and the coast of China. These "hurricanes of the east" are among the most severe in the world. When they hit Taiwan—usually in July, August, and September—they often cause damage to buildings and crops, as well as flooding.

Taiwan's lowland plains and valleys generally have rich alluvial topsoil since much of Taiwan's land is either volcanic or partly volcanic and thus quite fertile despite centuries of farming. The soil in the uplands and at higher elevations, however, is leached, acidic, and infertile, and it has been subjected to considerable erosion, though it remains rich compared to that of most mountainous areas elsewhere in the world. Because of its good soil and plentiful rainfall, Taiwan's forests have survived extensive cutting for many years and still cover half the island's land surface.

Owing to the variations in soil quality, elevation, climate, and other factors, Taiwan enjoys a diversity of flora. Of its more than 190 plant families and nearly 4,000 species, about one-third are considered indigenous. From sea level to about 6,000 feet, plants tend to be either tropical or subtropical. Mixed forests of broad-leafed deciduous trees and conifers occupy the higher areas. Conifers grow primarily at the highest elevations.

More than sixty types of mammals have been found in Taiwan, about forty-five of which are native species. The largest predatory mammal is the Formosan black bear. Foxes, flying foxes, deer, wild boar, bats, and squirrels inhabit the less populated areas. Taiwan has 330 species and subspecies of birds, just over 30 of which are indigenous. And there are more than 65 species of reptiles and amphibians. Snakes are found throughout the island; 13 species are poisonous. Many of the animals native to Taiwan are not found in China or elsewhere in the region. The plant and animal life on the island offers evidence for both Taiwan's early birth and for the view that it was in the past connected to the Mainland.

Taiwan's farmers produce a variety of crops. Rice is the staple, and the two or three harvests each year usually produce high yields. Other grains are less common. Fruits—considered among the best tasting in the world—and vegetables are also important crops. Taiwan has been self-sufficient in most food commodities and in the past exported large quantities of sugar and rice, and more recently sizeable quantities of fruits and vegetables and canned foods; but it now imports significant amounts of meat, grains (other than rice), and animal feed. Taiwan has a dairy industry and its farmers raise cattle for meat, but both are new to Taiwan and remain rather small in their economic importance. The nation's fishing industry has been important as a source of employment and food. In recent years, though, because fishermen have had to sail much farther from Taiwan's shores, fish farms have become common and profitable. Agriculture has shrunk in importance as a result of industrialization; and now that Taiwan is a member of the World Trade Organization (WTO), many farmers' livelihoods are threatened by foreign competition.

Taiwan is not well endowed in mineral or energy resources. Twenty minerals can be found on the island, but none in commercially significant amounts. Coal, which in Taiwan's early history made the island a port of call for merchant ships, was once important to the economy. Although coal was mined until just recently (primarily in the northern part of the island), production was very labor-intensive because the seams are so small.

Gold and copper have been mined in the northern part of the island for a century, although neither metal is currently of economic importance. Taiwan has small deposits of sulfur in the form of pyrite, dolomite (a source of magnesium), and nickel. Marble and a low-quality jade mined in Taiwan are used mostly for vases, jewelry, and other decorative items. Some oil and natural gas have been found recently, both onshore and off, but not in the commercially meaningful quantities once thought possible.[13]

One thing is clear when looking at Taiwan's natural resource base: Taiwan has very little. This means that it must develop another resource: its human talent.

Population

Taiwan's population numbers close to 23 million. Given its small area this makes the island one of the most densely populated places on earth, the number of people per square mile being nearly double that of Japan and almost five times that of China. If Taiwan were a province of China, it would be its most densely populated one. As more than two-thirds of Taiwan's surface is covered by mountains, the island's real population-to-land ratio should be regarded as even higher than the numbers indicate.[14] The population density of the lowlands, in fact, surpasses the island's average of more than 1,600 per square mile (635 per square kilometer) by a very large margin. If regarded as a nation-state, Taiwan would be the most densely populated nation in the world after Bangladesh (excluding, of course, some ministates and city-states).[15] Considering the large mountainous area in Taiwan that cannot be inhabited, though, Taiwan's population density may be said to exceed even that of Bangladesh.

Taiwan's high population density, however, is of recent origin. In 1940, the island's population was only 5.8 million. An influx of people fleeing the Mainland after the Communist takeover in 1949 and a very high birthrate after that for a decade and a half pushed Taiwan's population to more than 10 million by 1960.

The birthrate in Taiwan in 1952 was 4.66 per 1,000 population annually, one of the highest in the world. In response, in 1964 the government established an official birth-control program to expand population control measures that had been unofficially in effect in the cities for some time. As a consequence Taiwan's birthrate fell to 3.27 by 1965, and by 1980 to 2.34—just about the world average. By reducing the fertility rate by more than 100 percent in twenty years, Taiwan accomplished what it took most Western countries a century to do. After 1980, the birthrate fell to a figure well below the world's average. In 2001, the increase was 0.6 percent. In 2007, it was 0.3 percent. It is anticipated that Taiwan's population will reach zero growth around 2016, after which it will decline—by an estimated 4 million by 2051.[16]

Paralleling the decline in the birthrate, Taiwan's death rate dropped significantly, falling from 18.2 per 1,000 people in 1952 to 5.92 in 2006. Meanwhile, the infant mortality rate dropped from 44.7 per thousand to 4.6 per thousand during that same period. Increases in life expectancy have thus been extremely high over the past forty-five years. From 1951 to 1991, the life span of Taiwan's population rose from just over 55 (53.1 for males and 57.3 for females) to almost 75 (71.5 for males and 76.9 for females). Now it is 74.6 for males and 80.8 for females—even higher than the life expectancy figures in many European countries, and ten years above the world's average.[17]

Owing to the success of Taiwan's efforts to reduce the birthrate, together with dramatic decreases in the death rate, the average age of Taiwan's population has risen markedly in recent years. In 1964, 45 percent of the population was under the age of fifteen; just 2.6 percent was over the age of sixty-five. (In the United States the relevant numbers were 30.9 percent and 9.3 percent, respectively.) By 1986, nearly one-third of the population was still under fifteen. Since then, the age of Taiwan's population has increased very fast. In 1992, only about one-fifth of the population was under the age of fifteen; 6.8 percent of the population was over sixty-five. In 2008, 17.3 percent was under fifteen, and 10.5 percent was over sixty-five.[18]

The gender ratio of Taiwan's population has also been an issue of concern. Because more of those who fled to Taiwan in 1949 were male, the ratio of men to women was quite unbalanced for some time, and as a result many men could not find wives. This situation subsequently improved, but in 1964 there were still 109 males for every 100 females. Even today there remains an imbalance of men over women in most age groups. Only in the population over the age of sixty-five are there more females than males. Recently, after seeing the male-female sex ratio gap close for a number of years, it has increased again for a different reason: A 1985 law allowing abortions twenty-four weeks into pregnancy in order to prevent the birth of babies suffering congenital defects produced a rise in the proportion of male to female babies from 106.7 (versus 100 females) in 1985 to 110.3 in 1991. In other words, the use of scientific tests to determine the sex of babies before they are born has resulted in more abortions of female fetuses. Very recently, the imbalance has diminished slightly, but it is still a problem. Now the ratio is 109.5:100 (105:100 is the world's average).[19]

Because of the imbalance in the sex ratio and also the fact that many men perceive Taiwan's women to be too liberated, they seek wives from other countries. In 2007, 18 percent of marriages were with a foreign spouse—87 percent of which were brides, mostly from China (nearly two-thirds) and Southeast Asia. During the Chen Shui-bian presidency the government tried to limit the number of foreign spouses in various ways, including restricting their right to vote since they generally did not favor the DPP. This resulted in a slight decline in their numbers.[20] President Ma Ying-jeou has promised fewer restrictions on marriages with foreigners and better treatment of brides from other countries.

After 1949, Taiwan had almost no immigration. This and low birth and death rates caused the population to become static for a number of years. This is not the case now, however. In the last fifteen to twenty years, Taiwan has attracted immigrant labor as a result of a shortage of workers and high wages in Taiwan compared to most other parts of Asia. By the late 1990s, there were one-third of a million foreign workers in Taiwan.[21] In 2000, the government moved to reduce the number of employees recruited from other countries. Still the number increased to 424,000 in 2006. Most of these, 69 percent, were guest workers and were supposed to return to their native countries at the end of a contract. But some sought to stay, and this created controversy. At times they have also evoked scandal when they complained of ill treatment and, on one occasion during the Chen administration, rioted and exposed serious government corruption.[22]

Still another population issue is the number of citizens who have gone to China, most to do business or, since Taiwan's economic downturn in 2001, to find jobs. Probably a million or more people from Taiwan currently live in China, mostly in the southern coastal areas.[23] A large number seem to have settled there semipermanently. Many men have found wives in China, some second wives, and a good proportion of both groups have children there. This and the rumored large numbers of Chinese from China residing in Taiwan illegally, plus the growing number of Taiwan's men finding wives in China, have given rise to concern, sometimes alarmism, over Taiwan's "demographic unification" with China.

Still another population issue is urbanization. In 1920, only 4 percent of the people in Taiwan lived in cities with populations of more than 100,000. The proportion changed in 1949 because of the influx of Chinese from the Mainland, who, to a large extent, became city dwellers. In the middle and late 1950s, as a result of land reform and the enhanced productivity in the agricultural sector, people began moving to the cities in large numbers. This process accelerated in the 1960s as factories proliferated in or near Taiwan's large and medium-sized cities. By the early 1970s, Taiwan's population was two-thirds urban.

Urbanization was accompanied by an especially rapid growth of Taiwan's largest cities. In 1952, just over 47 percent of the population lived in cities of more than 50,000 population. By 1980, the proportion had risen to 78 percent (compared to the world's average of 43 percent)—ranking Taiwan twenty-eighth in the world (higher than Japan, 77 percent, or the United States, 75 percent) in terms of the percentage of the urban population. In the last decade or so this has reversed a bit with many people moving to the suburbs, and the percentage now is 68.7.[24]

Taipei's population, which was less than 326,000 in 1947, grew to more than 1 million in 1966—an increase of 260 percent. Another 1 million people were added by 1974. Other large cities in Taiwan have grown at a similar rate, nearly doubling or tripling in size between 1947 and the mid-1960s, while experiencing high growth even into the 1990s. Taiwan's four largest cities now account for nearly 30 percent of the population and 60 percent of the island's urban residents. Taipei's population is currently 2.6 million; Kaohsiung's is 1.5 million; Taichung is 1.1 million; Tainan is 762,000; Panchiao is 537,000; Keelung is 401,000.[25]

Since the mid-1990s, migration to most of Taiwan's large and medium-sized cities has slowed because of urban crowding and other problems. In fact, Taipei and some other cities have experienced a population decline since 1978. Satellite or "urban towns" near Taipei, Kaohsiung, and Taichung, built to reduce the population pressures there, have caused part of this decline. The population of Taipei County now exceeds that of the city, and it is close in Kaohsiung.[26]

Nearly all of Taiwan's population resides on the island of Taiwan itself: 99.7 percent. The population of the Pescadores is just over 90,000; Quemoy is 50,000; Matsu is around 8,000. Not included in Quemoy or Matsu's population figures, however, are the large numbers of soldiers garrisoned on these two islands. Islands off Taiwan's east coast have even smaller populations, and islands under Taipei's jurisdiction in the South China Sea lack civilian populations.

Ethnic Groups

Taiwan's population is made up of four major ethnic or subethnic groups: the Aborigines, two groups of "Taiwanese" Chinese (Fukienese or Hoklo and Hakka), and "Mainland Chinese."[27] The Aborigines are usually seen as ethnically distinct from the Chinese. However, they may or may not belong to a single ethnic group; different tribes are sometimes considered distinct ethnic groups. The three Chinese groups are more accurately described as being different from each other according to their provincial origins and the time they arrived in Taiwan, as well as the language or languages (dialects) they speak, rather than ethnicity. The terms "early arrival" and "late arrival" Chinese have also been used to describe the differences between the Taiwanese and the Mainland Chinese. This view, of course, is an oversimplification and has often been challenged.

The Aborigines have long been considered to have migrated from Southeast Asia or South China several millennia ago, though some tribes in the northern part of the island might have come from the north—meaning other parts of China or Japan. The languages of the Aborigines resemble Bahasa (the language spoken in Brunei, Indonesia, and Malaysia) in structure and vocabulary. Aboriginal culture for the most part seems to have originated in Southeast Asia, though it obviously evolved considerably in Taiwan. On the other hand it may be that the Aborigines populated Taiwan much earlier and migrated from Taiwan to other parts of Asia, rather than the other way around; some recent DNA studies suggest they are the ancestors of the natives of New Zealand and some of the Pacific Islands.[28]

The government lists thirteen major Aboriginal tribes: Amis, Atayal, Bunun, Kavalan, Paiwan, Pinuyumayan, Ruki, Saisiyat, Thao, Ruuku, Tsou, Yami, and Sakizaya. Other tribes can be identified, but all are either small and/or are being rapidly assimilated. Some tribes have virtually vanished. Around a tenth of Aborigines do not identify with a tribe. More than one-third of Taiwan's Aboriginal people are of the Ami tribe. All the Aborigines are less urban than the three Chinese groups mentioned above, and with the exception of the Yami tribe living on the Orchid Island off Taiwan's southeast coast, most reside in the Central Mountain Range area or on the east coastal plain. Although the Aborigines vary considerably from tribe to tribe in physical appearance, they are generally short and have rugged features, with larger noses and eyes than the Chinese. Most are identifiable because of their looks and by tattoos, clothing, and manners.

The Aborigines have long been assumed the original inhabitants of the island, though there is no definitive proof of this. In fact, some anthropologists say there were probably people on the island before the Aborigines. Nonetheless, the Aborigines regard themselves as Taiwan's first inhabitants; certainly they populated the island long before the arrival of any Chinese. It is difficult to say when the first Chinese arrived on the island, but it was probably around a thousand years ago. It is known that early Chinese emigrants were few in number, and most went to Taiwan only temporarily—for seasonal work or to trade. Major migrations occurred beginning in the seventeenth century, and at that time most of the immigrants sought to stay in Taiwan permanently.

When Chinese immigrants arrived, they identified two groups of Aborigines: sedentary groups who lived in the lowland areas and practiced agriculture, and less sedentary tribes who lived in the mountains and survived by hunting and fishing. The Chinese killed many of the former during frequent armed conflicts and drove many more into the mountains. Many were also assimilated. Therefore, now most of the Aborigines are mountain Aborigines.[29] While all of the Aboriginal population is said to be "acculturated"—speaking the national language and knowing both Taiwanese and Mainland Chinese customs while living amicably under the law and political system of the country—most still reside in the less-populated areas, especially the mountains. Many also keep their tribal ways. Some observers see many similarities between Taiwan's Aborigines and Native Americans.

Early Chinese migrants to Taiwan hailed mainly from Fukien and Kwangtung (Canton) provinces. They are now called "Taiwanese" or sometimes "native Taiwanese." However, there are two distinct groups of Taiwanese. The Fukien Taiwanese came mostly from the southern part of Fukien Province, especially the area near the city of Amoy. Hakka Taiwanese, or just Hakkas, also came from southern Fukien; but most came from Kwangtung. The migration of both groups was concentrated during specific spans of time; one might say they came in waves. The fall of the Ming Dynasty in 1644 brought a particularly large wave of migration from Fukien Province to Taiwan. Some Cantonese or non-Hakka Chinese from Kwangtung Province were among these early immigrants to Taiwan, but most turned out to be only temporary residents.

There were likely some Hakkas in Taiwan before the first Fukienese arrived, though this is not a certainty and their numbers were in any case small. The Hakkas were a persecuted minority in China, having been driven from their home area in northern China around 1,500 years ago. They became itinerants who took up residence in various parts of China. Some writers have likened them to the Jews in Europe. Recent evidence from DNA tests and linguistic studies indicate the Hakka people might have once resided in Mongolia.[30] In any event, many migrated to southern China and engaged in fishing and trading in the coastal areas, and from there, they migrated to the Pescadores and then on to southern Taiwan. Some migrated to Southeast Asia and elsewhere. By about AD 1000, there were a number of Hakka settlements in southwest Taiwan. The last large-scale migration of Hakkas to Taiwan occurred in the late 1860s after the very destructive Taiping Rebellion in China. Because a Hakka led the rebellion, Hakkas incurred considerable blame, resulting in even worse persecution than they had faced before; consequently many fled to Taiwan.

Fukienese, mostly farmers and fishermen, came in such large numbers that they pushed many Hakkas inland, sometimes into enclaves. The Fukienese then inhabited most of the western plain. The Fukien Chinese later called themselves *pen ti jen* (natives) or *ben sheng jen* (local province people); they labeled the Hakkas *ke chia jen* (guest people, which is what Hakka literally means), and they named the Aborigines *shan ti jen* (mountain people).

Notwithstanding this rather long period during which Chinese migrated to Taiwan, as late as the mid-seventeenth century, when the Dutch took control of Taiwan, it is estimated that there were only 25,000 Chinese on the island.[31] It was not until the nineteenth century that Chinese constituted a majority of the island's population, and even then they occupied considerably less than half of the island's land area. The Dutch encouraged the migration of Chinese to the island, as did the local governments that ruled Taiwan after the Dutch departed. However, the government of China during various periods banned emigration to Taiwan, often under the penalty of death. In addition, for long stretches of time, the government prohibited women or children from going.

In 1949, when the Communists defeated Nationalist Chinese armies and assumed political control of the mainland of China, another wave of more than 1.5 million Chinese immigrants arrived on Taiwan's shores. Because they hailed from various parts of China, they were known simply as Mainlanders, or *wai sheng jen* (outside-province people). Most, though, came from China's coastal provinces, more from the south than the north because Chiang Kai-shek's base of support was near Shanghai in southeast China, and thus more of his army and government were people from that area; also, the Communists took control of China from the north and isolated much of the west, keeping the people there from escaping.

Taiwan's population today is grouped as follows: Mainlanders, around 14 percent; Taiwanese, slightly more than 84 percent (the Hakkas make up 10 to 15 percent of this group); and Aborigines, around 2 percent. The birthrate is slightly higher among the two groups of Taiwanese mainly because they are more rural and less educated than the Mainland Chinese. The death rate is higher among the Aborigines. These and other population trends, however, do not greatly affect the ethnic ratio in Taiwan.

The early Chinese who immigrated to Taiwan did so mostly because of poverty, difficult conditions at home, and the prospects for a better life in Taiwan. Most emigrated for the same reasons Europeans left for America—except that few, if any, went to Taiwan because of religious persecution. Like the Europeans who flocked to the New World, most Chinese who settled in Taiwan severed ties with their homeland. For some time, as noted above, even when Taiwan was ruled by China, it was illegal for Chinese to emigrate, and those that did were punished, sometimes severely, if they returned to China—another reason the move was considered permanent by those who went to Taiwan. Few maintained or tried to reestablish broken family ties; indeed, such efforts were banned during the Japanese period, and after 1949 until the 1980s, because of the bitter military and political struggle between Taipei and Beijing.

The Mainland Chinese who fled to Taiwan in 1949 did not consider the move permanent. They hoped that the Nationalist Chinese military could regroup and counterattack and that the mainland of China could be liberated from the Communists, after which they would return home. After a while, most Mainlanders began to call Taiwan home and gave up any serious thought of returning to China. Their resignation to living permanently in Taiwan was at first more evident among younger and more successful Mainlanders, but after years of separation, Taiwan's miracle economic growth, and lagging growth in China, most Mainlanders came to view Taiwan as home.[32]

By the mid-1980s, more than half the Mainland Chinese population of Taiwan was born on the island. At that time, of the total population of the Republic of China, less than 6 percent was born in China.[33] As a result, it seemed that, at least as reflected in Taiwan's demographics, ties between Taiwan and China were weakening fast, amplified also by growing economic and political differences. Beginning in the 1980s, however, these trends changed as people from Taiwan began visiting China in large numbers, thereby encouraging economic links to grow. Soon many Chinese residents of Taiwan, Taiwanese and Mainland Chinese both, began to think differently about ties with China.

Culture

Taiwan's culture, for the most part, is of Chinese origins. It was brought by early Chinese immigrants from Fukien and Kwangtung Provinces and, after World War II, from various parts of China, and it contains elements of both regional cultures as well as the national culture in China.[34] The Chinese from Fukien and the Hakka Chinese brought cultures with them that were different from each other in many ways, though both reflect their southern coastal and rural origins. As stated earlier, Aboriginal culture may have been transplanted to Taiwan from somewhere else or it may have largely evolved in Taiwan. Whatever their origins, however, Aboriginal customs influenced Chinese culture in Taiwan, albeit the predominant influence was the other way around. Nonetheless, the customs and culture of many Aboriginal groups, especially those of the mountain Aborigines, remain intact. Furthermore, missionaries and scholars from China and the West, as well as merchants from throughout East Asia and then later from Europe and the United States also influenced Taiwan's culture. Additionally, Japanese culture had a strong influence on the mix during Japan's rule of Taiwan, and the United States has had a major cultural impact for the past sixty years.

Western cultural influence came to Taiwan through early missionary activities and in a host of other ways during the period of Dutch colonial rule in the seventeenth century, however brief. The Japanese had a major effect through the Japanese language and educational system, which were imposed on Taiwan during the Japanese colonial period. But many other facets of Japanese culture are to be found in Taiwan, among them music, art, literature, culinary skills, religion, and martial arts. During the Japanese period, Western influence continued to find its way to Taiwan, but it was largely filtered through Japan. Then, as a result of war between China and Japan, which started in 1937, Tokyo restricted Taiwan's contacts with China; thus, Chinese culture, albeit well rooted in Taiwan, was cut off from its source.

With the transfer of political control to the Republic of China in 1945 came a marked increase in Chinese influence and a Chinese cultural revival. The Nationalist government, especially after moving to Taiwan in 1949, sought in a variety of ways to propagate traditional Chinese culture. Chiang Kai-shek's personal cultural interests, which favored Chinese calligraphy, classical painting, opera, and folk arts, had a strong influence. Because the political leadership considered acculturation a necessary process to be applied to the population in Taiwan after half a century of Japanese control, the government sponsored cultural activities of various kinds. In fact, specific efforts were made to eradicate Japanese cultural influence. Anti-Soviet and anti-Communist themes were also in evidence and reflected the government's views and Taiwan's international status. Yellow journalism, pessimism, and defeatism were seen as bad for the society and were thus discouraged or banned.

The government promoted cultural change in large part through the Ministry of Education. In the early 1950s, the ministry launched a project to preserve the Chinese classics, and it subsequently sponsored cultural organizations and various awards. The Nationalist Party supported many cultural activities while the central government financed national museums, the National Central Library, concert halls, and Chinese opera theaters. The Taiwan Provincial Government budgeted funds for libraries, fine arts museums, and music halls in all counties and large cities. The Ministry of National Defense took an active role in encouraging cultural pursuits in the military. Besides efforts to expand social and political control, considerable government funding of culture is explained by the fact the Constitution mandates that 15 percent of the national government's budget be used for education and culture.

The government's efforts to promote culture were also facilitated by the many national treasures brought to Taiwan in 1949. Many antiques and other artifacts were stored until the National Palace Museum, described by many now as one of the best museums in the world, opened in 1965. Meanwhile, Taiwan's economic prosperity in the past four decades has been accompanied by an increased interest in cultural pursuits by a large segment of the population as well as individuals starting collections of art, books, and antiques.

Although culture was to a considerable extent manipulated by the government for political reasons in the years after 1949, this influence did not discourage the freedom of cultural expression unless it was considered subversive or in poor taste. Nor did the government's claim that it was the preserver of Chinese culture mean that Western ideas were unwelcome (except for pornographic materials and pro-Communist writings). In fact, Western—especially US—influence in Taiwan in the 1950s and 1960s (unlike in China) was very evident: Schools of thought such as symbolism, surrealism (especially among Taiwan's poets), existentialism, Freudianism, modernism, and sometimes even nihilism appeared in public debate and in local publications. Popular Western movements in art and literature also influenced Taiwan's local culture as many Western words and concepts became part of the language spoken in Taiwan—a marked contrast to the situation in the People's Republic of China.

In the 1970s, cultural developments in Taiwan reflected pragmatism (generally attributed to rapid economic growth), nationalism, nativism, and realism. Western influence increased markedly in the 1970s and thereafter as Taiwan's economic development became more dependent on exports and as more people gained access to Western newspapers, magazines, movies, and music. The culture also mirrored the changing nature of politics in Taiwan, especially as it became more acceptable to expound political ideas and as political and literary writing often merged. Modern scientific thought and new trends in the West in particular had a growing influence on Taiwan's culture.

The 1980s saw the development of informational literature, science fiction, feminism, and the extensions of trends from the 1970s.[35] Taiwan's growing cosmopolitanism and cultural self-confidence also became more evident. Culture, meanwhile, became less subject to government regulation and more pluralistic in nature. Official support and the encouragement of cultural pursuits continued, however, because the public believed tax money should be spent on culture and the government still sought to maintain some control over culture.

Chinese calligraphy, opera, and traditional music and dance currently appeal to the more educated and conservative segments of the population. Writing Chinese characters as a form of art was traditionally an avocation of the educated class, in part because Chiang Kai-shek encouraged it and, for some time, it was a part of the civil service exam. Additionally, after 1967, musical education became part of the required curriculum in primary and secondary schools in Taiwan. Mostly older, more educated people enjoy Chinese opera.

Sculpture, which never became popular in China because it was associated with manual labor, gained favor in Taiwan as it reflected traditional Taoism and contemporary political and social themes. While architecture during the Japanese era followed styles that were either Japanese or culturally neutral, most museums and other cultural buildings are now constructed in traditional Chinese or Western forms.

Many cultural expressions now reflect a "people's culture," although these are also merging with elite norms. Folk art reveals religious themes, whereas cartoons and posters are often political or avant-garde. Photography mirrors Western influence, but puppet shows, especially the traveling type, draw on local rural culture. The decision in 1987 to allow residents of Taiwan to visit China has resulted in a surge of Chinese cultural influence from the Mainland.

In Taiwan, movies attract large audiences.[36] Taiwan produces classical Chinese movies as well as modern dramas, romance stories, and adventure movies. Taiwan's filmmakers, although in critical disfavor for many years, have recently won various awards for their movies. Films made in Hong Kong and the West, and particularly American films, are popular in Taiwan. Japanese films, banned for some years, are now shown and attract fairly large audiences. Recently, films made in China have been shown, but the initial intense interest in them, in large part driven by curiosity, has not increased much, if any. Actors, regarded as low class in the past, now enjoy a decent social reputation. Many have become famous; some have even become social models, and a few have entered politics.

Because literature was discouraged during the Japanese era, Taiwan's writers are generally young, and there is a high proportion of woman writers compared with other countries, including China. Common earlier themes among writers were poverty, communism, the differences between the Mainland Chinese and the Taiwanese, and local culture. Now, however, romance and social problems are more common topics, as is Taiwan's sense of identity.[37] Freer expression in recent years, the growth of democracy, and increased foreign travel have broadened the interests and concerns of writers. Western books, like foreign music and movies, are very popular in Taiwan.

Transportation and Communications

Until the late 1800s, Taiwan did not have a transportation or communications network that linked different parts of the island. Roads were local and there were few good ones. Contacts between people living in different areas were hence limited to travel to places accessible by foot, oxcart, or boat. At the end of the nineteenth century, new roads, railroads, and ports were built, though much more was done under the Japanese. In recent years, major new construction in transportation and communications facilities has paralleled Taiwan's rapid economic growth.

For some time, railroads were one of Taiwan's most important means of carrying goods and transporting people. The Japanese built a network of narrow-gauge tracks that served the island well, and then more and better lines were built during the 1950s and thereafter. During the 1960s and 1970s, usage increased at a rate of from 5 to 10 percent annually. In the mid-1970s, railroads accounted for nearly half of the freight moved and passengers carried over more than a short distance.[38] After that, usage fell because of competition from other means of transport, especially trucks and buses using the new expressways. At its lowest point, in the last fifty years rail travel accounted for just 10 percent of the country's passengers and cargo.

In recent years, highway congestion and the greater comfort and safety that trains provide to passengers, together with faster service brought by better trains and double tracks, has caused a rise in rail travel. In 2006, the rails carried 463,000 passengers. In 2007, a high-speed train that runs at a speed of 186 miles per hour (300 km/h), making the trip from Taipei to Kaohsiung in around ninety minutes (two hours if stopping at all stations), was completed at a cost of US$15 billion. It was the first such infrastructure project undertaken by the private sector in Taiwan and will improve rail service and make the trains more competitive.[39]

Taiwan has approximately 33,000 miles of roads, most of which are paved. In fact, when it comes to road quality, Taiwan is considered one of the world's most developed nations. In 1978, a national expressway, the Sun Yat-sen Freeway (also called the North-South Freeway), was completed. Running almost the length of the island, this highway made it possible to travel between Taiwan's two largest cities, Taipei and Kaohsiung, in less than four hours. After it opened, traffic increased around 11 percent annually for more than a decade. A parallel expressway, the Formosa Freeway, was completed in 2004. Both freeways are on Taiwan's west side, the latter further inland. A new freeway is also under construction on the island's east coast.[40] Taiwan's freeways are toll roads, the tolls being adjusted upward at times in order to reduce the heavy traffic flows.

In the past, most automobiles were used as taxis or were company cars. However, this changed dramatically in the 1970s and 1980s and, by 1999, there were more than 16.3 million motor vehicles in Taiwan (around 10 million of which were motorcycles), up from 5 million in 1980. Now there are 5.6 million passenger cars registered, plus 13.6 million motorcycles.[41] A large portion of this growth came from individual use of vehicles. The rapid increase in private ownership and use of vehicles mirrored both Taiwan's prosperity and the reduction of tariffs on imported vehicles. Now more than 50 percent of families in Taiwan own cars.[42] The number of vehicles per capita in Taiwan compares to that of most developed nations, and, as is the case in other developed nations, the downside of this is serious traffic jams in Taiwan's largest cities.

The nation has six seaports that accommodate oceangoing vessels, and most were modernized and improved during the 1970s. Kaohsiung, the largest, handles the lion's share of Taiwan's imports and exports and, for some years, had the distinction of being the world's third largest container port (after Hong Kong and Singapore). In the past, Keelung, Hualien, and Suao followed in traffic volume. Recently, a new man-made port constructed near Taichung has become Taiwan's third largest harbor.[43]

Taiwan's merchant marine, 112 shipping lines with a total of 261 vessels of more than 100 gross tons, is one of the world's largest and is still growing in size and importance. Evergreen Marine Corporation, a private company founded in Taiwan, is the second largest container forwarder in the world.[44] Taiwan's shipping industry is large not only because Taiwan is a major trading nation but also because the government fears China might try to blockade or quarantine the island and has therefore encouraged shipping to grow for security reasons.

Taiwan has two international airports. The larger of these is Taoyuan International Airport (called Chiang Kai-shek International Airport before 2006), which is located outside of Taipei, and the smaller is Kaohsiung International Airport. Several foreign international carriers use the two international air terminals, as well as Taiwan's flag carrier, China Airlines (CAL), the privately owned EVA Airways, and some other local airlines. Additionally, Taiwan has sixteen domestic airports. Domestic air travel has been growing at 10 percent a year and is expected to grow at this rate for another decade.[45]

In Taipei, Taiwan's most congested large city, construction was begun on a subway system in 1988 and was completed in 1996. Its construction was delayed for some time because of the high cost of building such a system in a city that lies in a basin and is gradually sinking. At a cost of US$18 billion, it was the most expensive system in the world. It currently includes 46 miles of track with another 168 miles planned and forty-some of that under construction.[46] The system carries hundreds of thousands of passengers each day. A link to Taoyuan International Airport is scheduled to be opened in 2012. Kaohsiung had a similar, though less serious, traffic problem, and in early 2001 work began on a mass transit system there. It was plagued by construction problems, accidents, and scandals involving political kickbacks and riots by foreign workers helping build the project, and, as a result, its opening date has been delayed.[47]

Various forms of communications have supplemented the main traditional form in Taiwan, the mail, in the past few decades, though it has nonetheless continued to grow in size and efficiency. There are six or more pickups a day in most of Taiwan's large cities, making it possible to get a letter to another party in the same city within a few hours, and to most cities throughout the island the next day. Most foreign visitors to Taiwan are very impressed with its postal system.

Telephones came into popular use in the 1960s. During the 1970s, the number of telephones increased eightfold to more than 2.5 million by the close of the decade. Pagers soon became popular and then cellular telephones. International satellite long-distance and direct-dial calls can be made to and from Taiwan, and a trans-horizon microwave system is in service to Hong Kong and the Philippines. Video-telephone service is available between Taiwan and the Pescadores as well as between Taiwan and Quemoy.

Taiwan's meteorological services are also well developed. Numerous weather stations and radar and satellite information centers provide constant weather data, and typhoon and tidal wave predictions are considered accurate by global standards. There are several seismological stations for predicting and measuring earthquakes. The country also has systems for measuring radioactive fallout, sea conditions, and astronomical and ozonic changes.

Internet usage has grown very fast in Taiwan in recent years. Residents use the Internet for research, sending and receiving e-mail messages, entertainment, and other purposes. Visitors to Taiwan find it easily accessible. Wireless Internet availability is common. In 2006, Taiwan ranked tenth in the world in Internet usage according to the Digital Opportunity Index.[48]

The Media

Understanding the role of the media in Taiwan and the profound change it has undergone is vital to understanding the nation, its past, its present, and its future. Economic modernization and its side effects, such as affluence, increasing literacy, urbanization, a growing middle class, and higher levels of education, have been the driving forces behind the transition to a new and forceful media in Taiwan. So has political development, including the end of martial law, the growth of political parties, and the shift in ruling parties in 2000.

In the distant past, the common mode of mass communications was to paste written bulletins on walls in public places, but during the Japanese period radio and newspapers became common. Five stations operated in Taiwan, and there were nearly 100,000 receivers by the mid-1940s. Then, in the 1960s television came to Taiwan. Today, Taiwan is modern and up-to-date in communications and has numerous and different kinds of newspapers, magazines, radio stations, television stations, and movies.[49]

The Central News Agency (CNA), Taiwan's largest news agency, disseminates news in Chinese, English, and Spanish. CNA was established in China in 1924 and moved to Taiwan in 1949. In 1996, CNA became Taiwan's national news agency. Meanwhile, in 1990, it became fully computerized, and in 1997 it added a website that became very popular. CNA has correspondents in all of Taiwan's cities and counties and more than thirty foreign countries. Though there are more than a thousand other news agencies in Taiwan, they are much smaller and, except for some that disseminate economic news, none is very important.[50]

In the past, Taiwan's two largest Chinese newspapers were the *China Times* and the *United Daily News*. Both claimed to be the biggest paper in Taiwan; it is uncertain which actually was. The *China Times* was reputed to be a bit more liberal and the *United Daily News* a bit more conservative. Both publish other papers, including economic and local editions. The *United Daily News* publishes the *World Journal*, which is the most popular Chinese newspaper in North America. Today these two papers remain competitive, though both are said to represent the pan-blue or KMT view.

In recent years the *Liberty Times* has become Taiwan's largest newspaper, with a ranking of number thirty-five in the world. (*United Daily News* and *China Times* rank at forty-seven and forty-eight respectively). The *Liberty Times* favors the DPP. *Apple Daily*, a popular newspaper that tends toward simplifying or sensationalizing its coverage, also ranks in the top one hundred in the world and claims to be one of Taiwan's top papers. It says its ranking would be much higher if newsstand sales, rather than subscriptions, were counted.[51] There are three English dailies in Taiwan: the *China Post*, *Taiwan News*, and *Taipei Times*. The *China Post* is conservative and pro-KMT, while the *Taipei Times* and *Taiwan News* are liberal and pro-DPP. The Government Information Office publishes the *Taipei Journal*, a weekly information paper. The *Asian Wall Street Journal* and the *International Herald Tribune* are printed and sold in Taiwan and are available in most hotels. The trend in Taiwan has been toward larger papers and as a result many small and local papers have suffered from declining circulation. Some commercial papers and religious papers have been the exception.

Magazine publishing in Taiwan has had an even more interesting political history than newspapers and other forms of media. In 1960, Lei Chen, who published the *Free China Fortnightly* for a short time, formed the China Democratic Party (which was an illegal act at the time) and was arrested and jailed. His publication died with him. The founding of the *Taiwan Political Review* in 1975 by Kang Ninghsiang, some say, marked the beginning of a real political opposition in Taiwan even though the magazine was closed soon after it started publishing. The *Eighties*, another magazine published by Kang and his associates at this time, was more moderate and lasted longer. In 1979, a group of opposition politicians associated with the *Formosa* magazine formed the "Formosa Group" and organized a protest demonstration in Kaohsiung; the gathering turned violent and lead to the arrest and imprisonment of several oppositionists who later became DPP leaders, including Vice President Annette Lu and two former heads of the Democratic Progressive Party. In 1989, the editor of the *Freedom Era Weekly* published a proposed new Constitution; when an arrest warrant was issued, he set fire to the building and died in the blaze. In 2002, police seized the current issue of *Next* magazine when it published a story about government corruption.[52]

Currently Taiwan has a large number of magazines, some of them published by newspapers, some by book companies, and some by individuals. There are both general interest and specialized magazines. Many focus on social and political conditions, business, and fashion. The *China Times Weekly* and *Next* are well known for news and inside stories, respectively. *CommonWealth* is a popular financial magazine, and various other magazines deal with health issues, computers, and the English language. Because of a better educated population in the north, magazines sales are much larger there—60 to 65 percent of the total.[53]

Book publishing is also a big industry in Taiwan and continues to grow. Over 40,000 titles are published yearly—a large number considering Taiwan's population. Chinese books are sold both locally and in other Chinese-speaking areas in East Asia. A number of publishers have agreements with foreign publishers and copublish English-language books in Taiwan. Although foreign books used to be pirated in Taiwan, this is now a thing of the past. Books are marketed through bookstores and newsstands, while online bookstores have seen a growing business in recent years. In addition to these means of marketing and distribution, Taipei also holds frequent international book exhibits.[54]

Radio stations have proliferated in the last decade. Before 1993, there were only 33 stations; in 2001, there were 142 and more under construction. In the past, radio was devoted to dramatic, cultural, educational, and children's programs. Now radio broadcasts concentrate more on news, traffic, market reports and financial analysis, and talk programs, though music stations are the most popular. Broadcasts are in Mandarin Chinese, Taiwanese, Hakka, and English. Taiwan has private and government-owned services and stations; the most well-known government-owned service is the Broadcasting Corporation of China (BCC). Recently stations have also broadcast in Aboriginal languages as well as in Thai, Indonesian, and Vietnamese.[55]

Television began broadcasting in 1962 with the National Educational Television station. Taiwan Television Enterprise followed that same year, and China Television Company in 1969. Chinese Television System began operation in 1971. For some time, opposition politicians complained that the Nationalist Party controlled the television media. They tried to counter this and even established broadcasting systems on ships parked offshore. Formosa Television began broadcasting in 1997 and represented opposition politicians. Public Television Service followed the next year. Meanwhile, a large number of cable operators started doing business, many of them illegally, including individuals who set up cable operations to serve a large apartment building or a square city block. The practice was brought under control to some extent when the Cable Television Law was passed in 1993. Meanwhile, legal cable hookups have made many more programs available, with 60 percent of the population having access in 2005. By 2006, fifty-six domestic and seventeen foreign companies were offering ninety-two cable and forty-three satellite channels.[56]

Taiwan's movie industry has encountered moderate success, marketing its products (especially Mandarin-speaking movies) not only in Taiwan but also in Hong Kong and elsewhere in Asia. In the mid-1990s, however, the industry declined due to foreign competition (especially after the government lifted quotas on foreign films in 1986) and fewer movies were produced. Seventeen movies were released in 2001 compared to thirty-five the previous year. By 2006, licenses were issued for only 27 local productions. That year, 302 foreign films were shown in Taiwan, including 32 films from Hong Kong and 11 from China. At that time, Taiwan had 161 theaters operating 675 screens.[57]

The ending of martial law in 1987 and democratization at the national level during the 1980s and 1990s enhanced freedom of the media, which increased gradually in the 1960s and 1970s, considerably. Other than the movie industry, all other forms of media have experienced quite spectacular growth in recent years: Cable television reaches 80 percent of the population, newspaper readership is high, and books sell well. In 2001, there were 454 newspapers, 7,236 magazines, and 7,810 book-publishing companies in Taiwan—nearly double figures of a decade earlier.[58]

Tourism

After the Chinese government acquired Taiwan from Japan at the end of World War II, it did not welcome foreign visitors because of the conflict on the Mainland and with the communist regime in China after 1949: Tourism, it was thought, would create a security problem. There was little realization that considerable money could be made from tourists and that this revenue would help resolve Taiwan's foreign exchange shortage.

Although Chiang Kai-shek established a new policy regarding tourism in 1956, still, that year only 14,974 tourists visited Taiwan. Subsequently, however, the industry did take off, experiencing a growth rate of more than 23 percent annually for the next two decades. In 1976, more than 1 million tourists visited Taiwan. At this time visitors provided Taiwan with considerable foreign currency and a significant source of employment. In the mid-1980s, however, the rate of growth fell in part due to competition from China as a place foreigners wanted to visit. Nonetheless, the number of tourists continued to grow at about 10 percent a year. Almost 2 million visited Taiwan in 1988, and in 2006, Taiwan hosted an estimated 3.75 million tourists.[59]

By far the largest number of visitors to Taiwan are from Japan—more than one-third. Hong Kong is second; the United States is third. Singapore, Indonesia, and the Philippines follow in that order. Australia and several European countries trail the Philippines. This list has not changed much in recent years except that the number of visitors from Hong Kong has increased significantly. There are two other changes in tourism trends: First, more of Taiwan's citizens are visiting other countries than visitors from abroad are visiting Taiwan, and second, Chinese tourists are now visiting Taiwan. The number of Chinese tourists was strictly restricted during the Chen period, but has since increased.

Tourists visiting Taiwan typically go to the National Palace Museum near Taipei to see the world's largest collection of Chinese artifacts, antiques, jade, paintings, and other historical objects. When the Nationalists left China in 1949, they took with them the best treasures from a number of the best museums in China. The government in China accused Chiang Kai-shek of "stealing" China's precious possessions. This was subsequently seen as a good thing, however, as many would have been destroyed during Mao's Great Proletarian Cultural Revolution in the late 1960s and early 1970s had the treasures remained in China. Returning the treasures was mentioned during the Chen Shui-bian era if the KMT were to dispense with its assets accumulated at the time, but there was no public support for this. The Chiang Kai-shek Memorial Hall (renamed National Taiwan Democracy Memorial Hall) is also popular. Located in downtown Taipei, it is devoted more to Chinese history and contains the National Theater and the National Concert Hall. Another attraction is Taipei 101—the tallest building in the world.

Taipei's night markets are the most frequently visited place by tourists while department stores and small shops are favorite places for travelers to purchase local goods. Taipei is often said to have the best restaurants and most variety in cuisine anyplace in the world because famous chefs from all over China fled to Taiwan in 1949. Eating places in Taipei, in fact, serve food representing cuisine from nearly all areas of China, and this means variety. There are also many very good Japanese, Korean, and Western restaurants in Taipei.

On the more exotic side is Lungshan Temple in Taipei, one of Taiwan's oldest. Nearby is "snake alley," where one can see local showmen play with poisonous snakes and offer the daring observer the snake's blood to drink (which is said to be good for the health). Visitors can also see habu-mongoose fights (the habu is a poisonous snake similar to the rattlesnake); the mongoose usually wins and kills the habu. In earlier days there were restaurants in the area that served dog and cat meat; snake, turtle, and other unusual things can still be found on menus.

North of Taipei is Yangmingshan Park, where there are hot springs, volcanic craters, and waterfalls, as well as a good view of Taipei. South of Taipei, in Wulai, visitors can see waterfalls, mountains, and Aboriginal entertainment provided by the Atayal tribe. In Yehliu, north of Taipei, one can view unusual rock formations made by the wind and water from the ocean, many of which look like mushrooms.

In central Taiwan is the famous Sun Moon Lake, one of the most serene places anywhere say many visitors. There is also Ali Shan (Mount Ali), Yu Shan (Jade Mountain), and a giant Buddha statue near Changhua. In the south is Tainan, the island's oldest city, which has forts from the Dutch period and other interesting sights. Also in the south is Kaohsiung, Taiwan's second largest city, and nearby are the island's largest Buddha, Moon World, and some beautiful beaches further south. In eastern Taiwan are Taroko Gorge, a marble-walled cliff, and other spectacular scenery.

Visiting Taiwan at the time of national holidays is more interesting then usual. The most important is Chinese New Year, or Lunar New Year. It comes early in the year, but not at the same time each year. The Dragon Boat Festival is held in the summer, followed by Mid-Autumn Festival, or Moon Festival (again according to the lunar calendar), Confucius's Birthday (or Teachers' Day) in September, and Double Ten Day, or National Day, on October 10.

Notes

1. For details on Taiwan's geography and the territorial claims made by the Republic of China, see *The Republic of China 1994 Yearbook* (Taipei: Government Information Office, 1994), chapter 1.

2. "Geography of Taiwan," *Wikipedia* (online at wikepedia.com, viewed March 2008).

3. For details, see Michael Hindley and James Bridge, "Disputed Islands," *Free China Review* (August 1994): 42–47.

4. Jane Rickards, "Taiwan Stakes Its Claim on Disputed Isle," *Washington Post,* February 3, 2008, A18.

5. For further details on this controversy, see John F. Copper, "The Fishing Islands Controversy," *Asia Quarterly* (1972/1973): 217–227.

6. See Chiao-min Hsieh, *Taiwan–Ilha Formosa: A Geographical Perspective* (Washington, D.C.: Butterworths, 1964), 2–4.

7. See ibid., 20, regarding the frequency of earthquakes in Taiwan.

8. *The Republic of China Yearbook—Taiwan 2002* (Taipei: Government Information Office, 2002), 25. Also see Hsieh, *Taiwan–Ilha Formosa,* chapter 6, for further details.

9. See W. G. Goddard, *Formosa: A Study in Chinese History* (East Lansing: Michigan State University Press, 1966), x–xi.

10. For a list of Taiwan's rivers and their lengths and watersheds, see *Taiwan Yearbook 2007,* (Taipei: Government Information Office, 2007), 14.

11. Daniel P. Reid, *Taiwan* (Hong Kong: APA Publications, 1984), 24.

12. See chapter 4 of Goddard, *Formosa,* for details.

13. See "Taiwan," *Wikipedia* (online at wikipedia.com, viewed March 2008).

14. Taiwan ranks number five in the world in the percentage of its surface covered by forest. See *Asiaweek,* 7 December 1994, 17.

15. Yueh Ching, "Taiwan's Population Density Ranks No. 2 Around the World," *Free China Journal,* September 8, 1995, 4; *The Republic of China Yearbook—Taiwan 2002,* 22.

16. Philip Courtenay, "Taiwan faced with aging society," *Taiwan Journal,* August 17, 2007, 6; *Taiwan Yearbook 2007,* 27. Taiwan's fertility rate in 2006 was 1.12 compared to 1.3 for Japan, 1.9 for France, and 2.0 for the United States.

17. *Taiwan Yearbook 2007,* 180.

18. See Wen-hui Tsai, *In Making China Modernized: Comparative Modernization Between Mainland China and Taiwan* (Baltimore: University of Maryland School of Law, 1993), 135, for early data; and Phillip Courtenay, "Aging Societies Can Deliver Advantages to All," *Free China Journal,* July 10, 1998, 6. For recent figures, see Jane Rickards, "The Aging Taiwanese," *Topics* (February 2007): 18–21. The most recent data comes from the CIA's *World Factbook* (online at cia.gov).

19. *The World Factbook* (online at cia.gov).

20. Hungfu Hsieh, "Foreign spouses seen taking up 18% of marriages in '07," *Taiwan News,* January 21, 2008 (online at taiwannews.com, viewed on January 25, 2008).

21. *The Republic of China Yearbook—Taiwan 2002,* 347.

22. See *Taiwan Yearbook 2007,* 28, for data on the number of foreign workers.

23. Willy Wo-Lap Lam, "China Wages 'Big Bucks Diplomacy,'" *CNN,* June 19, 2002.

24. "Urbanization at Full Speed," *Free China Journal,* February 17, 1995, 4.

25. "2005 population estimates for cities in Taiwan," Mongabay.com (online at mongabay.com, viewed February 20, 2008).

26. Tsai, *In Making China Modernized,* 129.

27. For details on Taiwan's ethnic groups and the settlement of Taiwan, see Ronald G. Knapp, ed., *China's Island Frontier: Studies in the Historical Geography of Taiwan* (Honolulu: University of Hawaii Press, 1980), part 1.

28. John Nobel Wilford, "Pacific Islands' Ancestry Emerges in Genetic Study," *New York Times,* January 12, 2008 (online at lexisnexis.com).

29. *The Republic of China Yearbook—Taiwan 2002,* 27.

30. See Eugenia Yen, "Still Guests After All These (Fifteen Hundred) Years," *Free China Review* (October 1993): 12.

31. James W. Davidson, *The Island of Formosa: Past and Present* (New York: Oxford University Press, 1988), 561.

32. This is demonstrated by various studies and opinion polls. Further discussion on this issue will follow.

33. Wen-lang Li, "Social Change in Taiwan and the Solution to Ethnic Problems," *United Monthly* (May 19, 1987): 2, cited in Hung-mao Tien, *The Great Transition: Political and Social Change in the Republic of China* (Stanford: Hoover Institution Press, 1989), 36.

34. For further details on culture, see James C. Hsiung, ed., *Contemporary Republic of China: The Taiwan Experience, 1950–1980* (New York: Praeger, 1981), part 1. Also see *The Story of Taiwan* (Taipei: Government Information Office, 2000).

35. See *The Republic of China, 1988: A Reference Book* (Taipei: Hilit Publishing, 1988), chapter 39.

36. In 1983, Taiwan ranked eleventh in the world in per capita movie attendance. Its rank dropped in subsequent years, however, as videotapes and other forms of entertainment became popular. See *Asiaweek,* December 14, 1994, 18.

37. For details about this and some of the changes in culture mentioned previously, see Thomas B. Gold, *State and Society in the Taiwan Miracle* (Armonk, NY: M. E. Sharpe, 1986), 130–134.

38. See *The Republic of China 1995 Yearbook* (Taipei: Government Information Office, 1995), 281. In 1993, 158 million passengers used the railroads. In 1992, 30.6 million tons of cargo was hauled.

39. "Taiwan High Speed Rail," *Wikipedia* (online at wikipedia.org, viewed on January 25, 2008).

40. *Taiwan Yearbook 2007*, 160.

41. Ibid.

42. Ibid., 219.

43. Ibid., 221.

44. Ibid., 219.

45. Ibid., 163.

46. Ibid., 161.

47. "Kaohsiung Mass Rapid Transit," *Wikipedia* (online at wikipedia.org, viewed February 20, 2008).

48. *Taiwan Yearbook 2007*, 164–165.

49. Tien, *The Great Transition*, 196–197.

50. *Taiwan Yearbook 2007*, 190.

51. "World's 100 Largest Newspapers," World Association of Newspapers (online at wan-press.org, viewed February 20, 2008).

52. *The Republic of China at a Glance—Taiwan 2001* (Taipei: Government Information Office, 2001), 27.

53. *Taiwan Yearbook 2007*, 192.

54. Ibid., 193.

55. Ibid., 194–195.

56. Ibid., 195.

57. Ibid., 197.

58. Ibid., 229.

59. *The Republic of China 1989 Yearbook* (Taipei: Government Information Office, 1989), 459.

2

HISTORY

TAIWAN'S PAST IS OFTEN CITED AS EVIDENCE for both those who advocate that it is part of China, or should be, and those who do not. As noted in chapter 1, studies of its prehistory suggest links with Southeast Asia, China, Japan, and possibly some other parts of Asia. Early historical records indicate connections with China; but those ties were tenuous and do not support very strongly, if at all, the People's Republic of China's legal claim to the island. Yet Taiwan's early record does not offer any proof it should be seen as connected to or belongs to any other country. For a brief period in the seventeenth century, Taiwan was a Western colony. It subsequently enjoyed a short span of self-rule before it was governed by China for more than two hundred years and then by Japan for fifty years. At the end of World War II, Taiwan was returned to Nationalist China, but just four years later, that government was deposed by the Communists and fled to Taiwan, at which time Taiwan became the home of the Republic of China and, to many people, synonymous with it. For over twenty years, until 1971 when Beijing obtained the China seat in the United Nations, Taipei represented China in international affairs. Since then, Taiwan has been diplomatically—though not in other ways—isolated as a result of Beijing's efforts to undermine the Republic of China's and/or Taiwan's claim to sovereignty. Meanwhile, for nearly four decades in the post–World War II bipolar world, there occurred conflicts (two or more almost leading to a global war), but otherwise there were few interactions between Taiwan and China. From the 1960s on, Taiwan's economic success, then its rapid democratization and the growth of a local identity, made Taiwan very different from China. Most of its residents perceived that separation was both desirable and inevitable. But during the past three decades, economic ties with China proliferated and, with China becoming a formidable economic and military power, this view changed. One might say Taiwan has become separate from China politically as a result of democratization, yet economic ties and, to a lesser degree, people-to-people ties, have made the two closer.

Prehistory and Early History

Evidence of human life in Taiwan dates back to the Paleolithic Age, or 20,000 to 30,000 and possibly 50,000 years ago.[1] Whether Taiwan's earliest inhabitants were the ancestors of the present Aboriginal population is uncertain. In any event, the Aborigines are the first people known to reside on the island. Formerly most anthropologists believed they hailed from Southeast Asia, perhaps via the Philippines, and are kin to the present-day Malay people who inhabit Brunei, Indonesia, and Malaysia. There are remarkable cultural similarities, and as many as two-thirds of the words in several of the Aboriginal languages are similar to Malay, even though the two peoples have had no direct contact in recorded history. There are also similarities in physical characteristics, social organizations, and crafts.[2] However, some scholars say the Aborigines migrated to Taiwan from China, originally living in what is now northern Myanmar and are likely related to the Miao people in south China because of the many linguistic and cultural similarities between the two groups.[3]

An alternative view is that the Aborigines have several origins and that some of their ancestors, perhaps of two tribes, migrated from the north, from either Japan or northern China. Some myths seem to link them to one or two minority nationality groups in North China, and there are some cultural similarities with the Ainus, the original inhabitants of Japan. When the Japanese governed Taiwan, they advanced the theory that the Aborigines were of Japanese origin, and some Western anthropologists agreed. Some Mainland Chinese scholars say the Aborigines of Taiwan migrated from southeast China sometime around 1700 BC in search of better land.[4] Still other scholars have suggested connections elsewhere, such as with India.[5] Very recently, researchers, using DNA tests, have connected the Aborigines to the native populations in Australia, New Zealand's Maoris, and to some inhabitants of the South Pacific islands and advance the theory that Taiwan is the origin of the Australasian people.[6]

The examination of fossils, pottery, and other artifacts in Taiwan has established some generally accepted information: that the Aboriginal population was fairly evenly distributed throughout the island; that their livelihood came from fishing, hunting, and some shifting agriculture; that land was usually owned in common; and that the political and social systems were tribal. Most Aboriginal tribes were patriarchal and patrilineal; some, however, were matriarchal and matrilineal. The Aborigines had contacts several centuries ago with other peoples in East Asia. However, detailed or genuinely historical information about Taiwan's Aborigines begins in the seventeenth century when the Dutch rendered some of their languages into a written form.[7]

There is mention of Taiwan in early Chinese records, which is quite natural inasmuch as the island is visible from Fukien Province on a clear day, and travel to Taiwan by boat was possible more then two millennia ago. However, Taiwan was not often cited in early Chinese historical writings, which are essentially chronicles of each ruler or dynasty. When mentioned, early court records seem to indicate that Taiwan was not regarded as part of China.[8] This view, of course, was to be expected, since early in its history China occupied only what is today part of North China, and the seat of the Chinese government was, throughout the centuries, usually in the north—a great distance from the part of China now adjacent to Taiwan. Furthermore, throughout most of its history and even in modern times, "China" was defined more by culture than by territory; Chinese governments did not propound the concept of territorial sovereignty or boundaries, as nation-states did in the West.

Before the Han Dynasty (206 BC–AD 222), Taiwan was known in China as the land of Yangchow. During the Han and the Three Kingdoms period that followed, it was called Yinchow. The first official contact mentioned in Chinese historical records was in AD 239: The Chinese emperor at that time sent a 10,000-member expeditionary force to Taiwan, apparently to explore the island. This, Chinese leaders in Beijing now say, constitutes grounds for a legal claim to the island based on discovery.[9] But no territorial claim was mentioned in Chinese court records, and no follow-up missions were sent. Moreover, at that time Taiwan was referred to as an area "outside the pale of Chinese civilization."[10]

Almost four centuries later, in AD 605, the Sui Dynasty emperor sent a second expedition to Taiwan. The leader of the mission brought back several Aborigines, who were taught Chinese. A more serious follow-up expedition sent six years later, accompanied by an interpreter, brought back considerably more information about Taiwan. Though there were no subsequent visits and this mission ultimately had little impact, it has also been cited as the basis of a Chinese claim to Taiwan.[11]

After this, China sent no official expeditions or missions to Taiwan for some time. Some say this was because China did not seek colonies or the expansion of its territory across the seas. Taiwan's Aborigines, meanwhile, having ceased to be seafaring, initiated few contacts with China. Outsiders visiting the island in ensuing years were mainly pirates from the Ryukyu Islands and areas on the China coast adjacent to Taiwan.[12]

If China's historical visits to Taiwan were infrequent and established neither Chinese civilization on the island nor grounds for a territorial claim, the early migration of Chinese to Taiwan afforded a meaningful Chinese presence there and seems to provide the strongest rationale for a legal claim by China based on history. Yet it is uncertain when the earliest migration of Chinese occurred, whether they were Hakka or Fukienese, or even whether Chinese migrants preceded Japanese settlers on the island.[13] It is thought Chinese farmers and fishermen settled on the Pescadores as early as the seventh century; they were certainly to be found on Taiwan before the twelfth century AD.[14]

By the thirteenth century, there were a significant number of permanent Chinese settlements on Taiwan, and the Fukien Chinese were already displacing the Hakka from choice land.[15] There were no Japanese or other settlers on the island. If Japanese had migrated to Taiwan earlier—as seems to have been the case—there was no evidence of them at this time. Notwithstanding the number of Chinese communities on the island, the Chinese government apparently did not know much about emigration to Taiwan, or did not consider it important, since no records were made of it. Also, as was noted in Chapter 1, throughout much of Chinese history, going to Taiwan was a violation of Chinese law. As a result, most who went there did not plan to return to China and did not contemplate claiming the island for China; they simply sought land and a better life in Taiwan.

During the Yuan Dynasty (1263–1368), when the Mongols ruled China, the Peking government's interest in the "eastern and southeastern seas" areas grew, and the Pescadores were brought under its control, though Taiwan remained outside of Chinese (or, more accurately, Mongol) jurisdiction. Moreover, court records indicate that there was still confusion about whether Taiwan was part of the Ryukyu Islands to the north. Further, no mention was made of Taiwan's being Chinese territory or a part of China. The Mongols sought to conquer Japan, an ambition that prompted their expeditions to the Taiwan area. But this had no lasting impact.[16] Meanwhile, Chinese and Japanese pirates and Chinese farmers wrested control of some parts of the western coastal plain areas of Taiwan from the Aborigines. Chinese occupied some of the southwestern parts of the island, and Japanese settlers, who had meanwhile reappeared on the island, held some northern coastal areas.[17]

In 1430, during the Ming Dynasty, the explorer Cheng Ho landed on Taiwan's west coast and made contact with the Aborigines. His visit, however, was inadvertent: He had been shipwrecked there while returning to China from Southeast Asia. He obtained supplies and herbal medicines, that were said to have "miracle powers," from the Aborigines. When he returned to China, Cheng provided the emperor with a written account of his experiences. Cheng Ho's visit is thus cited as evidence of China's claim to Taiwan. But there were no subsequent visits. In ensuing years, Chinese court chronicles described Taiwan as a "base for pirates."[18] It also may be significant that Chinese historical records do not indicate that Cheng Ho, explorers, or other visitors to Taiwan had contact with Chinese residing there.

Having said all this, however, one must bear in mind that no other country has made a claim to Taiwan based on historical ties, and if one were to do so, its claim could not seriously compete with China's. Thus if history is to serve as the basis for a territorial claim, China has the best case to make. Finally, it is important to note that there was no central political authority on the island historically to justify an argument that Taiwan was self-governing or had the attributes of a nation-state, or even something that might have evolved easily into one.

Western and Chinese Rule

The Captain of a Portuguese vessel sailing through the Taiwan Strait en route to Japan in 1517 sighted Taiwan and wrote in the ship's log the words "Ilha Formosa," or beautiful island.[19] This was the first Western encounter with Taiwan. But the Portuguese ship did not stop or lay claim to Taiwan. Just over a century later, in 1622, Dutch forces landed on the Pescadore Islands and subsequently established a military presence there. They then used the Pescadores as a base for monitoring ship traffic in the Taiwan Strait while harassing Portuguese trading vessels sailing between ports to the north and south. The next year, a local Chinese official signed a treaty with Dutch representatives granting Holland a post on Taiwan and other privileges in exchange for their withdrawal from the Pescadores. Chinese officials at this time suggested that China had jurisdiction over Taiwan, but presented no evidence to support this claim.[20]

In 1626, Spanish forces seized Keelung and subsequently expanded their control to Tamsui on the northwest coast. Spanish colonial efforts were facilitated by an isolationist policy adopted by the Tokugawa Shogunate that, in 1628, led to the departure of Japanese settlers on Taiwan. Spanish settlers arrived, but Dutch forces drove them out in 1642. Shortly thereafter, the Dutch quelled Chinese opposition to their presence with the help of the Aborigines and established nominal jurisdiction over the entire island.

Taiwan economically and politically became a Dutch colony. It was governed by the Dutch East India Company, which claimed sovereignty over the island for Holland. The company rented land and farm implements to Chinese settlers and introduced oxen to till the fields, enabling the peasants to grow sugarcane and other cash crops. Dutch East India Company rule led to an expansion of commerce on the island and trade with merchants in China, Japan, and elsewhere in the region. The Company built castles, dug wells, conducted land surveys, created a writing system for the Aboriginal languages, and converted some of the population to Christianity. Though the Dutch East India Company exploited the island for profits, Taiwan experienced significant progress under Dutch rule.[21]

At the beginning of the Dutch period, the Chinese population was small; the Aboriginal population was several times larger. Chinese immigration increased under Dutch rule, however, and more Chinese became permanent inhabitants rather than seasonal workers. Still, most Chinese settlers on the island did not willingly or readily submit to Dutch rule; in fact, they rebelled against Dutch authority in 1640 and again in 1652. Most of the Chinese inhabitants preferred to be governed by China or wanted self-rule.[22]

Meanwhile, in China, the Ming Dynasty came under threat from the Manchus (a non-Chinese people who inhabited Manchuria). In a last-ditch effort to protect China from a Manchu invasion, Emperor Sze Tsung appointed Cheng Chih-lung, a pirate operating from a base in Taiwan, to command remnant Ming naval forces. Though successful in winning some important battles, Cheng Chih-lung failed to prevent a Ming defeat, and the Manchus established a new dynasty in 1644, the Ch'ing, which ruled China until 1911.

Cheng Chih-lung's son, Cheng Ch'eng-kung (also known as Koxinga), born in Japan to a Japanese mother, inherited his father's military forces. The Dutch at first saw him as a pirate of little consequence and allowed him to operate in areas in northern Taiwan. They even let Cheng bring large numbers of Chinese, mostly refugees fleeing Manchu rule, to Taiwan to become soldiers and/or to settle. Cheng was thus able to raise an army of 100,000 men and an armada of 3,000 junks in order to fight the Manchus for more than a decade (from 1646 to 1658), at one point nearly capturing the city of Nanking. However, after repeated failures to oust China's Manchu rulers, he was forced to limit his military activities to the coast of southern China.[23]

In 1661, having abandoned his efforts to reestablish the Ming Dynasty, Cheng launched an attack on the Dutch stronghold of Zeelandia, near what is now the city of Tainan. With 30,000 men, he besieged forts that were defended by 2,000 Dutch soldiers. After two years of fighting, the Dutch conceded defeat and reached an agreement with Cheng whereby they were allowed to peacefully evacuate. This brought an end to a generation of Dutch colonial rule of the island.

Cheng Ch'eng-kung established a Ming-style government on Taiwan, complete with a Chinese legal system, a court, scholars, and advisers. Some say he established the first Chinese government on Taiwan.[24] Cheng also promoted Chinese culture and religion. His rule, however, depended on the support of powerful local Chinese families; in this and other ways, his government resembled a feudal system more than it did the Chinese scholar-bureaucratic system. Moreover, since Cheng continued to regard the Manchu government as his enemy, he never established official ties with China.

Cheng successfully encouraged the growth of the Chinese population on Taiwan, and in that way he also made the island more Chinese. The Manchus inadvertently helped him in this effort: For a number of years, fearing that Cheng might land forces on the China coast and wanting to preclude local support for him and his armies, the government in Peking ordered the evacuation of the coastal areas of

China adjacent to Taiwan, causing severe deprivation to numerous villages there. Many inhabitants of coastal Fukien Province, bereft of their former livelihood of farming and fishing, fled to Taiwan.

Cheng promoted trade with Japan, the Philippines, Indochina, Siam, and the East Indies. Because Taiwan had several of the busiest commercial ports in East Asia during this time, the island absorbed cultural influences from these contacts and, unlike most of China, became quite cosmopolitan. Still, however, Cheng dreamed of restoring the Ming Dynasty, which he regarded as genuinely Chinese, and making Taiwan part of it.

Part of Cheng's undying desire to drive the Manchus out of China and restore the Ming Dynasty involved a plan to establish control over the Philippines. On several occasions, he sent representatives to Manila to meet with leaders of the Chinese population there. Worried about a rebellion, in 1661 Spanish rulers massacred 10,000 Chinese inhabitants, after which they sent a messenger to Cheng telling him they had killed all Chinese residing in the Philippines. A livid Cheng wanted revenge, but he died two years later, at age thirty-eight—some say of a heart attack precipitated by the news of the slaughter of Chinese in the Philippines.[25] Cheng no doubt would have accomplished much more, including possibly defeating Spanish forces in the Philippines, had he lived longer. Notwithstanding this, for his accomplishments Cheng is acclaimed a hero in Taiwan. Ironically, historians in China regard him highly as well for his liberating Taiwan from Western colonial rule—the earliest instance of this in Asia.

After Cheng Ch'eng-kung's death, his son, Cheng Ching, whose power base was in Fukien Province, vied with his uncle in Taiwan for the right of succession. The son, with his superior military forces, coerced the armies of his father's brother into surrender. A link between Taiwan and the adjacent area of China was formally established as a result. Cheng Ching, like his father, led several expeditions against the Manchus in his efforts to realize the dream of restoring the Ming Dynasty. But, after four years of failed efforts, he retreated to Taiwan, where he, too, died at a relatively young age.

After Cheng Ching's death, the Cheng house was plagued by palace intrigue, internal dissension, and unrest. Sensing an opportunity, the Manchu government sent a naval expedition to the Pescadores, where it destroyed the Cheng government's fleet and set the stage for an assault on Taiwan. When Manchu troops landed on the island, local military forces promptly surrendered, ending just over twenty years of Cheng family rule of Taiwan. Summing up the Cheng period, Taiwan was self-governing, but wanted ties with China. Some now draw a resemblance to the Chiang Kai-shek era from 1949 to 1975.

From 1683 to 1895, Taiwan was ruled by China. For most of this time—until 1886—the island was administratively part of Fukien Province. Officials assigned to Taiwan, who were mostly Chinese rather than Manchus, were generally lazy, inefficient, and corrupt. They enforced laws and edicts with cruelty and generally disregarded the welfare of the population, prompting numerous uprisings and such political and social instability that Taiwan became known as "the land of rebellion and unrest." From 1683 to 1843, there were fifteen major rebellions against the government.[26] Peking generally ignored Taiwan's problems. Official Chinese records during this period called Taiwan a "frontier area." Chinese, primarily from Fukien, continued to emigrate to Taiwan, even though during much of this period, specifically until 1732, the government officially prohibited it.

Citing the Peking government's general neglect of the island, not to mention the numerous revolts against Chinese authority, some scholars claim that China did not consider Taiwan to be part of China.[27] One must keep in mind, however, that China was ruled by the Manchus at this time, and they, to some degree, feared the "Chineseness" of Taiwan, especially since it had been a base of anti-Manchu military operations under Cheng Ch'eng-kung. Also, in spite of poor governance, Chinese culture flourished on the island, and the Chinese population increased rapidly.

After 1800, a rapid increase in Western commerce in the area and Taiwan's expanding imports and exports again caused Western powers to express an interest in the island. Another reason for Taiwan's attraction was that, through the publication of several books about Taiwan by European authors, Westerners had learned much more about the island and its presence on the world stage.[28] In addition, at that time ships became propelled by steam engines that burned coal—and Taiwan had coal.

But it was not until the Opium War (that started in 1839) that the foreign powers' desires to control Taiwan became serious. During the fighting, Chinese forces on Taiwan were mobilized. Subsequently, for strategic reasons stemming from Taiwan's possible role as a base of operations in a broader war, the government of China paid greater heed to the island. Though concern over Taiwan on the part of Chinese leaders soon faded, events had generated an opinion among some Chinese officials that the island had strategic value to China, a view that was to be revived later.

In ensuing years, Peking punished officials in Taiwan for mistreating British sailors who ran into trouble with local authorities, fearing London might use these incidences as a pretext for seizing and colonizing the island. In 1854, Commodore Matthew C. Perry urged the US government to establish a presence on Taiwan. A few years later, Townsend Harris, the US representative in Japan, suggested that the US government negotiate with officials in Peking for the purchase of the island. Because Peking consistently refused to accept accountability for difficulties foreign powers encountered in Taiwan, British and US officials concluded that China did not claim sovereignty over Taiwan or the Pescadores.[29] Nevertheless, neither London nor Washington made a decision to colonize Taiwan.

In the late 1850s, Keelung and Tamsui became important ports of call for Western ships. Accordingly, several European countries and the United States set up trading posts and consulates on Taiwan. Japan's contacts with Taiwan increased, particularly after Tokyo incorporated the nearby Ryukyu Islands in 1879. On several occasions, the Japanese government protested the abuse of Japanese sailors shipwrecked on the coast of Taiwan; Peking's authorities, as usual, denied responsibility. Again demonstrating China's lack of attention to Taiwan, in 1869 the heads of several Aboriginal tribes signed treaties with the United States.

China's neglect of Taiwan, however, ended in the late 1880s. When widespread rebellion broke out in southern China, the threat to Manchu rule there prompted officials in Peking to recognize anew that Taiwan was strategically important. Even the Imperial Court accepted this view after French forces blockaded and bombarded forts on the island during Sino-French hostilities over Indochina. In 1884, the government reorganized its political administration of Taiwan and appointed a capable official, Liu Ming-ch'uan, as governor. Two years later, Taiwan was elevated to the status of province.

Chinese rule under Liu Ming-ch'uan was efficient and enlightened. Liu built roads, railroads, and harbors. He improved and modernized Taiwan's economy and strengthened the island's defenses. Taiwan prospered, and its population developed better feelings toward China. Liu would have accomplished much more had it not been for jealous colleagues who saw him as a threat, and had not the Chinese government recalled him precipitously. Historians in both China and Taiwan regard Liu Ming-ch'uan highly; today, he is one of Taiwan's most renowned figures.

Part of the Japanese Empire

In 1894, China and Japan went to war over their conflicting interests in Korea. Surprisingly to many, Japan won, and won handily. The Treaty of Shimonoseki that ended the war in 1895 contained, among various provisions a phrase whereby China ceded Taiwan and the Pescadores to Japan "in perpetuity." The Western powers viewed the treaty as legally binding and thus regarded Taiwan's transfer to Japanese rule as legitimate.[30]

Meanwhile, when news of the treaty reached Taiwan, local leaders proclaimed independence and established the "Republic of Taiwan"—Asia's first republic. But the effort was ill-fated, and the new republic lasted but ten days. Part of the reason was that Taiwan had no central government to organize a meaningful effort to challenge Japan. Likewise, there was no island-wide support for any of the several contending political or military leaders because the island's population was divided by ethnic and clan differences. Finally, many residents of Taiwan at the time despised the warlordism and banditry that plagued the island and felt that Japanese rule might bring an end to these problems. They also felt that opposing Japan was futile.

The Chinese government in Peking did nothing to aid the resistance. China offered no support—not even recognition. In fact, during a formal ceremony in Keelung shortly after China signed the Treaty of Shimonoseki, an official sent from Peking formally transferred control over Taiwan to Japanese authorities. Most Chinese in Taiwan gave up hope of help from China, and many expressed bitterness about China's betrayal.[31]

Within three years, the Japanese military was no longer needed to keep order in Taiwan. The international community was somewhat apprehensive about Japan's colonizing effort because other countries wanted to continue to use Taiwan as a port of call. Not yet powerful enough to challenge most Western nations, even in Asia, Japan allowed foreign ships to stop in Taiwan and left open Taiwan's ports to trade and other contacts.

As Japan's first colonial effort, its rule of Taiwan was an experiment, and its policies often seemed inconsistent. Even though Japanese leaders complained about population pressures at home and later rationalized Japan's expansionist imperial policies by claims that it needed more space, it made no effort to populate the island with Japanese people. Japanese leaders regarded Japan (in contrast to its empire) as sacred ground and the Japanese people as descendants of the gods; transplanting them to areas already populated with non-Japanese contradicted these notions. Except for a few farmers, those Japanese who took up residence in Taiwan during the colonial period were either part of the military government or were in business.

Japanese colonial policy may be described as beneficial and progressive on the one hand, yet discriminatory and predatory on the other. It was efficient and in many ways enlightened, but it did not lay the groundwork for self-rule, much less democracy. Some observers have described Japan's intent as expansionist and militaristic from the outset, but those claims are difficult to prove.[32] It seems more accurate to say these aims developed gradually and/or happened in anticipation of World War II.

Tokyo's first objectives after it acquired Taiwan were to establish order and promote economic development. Both were seen as enhancing the power and prestige of Japan. Warlordism was eradicated, and law and order were established quickly, albeit by harsh means. Decrees issued by Japanese colonial authorities amounted to criminal law and were applied retroactively, sometimes without legal precedent. Tribunals were used, rather than civil courts, and capital punishment was employed frequently.

In the economic realm, Japan's first priority was to increase Taiwan's agricultural productivity. Tokyo encouraged the cultivation of rice in the northern part of the island and sugar in the south. Rice was considered a staple, sugar a cash crop. Using new strains of rice and more efficient production techniques, yields increased rapidly. By the 1930s, Taiwan produced twice as much rice as the population consumed. Nearly a million tons were exported to Japan annually, as well as about the same amount of sugar—or two-thirds of Taiwan's crop. Food production increased to such a degree that, by the 1920s, the consumption of meat, vegetables, and fruits in Taiwan was higher than that of any province in China and even higher than in some parts of Japan.[33]

Japan also upgraded Taiwan's economic infrastructure. Before 1895, Taiwan had 30 miles of railroad; by 1905 it had 300, and 7,000 more were either planned or under construction.[34] The Japanese constructed roads and harbors, and communications facilities were built or upgraded. In 1903, hydroelectric generators went into service near Taipei, making Taiwan the first place to use electricity in Asia outside of Japan.[35] Electrification spawned small industries, such as glass factories and paper mills, and made possible the mechanization of harbors. Tokyo standardized the monetary system, established banks, and promoted uniform commercial practices, thereby transforming commerce from a barter system to one based on money. After World War I, Taiwan's economy received a boost when Tokyo banned foreign enterprises from the island. New industries such as textiles, chemicals, and machinery sprang up quickly. In the 1930s, as a result of Tokyo's expansionist policies, the Japanese government began promoting the development of heavy industries in Taiwan. In the process, Taiwan's foreign trade increased markedly. However, Taiwan's enviable economic growth and modernization not only helped Taiwan's population, but it also served the colonial rulers. The island's economy was linked to Japan's, just as European nations tied their colonies to the metropolis. Before World War II, 90 percent of Taiwan's exports went to Japan. For Tokyo, Taiwan's economic growth was proof of Japan's enlightened colonial policies, but for Taiwan, it increased the island's dependency on Japan.

Meanwhile the Japanese improved public hygiene in Taiwan radically. The island, which had been known as the pesthole of Asia, became second only to Japan in the region in sanitation. By the early twentieth century, bubonic plague had been eradicated, cholera was rare, and smallpox was much less widespread. Dysentery and malaria were drastically reduced. All these diseases remained rampant in China.[36] Japanese rule also brought social change. Taiwan's educational system was improved markedly. The island's literacy rate, technological skills, and knowledge of world affairs soon exceeded that of any part of China or, for that matter, any other area in Asia outside Japan. Laws and customs that kept lower socioeconomic groups perpetually in debt were banned. In 1910, the practice of binding women's feet was outlawed.

Political governance was less enlightened. Japanese colonial governance was facilitated by *pao chia* (a system of common responsibility), which divided the Chinese population into groups of one hundred households each and made the head of each group accountable for the behavior of those families under his authority.[37] This person in turn held each family head accountable for the conduct of that family. Informants and severe punishments ensured effective Japanese political control. Important decisions on almost all matters were made in Tokyo to be administered by the Japanese colonial authorities. Although policies were somewhat more democratic before the 1930s, when the military grasped control of the Japanese government, there was still little evidence that Taiwan was heading toward self-rule or democracy.

The Aborigines proved difficult to control and incorporate into the society. The Japanese were generally successful in disarming them and forcing them to give up headhunting, but even as late as the 1940s, many were not "pacified" because the Japanese could not effectively police all of the mountainous areas in Taiwan. In fact, strong resistance by the Aborigines to Japanese rule led the Japanese colonial government to ignore parts of central Taiwan.

Japanese policies had other drawbacks. Japan's social policies, although generally progressive, were carried out with little thought or understanding of Taiwanese customs or feelings. Educational policies forced Taiwanese to learn Japanese, and neither standard Chinese nor the Taiwan dialect of Chinese were taught in school. Taiwanese students were encouraged to study medicine, engineering, science, and technology-related subjects, but not law, politics, or any of the social sciences. Reflecting their attitudes of ethnic superiority, Japanese officials and most other Japanese in Taiwan attended their own schools and resided in separate areas.

World War II

Japanese rule of Taiwan just prior to and during the war was not without problems. The colonial government faced a fundamental dilemma regarding its philosophy and its style of ruling Taiwan. Many Japanese officials advocated a policy of tough rule, thinking that the population of Taiwan opposed Japanese control. But they also assumed the island should remain a colony of Japan indefinitely. Others considered Taiwan's colonial status to be temporary and pushed for a different approach, called the "Formosa Home Rule Formula." Still others proffered a policy called *kominka*, or assimilation. *Kominka* had official support, but because most Japanese opposed granting equality to Taiwan's population, an assimilation policy was not realistic and was carried out only halfheartedly.[38]

In 1935, after Lin Hsien-t'ang and his Home Rule Association had for several years advocated the transfer of political power to a locally elected assembly, Tokyo's leaders announced the establishment of an elective government in Taiwan, but this applied only to local government and Japanese colonial officials retained veto power over important decisions. Still, an election was held, and some democratic change was in evidence. Progress toward more democratic rule, however, was reversed a year or two later when Japanese politics became dominated by the military and as Japan headed for war.

In 1936, Taiwan's colonial governors once again became military officers. The next year, when war broke out with China, martial law was put into effect in Taiwan. The Japanese navy referred to Taiwan as an "unsinkable aircraft carrier" and began to use it as a military staging area. Large numbers of Japanese troops were stationed on Taiwan and trained there. Many of Taiwan's newly created industries were expanded, and they prospered as a result of their vital role in supplying the Japanese war machine. In 1941, Taiwan was the site from which Japanese forces launched the invasion of the Philippines and of other offshore countries to the south.

Even before 1941, the Chinese population of Taiwan for the most part had forsaken their ties with China and saw little reason to reestablish them. Most supported Japanese rule—or at least had accommodated to it. There had been no meaningful protest in Taiwan to Japan's taking and colonizing Manchuria in 1931 or to its war with China, which started in 1937. Those for whom Japan's invasion of China was a problem or those who felt strong ties to China were allowed to leave and return to China. Few did so.

Many Taiwanese worked in war-related industries or in other ways abetted the Japanese war effort.[39] During the war, many Taiwanese volunteered for military service. Their defection rate was low, and there was little or no protest against military life. A large number of Taiwanese fought in combat in China (including in Nanking, where they participated in atrocities against Chinese civilians). According to one source, 207,183 Taiwanese were conscripted into the Japanese military; 30,304 were casualties during the war.[40]

As Japanese forces retreated in the Pacific, the population of Taiwan was readied for US attacks and, eventually, an invasion. Taiwanese served in units that prepared to defend the island. As it turned out, however, US forces limited their military actions to the bombing of oil storage depots, in addition to infrastructure and military targets. There was no saturation bombing or targeting population centers. In fact, Taiwan was spared the war damage that Japan and many other parts of East Asia suffered. There were shortages of many goods, but, again, Taiwan was more fortunate than most parts of the region.

Toward the end of the war, the US Navy discussed plans for invading Taiwan, but it soon abandoned the idea. US military strategists possessed few good maps of the island and, more important, realized that the Taiwanese were unlikely to rebel against their Japanese colonial rulers and would instead battle US forces to help defend the island.[41] To avoid the possible embarrassment of fighting local Chinese defenders of Taiwan, the United States instead invaded Okinawa, the largest of Japan's Ryukyu Islands, leaving Taiwan (unlike Japan proper and China) generally unscathed.

Meanwhile, because of Chiang Kai-shek's special role as an ally of the United States during the war, he was afforded the opportunity to request that "territories occupied by enemy forces since 1937 or 1939," as stated in the Atlantic Charter and as suggested by Winston Churchill, also include those lands taken from China by Japan during the Sino-Japanese War. Chiang had not made a serious effort to make a claim that Taiwan belonged to China before this, as witnessed by the fact that the constitutions written in 1925, 1934, and 1936 did not list Taiwan as a province of China. Moreover, "lost territories" cited in Sun Yat-sen's Three People's Principles included all or parts of Korea, Vietnam, Burma, the Ryukyu Islands, Bhutan, and Nepal; Taiwan was also cited but was accorded no special status.[42]

In any event, it became the policy of the United States and its allies during the war that Japan could not keep its empire, and that policy covered Taiwan. At the Cairo Conference in December 1943, the United States and the United Kingdom reached an agreement with Generalissimo Chiang Kai-shek to the effect that Taiwan would be put in the category of territories "stolen" by Japan, and that Taiwan "shall be restored to the Republic of China." This agreement was reaffirmed in the Potsdam Declaration in July 1945 when Japan's defeat was imminent. Yet Taiwan's legal status remained undecided pending the signing of a peace treaty.

In the fall of 1945, Japanese—one-eighteenth of Taiwan's population—departed the island. This large contingent of Japanese included most officials of the colonial government, the military, the police, businessmen, many professional people, and some farmers. Chiang Kai-shek sent military forces to keep order and officials from the government of the Republic of China to replace the Japanese colonial administration. It was thus assumed that Japan had surrendered Taiwan to Chiang's forces and that the island was to be returned to China; indeed, there was no other logical choice. The Cairo agreement said this (even though it was a wartime declaration and not a formal treaty). Mao's forces were capable of little more than launching guerrilla operations in the interior of China at this time, and besides, he and the Chinese Communist Party had expressed no interest in Taiwan.

Not unhappy that Japan was defeated, or at least fully accepting it as reality, Taiwan's population welcomed the arrival of Nationalist Chinese officials. Most of the population was tired of war and looked forward to the end of colonial rule. A large number of citizens wanted democracy and self-rule. Many wanted to restore family ties in China.

Nevertheless, many were apprehensive about Taiwan's future. A small minority in Taiwan advocated independence. A few suggested that Taiwan should become a

United Nations trust territory. Some even proposed that Taiwan should become a territory governed by the United States.[43] Others wanted guarantees about the island's future status should it become part of China again. Taiwanese who participated in the surrender ceremony asked for a provision giving "special status" to Taiwan because the island had been a Japanese colony for fifty years and, therefore, was different from China in many ways.[44] The American public wanted the troops to come home while its government focused more on problems in Europe than Asia. Taiwan was thus destined to share in China's turmoil and civil war.

Part of China Again

On October 25, 1945 subsequently celebrated as Retrocession Day, Taiwan officially became a part of the Republic of China. But Taiwan was not made a province of China, as had been expected. Similarly, no efforts were made to establish a democratic government. Chiang Kai-shek appointed Ch'en Yi governor-general and supreme commander and gave him the same kind of near-absolute power the Japanese governors had enjoyed.

Making matters worse, Ch'en, along with many of the Mainland Chinese soldiers sent to Taiwan at the time of the Japanese evacuation, regarded Taiwanese as traitors for not having opposed Japanese rule. Chen and his Mainland Chinese administration, as well as the military, also perceived that the Taiwanese had been tainted for fifty years by what they considered foreign and inferior Japanese culture. Few Mainland Chinese soldiers or officials spoke Taiwanese, and few Taiwanese spoke the Chinese national language. Although some Nationalist soldiers and administrators hailed from Fukien Province and spoke the dialect from which Taiwanese was derived, even that did not guarantee good communications. In any event, Ch'en wanted Taiwan to become "Chinese."[45]

The Nationalist Chinese government and the Nationalist Party soon came to be seen by many Taiwanese as a carpetbag regime, much the same way that the South in the United States viewed the harsh post–Civil War rule imposed on it. Disappointed that they had little voice in the political decision-making process and finding the Mainland Chinese by no means fair, honest, or likable, the Taiwanese came to regard the Nationalist government as no better than its predecessor and, in many important ways, much worse. They had expected better.[46]

More crucial to what transpired than the political and cultural factors were Taiwan's economic well-being, public health standards, and social order, all of which deteriorated dramatically at this time. Nationalist Chinese leaders were preoccupied with civil war in China and did not regard Taiwan's problems as important. Public and even private buildings were stripped of machines, tools, and sometimes plumbing—anything metallic—to send to the Mainland. Food shortages developed when large quantities of grain were commandeered to feed Nationalist armies fighting the Communists. Public health services almost ceased to function, causing outbreaks of cholera and bubonic plague. Rumors spread that Nationalist soldiers had brought these diseases to Taiwan. Public works were allowed to fall into disrepair and the education system deteriorated badly.[47]

Just as the Mainland Chinese perceived the Taiwanese as traitors lacking Chinese culture, the Taiwanese perceived the Mainlanders as dirty, dishonest, and technologically backward. Stories circulated about Mainland Chinese who stole bicycles and did not know what they were, and about others who spent hours staring at elevators they had never seen before. Clearly, Mainland Chinese officials were unable to maintain the basic public services, including power plants, trains, and buses, largely because of their lack of technological expertise. The Taiwanese also had to adjust to a new legal system. Nationalist soldiers often claimed ownership of houses and land based on forced occupation; the Taiwanese considered this stealing. Other laws were not understood and many were not enforced.

The ill feelings between the two groups came to a head on February 28, 1947, when plainclothes police officers killed a Taiwanese woman who had been selling black-market cigarettes to make a living. An angry mob formed and threatened the police, whereupon they fired into the crowd, killing four people. Widespread civil disobedience, and what seemed to some to be a rebellion, erupted, an event now known as *er er ba* (or 2-2-8, for the second month, twenty-eighth day).

Most historians blame Governor-General Ch'en Yi for the incident. Although Ch'en could speak Japanese and Taiwanese, he refused to use either language in conducting affairs of state. He expected Taiwanese to learn Mandarin Chinese, which older Taiwanese could not do easily. He also ruled as an aloof Chinese official—by example rather than by contact with the people. Trying to govern in a moral way, Ch'en sought to maintain social order with only a fraction of the police and troops Japan had used. And, though he was generally hardworking and principled, many of his subordinates were lazy, corrupt, and incompetent. Ch'en's agenda for Taiwan included creating a socialist economy with considerable state control, but this was a mistake. Finally, instead of taking action to defuse social unrest in early 1947, he temporized. Worst of all, he treated complaints and protest as pro-Communist, even though Taiwanese had virtually no connections with (or even much knowledge of) Communists on the Mainland or anywhere else.[48]

During the protest or rebellion (there being disagreement about which it was), Taiwanese killed or injured a large number of Mainland Chinese, including many unarmed, innocent civilians. In some instances, they beat or killed anyone who did not speak Taiwanese, including Hakkas. The killing and the virulent opposition to the government looked like a revolution to Nationalist authorities in China, even though what was happening in Taiwan was by no means well organized. On March 8, 1947, a large contingent of Nationalist Chinese troops arrived that used their weapons with little restraint against unarmed Taiwanese. Though official reports of this incident denied this charge, it seems that the troops acted out of vengeance for the killing of their fellow Mainland Chinese. In any event, the Nationalist government felt what happened in Taiwan was an unwanted distraction, one that helped the Communists in China with whom they were engaged in a life-and-death struggle. By the end of March, order was restored, but not before thousands of Taiwanese had been killed, including the core of Taiwan's potential local leadership.[49]

Chiang Kai-shek briefly turned his attention from events on the Mainland to Taiwan after the February 28 Incident. He removed Ch'en Yi from his post, along with a number of other high officials. He made Taiwan a province, rescinded military rule, and appointed some Taiwanese to top positions in the government. Various government monopoly enterprises were sold, and efforts were made to alleviate unemployment. However, serious damage had already been done to the Nationalist government's credibility, and Taiwanese hatred of both the government and Mainland Chinese would not soon subside.

In ensuing years, seldom was there mention of what happened in February and March 1947. The government's policy was to erase the incident from history and from public memory. However, with democratization in the 1970s and 1980s, and particularly with the end of martial law, opposition politicians began using *er er ba* as a rallying call. The government subsequently changed its stance and, with the help of scholars, launched an investigation into what happened and why. In 1992, a detailed report was published on the incident.[50]

Yet many politicians would not let the issue die, or sought to exploit it. Taiwan's new political parties and even their factions differed sharply over whether February 28 should be made a holiday or a day of mourning, and whether statues or buildings should be built in remembrance. In 1995, on the forty-eighth anniversary of *er er ba,* President Lee Teng-hui, following the erection of a monument in Taipei's New Park, issued a formal apology on behalf of the government to the families of victims. Taipei's mayor, Chen Shui-bian, representing the opposition party, subsequently announced that the park would be renamed "2-2-8 Peace Park" and that February 28 would be "peace day." The Legislative Yuan meanwhile passed a bill to provide compensation to victims' relatives and made February 28 National Memorial Day. In 1997, February 28 was made a national holiday.[51]

After Chen Shui-bian became president in 2000, he and the Democratic Progressive Party used the event in election campaigns and on other occasions to rally his supporters against the KMT. At times this worked well. But the DPP seemed to overreach and appeared unaware that Taiwan's youth did not know of *er er ba* from direct experience and didn't care about it as much as their parents, while to most it was not a substitute for good government or astute management of the economy.

Taiwan as the Republic of China

By late 1949, Chiang Kai-shek's Nationalist forces had been defeated in most of China by Mao Tse-tung's (now spelled Mao Zedong) Communist armies. Chiang and a portion of his military and government fled to Taiwan, where they hoped to regroup and counterattack. With that, Taiwan had to absorb more than 1.5 million people at a time when the economy was in dire straits and social conditions were going from bad to worse. This influx of people aggravated an already stressed infrastructure as well as relations between the Taiwanese and the Mainland Chinese. Chiang ordered Ch'en Yi executed in public and purged the government and the Nationalist Party of the most corrupt and incompetent officials. But these actions, although sincere and in many ways effective at the time, had but a marginal effect toward improving relations with the local population.[52]

However, in spite of their dislike of the Mainland Chinese and the government and the fact that Chiang Kai-shek had little credibility internationally, most Taiwanese saw no realistic choice but to accept Nationalist rule. The likely alternative was worse. Few Taiwanese wanted to be governed by the People's Republic of China: Communism was in no way attractive, philosophically or otherwise. Moreover, Mao had no organization or base of support in Taiwan and consequently he had no means of launching an effective movement against Nationalist rule. To "liberate" Taiwan, Mao would have to invade the island, which everyone in Taiwan knew would be a very costly affair in terms of loss of life and property damage.

Mao's People's Republic of China laid legal claim to the island when the Nationalists were defeated (based on the argument that it was a successor government to the Republic of China), even though Mao had earlier spoken of Taiwan as if it were not part of China. In fact, Mao had some years earlier put Taiwan in the same category as Korea and other would-be "friendly territories" on China's periphery. Even in the late 1940s, Mao expressed no interest in Taiwan and made no effort to launch a Communist insurgency movement there, not even after the Japanese left. He apparently perceived that the success of his revolution would eventually persuade all of Asia—particularly areas or countries near China—to adopt communism, and, in this context, territorial issues did not matter.[53]

Conclusions about Taiwan's legal status at the time seemed academic anyway: The island's future would be determined by military force. In fact, in the spring of 1950, Mao formulated plans for an invasion of Taiwan. But, because the Nationalists had taken with them much of the Chinese navy as well as the large ships of the merchant marine, this required using thousands of small boats. In water holes in Fukien Province, he trained his soldiers to swim because they would have to reach Taiwan's shore after being dropped from boats a mile out. But many of Mao's troops became infected with a liver fluke, found locally in the soil, forcing a delay of the invasion plans by a few weeks.[54] In the meantime, war broke out in Korea, and the United States, having abandoned Chiang Kai-shek in January (when Secretary of State Dean Acheson described Taiwan, along with Korea, as not within the US "defense perimeter"), now reversed course and sent the Seventh Fleet to the Taiwan Strait to shield Taiwan from an invasion.

The Nationalists quickly took advantage of the respite from conflict. With the United States guaranteeing the island's security, Chiang Kai-shek implemented various kinds of political reform to create a more honest and efficient government. In particular, he took steps to rid the government and the ruling party of corrupt, lazy, and incompetent officials. Chiang even organized elections and made other efforts to democratize Taiwan's political system at the local level.

Because of the Korean War and China's role in it, and owing to Nationalist China's adamant stance against communism (not to mention the considerable support Chiang and the Nationalists once had, and again enjoyed, in the United States), Taiwan became a valued member of the Western bloc. With the polarization of the world into two camps, and because the Republic of China continued to represent China in the United Nations and most other international organizations (which regarded the government in Peking with hostility, and vice versa), Taipei was at center stage in the East-West struggle.

In the ensuing months and years, however, the Nationalists' hopes of reconquering the Mainland dimmed. Nationalist leaders began to think of Taiwan as a permanent home. Furthermore, they felt they were needed in Taiwan, where political leadership and administrative talents were lacking. In addition, they saw they had a chance to redeem themselves and prove that their ideology was superior to communism. Meanwhile, many Taiwanese began to realize that their animosity had to be put aside if Taiwan was to survive and prosper. As time passed, this attitude became more and more prevalent.[55]

With the benefit of a period of peace for the first time in more than a decade and the help of US economic and military assistance, Chiang Kai-shek instituted new plans aimed at promoting economic development. The first, and one of the most important ones, was land reform. It was a resounding success—so much so that it still provides a model for other countries to study and emulate. Land reform and Taiwan's overall successful economic development plans, both of which were overseen by US aid advisers, made Taiwan a showcase of US foreign aid and improved Taiwan's economic situation and the Nationalist government's image in the international community.[56]

Although the United States protected Taiwan from an invasion by Mao's People's Liberation Army (PLA), the US government also tried to prevent the Nationalist Chinese from trying to destabilize Mao's government on the Mainland and/or from starting a conflict that might drag the United States into a war with

China and the Soviet Union. Keeping the two sides apart was not easy. Two crises erupted, in 1954 and 1958, over the Offshore Islands (the island groups of Quemoy and Matsu, which Communist forces had failed to take in 1949 and which remained in Nationalist hands), when the Chinese military bombarded the islands. Mao apparently saw an opportunity to test US resolve. In response, Washington demonstrated its mettle by supplying Nationalist forces on the islands and even threatening to use nuclear weapons against China.[57]

Chiang Kai-shek adopted the position, not unlike that espoused by the United States, that China was captive of the Soviet Union. In the US government, this attitude persisted until the Nixon administration, even though relations between Moscow and Beijing showed clear signs of strain. The Nationalist government thus failed to adjust to a changing world, in particular a thaw in the Cold War. Some observers later said that Taiwan failed to adopt policies that might have saved it from becoming illegitimate. Some historians in Taiwan, however, contend that changing course at that juncture would have separated Taiwan from China permanently. Others say that adopting a policy of separation or a one China, one Taiwan stance would have stimulated premature demands for democracy, which would have evoked political instability and ethnic conflict. Those who wanted an independent Taiwan say it was an opportunity missed. In any case, the People's Republic of China won the struggle to represent China in world affairs in the 1970s.

Taiwan was, however, ready for economic change. By the mid-1960s, after successful land reform and the beginning of its industrialization process, Taiwan was poised for an economic takeoff. In 1964, US aid to Taiwan stopped, and almost simultaneously, Taiwan's economy took off. Over the next two decades, Taiwan could boast of the world's fastest-growing economy. Economists since have observed that US aid helped Taiwan's economic growth get started and that its termination forced Taiwan to stand alone, which it did very successfully. Little more than two decades of Nationalist rule after 1949 made Taiwan more prosperous than it had ever been.

Economic development fostered social progress in manifold ways. Taiwan became permeated by foreign influence and culture, especially as trade increased and the population and government came to realize that economic prosperity depended on exports. Taiwan, as a consequence, became much more open and cosmopolitan; this happened at a time when China was becoming more inward-looking and increasingly hostile toward the rest of the world. As economic well-being increased, Taiwanese alienation decreased, even though Taiwan was still governed under martial law.

With economic growth, democracy began to bud. The Nationalist government had for some time encouraged democracy at the local level, where the Nationalist Party functioned as an intermediary among hostile Taiwanese factions. Nationalist Party leaders believed they could institutionalize democratic politics and apply it to the central government in the future—but only gradually and when Taiwan was ready for it. The Taiwanese felt that democracy at the local level would eventually work its way to the top. These opposing views did not cause conflict, but rather they provided two paths to democratization that became mutually reinforcing.

With economic and political change as well as a better understanding of the world that accompanied both, the myth that the Nationalists represented the people of China and that Mao's government was a temporary, outlaw regime could not be perpetuated, even though Peking's policies threatening Taiwan reinforced the Nationalists' recalcitrance. At times, it appeared Nationalist Chinese leaders were resigned to or even advocated Taiwan's separation from China. As early as 1958, Chiang Kai-shek said publicly that realizing the goal of returning to the Mainland "would be 70 percent political." This statement and the Nationalists' inability to oust Mao from power (and they made no serious efforts to do so after the early 1960s) told many observers that the government, privately at least, accepted the reality of two Chinas.[58]

However, the US escalation of the Vietnam War after the Gulf of Tonkin Incident in August 1964 resuscitated the bipolar structure of world politics in Asia and increased US support for Taiwan. In 1965, Mao launched the Great Proletarian Cultural Revolution, which turned politics in China quickly leftward and resulted in a self-imposed isolation of the People's Republic of China for several years. Both played into the hands of those in Taipei who resisted change and new policies.

But the events that gave Taipei a respite from pressures to reform were not to last. In 1969, relations between the governments in Washington and Peking (by now written Beijing) changed course as a result of US efforts to disengage from Vietnam and an escalation of Sino-Soviet border hostilities.[59] A rapprochement between Washington and Beijing, former archenemies, was mutually advantageous and was soon on the agendas of both governments. In 1971, National Security Adviser Henry Kissinger visited Beijing and arranged for President Nixon to go there the next year in what became a watershed shift in US-China relations. That same year, largely as a result of the thaw in US-China relations, the People's Republic of China was admitted to the United Nations, and the Republic of China was expelled. Subsequently, Taiwan's government suffered the loss of diplomatic ties with most of the nations with which it had formal relations, including almost all of the important nations of the world.[60]

In February 1972, President Nixon visited the People's Republic of China, where he signed the Shanghai Communiqué and engaged in talks that anticipated a rapprochement between the two countries while also anticipating the establishment of diplomatic relations. This historic shift in US-China relations was a shock to

Taiwan, but it was not as ominous as many in Taiwan had anticipated. Nixon had treated the "Taiwan issue" with deliberate ambiguity.[61] The United States did not abandon Taiwan. Although the credibility of the government and the ruling Nationalist Party were hurt, it could have been much worse. Leaders in Taipei did not lose public support at home because they had, after all, engineered Taiwan's miracle economic development. In addition, most observers in and outside of Taiwan took the view that little could have been done to prevent what happened. Clearly, there was no popular desire for Beijing to rule Taiwan.

In April 1975, Chiang Kai-shek's death symbolized the end of the Nationalists' hope of ruling a unified China—if anyone still espoused any optimism about this. The next year, Mao died, putting an end to the personal duel between two political factions-turned-governments that had been so much a part of China's modern history.

Taiwan Ruled by Chiang Ching-kuo

Following President Chiang Kai-shek's death, Vice President Yen Chia-kan became president of the Republic of China in accordance with provisions in the Constitution. But Chiang Kai-shek's eldest son, Chiang Ching-kuo, premier since 1972 and head of the Nationalist Party, *de facto* ruled (with Yen's cooperation, of course). In 1978, Yen declined to run for reelection when his term as president expired. Chiang Ching-kuo was nominated and elected president.[62]

Chiang Ching-kuo was not schooled in democratic tradition nor representative government. Instead, in his youth, his father had sent him to the Soviet Union, where he joined the Communist Party, supported Leon Trotsky, and married a Russian woman. Nor had he championed political reform during most of his political career in Taiwan. However, he realized the need for Taiwan to shed its authoritarian political system if it were to sustain its rapid economic growth and maintain important political ties with the democratic West.[63] He also understood that only through political change—meaning democratization—could Taiwan heal the wounds of ethnic ill will, parry Beijing's overtures to negotiate unification, and win support from the international community.

Chiang Ching-kuo lived by his convictions. In the early and mid-1970s, he recruited Taiwanese into the party and the government. As president, he launched an anticorruption campaign that was taken seriously by those both in and out of government, especially after he jailed high government officials for corrupt practices—including some of his own relatives. Ordering government offices to publish their telephone numbers and respond to citizens' requests and suggestions, Chiang compelled officials to be responsive to public demands and act as "employees of the people." The population applauded him and his actions and supported his efforts in building good government.[64]

CCK, as Chiang was called fondly by many, made frequent visits to the countryside to talk to farmers and ordinary citizens. Privately, he maintained an austere lifestyle, eschewing publicity and praise. His demeanor won him broad respect at home and good press abroad. He became a truly popular president.

But sometimes CCK had to force political change upon the ruling party and government by edict. In short, he brought democracy to Taiwan by quite disparate means. Many people felt the change was long overdue, having been envisioned by Sun Yat-sen and set forth in the Constitution. Some thought he moved too quickly. Nevertheless, in retrospect most perceived that no one else could have modernized Taiwan's politics as effectively as CCK did.

At a critical juncture, however, Taiwan was dealt a diplomatic shock that set back its democratization. In December 1978, President Jimmy Carter, without warning, announced that the United States would sever diplomatic ties with Taipei effective January 1, 1979 and end their defense treaty a year later. President Carter also acknowledged (in negotiations with Beijing) that there was only one China—the People's Republic of China. These statements mirrored a fundamental change in US-China/Taiwan policy.[65] Although Taiwan was inured to difficult situations, loss of official ties with its only important friend and its protector was a severe blow. Some observers at the time said the events were portentous: Taiwan was now illegitimate and isolated in the international community and would be compelled to become part of China.

However, altering and in some important ways reversing Carter's China/Taiwan policy, in April 1979 the US Congress passed a law called the Taiwan Relations Act (TRA). The TRA restored relations with Taiwan to a near-official level. Moreover, it included a defense provision that provided Taiwan US security guarantees. Leaders in Beijing, preoccupied by a war with Vietnam while the TRA was being debated and reluctant to disturb its new and valuable relationship with the United States, reacted to Congress's action with only token protest. Later, however, Deng Xiaoping made a concerted effort to undermine the legislation. He also declared that he would not renounce the use of force against Taiwan—a position still held by the Beijing government today.[66]

Losing diplomatic relations with the United States made CCK even more determined to press ahead with democratization. Meanwhile, opposition forces became more active when they saw how grim Taiwan's diplomatic situation had become. They thought that only profound political change (meaning rapid democratization) would save Taiwan from being isolated and then absorbed by the People's Republic of China. The opposition's efforts throughout 1979 climaxed in December with a protest demonstration in the southern city of Kaohsiung that resulted in widely publicized violence. At that point, public opinion, which had previously supported the activists' proposed reforms, shifted in favor of the government because most citizens feared chaos. The government jailed some of the demonstrations' leaders, but negotiated further democratic change with others. Reforms discussed included revising Taiwan's election law and reaching some gentlemen's agreements between the government and the opposition so that an orderly but competitive national election could be rescheduled.

As a result, in 1980 Taiwan held an unprecedented election. Whether it was "democracy from the top down," as some observers said who thought it was Chiang Ching-kuo's creation, or from the bottom up, as the opposition suggested, is difficult to say; it was both. Other observers said Taiwan was rebuffing Beijing's overtures to negotiate reunification by pushing democratization. In any event, the election reflected Taiwan's rapid evolution away from an authoritarian, one-party political system toward real democracy.

In 1983, Taiwan held its second national democratic election. Again the KMT performed well. Some critics said it should have, given its advantages in talent, money, and control of the media. Others said the opposition was too radical and, furthermore, had not learned the art of campaign politics. As a consequence of this second democratic national election, Chiang Ching-kuo and the Nationalist Party became more confident and willing to continue democratic reform.

In 1984, CCK was reelected president of the Republic of China, even though questions lingered about his health. He picked a new vice president, Lee Teng-hui, who was seen as highly competent and loyal to CCK and the Nationalist Party and also committed to democratic reform. Lee was soon considered CCK's heir. Because Lee was Taiwanese, his rise seemed to mark the beginning of the power transition from Mainland Chinese to Taiwanese. Seen in retrospect, it was.

In early 1986, at a Nationalist Party's Central Committee meeting, CCK called for several major reforms in government. These included restructuring the parliament, getting rid of martial law, and allowing new political parties to form. In October, in a widely heralded interview with Katharine Graham, owner of the *Washington Post*, President Chiang Ching-kuo repeated—some say formalized—these promises. This paved the way for the first two-party election ever held in a Chinese nation. In December of that year, the newly formed Democratic Progressive Party (DPP) vied with the ruling Nationalist Party for seats in the Legislative Yuan and the National Assembly. Performing well in spite of genuine competition while nominating mostly Taiwanese candidates, the Nationalist Party again burnished its image and expanded its mandate to rule Taiwan. It was clear that the days of a one-party dictatorship in Taiwan were over and that the Nationalist Party could lead a democratic nation.

Meanwhile, President Chiang Ching-kuo announced that none of his relatives would hold a position of political prominence after his death. He also took steps to ensure that the military would not play a significant political role in Taiwan after his demise. Instead, Vice President Lee Teng-hui was being groomed to become president. Other Western-educated leaders, many of them young by Chinese standards, were promoted to top positions in the government and in the ruling party. In July 1987, Chiang Ching-kuo seemed to put the final touches on political modernization by abolishing martial law. At the same time, trying to ameliorate ethnic differences, CCK noted that he had lived in Taiwan for forty years and should, therefore, be counted as Taiwanese.[67]

When President Chiang terminated martial law, the public did not strongly believe that it should end. Many felt it contributed to social stability and economic growth and should be kept. However, the Western media gave this decision more applause than it had given anything else President Chiang had done, and in this way CCK improved both his and Taiwan's global image considerably. The termination of martial law did have a salutary effect on the exercise of civil and political rights and made Taiwan's media free from military oversight and censorship. A few months later, CCK ended the ban on travel to China by Taiwan's citizens, thus paving the way for economic and other contacts between Taiwan and China that would boom and have a lasting impact.

In retrospect, one of the most salient questions about the Chiang Ching-kuo era is: Did CCK engineer the separation, or further split, of Taiwan from China? He had always advocated a one-China policy. His roots were in China. Yet he brought democracy to Taiwan, and that furthered separation. Some say he sought to create a model for China and saw democratization in China as the key to bringing the two together again.

CCK's biographers treat him as a great leader who understood the times and who acted with integrity and with the interests of the citizens of Taiwan at heart.[68] Future historians will no doubt see him as the leader who launched Taiwan's "political miracle" and kept Taiwan's "economic miracle"—launched by his father—on track. Recent public opinion surveys indicate he is Taiwan's most highly regarded president.

Taiwan Under Lee Teng-hui

When Chiang Ching-kuo died in January 1988, Vice President Lee Teng-hui succeeded him as president according to the Constitution and CCK's wishes. At an emergency meeting of the Nationalist Party, Lee was also made temporary head of the ruling party. However, "old guard" members of the party aligned against Lee to block him from assuming too much power. They feared that Lee, who was Taiwanese, would threaten Mainland Chinese rule of Taiwan and/or would advance Taiwanization too quickly. On the other hand, they could not dispute Lee's competence or that he was CCK's chosen successor. A motion to have a rotating party head was voted down and Lee became the party's undisputed leader.[69]

Lee symbolized an end of the Mainland Chinese minority's hold on political authority. Yet his leadership did not dampen the spirits of the opposition (mostly

Taiwanese), which perceived that the speed of democratization was still too slow. Interest groups and new political parties were also playing a new role in the democratization process. So, too, protest had become part of Taiwan's political process. In May 1988, farmers took to the streets to demonstrate, as other groups had been doing at the rate of about 150 per month. Seventeen hours of riots resulted in extensive property damage and injuries to more than 500 people. This typified the new political climate in which Lee Teng-hui had to rule.[70]

A few months later, the Nationalist Party held its Thirteenth Congress. Lee was officially elected chairman of the party, enabling him to further consolidate power. Lee was popular, and the democratization of party rules accomplished at the meeting worked in his favor.[71] Yet these changes meant that he did not have the kind of control over the party that CCK had and that party infighting and factional struggles were going to become serious problems. After the party congress, President Lee picked a new cabinet. For the first time, the majority was Taiwanese. Lee, however, chose the popular Lee Huan, a Mainland Chinese, to be his premier, thereby keeping a balance of Mainlanders and Taiwanese at the top.

Soon after this, President Lee and the Nationalist Party backed new laws to retire members of Taiwan's democratic bodies of government who were elected on the Mainland and subsequently frozen in office or replaced by appointment, the so-called "elder parliamentarians." In March 1990, although challenged briefly by the popular Taiwanese politician Lin Yang-kang and Chiang Wei-kuo (Chiang Kai-shek's second son and CCK's half-brother), respectively, Lee Teng-hui was elected in March 1990 to a new six-year term. Those who opposed him did so for a variety of reasons, saying that he was too dictatorial, that he was advancing democracy and Taiwanization too fast, and that he had difficulty filling CCK's shoes. His supporters said his detractors were simply opponents of democracy. In any case, Lee's popularity remained high.[72]

In May 1989, Taipei supported (though not with money, weapons, or material help) the student-led democracy movement in China. The massacre in Tiananmen Square that followed in June damaged China's global image severely. Yet Taiwan did not reduce its growing ties with China, realizing that trying to isolate China was neither feasible nor in consonance with the New World Order. Moreover, many perceived Taiwan and China as members of a "Greater China," or Pacific Rim bloc, in an era of global economic blocs.[73]

In early 1991, Taiwan embarked on a new Six-Year Development Plan, which its leaders hoped would catapult Taiwan into the top twenty nations in the world in per capita income by the end of the century. In April, Lee ended the Temporary Provisions of the Constitution that had circumvented the granting of civil and political rights. In so doing, he positioned Taiwan to democratize even faster. In December, after elder politicians agreed to retire, the electorate picked delegates to a new National Assembly. This was Taiwan's first nonsupplementary—or plenary—election. The Nationalist Party performed well, receiving, according to some observers, a democratic mandate it had never before enjoyed. The scope of the victory also aided President Lee and his party in their efforts to make further constitutional changes and extend reforms into the realm of systemic change.

The following March, the National Assembly met to amend the Constitution. Delegates to the National Assembly would henceforth serve for four years, the Control Yuan would become a semijudicial body, and the provincial governor and the mayors of Taiwan's two metropolitan areas would become elected officials. Other reforms followed, including the abolition of the Taiwan Garrison Command, which had been responsible for censorship and control of the population and was a symbol of past repressive government.[74]

Its push for reform notwithstanding, the Nationalist Party did not perform well in the Legislative Yuan election in December 1992. The party was divided along ethnic lines and over the issue of relations with China. Some said the KMT's problems were President Lee's fault. Yet his popularity did not suffer. Lee subsequently formed a new cabinet and replaced the Mainland Chinese premier, Hau Pei-tsun (who had succeeded Lee Huan and with whom he had been in considerable disagreement), with Taiwanese Lien Chan.

Meanwhile, a political rapprochement between Taipei and Beijing appeared increasingly likely. President Lee had formally ended the state of war with China in 1991, investment funds from Taiwan were pouring into China in large amounts (surpassing even those from Japan and the United States), and people were crossing the Taiwan Strait in large numbers to visit and/or to do business. In April 1993, Taiwan and China held preliminary but official talks to normalize relations. Called the Koo-Wang talks, these negotiations resolved some problems that were part of the five decades of hostility between the two sides.[75]

In August, the Nationalist Party held its Fourteenth Congress amid party infighting and concern about future election defeats. Factionalism had become a serious problem: In fact, several members of the nonmainstream faction of the party, a group made up mostly of Mainland Chinese who perceived that President Lee supported an independent Taiwan, left the party to form the New Chinese Party (later renamed the New Party). As a result, President Lee increased his control over the KMT, even though party rules had changed so as to give increased authority to members of the party who were elected to high office, notably legislators, some of whom competed with Lee for influence in the party.[76]

In 1994, the Republic of China's Constitution was amended again. One amendment provided for the direct election of the president and vice president (instead of by the National Assembly). Following this, in early 1995 President Lee announced that he would be a candidate. In March 1996, the electorate gave Lee another term in what was Taiwan's first popular election of its president. The event was widely acclaimed by the media in Taiwan and abroad to be the first such election of a chief executive in 5,000 years of Chinese history. Lee had indeed made a mark in history.

Meanwhile, in June 1995, as part of Taiwan's (created by Lee) "pragmatic diplomacy," Lee made a controversial trip to the United States at the invitation of his alma mater, Cornell University. The visit incensed Chinese leaders in Beijing who, in the context of a leadership succession, ordered missile tests in the Taiwan Strait. Beijing conducted even more provocative tests, including the firing of missiles armed with live warheads close to Taiwan's two biggest ports at the time leading up to Taiwan's 1996 presidential election. In response, President Clinton dispatched two aircraft carriers, each with accompanying ships, to the area, thereby putting Washington into a face-off with Beijing. Needless to say, ongoing talks between leaders in Beijing and Taipei were put on hold.[77]

The direct presidential election—although a victory for Lee and Lien Chan (Lee's vice-presidential running mate), the ruling Nationalist Party, and democratization in Taiwan—created burdens on Taiwan's political system. To resolve systemic political problems that resulted from multiparty politics and an increasingly pluralistic society, President Lee convoked a National Development Conference in December. Delegates recommended more constitutional changes, some of which were made in mid-1997. One of them, the virtual elimination of the provincial government, was the most debated. James Soong, Taiwan's first elected governor (in 1994) tendered his resignation in displeasure after the conference. Lee and Soong became enemies and, this together with crime and corruption worsening, caused Lee's image to suffer.

The United Kingdom's transfer of Hong Kong to the People's Republic of China in July 1997 created another problem for President Lee. According to leaders in Beijing, Taiwan was next. President Lee rejected Beijing's reunification proposals and its "one country, two systems" formula for uniting China. He asserted that Taiwan was not a colony and could, moreover, defend itself. Subsequently, the resounding defeat of the Nationalist Party in local elections in November—thus giving the opposition Democratic Progressive Party (which called for Taiwan's independence) jurisdiction over more than 70 percent of the population at the local level—caused Taiwan's formal separation from China to become a matter of concern not only for the ruling party but also for Beijing and Washington.

Taiwan weathered the storm of the so-called Asian economic meltdown in 1997 and experienced quite normal economic growth in 1998, though its currency floated downward a bit. Economic problems elsewhere, however, provided Taiwan with better opportunities for investment in the region. Economic stability, among other factors, explained the Nationalist Party's good performance in the December

1998 election, wherein the ruling party made gains in the lawmaking body of government and Ma Ying-jeou recaptured the Taipei mayorship for the KMT from the opposition DPP's Chen Shui-bian.

In 1999, President Lee, during an interview with a German radio station, stated that relations with China had to be considered as state-to-state relations or special state-to-state relations. Some observers said that Lee was in essence declaring Taiwan legally independent, while others said he was simply explaining what was obvious. Lee may have been responding to President Bill Clinton's "three no's" (no two Chinas; no one China, one Taiwan; and no to Taiwan's joining international organizations that assume statehood for membership) statement made when he visited China in 1998. In any event, leaders in Beijing were incensed at Lee's proclamation and harshly criticized him. Some said China-Taiwan relations were deeply and perhaps permanently scarred as a result.[78]

Chen Shui-bian's Taiwan

In March 2000, Taiwan held its second direct presidential election. President Lee Teng-hui was in his mid-seventies and had held the nation's highest office for twelve years. He decided not to run again. Chen Shui-bian of the opposition Democratic Progressive Party won the election and was inaugurated the fifth president of the Republic of China in May. How Chen won, the significance of a change of ruling parties, corruption, the Chen administration's governance, its management (or mismanagement) of the economy, and how Chen handled foreign relations— especially with the United States and China—are all telling.[79]

President Lee supported his vice president, Lien Chan, for the ruling Nationalist Party nomination. Lien was eminently qualified; indeed, his experience easily exceeded that of the other candidates. Born into a famous local family, Lien had earned a Ph.D. in political science at the University of Chicago. He returned to Taiwan and, a few years later, became the youngest minister in the nation's history. He served in several cabinet positions, was governor of Taiwan, premier, and vice president. Lien was Taiwanese, but had close contacts with Mainland Chinese in the party and the government. Notwithstanding the many factors that favored Lien, Taiwan by this time had evolved into a popular democracy, and Lien was not so much a man of the people.

James Soong was, and his popularity ratings were much higher than Lien's. Soong was also highly qualified: a Ph.D. from Georgetown University, name recognition from several years of heading the Government Information Office, and experience as the party's secretary-general. He was also the first-ever elected governor of Taiwan. Soong wanted the nomination and, like many others, felt he should get it. But President Lee opposed it. Some said that Lee didn't want a non-Taiwanese president, but others cited different reasons. In any case, when Soong decided to run as an independent, the conservative—or KMT—vote split.

During the early months of the campaign, Soong's poll numbers were better by a large margin than those of either Chen Shui-bian or Lien Chan. But, as the election approached, a KMT legislator (many thought upon Lee's order, though Lee denied this) released information indicating Soong had diverted party money into his own bank accounts and to those of his relatives when he was party secretary-general. Though he was later exonerated, the charges severely hurt Soong, who had a reputation for honesty. Soong was further handicapped by lack of a party, a good campaign organization, and money.

This situation played into Chen Shui-bian's hands. Meanwhile, Chen won the nomination of his party without difficulty, and his party was more unified than usual. Chen also ran a masterful campaign. He handled controversial issues deftly. Most important, he played down his previously strong stand for independence. His party and his campaign team exploited ethnic politics, the KMT's corrupt image, and the split between Lien and Soong. Finally, Chen convinced many voters that a change in ruling parties would bolster Taiwan's democratization.

Down the stretch, some noted business leaders announced their support for Chen, as did Nobel Prize winner Lee Yuan-tseh, who headed Taiwan's most famous think tank, Academia Sinica. Chinese leaders in Beijing, including the premier, publicly attacked Chen during the last days of the campaign and harshly warned Taiwan's voters not to vote for the "independence candidate"—meaning Chen. However, the strategy backfired and instead helped Chen win.[80]

But Chen won by a very small margin. Soong won just over 2 percent less of the popular vote. Lien was a distant third. Had the KMT not damaged Soong's campaign, Soong would have won. Had there been a runoff election (a provision in the constitutions of many nations, but not Taiwan's), Chen would not have been elected president. Soong won the majority of the vote from all of Taiwan's minority ethnic groups (Aborigines, Hakka, and Mainland Chinese). He won the female vote. He won in almost every part of Taiwan except the south. Chen won big among the Fukien Taiwanese and by a large margin in the south. After the election, many questioned Chen's mandate.

Not only did Chen not have a strong mandate, his party, the DPP, had never ruled and was by its history and makeup not prepared for that task. After the election, Soong formed a political party called the People First Party (PFP). Many of its members felt Soong should have been president. Despite hard feelings toward the KMT, the PFP joined the KMT to form an opposition bloc. Chen's party held only a third of the seats in the Legislative Yuan, so the new president faced a divided government of a very serious nature.

Making matters worse, because Taiwan's political system was a mixed one— presidential, parliamentary, and cabinet—the role of each branch of the government vis-à-vis the other was not clear. Nor were the powers of each well defined. So Chen spoke of building a coalition government and made moves in that direction. He gave up his positions in the DPP and appointed members of the KMT to cabinet positions—even his premier, Tang Fei. But Chen didn't consult with opposition party leaders and in so doing showed a lack of leadership while seriously underestimating the opposition. Alternatively he feared the legislature would usurp his powers and saw playing ethnic politics as his way out. In any case, coalition government was soon forgotten.[81]

Differences with the opposition parties worsened, and the hostility came to a head less than six months into Chen's presidency over the issue of building Taiwan's fourth nuclear plant. Chen's party had long opposed nuclear power, and he had campaigned fervently against it. The problem was that the plant had already been approved by a previous legislature. In response to Chen's decision to nix the plant, the opposition initiated an impeachment proceeding against him, but then withdrew it. Chen was embarrassed and his poll numbers dropped precipitously. His saving grace was that the impeachment effort also damaged the opposition. The result was intense political polarization, gridlock, and malaise.

The economy promptly went into a tailspin. The country witnessed negative economic growth (almost 2 percent for 2001), and unemployment figures that were higher than most citizens had ever seen. Chen blamed the opposition. He also attributed the downturn to the weak global economy. But many saw Chen's poor management of the economy as the main cause. Meanwhile, many industries, including many of Taiwan's "best and brightest" companies (especially computer and semiconductor enterprises), started moving all or part of their operations to China to take advantage of cheaper labor costs, lower taxes, and fewer regulations, and to be closer to a gigantic and booming market. Chen and his supporters were divided about whether to try to stop the exodus.

President Chen proclaimed that he would be able to accomplish more and could resolve many of the country's travails if his party could win the legislative election in December 2001. Former president Lee Teng-hui came out of retirement and formed a new political party, the Taiwan Solidarity Union (TSU), to help Chen. They were labeled the green bloc, or pan-green. Both Chen's DPP and the TSU resorted to playing ethnic politics during the campaign. DPP campaign strategists even named Adolph Hitler as a model person in some of their campaign advertisements, much to the consternation of many foreigners in Taiwan. The ethnic appeal worked, as did efforts to label the opposition parties as loyal to China and not Taiwan. The DPP increased the number of seats it held in the legislature by a sizeable margin, and the TSU performed well for a new party. The KMT performed very badly, but most of its losses were gains for Soong's People First Party, which made a bigger percentage gain than the DPP. Independents and other parties all but vanished. The opposition "blue team" (the KMT and the PFP) kept its legislative majority.[82]

Chen and his vice president, Annette Lu, won reelection in 2004, but under quite questionable circumstances. Both were shot, though their wounds were superficial, the day before the voting. President Chen ordered the police and the military to remain at their posts, depriving them of the opportunity to vote. Their vote would probably have been for Lien and Soong, who had joined forces to make a strong opposition ticket. This and sympathy voting for Chen and Lu gave them the victory, which they, the stock market, and those betting on the election didn't expect. The opposition didn't accept the election results and organized public protest demonstrations while challenging the election in court. As a result, political polarization got even worse.[83]

Meanwhile, corruption infected the Chen administration and the DPP. This and an economy that remained in the doldrums in the mind of citizens, together with President Chen's reputation for poor governance, playing on ethnic ill will, and ruining relations with the United States and China, caused DPP losses in the next three elections. In the run-up to the last one, in 2008, an election to choose the metropolitan mayors (Taipei and Kaohsiung) and city councils, many Chen administration officials were under indictment or in jail for corruption. Chen's wife had been indicted for perjury, falsifying documents, and stealing government funds. Chen's son-in-law was convicted of insider trading. The prosecutor said President Chen would have been indicted except that he was protected by presidential immunity. In the interim, Shih Ming-teh, a former DPP chairman and party hero, launched a mass movement against corruption and against Chen. A million or more turned out at some of his rallies. Chen survived, but his poll numbers fell into the teens, sometimes below.[84]

Several years before this, President Chen had become unpopular in the United States for playing ethnic politics and provoking China at a time when the Bush administration was preoccupied with the war on terrorism. US leaders retaliated by repeating America's one-China policy while warning Chen and even questioning Taiwan's sovereignty. Chen was not allowed transit stops in major US cities when traveling to Latin America and elsewhere, as had been the case early on in his presidency. US State Department personnel generally refused to talk to Chen or anyone in his administration.[85] This also hurt Chen's image.

In January 2008, the KMT defeated the DPP badly in the national legislative election, for which President Chen assumed blame. Chen forthwith resigned as chairman of the DPP. Frank Hsieh, a former mayor of Kaohsiung and premier for a short time under Chen, assumed the chairmanship of the party and won the party's nomination to run for the presidency in March. President Chen had supported someone else. Hseih campaigned for president with Su Tseng-chang as his vice presidential running mate, generally but not totally distancing himself from Chen. Ma Ying-jeou, the KMT's candidate running with Vincent Siew, defeated the

DPP's candidates, getting more votes than any presidential election ticket in history. Most observers in large part blamed Chen for the DPP's loss. This marked an ignominious end to the Chen presidency.[86]

Notes

1. This date has been pushed back even further by recent archeological discoveries. See Chen-wen Tsung, "Clues to a Distant Past," *Free China Review* (April 1991): 61.

2. W. G. Goddard, *Formosa: A Study in Chinese History* (East Lansing: Michigan State University Press, 1966), 3–5.

3. See *Area Handbook for the Republic of China* (Washington, D.C.: US Government Printing Office, 1969), 22, for a discussion of this topic.

4. See Goddard, *Formosa,* 16, 20. Also see James W. Davidson, *The Island of Formosa: Past and Present* (New York: Oxford University Press, 1988), 3.

5. See Chen-wen Tsung, "Building on the Past," *Free China Review* (June 1992): 85.

6. David Barber, "DNA Shows Maoris Came from Taiwan, Says Scientist," *South China Morning Post,* August 11, 1998 (Internet edition), no page number shown.

7. See Chiao-min Hsieh, *Taiwan–Ilha Formosa: A Geographical Perspective* (Washington, D.C.: Butterworths, 1994), 131–138.

8. Taiwan was either regarded as an "uncivilized" area, in contrast to China, which was civilized, or an area that was partly civilized and thus a tributary state. See John K. Fairbank, ed., *The Chinese World Order* (Cambridge, MA: Harvard University Press, 1968).

9. This claim was most recently mentioned in a twenty-four-page pamphlet titled "The Taiwan Question and the Reunification of China" (Beijing: Taiwan Affairs Office and Information Office, State Council, 1993), referred to hereafter as China's White Paper on Taiwan.

10. See John K. Fairbank, *The United States and China* (New York: Viking Press, 1967), 13.

11. See China's White Paper on Taiwan, cited above in note 9. The different viewpoints espoused by China and Taiwan are discussed in John F. Copper, "The Origins of Conflict Across the Taiwan Strait: The Problem of Differences in Perceptions," *Journal of Contemporary China* (June 1997): 199–227.

12. See Davidson, *The Island of Formosa,* 3–4. Also see Simon Long, *Taiwan: China's Last Frontier* (New York: St. Martin's Press, 1991), 5.

13. Some Japanese writers have suggested that Japanese may have been the first settlers. See Shinkichi Ito, "An Outline of Formosan History," in Mark Mancall, ed., *Formosa Today* (New York: Praeger, 1963), 44. Also see Davidson, *The Island of Formosa,* 6.

14. See *Area Handbook for the Republic of China,* 22.

15. Ibid.

16. See Davidson, *The Island of Formosa,* 4.

17. Ibid., 5.

18. See Long, *Taiwan,* 4.

19. For details on the period of Western colonial influence, see Goddard, *Formosa,* chapters 3 and 4. See also Hsieh, *Taiwan–Ilha Formosa,* chapter 11.

20. See Goddard, *Formosa,* 51.

21. See George M. Beckman, "Brief Episodes—Dutch and Spanish Rule," in Paul K. T. Sih, ed., *Taiwan in Modern Times* (Jamaica, NY: St. John's University Press, 1973).

22. Long, *Taiwan,* 10–11.

23. For details about Cheng Ch'eng-kung's life and accomplishments from quite different perspectives, see Cheng Cheng I-chou, *Cheng Cheng-kung Chuan* (biography of Cheng Cheng-kung), reprinted in Taiwan in Wen-hsien Ts'ung K'an, Collection of Works on Taiwan Series (Taipei: Office of Economic Research, 1960); Ch'u Ch'i, *Cheng Cheng-kung* (Wuhan: People's Publishing House, 1956); and George Phillips, "The Life of Cheng Cheng-kung," *China Review* 13, nos. 2 and 3 (1985).

24. See Parris H. Chang, "Cheng Cheng-kung (Koxinga): A Patriot, Nationalist and Nation-Builder," in Sih, ed., *Taiwan in Modern Times*.

25. See Davidson, *The Island of Formosa*, 52.

26. See Goddard, *Formosa*, 99.

27. See for example, Wen-hsiung Hsu, "Frontier Social Organization and Social Disorder in Ch'ing Taiwan," in Ronald G. Knapp, ed., *China's Island Frontier: Studies in the Historical Geography of Taiwan* (Honolulu: University of Hawaii Press, 1980). Hsu notes that there was, on average, an incidence of communal strife every 2.7 years during the 212 years of Ch'ing rule.

28. See Chan Lien, "Taiwan in China's External Relations," in Sih, ed., *Taiwan in Modern Times*, 88–89.

29. Joseph W. Ballantine, *Formosa: A Problem for United States Foreign Policy* (Washington, D.C.: Brookings Institution, 1952), 17. Note that the Chinese government at this time still did not completely understand the concept of sovereignty.

30. See George H. Kerr, *Formosa: Licensed Revolution and the Home Rule Movement, 1895–1945* (Honolulu: University of Hawaii Press, 1974), 27.

31. Ibid., 14.

32. Ibid., 17–20.

33. See Samuel Ho, *The Economic Development of Taiwan, 1860–1970* (New Haven: Yale University Press, 1978), for an analysis of Taiwan's economic development under the Japanese.

34. Kerr, *Formosa*, 88–89.

35. Ibid., 91. See pages 89–91 for additional data on railroad and other infrastructure building.

36. See Ming-min Peng, *A Taste of Freedom* (New York: Holt, Reinhart and Winston, 1972), 7. Peng notes that China was not concerned about public health problems and that because so many Japanese soldiers died in Taiwan in 1895, sanitation became a priority for Japan.

37. See Kerr, *Formosa*, 59–61. The *pao chia* system was called Hoko in Japanese.

38. See Harry J. Lamley, "Taiwan Under Japanese Rule, 1895–1945: The Vicissitudes of Colonialism," in Murray A. Rubinstein, ed., *Taiwan: A New History* (Armonk, NY: M. E. Sharpe, 1999), 240–242.

39. See Denny Roy, *Taiwan: A Political History* (Ithaca, NY: Cornell University Press, 2003), 52–53, and Tse-han Lai, Ramon H. Myers, and Wou Wei, *A Tragic Beginning: The Taiwan Uprising of February 28, 1947* (Stanford, CA: Stanford University Press, 1991), 38.

40. Christopher Hughes, *Taiwan and Chinese Nationalism, National Identity and Status in International Society* (London: Routledge, 1997), 22.

41. See George H. Kerr, *Formosa Betrayed* (New York: Da Capo Press, 1996), chapter 2.

42. See Hughes, *Taiwan and Chinese Nationalism*, 5.

43. See Kerr, *Formosa Betrayed*, chapter 3.

44. Ibid.

45. Roy, *Taiwan: A Political History*, 60–64.

46. Ibid., chapter 5.

47. Ibid., 173–182.

48. Historians sympathetic to both the Nationalist government and Taiwanese independence blame Ch'en Yi for the difficulties in Taiwan in the late 1940s—even problems that occurred after he was removed from office, because many of his supporters and appointees remained. For example, see Fred W. Riggs, *Formosa Under Chinese Nationalist Rule* (New York: Octagon Books, 1972), 45–48. Also see Kerr, *Formosa Betrayed,* chapter 6. For a less harsh treatment of Ch'en, see Lai, Myers, and Wei, *A Tragic Beginning,* chapters 3 and 4, especially pages 97–98.

49. The number of Taiwanese killed at this time is a matter of guesswork. Kerr (in *Formosa Betrayed*) puts the number at 20,000. Lai, Myers, and Wei say it is at most 10,000. For some years, government documents indicated that only several hundred were killed. In 1992, the government released a detailed report on the incident and put the number killed at between 18,000 and 28,000.

50. Roy, *Taiwan: A Political History,* 185.

51. See Murray A. Rubinstein, "Postscript and Conclusion," in Murray A. Rubinstein, ed., *Taiwan: A New History* (Armonk, NY: M. E. Sharpe, 1999), 495.

52. See Hung Chien-chao, *A History of Taiwan* (il Cerechio, 2000), 257–259, and Roy, *Taiwan: A Political History*, chapter 4, for different accounts.

53. See Edgar Snow, *Red Star Over China* (New York: Random House, 1938), 33–89.

54. See Frank A. Kierman, *The Fluke that Saved Formosa* (Cambridge: Center for International Studies, Massachusetts Institute of Technology, 1954).

55. See Fred W. Riggs, *Formosa Under Chinese Nationalist Rule* (New York: Octagon Books, 1972) for an early account of this process.

56. See Neil H. Jacoby, *U.S. Aid to Taiwan: A Study of Foreign Aid, Self-Help and Development* (New York: Praeger, 1966), chapter 17.

57. See A. Doak Barnett, *Communist China and Asia: A Challenge to American Policy* (New York: Vintage Books, 1960), 415.

58. Chiang Kai-shek had long spoken of the "liberation" of the Mainland as partly political. In the late 1950s, after the United States made it clear that it did not want to get involved in a war with China over the Offshore Islands, Chiang began to speak more of the political nature of the task. Some in Taiwan interpreted this to mean that the mission was being given up, or at least de-emphasized. In about 1958, Taiwan began making plans for economic growth and diverting its attention to the development of the island as opposed to an invasion of the Mainland.

59. I believe that the fighting on the Sino-Soviet border and a new administration in the United States brought about a change in US-China relations. Some scholars think the policy change occurred a year or two later.

60. Technically, the Republic of China withdrew from the United Nations, as it said it would do if Beijing received a majority of support from the UN members for its bid to membership. It is generally believed that the United States opposed Beijing's joining the United Nations at Taipei's expense, but, given the situation and the rules of UN membership, there was no alternative. Many US allies voted for Beijing, an indication that Washington had not asked its friends for votes of support for Taipei.

61. For details, see John F. Copper, *China Diplomacy: The Washington-Taipei-Beijing Triangle* (Boulder: Westview Press, 1992), 38–39.

62. See Ray S. Cline, *Chiang Ching-kuo Remembered* (Washington, D.C.: U.S. Global Strategy Center, 1989), for details on Chiang Ching-kuo's life.

63. See Peter R. Moody, Jr., *Political Change on Taiwan: A Study of Ruling Party Adaptability* (New York: Praeger, 1992), 186–187.

64. For details on Chiang Ching-kuo's leadership and political and economic development in Taiwan, see Shao-chuan Leng, ed., *Chiang Ching-kuo's Leadership in the Development of the Republic of China on Taiwan* (Lanham, MD: University Press of America, 1993).

65. In a sense, this represented a reversal in US policy inasmuch as previous US presidents had declared that Taiwan was part of China. President Nixon had stated that this was the view of both sides, but didn't set forth a US policy.

66. For details, see Copper, *China Diplomacy*, 67–75.

67. Jaushieh Joseph Wu, *Taiwan's Democratization: Forces Behind the New Momentum* (Hong Kong: Oxford University Press, 1995), 39.

68. See, for example, Ray S. Cline, *Chiang Ching-kuo Remembered: The Man and His Political Legacy* (Washington, D.C.: U.S. Global Strategy Council, 1989), and Shao-chuan Leng, ed., *Chiang Ching-Kuo's Leadership in the Development of the Republic of China on Taiwan.*

69. For biographical information on Lee, see Shih-shan Henry Tsai, *Lee Teng-hui and Taiwan's Quest for Identity* (New York: Palgrave-Macmillan, 2005). For information on Lee's presidency in his own words, see Lee Teng-hui, *Creating the Future: Towards a New Era for the Chinese People* (Taipei: Government Information Office, 1993). For a critical assessment of the Lee era, see Wei-chin Lee and T. Y. Wang, eds., *Sayonara to the Lee Teng-hui Era: Politics in Taiwan, 1988–2000* (Lanham, MD: University Press of America, 2003).

70. See Roy, *Taiwan: A Political History*, 178.

71. See John F. Copper, "The KMT's 13th Party Congress: Reform, Democratization, New Blood," in Cynthia Chenault, ed., *Modernizing East Asia: Economic and Cultural Dimensions of Political Change* (Jamaica, NY: St. John's University Press, 1989).

72. For details on the 1990 election, see Tsai, *Lee Teng-hui and Taiwan's Quest for Identity*, 177.

73. John F. Copper, *Playing with Fire: Looming War with China Over Taiwan* (Westport, CT: Praeger, 2006), 32–35.

74. For details, see Linda Chao and Ramon H. Myers, *The First Chinese Democracy: Political Life in the Republic of China on Taiwan* (Baltimore: Johns Hopkins University Press, 1998), chapters 10 and 11.

75. See Hungdah Chiu, *Koo-Wang Talks and the Prospect of Building Constructive and Stable Relations Across the Taiwan Strait* (Baltimore: University of Maryland School of Law, 1993).

76. See John F. Copper, "The KMT's 14th Party Congress: Toward Unity or Disunity," *Journal of Chinese Studies* (October 1994).

77. For details, see Copper, *Playing with Fire*, and John W. Garver, *Face Off: China, the United States, and Taiwan's Democratization* (Seattle: University of Washington Press, 1997).

78. See Sheng Lijun, *China and Taiwan: Cross-Strait Relations Under Chen Shui-bian* (London: Zed Books, 2002), chapter 3.

79. For Chen's autobiography, see Chen Shui-bian, *The Son of Taiwan: The Life of Chen Shui-bian and his Dreams for Taiwan* (Taipei: Taiwan Publishing Company, 2002).

80. See John F. Copper, *Taiwan's 2000 Presidential and Vice-Presidential Election: Consolidating Democracy and Creating a New Era of Politics* (Baltimore: University of Maryland School of Law, 2000).

81. For details, see John F. Copper, "Taiwan in Gridlock," in John F. Copper, ed., *Taiwan in Troubled Times: Essays on the Chen Shui-bian Presidency* (Singapore: World Scientific, 2001), 19–52.

82. See John F. Copper, *Taiwan's 2001 Legislative Magistrates and Mayors Election* (Singapore: East Asian Institute, Contemporary China Series, World Scientific, 2002).

83. John F. Copper, *Taiwan's 2004 Presidential and Vice Presidential Election: Democracy's Consolidation or Devolution* (Baltimore: University of Maryland School of Law, 2004).

84. For details on corruption in the Chen administration, see John F. Copper, *The Blight of Corruption in the Chen Administration in Taiwan*, Background Brief, East Asian Institute, December 2007.

85. See John F. Copper, "Why the Bush Administration Soured on Taiwan," in Shuisheng Zhao, ed., *U.S.-China Relations: Cooperation and Competition in Northeast Asia* (London: Palgrave/Macmillan, 2008).

86. John F. Copper, *Taiwan's 2008 Presidential and Vice Presidential Election: Maturing Democracy* (Baltimore: University of Maryland School of Law, 2008).

3

SOCIETY

TAIWAN'S SOCIETY AND THE CULTURE upon which it is built are basically traditional and Chinese. More specifically, they are rural southern Chinese in origin. Taiwan also has an elite culture that is somewhat different. Both have evolved considerably in Taiwan—affected by interactions with the Aborigines, the population's contact with other people in the region, European and Japanese colonization, and considerable Western influence in recent years, particularly American. Rapid economic growth has given rise to materialism, not to mention Taiwan's rapid democratization, and has produced profound social change, giving rise to many of the problems present in Western countries. The breakdown of traditions, the weakening of the family, increasing alienation, and other pains of a society in rapid transition are prevalent. Urbanization, crime, youth problems, divorce, and drug use are all regarded as serious issues. While Taiwan's problems are less acute than those in most other rapidly modernizing or modern countries, most citizens view many of these problems with alarm. The strength of Chinese culture and the strong family tradition seem to explain this. Social change in Taiwan is worthy of study because it has been so rapid, and some of the solutions to problems, and the new society itself, are unique. The differences in culture among the ethnic groups help explain Taiwan's diversity and to some extent its colorful and at times raucous politics. Finally, Taiwan's culture and society connect intimately to the issue of Taiwan's identity and whether Taiwan is essentially China or is different and whether its future is with China or separate. Culturally, Taiwan has been growing apart from China for many years, though recently an increase in cross-strait contacts and China becoming capitalist while returning to its traditional culture has reversed this trend.

Social Structure and Order

Before the twentieth century, for a number of reasons the various groups of people inhabiting Taiwan had little contact with each other and, therefore, maintained quite distinct social systems.[1] The Aborigines' social systems were tribal, though their social order differed markedly between two broadly defined groups: the mountain Aborigines and the lowland Aborigines. The mountain Aborigines' social structures were more communal and less settled; the lowlanders' social systems were more sedentary and in some important ways resembled those of Chinese agrarian society. Customs, mores, and social systems varied considerably among the tribes. In tribal organization, some groups were classless, while others distinguished between the chieftains and the common people or followers. In some tribes, social status was determined largely by age. Most, but not all, were male-dominant: patriarchal and patrilineal. Depending on the tribe, married couples lived with a spouse's parents or apart. All of the Aboriginal groups were monogamous.[2]

Today, the mountain Aborigines' social systems are much more in evidence than those of the lowlanders. With the coming of Chinese migration, many lowlander Aborigines were either killed or assimilated by the Chinese; others retreated into the mountainous areas, whereupon they adopted the mountain Aborigines' societal patterns. In addition, the mountain Aborigines resisted change and assimilation more than the lowland Aborigines.[3]

Chinese immigrants brought their customs, mores, and norms to Taiwan—except they did not bring with them the ancient Chinese prejudice against physical work; alternatively, need forced them to abandon that facet of their culture. Nor did education become the basis of elite class status in Taiwan as it had been in China. Social position was founded more on differences in privileges between the rulers and the ruled, and the possession or control of arms, wealth, and sometimes positions in secret societies. Taiwan was a dangerous land, which the Chinese were constantly made aware of by the Aboriginal practice of headhunting. The authority and status accrued by weapons and money translated into a social order and a political system similar to those in feudal Europe and Japan and, in many respects, quite unlike that in China.

Social relations among the Chinese immigrants were, from the onset of their migration to Taiwan, founded on the village, which was typically controlled by one or a few powerful families. Dominant families chose village leaders who regulated land tenure and were responsible for security. Social norms and rules were established and enforced by family elders. The important families frequently controlled large sections of the flat land of the island, including most of the farmland.[4] Thus, a social hierarchy was to a large degree founded on land tenure.

The landlord system that took root in Taiwan several centuries ago eventually evolved into a mixture of traditional feudalism and government-controlled land rights—the latter a product of Taiwan's experience with Western colonialism. Later, landlords subcontracted with cultivators, who then hired farm laborers. Some landlords supervised the use of land, while others held official government positions, maintaining their authority and privilege in that way. Those who could provide the Chinese population with protection against Aboriginal raids also acquired rights over land. Serfdom did not become part of Taiwan's feudal order, but indentured servitude, male and female, was common. Males worked in the fields, females in the home. Female indentured servitude lasted until the Japanese colonial period, when Tokyo abolished it.[5]

The social hierarchy of the Chinese population of Taiwan was patriarchal and patrilineal. Only males were heirs, and as a consequence female children were seen as temporary members of the family and thus were trained in household skills so, at the proper age, they could be married into a friendly and, if possible, rich and powerful household. A family lacking a male child would adopt one, usually an infant, usually from a relative. Alternatively, the family would "adopt" a son-in-law, who would agree his children would take his wife's family name; but this practice was considered a loss of face for the man and was less common than infant adoption.

Until the age of about four, male and female children were raised together, with few distinctions based on gender. Typically children were given little responsibility until the age of about six. By the age of sixteen, children assumed many adult duties, and by eighteen they were usually working. Although families were large, children were generally treated with considerable kindness and were regarded as precious possessions. The mother was mainly responsible for rearing the children, but grandparents and older siblings also played a role, as did more distant relatives at times.[6]

Authority within the Chinese family was to a large degree based on age, especially when the extended family lived in one house. Respect for elders also extended throughout society. Older people, even when barely able to work, would often maintain positions in businesses or government because of the social taboo against forced retirement. Elders served as a stabilizing influence in society, though age did not necessarily equate with authority outside the household unless combined with high social class or important business or political connections.

In terms of the social-class hierarchy, working for the government or in education conferred elite status. However, as Taiwan began to develop economically, there was another route to the higher class: commerce. Some scholars thus identify two middle classes in Taiwan: the first, those belonging to a scholar-official class as in China before 1949, and the second, those who found wealth through business. Though both were modernizing forces, over time they merged to some degree with the impact of money in politics.[7]

In Taiwan—as in China, Japan, and other Asian countries—parents or other relatives arranged marriages. These marriages bonded families, and young men and women frequently had little or no say about the selection of their mates. In fact, it was not uncommon for a couple to have had no acquaintance before marriage; sometimes they had not even seen each other. Young married women were usually subservient to their husbands and to the elders in his family; but their status was no lower and, in fact, was generally higher than that of women in most traditional societies. Married women's status usually increased over time because of the respect for age in Chinese culture.

In terms of social structure, norms and mores, early on, Taiwan was not much different from China. But when the Communists took control of China in 1949, they sought to reconstruct the society, and, in the process, they deliberately weakened the family system and redirected the individual's loyalty toward the state and the Communist Party. This had a profound impact on the culture. Nothing similar happened in Taiwan, although the government endeavored to nurture nationalism for the purpose of building the state, and the central role of the family in the society suffered somewhat in the process. The modernization processes, on the other hand—especially urbanization, mass education, consumerism, materialism, and Westernization—profoundly affected the family system in Taiwan. These forces of change have been gradual but very strong and have generally favored a weaker family structure and the nuclear family over the extended family. In China, since the death of Mao, the family has to some degree been restored to its central societal role; in this respect, there is convergence with Taiwan.

Ethnic Issues

As noted earlier, four ethnic or subethnic groups populate Taiwan: the Aborigines, Hakkas, Fukien Chinese (also called Fukienese or Hoklo), and Mainland Chinese (or Mainlanders). There is disagreement about whether the term "ethnic" accurately describes the Chinese groups; some prefer "subethnic" or "provincial." The Aborigines, on the other hand, are generally considered "ethnically" different from the three Chinese groups; in fact, they are sometimes said to be a different race from the other three. The three categories of Chinese may be said to constitute different groups—at least distinct in culture, language, and in some other ways—although the Mainland Chinese are much more heterogeneous and lack most of the qualities of an ethnic or even subethnic group. The three Chinese groups all consider themselves Han people that make up around 90 percent of the population of China. If self-identification by the four groups is considered important, then they constitute discrete groups.

In the past, the Aborigines were severely discriminated against by the Chinese population, due to the danger they posed to the Chinese communities and the strife between the two groups that lasted for centuries. Stereotypes of the Aborigines as headhunters and the associated fear this caused the Chinese lasted long after this practice became uncommon and even extinct. Prejudice against the Aborigines, based on their "primitive" lifestyle and less success in education, business, etc.—and their not being Chinese—persists to this day.[8]

Under the Japanese, the Aborigines were kept separate from each other and the rest of the population, but Nationalist Chinese policy was to integrate them into Chinese society. It seemed that neither worked. The Aborigines have a lower socioeconomic and educational status than other ethnic groups living in Taiwan. As a group, they are afflicted with higher rates of unemployment, alcoholism, adolescent prostitution, and various other social ills. Because of this, the Aborigines have for some time received special education, job training, and other benefits through provisions in the Constitution to help minority groups and the poor. In recent years, social welfare and other such programs to help the Aborigines have proliferated. Still, the Aborigines remain largely outside the mainstream of society and are considered underprivileged. Most do not want to be assimilated, and many view social programs as counterproductive, conferring few real benefits while causing a further cultural breakdown in Aborigine communities.

The Aborigines may face an even more serious problem. According to government figures, Aborigines living in special communities have a combined population of 458,000—around 2 percent of Taiwan's total population. Their birthrate is lower than that of other ethnic groups, and, as a result, they are a declining percentage of the population. Meanwhile, an estimated 80,000 Aborigines have permanently or semipermanently migrated to the cities in search of work, compared to 5,000 that lived in cities in 1960 and 30,000 in 1980. Because their numbers are declining, the histories of the various Aborigine tribes, which are mainly oral, are being lost; so are their languages, arts, and songs. Some say the Aborigines are heading for assimilation and extinction.[9]

Prosperity and democracy, on the other hand, have begun to transform the Aborigines into vocal minority groups that have become unified politically. Most Aboriginal organizations advocate policies of separateness so as to preserve their society and culture. Thus their social integration and the obliteration of their culture are not foregone conclusions. Anyway, the integration and assimilation of the Aborigines are not firm government policies and may be changed.

The culture and social structure of the Hakka Chinese was unique in China before they migrated to Taiwan. Hakka people originally inhabited North China, but were driven out to become a people "without a homeland." Some Western writers have compared them to the Jews or Gypsies. They took up residence in various parts of China, but most settled in southern, coastal China. Hakkas long suffered from various forms of prejudice; they were even barred from taking the imperial examination throughout various periods of Chinese history. Because the leader of the Taiping Rebellion, which caused massive killing and widespread destruction in what amounted to a civil war in China in the mid-1800s, was Hakka, further discrimination against Hakkas resulted.

Inasmuch as the Hakkas had long-known persecution, they took with them to Taiwan a strong sense of separateness and "clannishness." They retained this because of the dangers of living in close proximity to the Aborigines—which was closer than that of the Fukien Chinese, who forced the Hakkas from good farmland close to the shore and into hilly areas—and also their minority status in Taiwan vis-à-vis Fukienese Taiwanese with whom they frequently fought. Notwithstanding the cultural homogenization Taiwan has experienced in recent years, the Hakkas self-identity and different culture remain, and many Hakkas still live apart or in Hakka communities.

Hakka social customs and mores still differ noticeably from those of the Fukien Taiwanese and the Mainland Chinese. Hakka women, for example, engage in physically taxing work such as road building, construction, and agriculture. Yet they are typically more passive and self-effacing than other Chinese women. Some observers note that Hakka men favor certain professions or businesses (such as railroad jobs, police work, fishing, small business, and trade) because in the past they were unable to acquire good land or lost it to the Fukien Taiwanese. Some have also noted a stronger family system among Hakkas because of the discrimination they faced both in China and in Taiwan.

Hakkas can be identified by their customs, ancestral records, and language (or dialect, which Fukien Taiwanese and Mainland Chinese seldom speak). Many Western authors, though, do not distinguish between the Hakkas and the Fukien Taiwanese, simply lumping them together under the term "Taiwanese." This is odd since the two groups have a history of conflict that has resulted in mutual distrust and even hatred. Earlier, their disagreements were mainly over land, but recently, they have involved language and other issues. Due to the treatment Hakkas faced earlier in their interactions with Fukien Taiwanese, when strong antagonisms developed between the Fukien Taiwanese and the Mainland Chinese that culminated in 1947 in the February 28 Incident, many Fukien Taiwanese questioned whether the Hakkas would side with them or the Mainland Chinese in the event of a broader conflict. Even years later, they continued to harbor doubts.[10]

Hakkas call themselves Taiwanese (since they regard Taiwan as their home and have even fewer familial ties with China than the Fukienese Taiwanese). In many respects, they do not consider themselves "mainstream" Taiwanese, as do Fukien Taiwanese, nor do they regard themselves as part of the majority Taiwanese group. They got along with the Mainlanders better than the Fukien Taiwanese did in the past and, indeed, still do. In various ways, they see themselves as a minority group like the Mainland Chinese. They feel they are culturally and socially unique, and many want to remain that way. Recently, they have become more conscious of their separate status, and this put them at odds with Fukienese Taiwanese during the Chen Shui-bian. One of the serious disagreements between the two groups involved the efforts of many Fukien Taiwanese to make Taiwanese the official language of the country. Clearly, it is not accurate to say the Hakkas are simply Taiwanese.[11]

Hakkas probably number 2 to 3 million, or 10 to 15 percent of the population. Some claim that the figure is closer to the larger figures or even more because many Hakkas lost their identity when they stopped speaking their language or intermarried with Fukien Taiwanese. Hakkas dwell in many parts of China, but they generally do not have significant ties with their island counterparts. Nevertheless, many Hakka, people say, identify less with Taiwan than do the Fukienese Taiwanese and are more cosmopolitan because they identify with and admire Sun Yat-sen, Deng Xiaoping, and Lee Kuan Yew, all of them Hakka.

Hakkas have adjusted to modernization quite well, much better than have the Aborigines. Additionally, while their incomes are lower than other Chinese on average, many Hakka have done well economically. They have also been successful in politics. Former president Lee Teng-hui is Hakka (though he doesn't speak Hakka), as well as Wu Poh-hsiung and a number of other top figures in the Nationalist Party. In recent years, Hakkas have come to comprise an important voting bloc and have thus increased their political influence at election time. The Democratic Progressive Party has tried to woo their vote, but with little success.

The Fukien Taiwanese brought their social structure and organization with them from China, specifically southern Fukien Province. Their culture was Chinese, but differed from that of other parts of China. Fukienese culture, like Hakka culture, gradually changed in the absence of ties with China, numerous contacts with foreign countries, and fifty years of Japanese rule. The Fukien Taiwanese were originally mostly farmers, fishermen, and traders, and though many still are, increasing numbers of them have entered business—usually family businesses or firms owned and operated by other Fukien Taiwanese. Today, they dominate the business community, and for this reason, their socioeconomic status has improved faster than that of any other ethnic group in Taiwan.

The Fukien Taiwanese have also become active politically, early on joining the KMT (even former president Chen Shui-bian) and later the DPP, running for office as independents and also applying for government jobs. Many started careers in local government or in law. Their status and influence expanded from the 1970s on to such a degree that they are now the dominant ethnic group in Taiwan politically. Democratization has clearly favored the Fukien Taiwanese.

Because the Fukien Taiwanese constitute a numerical majority, around 70 percent of the population, they often regard the other ethnic groups as minority groups. As mentioned above, the Fukienese lived apart from and often engaged in conflict with the Aborigines and the Hakka in the past. This was overshadowed by ill feelings toward Mainlanders that grew in the mid- to late 1940s, particularly after the February 1947 "massacre." After 1949, this tension worsened because of the influx of Mainlanders who fled to Taiwan after the defeat of the Nationalist armies on the mainland. Mainlanders at this time not only arrogated nearly all important positions in the national government and in education, but also assumed a higher class status based on cultural and linguistic ties to China. All of this caused resentment among Fukienese.

Though Fukien Chinese trace their ancestry to Fukien Province, until recently few had been there. Like the Hakka, most did not plan to return to China when they left. Years of separation from the mainland have led them to identify with Taiwan and to see the island, rather than China, as their home. Many have come to regard themselves as Chinese only in the limited sense that European Americans see themselves as Europeans. Some Fukien Taiwanese have even made the argument that they are not Chinese. They point out that because women were not allowed to migrate to Taiwan for long periods, many men found wives locally; thus they are a "mixed race." This point has been used by pro-independence advocates in the DPP in order to assert that Taiwan and China are different places and should be separate. The whole story, however, should include the fact that many Mainland Chinese soldiers found Aboriginal wives in 1949 and after, and that 90 percent of Fukienese and Hakka have some Vietnamese ancestry.[12]

The Mainland Chinese came to Taiwan from various provinces of China after 1945, but most in 1949. The majority were either soldiers or government officials. They represented all parts of China, though a disproportionate number hailed from the south and central parts of China, especially the coastal provinces. Few came from the northern and western provinces. For some time, an inordinately large number of top government officials in Taiwan came from Chekiang, the province where Chiang Kai-shek was born; indeed, for some years, Mainland Chinese from parts of China other than Chekiang experienced some discrimination—certainly disadvantages—when seeking government jobs. Many say this bias was also apparent in education and other areas.

After they fled to Taiwan, the Mainlanders sought to preserve Chinese cultural traditions. They spoke Mandarin Chinese (which was the national language of

China and traditionally the language of the educated) and, compared with the other Chinese groups residing in Taiwan, had greater—or at least more recent—contact with the fount of Chinese culture. As the self-designated protectors of Chinese civilization, many Mainlanders expressed condescending attitudes toward Taiwanese, while others emulated their group's elites or saw preserving Chinese tradition as a matter of pride or self-identification. In addition, Mainland Chinese made a claim of cultural superiority on the basis of the years of Japanese colonial rule of Taiwan, which "Japanized" the island's population. Because of their experiences at the hands of the Japanese military during World War II, the Mainland Chinese generally disliked or even hated the Japanese. For this reason, when they arrived in Taiwan, they felt that Japanese culture, to which many, especially Fukienese Taiwanese, had adopted, should be eradicated as quickly as possible.

Taiwanese do not espouse such an attitude, and many, especially higher class Taiwanese, speak of the period of Japanese colonization as better than the periods of "Chinese colonization" before and after that. Many perceive that Japan ruled Taiwan very well. Many admire Japanese culture. This admiration has been an ethnic "identifier"; indeed, foreigners have often observed that one can discern the difference between the Mainland Chinese and the Taiwanese by their attitudes toward the Japanese and by the presence or absence of Japanese items in their homes.

Mainland Chinese are urban dwellers more than are the other groups, with more residing in Taipei proportionally than anywhere else. In fact, certain districts or suburbs of Taipei are predominantly Mainland Chinese.[13] Recently, Mainlanders have developed a new type of exclusivity that stems from being a minority in the context of Fukien Taiwanese gaining political power. Many, in fact, prefer to live in their own areas.

When they came to Taiwan, many Mainlanders brought wealth with them or had good jobs in the government or elsewhere through family connections. They filled most of the official positions formerly occupied by the Japanese, and a few took over Japanese businesses. Their education level was higher than that of the other three ethnic groups and remained higher. The socioeconomic status of Mainland Chinese, however, has fallen over the years due to the success of the Taiwanese in business and the failure of public-sector salaries to keep pace with those in the private sector. The children of Mainlander families now frequently work at menial jobs; daughters are even employed as bar girls—formerly a job for Taiwanese. In fact, many regard the retired Mainlander soldiers as the most hapless of any segment of the society, having neither family roots nor economic wherewithal. It is certainly no longer accurate to say that the Mainlanders exploit Taiwanese or that Taiwanese are a disadvantaged or oppressed group. In some important ways, it is just the opposite.

It is crucial to point out, however, that for the most part, ethnic prejudices and differences have faded in recent years with amazing speed. Ethnicity was once easily discerned from accent, physical appearance, and even mannerisms, but this is no longer so. Now it is often difficult to know the ethnic group of young people without asking. Since ethnic identity is defined more by language than most other factors and because the younger generation has grown up with both Mandarin and Taiwanese, the biggest reason for ethnic separation will soon disappear. In sum, ethnic and provincial identification in many respects are evaporating quickly and will likely be much less important in the future.[14]

Ethnic barriers have also diminished much faster than most observers anticipated three or four decades ago because of Taiwan's rapid economic growth and the material culture it has created and also because virtually all ethnic groups have shared in Taiwan's prosperity. A considerable amount of Westernization has also contributed, as have urbanization and intermarriage. Similarly, government policies have helped, including policies that favored Taiwanese in recruitment and hiring beginning in the 1970s. Finally, almost the entire population of Taiwan—and certainly all its ethnic groups—shared a common desire to remain independent of the People's Republic of China for as long as it was poor and Communist.

Despite all this, it is quite apparent that ethnic tension increased in Taiwan after the election of Chen Shui-bian to the presidency in early 2000. He appealed to Fukienese voters on the basis of ethnicity and won the election that way. All other groups in 2000 voted more for another candidate, James Soong. Subsequently, Chen and the DPP played the "ethnic card" in order to govern without sharing power. The three minority groups complained of discrimination by the government that favored Fukien Taiwanese. They also noted discrimination spilled into social interactions and that they are often treated with scorn and prejudice in daily life. Ethnic relations were thus strained during the time the Chen administration was in power. In 2008, Ma Ying-jeou, a Mainland Chinese, campaigned on a platform of healing ethnic relations, and he won the election by a wide margin. This indicated the electorate had come to disapprove of the Chen government's policies of ethnic divisiveness. At that juncture, many looked forward to a return to the trend of fading ethnic differences.

Languages and Religions

The overwhelming majority of both the Chinese (all groups) and the Aborigines in Taiwan speak Mandarin Chinese, or *kuo yu* (meaning "national language"), which derives from the Beijing dialect in a somewhat similar way as American English comes from British English.[15] There are differences in accent, but this does not prevent Mandarin from being a language nearly everyone can use for at least basic communications. The two Taiwanese groups also speak their own languages or dialects (different languages in the sense that they are mutually unintelligible, though they are very similar, almost identical, grammatically and in the written form—Chinese not being a phonetic language but rather one that employs pictographs and ideographs). Most Mainland Chinese, with the exception of the young in decreasing numbers, know the regional dialect of the province or area that they or their parents came from. Thus, while the Chinese residents of Taiwan often do not understand what others are saying, they do have mediums of communications that enable them to talk to each other. Ease of communicating is also enhanced by Taiwan's high rate of literacy, the difficulty of written Chinese notwithstanding.

The Aborigines speak languages that resemble Malay in structure, and many words are similar. Yet the Aboriginal languages, or dialects, differ considerably, and the various tribes cannot communicate with others in any of their tongues. The Aboriginal languages were not written until the Dutch period, when they were rendered into an alphabetic form and taught in schools. In recent times, Aboriginal languages have been dying out with modernization, though both official and unofficial efforts have helped revive and preserve them.

Fukien Taiwanese speak Taiwanese, a derivative of the Amoy dialect of Chinese, or Amoy Fukienese, the language spoken in southern Fukien Province. Most also speak Mandarin Chinese. Hakkas speak the Hakka dialect, which originated in north China, but was influenced over the centuries by various dialects in southern China, where many Hakkas lived. Most—indeed, nearly all—of the Hakka population of Taiwan also speak Taiwanese and Mandarin. Some Hakkas do not speak Hakka, especially if they grew up in a non-Hakka community or their parents didn't teach them. Some older Taiwanese do not speak Mandarin Chinese, but rather speak Japanese. Many younger Mainlanders speak Taiwanese, especially if they have grown up outside of Taipei. Most Aborigines speak Mandarin Chinese and Taiwanese; some speak Japanese. In short, almost all the Republic of China's people speak two or more dialects or languages.

There are regional accents in both Taiwanese and Hakka. Most Taiwanese, for example, can be identified from their speech as being from the northern or southern part of the island. Older Mainlanders have accents coming from their provincial dialects. Local accents, however, are rapidly disappearing because of social mobility and the influence of national radio and television.

Some differences have evolved in the versions of Mandarin Chinese (called *pu tung hua,* meaning "common language," in the People's Republic of China) spoken and written on the two sides of the Taiwan Strait. These differences come from more than four decades of almost total separation as well as from Western influence in Taiwan and the lack of it in China. There have also been calculated efforts by the government of the People's Republic of China to reform the language. In China, many of the characters have been simplified (sometimes for ideological reasons), whereas the traditional ones remain in use in Taiwan. Words, phrases, and slogans based on Communist teachings or ideology or used in Mao's various campaigns are often not understood by people in Taiwan. Yet with the proliferation of contacts, the increased travel by people from Taiwan to China in the past three decades, and less censorship on both sides, the number of terms and phrases unfamiliar to people on one side or the other of the Taiwan Strait has decreased rapidly.

Controversies have arisen over language use and policies in Taiwan. When Taiwan reverted to China after World War II, the Nationalist government made Mandarin the official language and tried to discourage the use of all dialects. Taiwanese found it difficult to adjust to this policy because it meant learning a new spoken language. Also, many felt that Mandarin Chinese was being forced upon them, as Japanese had been forced on them fifty years earlier.[16] Government officials, however, perceived this policy as a necessary part of nation-building and modernization.

Because Mandarin Chinese boasts more speakers than any other language in the world and is very useful for reasons ranging from travel and commercial relations to research, many Taiwanese and Aborigines have long supported its use in the education system, government, and elsewhere. Opening contacts with China in the 1980s and China's economic boom have amplified this argument. Yet there have also been movements in Taiwan to use Taiwanese and Hakka more. Three decades ago, demands for radio and television programs in Taiwanese began to emerge; demands for Hakka soon followed and, more recently, the Aboriginal languages.

Currently, many Fukien Taiwanese see the use of their language as an expression of ethnic pride and their dominance in politics and thus as mirroring the democratization of Taiwan. Indeed, many Taiwanese politicians make it a point to speak Taiwanese when campaigning and sometimes use it in government meetings, to the embarrassment of many older Mainland Chinese who do not understand it. Some Fukien Taiwanese, especially those advocating a separate or independent Taiwan, argued that Taiwanese is a unique language, very different from Mandarin Chinese. It is true that it contains different sounds and that the system of tones is not the same; it is therefore unintelligible to Mandarin speakers. Nevertheless, Taiwanese remains very similar to the dialect of Chinese spoken in southern Fukien Province in China. Also, interestingly, it is structurally much more like ancient Chinese than is Mandarin Chinese. Thus, some say Taiwanese is more Chinese than Chinese (meaning Mandarin Chinese).

Despite the posturing and occasionally bitter debates about language, there have been no language riots in Taiwan as there have been in some other countries. Though continued controversy over language is likely, Taiwan will no doubt remain a bilingual or multilingual country. The majority of Taiwan's population has been raised speaking more than one language or dialect, and most see an advantage in keeping a multilingual population in Taiwan. Those who have advocated making Taiwanese the sole official language of the country to accord with majority rule have not had much success since Taiwanese is not very useful outside of Taiwan, except for some Chinese communities in Southeast Asia. Furthermore, Taiwan is increasingly dealing with China commercially and in other ways, and thus Mandarin Chinese needs to be kept.

In addition to Chinese, English and some other Western languages and Japanese are taught in the schools from primary grades through college and university, though among foreign languages, English predominates. In fact, English is now compulsory beginning in the third grade. Many English textbooks are used in Taiwan's colleges and universities, especially in the technical fields. Chinese language texts are generally not as good or are not considered up-to-date. Also, students feel a need to know the vocabulary of their field in English so they can attend graduate school abroad and communicate with foreigners in their profession. Citizens who travel abroad frequently also use English in business meetings.

Language is not the only way Taiwan is diverse: So are its religious beliefs and practices. Many, when asked what religion they adhere to, mention several. For this reason and the fact that Taiwan's religions are not exclusive, nor have religion and politics become intertwined, religion seldom has been the basis for discrimination, ethnic hatred, or social conflict. Some observers have described Taiwan as a nation of extraordinary religious tolerance. Indeed, it might be the foremost nation in the world as far as religious freedom is concerned.[17] Many religions are practiced in Taiwan without difficulty or interference.

The Aborigines of Taiwan practice animism, nature worship, and various kinds of animal sacrifice. They also combine ancestor worship with agrarian rites. Their belief systems are polytheistic, and they make no distinctions between gods and spirits. Except for two groups, the Aborigines do not espouse the concept of a god-creator. In the past, some tribes practiced headhunting as a source of religious prestige and to enhance their qualifications for marriage. This, of course, is no longer true.

Chinese migrants brought Taoism, Confucianism, and Buddhism to Taiwan as well as some other religions. The Dutch brought Protestant Christianity, the Spanish brought Catholicism, and the Japanese brought Shinto. When the Communists captured China in 1949, many religious organizations and their officials, as well as ministers and priests, fled to Taiwan, adding to Taiwan's religious mix.

The principal religions of Taiwan—by number of followers—are Buddhism, Taoism, Christianity, and I-Kuan Tao (or the Religion of Unity). Buddhists are said to number 8.1 million and Taoists 7.6 million. Christians total 903,000 (605,000 Protestants and 298,000 Catholics). There are 845,000 I-Kuan Tao followers. Several other religious groups claim adherents numbering more than 100,000. There are nearly 60,000 people of the Islamic faith in Taiwan, most having come from China in 1949, though Islam was practiced in Taiwan before that.[18] Having said this, there is a major caveat: Many say all Chinese are Confucian. But this means espousing Chinese culture, philosophy, and certain ethical principles rather than holding to special religious beliefs, though many people also regard Confucianism as a religion.

Taoism is the oldest of the Chinese religions on Taiwan, tracing its origins to the teachings and writings of Lao Tzu, who lived in the sixth century BC. Lao Tzu taught individual freedom, laissez-faire attitudes about government, human spontaneity, living in accord with nature or the Tao (meaning the way or path), and mystical experience. Taoist teachings became more spiritual in nature in the third century BC, after which Taoism evolved into an organized religion. Central to Taoism's religious side is belief in the attainment of immortality. People who live in harmony with their natural environment, according to Taoist teachings, are able to become immortals. Taoism also incorporates the theory of opposites, or *yin* and *yang,* which must be reconciled to strike an essential equilibrium or balance in the universe. During the seventh through the ninth centuries AD, Taoism became the religion of the court in China. Subsequently, it adopted aspects of Buddhism and Confucianism and fragmented into different sects or schools. The *Tao-te Ching* is the classic text, or "bible" of Taoism.

Taoism was brought to Taiwan by the earliest Chinese immigrants and was preserved and practiced on the island by the various Chinese communities. During the Japanese period, however, Taoism was suppressed because it was associated with Chinese patriotism and nationalism. As a result, many Taoist temples were reregistered as Buddhist temples. After World War II, Taoism made a revival. In 1950, Chang En-pu, a Taoist priest from China, established a Taoist fellowship, creating a more organized form of Taoism in Taiwan. There are now more than 18,000 Taoist temples, more than any other religion, and a large number of clergy in Taiwan, as well as a college, various other schools, hospitals, and a library.[19]

Buddhism originated in India in the sixth century BC from the teachings of an Indian prince, Siddhartha Gautama, who renounced his royal status and lifestyle to search for truth. Better known as the Buddha, he taught the Four Noble Truths: Life is suffering, suffering is the result of one's desires, one should control one's desires, and the way to eliminate desire is the Eightfold Path. The Eightfold Path consists of right views, intentions, speech, conduct, livelihood, effort, mindfulness, and concentration. In the second century BC, Mahayana (or the Greater Vehicle) Buddhism developed the belief in Bodhisattvas, or enlightened people capable of saving sentient beings, and the idea that attainers of merit (for doing good deeds) would reach a state of release called Nirvana. These ideas were similar to many

Taoist beliefs prevalent in China, an affinity that helped Buddhism gain acceptance there.

Brought by early Chinese immigrants, Buddhism became more popular in Taiwan in the late sixteenth century when Cheng Ch'eng-kung built many Buddhist temples and supported the religion in other ways. Some of the temples were used by practitioners of Taiwan's folk religions, thus giving Buddhism a local flavor. The main Buddhist sect that prospered in Taiwan was *Chan*. During the Japanese period, when Japanese Buddhists of various sects proselytized in Taiwan and Japanese monks took leading positions in the temples, Buddhist teachings and doctrine changed to resemble Japanese Buddhism in many ways. Moral and disciplinary codes and education were particularly affected. In 1949, many Buddhist monks fled to Taiwan from China and brought with them Buddhist practices and traditions not known previously in Taiwan.

In recent years, Buddhist organizations in Taiwan have been socially active, especially in working with the island's youth. They have also taken an interest in education, even building institutions of higher learning and sponsoring religious programs on television. Taiwan has numerous Buddhist temples. There are also a number of Buddhist seminaries, universities, colleges, orphanages, hospitals, retirement homes, and libraries. In addition, Buddhist organizations have been heavily involved in social welfare. In 1991, Master Cheng Yen, a leading Buddhist priest, received the Roman Magsaysay Award (Asia's version of the Nobel Peace Prize) for his contributions to the society. That same year, the Tzu Chi Foundation raised US$16 million for flood victims in China. In 1996, several Buddhist organizations supported Chen Li-an for president though their help did not prove critical to his campaign. In March 1997, the Dalai Lama visited Taiwan for five days and met with President Lee; he visited again in April 2001.[20]

Confucianism originated in China in the pre-Christian period based on the teachings of Confucius, who was born in 551 BC. Confucius is said to have edited or written several classic books: *The Book of Songs, The Book of History, The Book of Rites, The Book of Change,* and *The Spring and Autumn Annals.* The ethical teachings of Confucius are recorded in *The Analects* and *The Great Learning.* The metaphysical aspects of Confucianism are found in *The Doctrine of the Mean.* Through their teachings and writings, Mencius and Hsun Tzu, Chinese philosophers who lived two centuries later, contributed to what later became Confucian doctrine.

Confucianism, in its original form, may be said to be more an ethical code or handbook for behavior than a religion. When it became the official ideology—or the Imperial Court's political philosophy—during the Han Dynasty (206 BC to AD 221), it embraced a broad spectrum of ideas (some of them contradictory), though its central themes were rationalism and worldliness. Confucianism later took on the characteristics of a philosophy and a religion, but this transformation did not overshadow its rational side nor did it affect the opposing ideas it holds about human nature, social order, and the like. For example, Mencius taught that man was basically good, whereas Hsun Tzu was pessimistic. Mencius was democratic, Hsun Tzu legalistic. Confucianism, despite its eclecticism, expresses a unique reverence toward heaven and supports ancestor worship, and in these ways it is more a religion than a philosophy.

Confucianism came to Taiwan with the early Chinese, though Chinese officials who came to govern Taiwan later propagated it more. Though thought of as a political philosophy or ethical code for officials, it is also a "people's philosophy" and contributed to ideals about the family and interactions among people. There are Confucian temples in Taiwan, though some say they serve the purpose of honoring Confucius and are not strictly for worship. Over the years, Confucianism incorporated many local religious beliefs in China. It did the same in Taiwan.[21]

Christianity's stature in Taiwan is more a function of its social and political influence than of the number of its followers. Christian missionaries have been actively involved in social-help programs and education, founding a number of schools (both secondary and higher) that are quite influential in Taiwan today. A number of Taiwan's top political leaders have been Christian. Chiang Kai-shek and his son Chiang Ching-kuo were Methodists (though how serious they were has been questioned). Lee Teng-hui is Presbyterian—a denomination that has actively supported Fukien Taiwanese interests and is pro-independence. Taiwan's Christians maintain ties with their organizations and followers in other countries, adding to Taiwan's cosmopolitanism and internationalism.[22]

There is little difference among the ethnic groups in Taiwan in religious beliefs or practices, though there are more Christians among Mainland Chinese and Aborigines due to Western influence and proselytism. Taiwanese more frequently say they are Buddhist. But the people and the government in Taiwan are very tolerant of religious beliefs and practices—some say as tolerant as the Communist regime in China has been intolerant. In China, religion has been viewed as a challenge to communism, an "opiate of the people," and a propagator of superstition; thus it has been the target of eradication or suppression. On the issue of religion there has long been little understanding between the people on the two sides of the Taiwan Strait. On the other hand, religious freedom in China has increased markedly in recent years, and the gap between China and Taiwan in this regard has closed a bit.

Early Forces of Social Change

As noted earlier, the Chinese who emigrated to Taiwan several centuries ago had to adjust to a new environment, and the culture and social organization in the Chinese settlements changed in response to an array of often harsh challenges presented by life in Taiwan: hostile Aborigines, ethnic feuds, civil unrest, violence, high crime rates, an imbalance in the sex ratio—societal traits that characterized "frontier areas" elsewhere in the world. The Chinese communities were thus organized more along ethnic lines and for defense rather than as farming communities as they had been in China. This injected individuality and an element of rebelliousness into Taiwan's culture.

Taiwan's Chinese population culturally also became more eclectic than most parts of China, being influenced by the mingling of customs, mores, and norms of the different ethnic groups, Western culture, and contacts with other peoples or nations in the region. Education and family origins did not remain the basis of class status as they had in China, or at least as much. The Chinese communities in Taiwan were confused about relations with China—and even about their roots. Their society and culture changed, yet they remained in many ways Chinese. However, a Taiwanese national identity did not develop. As a matter of fact, this helps explain why foreign influence on Taiwan's culture was considerable in ensuing years.[23]

Dutch rule brought significant social change to Taiwan, making Taiwan more cosmopolitan and Western, though its influence was limited to one generation, and it affected only a small portion of the population. The Dutch did, however, have a definite modernizing affect. Cheng family rule, which followed the Dutch period, generated a sense of local identity, but not among all Chinese living on the island and it did not last very long. Subsequent Chinese rule did not change Taiwan very much socially or culturally, and the Manchus (the rulers of China at the time) had little lasting influence in transferring their culture to Taiwan. Chinese culture was preserved on the island during this period; in fact, some aspects of Chinese society and culture that faded in China were retained in Taiwan.

After 1895, Japanese rule brought a new round of social change, both positive and negative. Tokyo abolished certain land use laws, namely the practice whereby the government granted permanent first title to land that was then transferred to secondary owners who, in turn, paid the first owners for its use and then cultivated or rented the land. Japan, as noted in Chapter 2, also got rid of the practice of buying servants, and foot binding, and eliminated a host of Chinese superstitions. Meanwhile, the building of a national economy created a new business class that included bankers and financial experts, not to mention entrepreneurs. The Japanese language was used in the education system and in official transactions, providing greater access to foreign—especially Western—technology and learning.

When Taiwan reverted to Nationalist Chinese control in 1945, Japanese social and other influences were eliminated by deliberate policies of the Nationalist government. The Japanese language was no longer used in government matters or in education, and Japanese newspapers, magazines, books, and movies were banned.

Mainland Chinese dominated Taiwan politically and socially, and the two were mutually reinforcing. The local, or indigenous, Chinese groups, as well as the Aborigines, had a difficult time adjusting. They had to learn Mandarin Chinese and the culture brought by the Mainland Chinese—difficult tasks considering there had been little contact between Taiwan and China for fifty years. They also had to adjust to a new legal and political system. In 1949, an influx of Mainland Chinese required housing, education social services, and jobs—all of which were in short supply. They displaced many Taiwanese from their jobs and land, and they dominated the upper echelons of the society via positions in the government and education. These developments, understandably, created further social instability and ethnic friction.

After 1945, social status in Taiwan depended largely on education and position in the government or the military and, of course, wealth. Success in business, except small businesses, depended to a large extent on connections with the government, since much of the economy, especially large enterprises, was in the public sector. Non-Mainland Chinese had opportunities to rise socially, but only by learning Mandarin Chinese and establishing ties in government, business, and educational circles, or in the Nationalist Party. In all these realms, Mainland Chinese and their culture assumed a dominant role.

Taiwan's new rulers engineered broad and deep social change on the island from 1945 on in other ways. The most important factor fostering social progress in the post-1949 period in Taiwan, particularly in rural areas, was land reform. Rent reduction, the distribution of public lands, and the land-to-the-tiller laws, which were put in effect between 1949 and 1953, were its main components. Together, they increased the percentage of owner-farmers from about one-third of rural residents in 1948 to nearly 60 percent in 1953. Meanwhile, the amount of land cultivated by owners increased to more than 75 percent of the total land tilled. Among its most immediate social impacts, land reform increased the proportion of farmers who owned their own land and undermined the feudal political and social structures that had existed in rural Taiwan for some time. This created more citizen participation and democracy in local government and benefited economic growth and the capitalist system. In China, Mao implemented land reform, but it had quite different results and was soon judged a failure.[24]

Land reform indeed had far-reaching effects on the culture and society. Landlords, mostly Taiwanese, who were compelled to sell their land, were compensated in the form of bonds in government corporations. Not happy with this policy while perceiving that the bonds had no potential for growth, most landowners sold them. Also, because land prices dropped in anticipation of the effects of land reform, the land was worth less than expected when it was sold. As a result, many landlords not only got less for their land than it was worth but also missed an economic windfall from subsequent increases in the value of the stocks they were given for their land. The socioeconomic position of the former landlords, an elite group in Taiwan's society, thus diminished dramatically. In short, land reform not only eliminated the landlord-tenant relationship that was a central part of the island's social system, but also reduced the landlord class to a small group with much less money as well as social and political influence. This helped wipe out gross inequities in wealth in rural Taiwan; in fact, it contributed more than anything else to the leveling of incomes in Taiwan before the onset of industrialization.[25]

Land reform in Taiwan brought other secondary or delayed social changes or effects. It prompted the restructuring of rural society. Soon, the family no longer commanded the unquestioning loyalty of its members. The relationship between men and women changed, as did the practice of filial piety. The birthrate dropped. Agriculture became more efficient, leading younger people to seek jobs in the cities and farm families to decrease in size and number. Rural society became smaller and much more mobile.

The success of land reform and the resultant increases in agricultural productivity gave rise to rapid urbanization, as was noted in Chapter 1. The urbanization of Taiwan's population during the 1960s and after had a profound and lasting social impact. On the positive side, it fostered greater job specialization, created broader employment opportunities, promoted social equality, reduced social and class barriers, and vastly increased cultural opportunities. On the negative side, it weakened the family and engendered social alienation, giving rise to serious increases in crime rates, juvenile problems, and drug addiction. Meanwhile, a high but rapidly falling birthrate and an extremely fast decline in the death rate together caused Taiwan's population to grow rapidly in the short term and then to age quickly. These social problems remain serious, as will be seen in a later section of this chapter.

The United States was also a catalyst for social change in Taiwan, especially after 1949. At first, US influence was exerted through American economic and military assistance, plus the presence of a sizable number of US military personnel on the island. After aid was ended in 1964, trade links with the United States became just as important, not to mention American capital investment. The presence of Americans and contacts with them brought ideas about democracy, social equality, and progress to Taiwan. American books and movies also had a noticeable social impact, as did the many students who returned to Taiwan after studying in the United States. (For some years, Taiwan sent more students to colleges and universities in the United States than any other country in the world.) The United States also served as a model for social as well as economic and political change.[26]

Because of the importance of foreign policy and Taipei's claim to be "Free China," the government was more responsive to and influenced by the global community than most countries. Furthermore, with export-driven economic growth,

Taiwan became a nation whose economic development and prosperity depended on international markets, and the island became increasingly penetrated by outside forces and ideas. Foreign travel, which became common in the 1970s and 1980s, helped make Taiwan's citizens global in their outlook. In short, Taiwan's society and culture were heavily influenced by the external world.

Underscoring the importance of the forces of change cited above, almost all the social evolution (or devolution) that occurred in Taiwan after 1945 became permanent because the attendant modernization was embraced heartily by most of the population and was seen as either progressive or inevitable, or both. The key expediters of social change—economic growth, greater social and geographical mobility, expanded educational opportunities, consumerism—were present in other countries of the world, but they caused especially vast social change in Taiwan. The change was greater than it would have been otherwise because many of the influencers of change were mutually reinforcing.

Economic Development and Social Change

Rapid economic growth has been a powerful force driving social and cultural change in Taiwan. Economic expansion, in fact, has been the major "driver" behind the evolutionary—and in many ways "revolutionary"—social change Taiwan has experienced for the past four-plus decades. To understand both the speed and profundity of the results, it is helpful to examine some of Taiwan's economic data, particularly as they show how prosperity engendered social change. (Taiwan's economy is discussed in greater depth in Chapter 5.)

From 1953 to 1970, farm output in Taiwan grew rapidly—at two to three times the rate of population growth. Extremely large productivity increases in the agricultural sector and then in industry in the mid-1960s caused personal incomes in Taiwan to skyrocket—from about US$50 per year in 1950 to $200 in 1964 to more than US$3,000 by the mid-1980s and more than US$10,000 in 1992. Putting this in perspective, during this period the average income of citizens in Taiwan increased two hundredfold. The mean income of Taiwan's citizens was US$18,000 in 2008 and was projected to reach US$20,000 in 2009 and US$30,000 in 2015.

Such rapid economic growth caused surplus labor to be quickly absorbed. Taiwan's unemployment rate (which was probably in the 20 percent range in the 1950s) fell to 5.2 percent in 1963, and to less than 2 percent in the 1970s—a level, economists say, that is needed to allow workers to change jobs or seek retraining. In subsequent years, unemployment remained consistently below 3 percent.[27] Low jobless rates caused base salaries—or the salaries of unskilled workers—to increase faster than others, markedly reducing the income gap between rich and poor. As a result, the income disparity ratio dropped from 15 (based on a comparison between the top 20 percent and the bottom 20 percent of the population) in 1952 to

4.9 in 1982 and to 4.1 a few years later. Taiwan's level of income inequality became not only one of the lowest among developing nations but was below that of either Japan or the United States.[28]

Growth with equity benefited almost everyone, causing Taiwan to become a mass-consumption society. Prosperity first had an impact on diet: From 1952 to 1981, caloric intake increased from an average of 2,070 per day to 2,830—a total that exceeded that of any other country in Asia. Protein consumption grew, and a greater variety of foods were added to the diet. Next it affected consumer buying. By 1986, 97.2 percent of families owned color television sets, 98.8 percent owned refrigerators, 78.5 percent had washing machines, 83.2 percent had telephones, 30.3 percent owned air conditioners, and 12.3 percent had automobiles. With the exception of automobiles, these figures were comparable to data for the United States and advanced Western European countries. By the mid-1980s, the number of color TVs, refrigerators, and washing machines per family in Taiwan was higher than in the United States. During this time, almost 80 percent of families in Taiwan became homeowners—one of the highest percentages in the world.[29]

This growing affluence affected Taiwan's society in important ways. A decline in the birthrate, an aging population, and rapid urbanization have already been discussed. The impact on education will be assessed in the next section of this chapter. The changing structure of employment and a new interest in politics will be discussed in subsequent chapters. Here, however, special mention needs to be made of changes in the social structure, both rural and urban; social classes; the status of women; the family; and leisure and travel.

In rural Taiwan, as a result of the economic boom (which, as noted earlier, the agricultural sector experienced first because of land reform), the social structure changed from a family- or kinship-based one to an "associated" society. In other words, the interactions among friends and associates became relatively more important than interactions among relatives. Rural society became less authoritarian and more democratic, with more people participating in decision-making. The "leveling effect" of economic growth also led to the creation of new social and political organizations that were generally much bigger and involved more diverse memberships. In the words of sociologists, social organizations became horizontal rather than hierarchical in structure. They also became more political. Paternal and kinship relationships were replaced by mutual-benefit relations, while friendships or collegial relations supplanted family ties in the daily lives of rural citizens. Societal leadership saw Confucian academics and the traditional gentry replaced by successful businesspeople, professionals, educators, heads of farmers' associations, community affairs leaders, politicians, and others.[30]

With increases in rural incomes came electrification, which made it possible for farmers to lead more active lives simply because they could stay up later. The popularity of radio and television, which followed, brought new forms of culture.

Schools became more the locus of social interactions and cultural activities. Meanwhile, higher crop yields and increases in the planting of cash crops linked farmers to a free market, thus cementing ties between farmers and the government through crop improvement efforts, subsidies, and farmers' co-ops. These relationships integrated rural Taiwan more fully into the national economy and broke down barriers between rural and urban Taiwan. Thus a national culture emerged.

In the cities, traditional culture broke down even faster and more completely as a result of Taiwan's rapid industrialization. People formed new bonds based on friendship, work, business, and school ties. The importance of family links declined. Many found new opportunities to change their social status. Professional groups became more specialized. Even more than in rural Taiwan, people looked to the government for solutions to their problems. Western culture became much more widely accepted and commonplace. Differences between rich and poor decreased, yet wealth became more important.

These developments heralded the creation of a large middle class in a society that had once been bifurcated into high and low classes. By the 1980s, when asked about their social-class status, three-fourths of the population in Taiwan said they were middle class—a 20 percent increase over the 1950s. More precisely, more than two-thirds of the population (according to a poll taken in 1986) ranked themselves between 4 and 7 on a social strata scale of 10. During this same period, over 60 percent said that their social positions were higher than those of their parents, an indication that, for the majority of the population, social change was positive. Social transformation resulting from economic growth had still other ramifications: The effect of a father's occupation on his son's became very small—about the same as it was in the United States. Profession became a more important indicator of class status (as self-defined, at least).[31]

Because of Taiwan's economic prosperity, women's roles changed markedly, especially in marriage and employment. Arranged marriage became a thing of the past, though arranged meetings, wherein either party had the right to refuse or reject the other, became common. Love came to be regarded as a desirable incentive to marry rather than a dangerous diversion from family prearranged pairings. Women also began marrying later: at an average age of 26.1 in 2000 compared to 22.2 in 1971. It rose to 29 by 2006.[32]

The number of women joining the labor force likewise increased very rapidly. In the past, women worked in the home, a situation that began to change significantly in the 1950s. By 1961, 35.8 percent held jobs outside the home. In 1990, the figure was 44.5 percent, and in 2000, 46 percent—about the same percentage as in the United States and the countries of Western Europe. Perhaps even more telling was the large percentage of married women who began to work or stayed in the workforce after marriage. Now, almost 50 percent of adult women work full time.[33]

The social status of women, of course, improved markedly, though it was never as low as many Westerners have perceived it to be. Women in Chinese societies traditionally had much more control over their husbands and broader authority in the family than is generally assumed. Thus the transition to a modern society was not as difficult as it may have appeared. Today, women in Taiwan have become active in politics, have formed their own organizations, and own or control a significant portion of the national wealth—more, proportionately, than women in the United States. They also travel alone more and are less frequently victims of crime and abuse than women in the United States. Yet feminism as it is known in most Western countries has not become popular in Taiwan.

Women do, however, report difficulties with their new roles. For example, many married women say they are burdened with working while retaining the primary responsibility for keeping the family together and raising the children. They complain that they cannot maintain close bonds with their children because they must put them in childcare centers or with relatives during the day. Many women complain that they are disproportionately the victims of crime and that they are severely discriminated against if they divorce. A large number of women say they do not enjoy the opportunities available to men in business and politics. Many more women now suffer from stress and say they cannot cope with social change.[34]

Economic and social change has wrought a profound transformation in the family structure in both rural and urban Taiwan. The extended family, which was the rule in the past, is now less common. By the early 1980s, more than half of families were nuclear, less than a quarter were extended, and more than 5 percent were single-parent households. Meanwhile, family size decreased from an average of 5.9 persons in 1951 to 4.0 in 1990. A large part of the shift was accounted for by the fact that Taiwan was no longer an agricultural society. By 1996, less than 11 percent of the working population was employed in agriculture. Most of those who quit farming went to the big cities to live. Soon 50 percent of the population lived in the four largest cities. These statistics, as well as the government's increasing spending on "social welfare" (nearly threefold in fifteen years), reflect the continuing weakening of the family.[35]

Still another facet of social change associated with economic growth, and one that seems to be more pervasive than all others, is the generation gap. Most older citizens in Taiwan have a rural background and have been involved in farming during much of their lives; the majority of younger people have not had this experience. Furthermore, social change has impacted the younger generation more than older people, who feel they have not been able to keep up. The youth, say elders, espouse "odd" views of society and the world, and they believe in different standards of behavior. Many elders complain that respect for age has been diminished by economic progress; they believe their children, and young people generally, have abandoned them for a different world.[36]

There are other major differences in life experiences between the older and newer generation. Older people remember the period of Japanese colonization, Japan's defeat in World War II, and the beginning of Nationalist Chinese rule. Younger people do not. Older people recall many hardships. Younger people do not know about poverty or deprivation from personal experience; instead they "suffer" from affluence. The younger generation is much more westernized. Even the early period of Nationalist rule is seen differently by those who experienced it and those who have only heard about it. Older people recall the serious problems that developed when the Nationalists came, and they remember when US aid was critical to Taiwan. Younger people do not know about these things from personal experience. Some of Taiwan's youth even think the United States has become a failed country where a large percentage of the population is poor—a view that seems all the more real when they see Americans coming to Taiwan looking for jobs and, sometimes, begging on the streets. Older Taiwanese identify with the Japan of the past. Older Mainland Chinese remember their life in China before Communist rule. Even Taiwan's political elite is split between those with traditional or no education and those holding foreign degrees, particularly Ph.D.s from top American universities.

Economic progress has fostered still other social and cultural changes. As Taiwan became affluent, recreation became more important. In response, the government has made more cultural activities available to citizens. Mountain climbing and walking in the parks are common spare-time activities. Kung Fu and archery, which were the traditional sports, are still practiced, but baseball, basketball, soccer, tennis, and golf have become more popular. Talking in the teahouses and visiting museums are common recreations, as are listening to music (in music halls or discos), karaoke, and dancing. Most people engage in recreational activities at home or close to home so as to avoid traffic and other problems. Many people spend a good portion of their free time watching television, videotapes, or discs—about the same amount of time spent by people in the United States and Japan. The advent of new cable stations in recent years has made television more popular. Yet many young people complain that they do not have as much leisure time as their counterparts in Western countries because they spend much more time studying and preparing for college entrance examinations or tests to study abroad.

The age factor also connects to the question of whether Taiwan should be independent or should reunite with China. Years of separation have created in Taiwan a unique society that is very different from that of the People's Republic of China. Aware of the political extremism and poverty in China under communism, most young people in Taiwan came to identify socially and politically with the United States, Japan, and, to a lesser extent, Western Europe. They did not understand or identify with China very much and saw themselves—and Taiwan—as a part of the international community, but hardly part of China.

Recently, this situation has changed. Economic ties between Taiwan and China have become extensive while most people in Taiwan now admire China's economic success. This has likely become a very meaningful catalyst for a future social and cultural convergence. Equally important is the proliferation of visits back and forth, especially by citizens from Taiwan visiting the Mainland. In 1996, more than 1.58 million visitors crossed the Taiwan Strait, of which 1.53 million went from Taiwan to China. Also, over 18 million postal items and 280 million minutes of telephone calls went from Taiwan to China or from China to Taiwan. In 2005, citizens from Taiwan made 41.3 million visits to China.[37] A very large portion of the population of Taiwan, including people such as taxi drivers and others who are certainly not wealthy, have visited China in recent years.

The new cross-strait contacts have altered the attitudes of the people of Taiwan in complex ways. The differences among Taiwan's ethnic groups add a special perspective to Taiwan's relationship with China. Taiwanese do not favor ties with China as much as Mainland Chinese and see Taiwan's future linked more to Japan and the United States. To some extent, they fear China. They are opposed to Chinese immigration. Mainland Chinese see more hope in a "Greater China," Hakkas are in between, and the Aborigines are less concerned about the issue. There are also divisions by profession. Businesspeople favor ties with the Mainland to enhance commercial opportunities and profits and, more than others, see Taiwan as part of a Pacific Basin or Greater China bloc.

With affluence, travel—both domestic and overseas—has increased markedly. In 1992, 4.2 million people made trips overseas, more than one-third of those visiting China. In 1993, the number reached 4.6 million, an increase of 10 percent. In 2001, 7.2 million traveled abroad. One would conclude from the number of trips that more than one-fourth of the population travels abroad each year. It has been said that the percentage of Taiwan's population that engage in foreign travel is one of the highest in the world.[38] The large proportion of Taiwan's citizens visiting other countries makes the population quite worldly and affects the population's view of Taiwan's place in the world, including whether Taiwan is part of China or is a separate country.

Rapid improvements in the standard of living also explain progress in raising education standards, providing welfare benefits, and addressing new—and sometimes serious—social problems. These three topics are discussed in greater depth below.

Education

Education has long played a special societal role in Taiwan. In the past, one's education correlated closely with his or her class status more than it did in most other places in the world, except China. In recent years, education has afforded an avenue for social mobility and social-class change, while it has also made the population more cosmopolitan and conscious of events elsewhere in the world. It has been a source for many new interactions and opportunities, and it has helped promote culture, economic growth, a sense of national unity, and democracy.[39]

Before the Japanese period, the educated portion of the population was small. Upon making Taiwan a colony, Tokyo promoted mass education and, within a few years, 70 percent of children attended elementary school. As a result, a basic education did not convey the elite status it once did.[40] Mass education had other effects: A broadly educated population fostered social change and helped facilitate economic growth. On the other hand, only a small portion of the population received higher education and, as noted in Chapter 2, few studied law, the humanities, or the social sciences. Furthermore, the best students went to Japan to study, leaving the second best to form student organizations in Taiwan that had less social impact than would have otherwise been the case. Under the Japanese, the Chinese classics fell into disuse and knowledge of the Chinese language and literature deteriorated.

The reestablishment of Chinese rule in 1945 brought continued support for educating the general population. The Constitution of the Nationalist government contained special provisions concerning education, including the right to education and a promise that education shall be provided free by the government to all children up to the age of twelve and to older people who have not received an adequate education. The Constitution also allocated 15 percent of the budget of the national government, 25 percent of the provincial government's budget, and 35 percent of municipal governments' budgets to education and culture. These constitutional provisions were fairly rigidly adhered to, and only defense accounted for a bigger portion of government spending.

Because of a tradition that emphasizes education and, more recently, strong public support for economic development (thought to be closely linked to improving the skills of the workforce), upgrading educational standards, keeping young people in school, and spending more money to do this had strong public approval. There was also support at the top. Chiang Kai-shek and the government under him viewed schooling as one of the most important tools for building social consensus and unity, as well as a means of promoting economic, social, and political progress.

Early on, the national government not only set about upgrading schools, but also planned the restructuring of the educational system. The Ministry of Education followed Sun Yat-sen's suggestions: that there should be compulsory education for six years (increased to nine years in 1968), that scholarships should be available to enable intelligent but poor students to attain further education, that education should be job oriented, and that teaching must be guided by government policies (to advance patriotism, national unity, and the like). Confucian learning was de-emphasized while Sun's writings, military strategy, and science and technology were accorded a higher place in the curriculum. In short, education was made more practical and goal oriented.

Some specific policies that were part of the government's educational reform program deserve special mention. To prevent cramming, examinations for entry to middle school were dropped. Girls were encouraged to go to school; thus, sex bias was removed from education. The government gave more financial support to vocational schools, which taught subjects that the economy and the job market required. Government actions thus further linked education to employment. Teacher training and parent-teacher organizations also received government support, as did schools that taught night and specialized courses.[41]

Textbooks and curriculum, approved by the Ministry of Education and uniform throughout the nation, were upgraded. Grade levels, curriculum, and the academic calendar were adjusted to follow the US system. Unlike the US system, however, Taiwan's system used national competitive examinations in order to restrict the number of college students and, to a considerable degree, determined their majors. For most students, passing the entrance examination to college or university was very difficult, although getting through courses and remaining in school to graduation was less difficult than in the United States.[42]

Meanwhile, from the early 1950s on, there was a phenomenal increase in the number of students at all grade levels. In primary schools, the number of students enrolled increased from less than 1 million in 1950 to nearly 2.5 million in 1985. The number of high school students rose even more dramatically: from 67,000 to more than 1.7 million, an increase from 8.8 percent of the student population to 44.6 percent. In 1950, 80 percent of school-age children attended school; by 1979, it was 99 percent. Now the enrollment rate for students eligible for primary education is 99.4 percent.[43] The number of colleges rose from 7 to 105, and the number of students pursuing higher education increased from 6,665 to 412,381 during this period. The student population of Taiwan overall increased markedly. In 1950, there were 139.6 students per 1,000 people; by 1979, the number was nearly double—262.3. Now, more than 25 percent of the population attends school.[44]

The social impact of greater educational opportunities was evident at both ends of the spectrum. At the one end was illiteracy. Although Taiwan's illiteracy rate was the second lowest in Asia (after Japan's) in 1950, it was still a concern to the government and the citizenry. By 1962, illiteracy fell to 24.8 percent of the population over age six. By 1990, it was reduced to 6.8 percent, and now it is 3.9 percent.[45] At the other end of the spectrum, more people attained higher education. In 1990, over half of those receiving an education got some secondary education, and Taiwan was rated one of the top countries in the world by the percentage of the population enrolled in college or university.[46]

By the 1980s, compared with countries at a similar level of development, Taiwan's quality of education was six times higher. UN statistics indicated that its standards exceeded those of all major underdeveloped and developing nations, an achievement that reflected the tremendous improvements in education in Taiwan over the previous three decades. Taiwan was even able to compete with developed countries in the educational level of its citizens. Before the close of the 1980s, there were twice as many college students in Taiwan per capita as in Great Britain.[47] By the 1990s, Taiwan was gaining accolades around the world for its educational system. In a survey assessing knowledge of science and mathematics among thirteen-year-old children, Taiwan ranked first in the world. One author attributed Taiwan's excellent educational system to standardized instruction, intense competition, more time in class, more homework, more exams, and special schools.[48]

Still another aspect of education in Taiwan that is important when assessing its societal impact is its globalization effect. At the college level, many of Taiwan's best students study abroad: 115,000 went between 1954 and 1989, 30 percent earning engineering degrees. Though a tiny country compared to most of its competitors, until 1989 Taiwan sent more students to the United States (where 90 percent of its students went for foreign degrees) than any other nation in the world.[49] Although an ever-increasing number of students from Taiwan go abroad—especially to the United States—to study, fewer are now going for advanced degrees because of the improvements made in local colleges and universities and the proliferation of graduate degree programs. Also, because Taiwan's primary and secondary schools are so much more demanding than Western high schools, and because going abroad now is affordable, more younger but less outstanding students have been going to the United States and elsewhere to study.

Another aspect of the internationalization of Taiwan's education can be seen in what Taiwan's students have done after going abroad. During the 1950s and 1960s, few of these students returned home after receiving their degrees. But this "brain drain" turned around in the 1970s and 1980s as a result of Taiwan's prosperity and the job opportunities that economic growth created (and, at the same time, unemployment became a serious problem in the United States). This reverse brain drain contributed immensely to Taiwan's research capabilities and to the growth of knowledge-intensive industries. Returned students also stimulated political and social change as they began to assume various leadership roles.

Meanwhile, Taiwan has attracted a sizeable number of foreign students to its colleges and universities. In 1996, 5,432 students from over fifty countries were studying the humanities (most studying Chinese) in various institutions in Taiwan.[50] Taiwan has thus had considerable influence on Western Sinology, having long provided language training and research facilities to foreign students and scholars. Even more important is the large number of overseas Chinese students who have enrolled in Taiwan's schools. From 1951 to 1992, 63,000 overseas Chinese students graduated from Taiwan's educational institutions. In recent years, more than 10,000 have attended various schools at any one time.[51] In the last decade, some students from the People's Republic of China have studied in Taiwan, and some students from Taiwan have studied and even pursued degrees in China. The numbers have been small, but they have increased steadily. Researchers have also crossed the Taiwan Strait in both directions. Educational exchange, however, is still in its infancy and does not yet provide much evidence of integration or convergence between Taiwan and China. It is also apparent from looking at the social role of education in Taiwan, as well as recent changes, that a big gap exists between Taiwan and China.

The political impact of foreign higher education can hardly be overestimated. In the 1990s, 70 percent or more of cabinet members had been educated abroad, and 60 percent or more typically held Ph.D. degrees. Taiwan's top echelon of government was often described as the world's most educated. With a change in ruling parties in 2000, less stress has been placed on education—notably educational qualifications for government jobs. Nonetheless, standards remain high compared to those in most countries of the world.[52]

Because of the rapidly expanding demand for education for a number of years, private educational institutions flourished. In the 1950s, almost all schools were public. In contrast, in the 1990s, private schools accounted for 23 percent of the nation's students, including 55 percent of all college and university students.[53] Today the ratio remains about the same. Private schools were, and still are, generally affiliated with a church or religious organization. The best schools, especially colleges and universities, however, remain public, although the best kindergartens and specialty schools are private.

With the expansion of educational opportunities, the number of college students has increased markedly in recent years as more colleges and universities have been built. Now few students who want to attend college cannot go. In fact, in recent years, there have been more slots in colleges and universities than applications. As a result, more students who attend college drop out or fail to earn degrees. Some say, as a result, there has been depreciation in respect for college learning and a devaluation of the college degree. In 1992, 43.8 percent of graduating high school students went to college or university; in 2002 it was 80 percent. In 1992, Taiwan had 50 universities with 278,000 students; by 2002, this had increased to 148 universities (89 of them private) and 780,000 students.[54]

During the Chen era, the government put much emphasis on revising textbooks to teach Taiwan's history rather than China's while using education to promote localism and Taiwanese identity. Critics said education was used to promote a political agenda rather than teach. Teachers were demoralized as a result of this as well as the government ending a holiday for teachers (also Confucius's Birthday). The government also did not try to resolve the problem of too many universities and the process of cheapening education that had been in process before 2000. Meanwhile, "Taiwanization" alienated many Overseas Chinese, who found going to Taiwan for an education less attractive and China more attractive. Less attention was given to higher education, with some officials feeling it was elitist and Chinese. Now, none of Taiwan's universities are rated in the top one hundred in the world, compared to six in China (three in Hong Kong), two in Singapore, five in Australia, four in Japan, and one in Korea.[55]

It seems likely that educational policies will change to fix these problems. Most college and university presidents believe that Taiwan should open up to students from China and that Taiwan should try to attract more Overseas Chinese students and do other things to improve the quality of education in Taiwan.[56] Officials in the Ma Administration have also decried the decline of educational standards.

Social Welfare

Welfare has an interesting history in Taiwan. Social programs were in evidence on the island when it came under Chinese rule in the seventeenth century.[57] These consisted almost exclusively of special aid to the poor, to women, and to children. Under Japanese rule, social welfare was expanded considerably in scope. Japanese colonial governors used welfare programs as a means of facilitating their political control. Indeed, this strategy was quite effective: Tokyo enhanced its popularity by eliminating poverty, equalizing incomes and wealth, and engaging in charity work—all in the name of the Emperor. The Japanese later used the term "social enterprises" to include education and research as well as social relief and economic help programs of various kinds.

When Nationalist China incorporated Taiwan in 1945, Governor Chen Yi, who regarded the welfare system as a tool used by the Japanese to destroy Chinese culture and render the population dependent, eliminated much of it, leaving intact only relief for the poor, medical care for the impoverished, and famine and disaster relief organizations.[58] However, when the Nationalist government moved to Taiwan in 1949, it took several social welfare programs with it. Need at the time also dictated either the expansion of existing programs or the creation of new ones. The aforementioned areas of welfare that were in operation in the late 1940s were expanded. New efforts focused on soldiers (a Military Servicemen's Insurance Law was passed in 1953). Newly arrived Mainland Chinese were given help in finding housing and jobs while Taiwanese who had been displaced from jobs or had suffered during the economic hard times of the previous half-decade were provided assistance.

In the 1960s and 1970s, as Taiwan began to prosper economically, the scope of welfare efforts grew to include vocational training, labor security, health, and public housing. New government agencies were created, and the number of social workers increased accordingly. The government at this time also assumed a new responsibility: child welfare. Taiwan received funds from the United States and from the United Nations and its related agencies for some of these efforts. But government spending also increased by large amounts. In total expenditures from all levels of government, funding soared from 2.8 percent of budgets in the early 1950s to over 10 percent in the early 1970s.[59]

In the 1980s, the government and the ruling Nationalist Party embarked on a variety of formerly untried social welfare projects and again greatly increased government spending on welfare. The motives were unique: The government faced a problem of legitimacy after the United States severed diplomatic relations in 1979 and established its embassy in Beijing. As disaffection with the government grew, many leaders perceived that they needed to take steps to defuse this potentially explosive situation. Some thought that increases in welfare spending would make the government popular both at home and abroad, inasmuch as welfare would alleviate poverty and convey the impression that the government cared for its citizens. Increased welfare outlays would also send the message that the country was democratic and that the voters, even poor voters, had an input in formulating government policies. In the late 1980s, the opposition Democratic Progressive Party pressured the government to expand welfare and the Nationalist Party–controlled government made similar or identical proposals in an effort to preempt an important part of the DPP's platform. Finally, it was widely perceived that the country could afford more social welfare.

The thrust of social welfare also changed again. Previously, it had been aimed at groups considered vital to maintaining political stability: The military, labor, and government employees were the main beneficiaries. It now shifted to help anyone who needed it. In the early 1980s, the government passed three pieces of legislation that reflected this change in attitude: The Aged Welfare Law, the Handicapped Welfare Law, and the Social Assistance Law. It also enacted laws to help youth and launched a new insurance program for teachers and administrative staff in private schools. In 1985, the Bureau of Labor Insurance was ordered to work on a program for giving farmers health insurance. In 1987, the government announced its intention to establish a national health insurance program.

All of this caused social spending to increase markedly during the 1980s. Welfare expenditures at the national level, which were under 2 percent of the gross national product in 1980, passed 3 percent by 1990. Spending at all levels of government was around 3 percent in 1980, and by 1990, reached more than 4.5 percent of gross domestic product. Social welfare expenditures peaked in 1996 and fell after 2001.

By 2006, increases resumed as welfare reached 5.1 percent of the gross domestic product.[60]

One of the big items that caused social welfare spending to increase was health care. In 1995, the legislature adopted the National Health Insurance Program that incorporated thirteen existing health insurance plans while extending coverage to an additional 7.5 million people. Participation was mandatory under the Health Insurance Law, essentially extending health benefits to everyone, though the main beneficiaries were those who did not have any insurance at all: the elderly, children, students, and housewives. A fierce debate soon raged about who would pay: the government, employers, or individuals. It was finally decided that employers would pay 60 percent of the cost, employees 30 percent, and the government 10 percent. Citizens over seventy paid no premiums. Between 70 and 95 percent of costs were covered for patients admitted to hospitals, and somewhat less for those seeing a doctor in an office or clinic.

National health insurance, however, was not without problems. The program's reputation was sullied when better doctors demanded additional money for their services or refused to accept the scheduled payments. Overuse, meanwhile, resulted in much higher costs than anticipated, while the program's effectiveness measured by increases in life expectancy and less health disparity among social classes were marginal. The Nationalist Party took credit for giving health insurance to virtually all citizens, but it did not win many kudos because of the attendant controversies and the fear that the increased tax burden might make Taiwan's exports noncompetitive in the world market.[61]

Meanwhile, the government got into new realms in social welfare. Added to the list of welfare causes were child protection services, campaigns against drug abuse, youth counseling and guidance, women's educational attainment efforts, women's services networks, divorce counseling and aid, elderly daycare, special services for the aged, services for the disabled, low-cost housing, and assistance to the Aborigines. In 2002, the government launched a program to help older citizens who received no pension or other such benefits. In mid-2007, the legislature passed the National Pension Act that was inclusive for all citizens age twenty-five to sixty-four who did not already participate in a program.[62]

The proliferation of welfare initiatives and the costs associated with them have engendered widespread debate in Taiwan. Many say that welfare has contributed to undermining and even destroying the family. Others contend that welfare has weakened the nation's work ethic and has hurt its competitiveness in the global marketplace. Some worry that the polity is evolving from a capitalist to a socialist one, a nanny state, and that welfare is "breaking the bank" of the country. In 2001, unemployment benefits skyrocketed due to an economic recession, and the worst earthquake ever struck the island, which brought this issue into focus.[63]

The issue of social welfare has also translated into fierce political discourse. The DPP, which had long stood for helping the poor and disadvantaged, soon after it became the ruling party in 2000 had to cut social welfare due to a poor economy. As a result, the party's poor and disadvantaged constituencies became alienated. Meanwhile, many citizens in Taiwan noticed that China, after its free market reform that had begun in the late 1970s, cut welfare spending and subsequently boomed economically.

Other Social Problems

Several of Taiwan's "social ills" deserve further discussion, some because they are serious, and others because they are new or unique. Taiwan's rapid economic, political, and social change has indeed made some already existing problems more acute or has created new ones.

Some say the most hapless group in Taiwan is the veteran. Around 150,000 soldiers came to Taiwan with Chiang Kai-shek and the Nationalist Party and government in 1949. They were promised land in China when they returned and were even given titles or deeds. These, of course, proved worthless. Because there was the large proportion of men in Taiwan at the time, and due to their low socioeconomic status, most soldiers could not find wives and thus lacked families. Now they are in their 70s and 80s, and their veterans' benefits have not kept up with inflation. Also, since government welfare budgets are now stretched and include numerous other groups, soldiers, as a consequence, receive less. They currently suffer from alienation, poverty, and various other social problems. Many want to leave Taiwan, but have nowhere to go. Making matters worse, during the Chen era, the Democratic Progressive Party sought to have their stipends reduced since the veterans mostly voted for the KMT.[64]

Still another social problem is the housing shortage in some cities and the fact that houses and apartments are too expensive for many people to afford. The rate of home ownership in Taiwan is high, but in recent years—because of the very fast appreciation in the value of land and property—many people who want to buy, especially for the first time, find it difficult or impossible. During the 1989 election campaign, the so-called "snails without shells" (or people who could not afford housing) staged massive protest demonstrations in exclusive areas of Taipei. The government at various levels has intervened and has built more public housing while also providing low-cost loans to workers and first-time buyers of houses or apartments. Still, the problem remains a serious one.

Related at least indirectly to the housing problem is the matter of low-income households. Poverty has been virtually eliminated in Taiwan (currently 0.7 percent of households) because of the economic miracle and the ease with which most people could find employment. Yet families with children still have difficulty making ends meet because of high rents and Taiwan's rapidly growing cost of living. The government has established programs to deal with both, but some people are overlooked. Also, some people who should qualify do not, and others, out of pride, are reluctant to collect government welfare.

Crime is a social problem that has appeared rather suddenly in recent years and is now regarded as quite serious by many of Taiwan's citizens; indeed, crime has consistently been among the top five issues of concern as reflected in public opinion surveys in recent years. Higher crime rates are generally considered the result of urbanization and the social alienation it has created, materialism, a weakening of the family structure, permissiveness, and Westernization. Some say that democratization has brought about lax law enforcement and less severe punishments, and that this accounts for dangerous streets and high crime rates.

The growth in crime began in the late 1960s—though recent increases have been much higher. In the past ten to fifteen years, the increases have been especially large, and violent crimes and juvenile crime have accounted for most of the increase: Violent crimes rose from 7.4 percent of the total in 1981 to 10.9 percent in 1990, and juvenile crimes went up from 12.8 per 10,000 in 1970 to 27.6 per 10,000 in 1990. In the late 1990s, violent and juvenile crimes declined, but people were still alarmed. The total number of crimes committed in Taiwan in 2000 was eight times what it was twenty years earlier. Larcenies increased nearly sixfold, robberies by about that, and rape by more than three times. In 2001, recession caused the crime rate to shoot up—12 percent overall and 40 percent for violent crimes.[65]

Of even greater concern to society, however, is that juvenile crime as a percentage of total crime has increased. The rate is alarming: from 17 per 10,000 in 1974 to 50 per 10,000 in 1992. The National Police Administration recently reported that the most recent crime statistics indicate that juveniles between the ages of twelve and eighteen committed almost 10 percent of all crimes and that the mean age of youths committing crimes is falling. The most common crimes are burglary, violence against persons or property, and drug use.[66]

Sensational crimes committed in recent years have made headline news, thereby making the crime problem appear much more serious and causing public alarm. The children of very wealthy citizens have been kidnapped and murdered. A famous singer's daughter was kidnapped and brutally murdered in 1998. These crimes are associated in the public mind with gangs, organized crime, and political corruption (which is seen as a reason for governmental laxity in this area). Accordingly, several organs of government and some high officials have seen their public opinion poll ratings drop.

Related to increases in the crime rate is the rapid growth in drug use in Taiwan. Although still low by the standards of Western countries, the number of drug users and the amounts sold and consumed has escalated rapidly in recent years. Arrest statistics reflect the seriousness of drug abuse. In the past, drug-related crimes were about 5 percent of the total, but this rose to 13 percent in 1991 and to 32 percent in 1993. In 1994, drug offenders and drug-related crime accounted for 63 percent of prison inmates, the largest of any category. In 1993, convictions for drug crimes increased 70 percent. That same year, the amount of marijuana seized by the police increased 133 percent. Meanwhile, heroin seized increased twenty-threefold from 1989.[67]

Drug use and related crimes declined in 1995 and after, and government actions were in large part credited for this. Several laws were passed to prevent smuggling and money laundering, and Taiwan was taken off the blacklist of transshipment countries by the US Department of State in 2000. Nevertheless, the drug problem is still seen as a very serious social ill. Some say drugs became a problem after the lifting of martial law, when sentences were reduced and pushers were seldom executed. Others say it is the product of modernization and Westernization. Still others relate it to organized crime and politics.

Another social problem that is a cause of concern is the increase in the divorce rate and the accompanying family dislocation. The divorce rate in Taiwan increased 10 percent or more a year, contributing to a nearly sevenfold increase in the forty-year period beginning in the 1950s. From 1985 to 2006, the rate of divorce more than doubled, growing from 1.1 percent to 2.8 percent.[68] The rate has since continued to increase. Now it is estimated that 25 to 30 percent of marriages end in divorce. Most divorces are initiated by the wife, with the most frequently given reasons being infidelity and irreconcilable differences. Some say this is the project of new laws, democracy, and a diminished loyalty to the family.[69]

Seemingly related to the rising divorce rate and the weakening of the family, child abuse has become a social problem of serious proportions, at least in perception, in recent years. The number of cases reported more than doubled between 1993 and 1996. Physical abuse is the most common complaint (40.9 percent), followed by neglect (24.3 percent), and substandard parenting (19.1 percent). The Children's Welfare Law was enacted in 1973 and was subsequently revised in 1993 to deal with this problem. The approach is both unique and severe. Names of offenders are published, and fines can be as high as US$11,000. Men have been most frequently charged under this law. Women, however, have also been punished as well for smoking, drinking, taking drugs, and chewing betel nuts while pregnant. The government has taken serious legal steps recently to deal with the problem.[70]

Rape, child prostitution, and other sex crimes are also attracting increasing attention in Taiwan. Although the frequency of these crimes is much lower than those in most other countries, these problems have generated grave concern among Taiwan's populace because they are increasing and because they attract attention from the media. They are widely reported in the press and cause alarm; consequently, many people blame society for becoming too permissive and for lax law enforcement.

A not unrelated problem—and said to be the outcome of the war between the sexes—is a sudden increase in the number of both men and women who do not want to marry. In the twenty year period between 1980 to 2000, the percentage of men in the eligible age range each year who marry had fallen from 6.7 percent to 4.65 percent. For women, it dropped from 9.19 percent to 6.37 percent. Taiwan in this respect seems to be following similar trends evident in Japan and some other countries, where more people don't want to marry, or at least don't marry. Some observers feel this trend will make the society unstable, threaten the family, and cause a further decline in population growth.[71]

Suicide has recently become a serious social problem; it is now the ninth leading cause of death in Taiwan. Of the more than 2,000 people who take their own lives each year (2,471 in 2000), one-quarter are less than twenty-five years of age, and the large majority are male (ten times the number of females). The number of student suicides is shocking to most of Taiwan's citizens, especially the number committed by those who fail college entrance or other examinations. It is the third leading cause of death for young people. Elderly people also commit suicide more than they do in other countries. Critics of the Chen administration noted that the rate of self-killing increased 200 percent during his first six years in office due to the country's bad economy.[72]

Still another problem is obesity. According to a recent survey, 20 percent of people living in Taipei over age twenty are overweight. Other data indicate that a fast-growing number of children are overweight. A large percentage of people living in Taiwan now consider their lives too sedentary and they feel they are unhealthy and need more exercise.[73]

Although Taiwan's social problems are not as serious as in the modern Western democracies, they seem to be worse because they have appeared so suddenly. This very abruptness might lead to quicker, better solutions, and Taiwan may be able to solve these problems as efficiently as it has dealt with so many others. The alternative is a worsening social environment that will adversely affect the society and much more.

Notes

1. The most detailed anthropological studies on Taiwan are to be found in Emily Martin Ahern and Hill Gates, eds., *The Anthropology of Taiwanese Society* (Stanford, CA: Stanford University Press, 1981).

2. Chen Kang Chai, *Taiwan's Aborigines: A Genetic Study of Tribal Variations* (Cambridge, MA: Harvard University Press, 1967), 43.

3. See Chiao-min Hsieh, *Taiwan–Ilha, Formosa: A Geographical Perspective* (Washington, D.C.: Butterworths, 1964), 127–131.

4. See Edwin A. Winckler, "Roles Linking State and Society," in Ahern and Gates, eds., *The Anthropology of Taiwanese Society,* 63–65.

5. Edgar Wickberg, "Continuities in Land Tenure, 1900–1940," in Ahern and Gates, eds., *The Anthropology of Taiwanese Society,* 212.

6. See Arthur P. Wolf, "Domestic Organization," in Ahern and Gates, eds., *The Anthropology of Taiwanese Society,* 341–361.

7. Murray A. Rubinstein, "Taiwan's Socio-Economic Modernization," in Murray A. Rubinstein, ed., *Taiwan: A New History* (Armonk, NY: M. E. Sharpe, 1999), 388–389.

8. See Hill Gates, "Ethnicity and Social Class," in Ahern and Gates, eds., *The Anthropology of Taiwanese Society,* 241–282.

9. For details, see "Taiwan's Aborigines," *Wikipedia* (at wikipedia.com).

10. Denny Roy, *Taiwan: A Political History* (Ithaca, NY: Cornell University Press, 2003), 6.

11. Some say the Hakkas constitute a buffer between the Mainland Chinese and the Taiwanese. Others say they identify with the Fukien Taiwanese but favor a government of Mainland Chinese. Hakkas have done very well in politics in Taiwan, and many hold top positions in various police organizations.

12. Hu Ching-hui, "Most Hoklo, Hakka have Aboriginal genes, study finds," *Taipei Times,* November 21, 2007, 1. According to the author, 85 percent of both groups have Aboriginal genes, though the study also indicated 90 percent have some Vietnamese ancestry stemming from their family origins on China's southeast coast and like the Chinese living in that part of China now.

13. See Gates, "Ethnicity and Social Class," 61. The author notes that one of the main reasons for this is that Mainland Chinese took houses evacuated by Japanese after 1945.

14. For further information on this topic, see Kuo-shu Yang, "Transformation of the Chinese People," in James C. Hsiung, ed., *Contemporary Republic of China: The Taiwan Experience, 1950–1980* (New York: Praeger, 1981), 268–281. In recent polls, nearly 40 percent of those asked said they were both Chinese and Taiwanese as compared to less than 30 percent in 1995. Also, the number saying they were Taiwanese decreased from nearly 50 percent to under 40 percent, and the number calling themselves Chinese fell from nearly 25 percent to just over 15 percent during the same time period. See "Cross Strait Breakthrough," *Topics* (November 1998): 13.

15. For details about the languages used in Taiwan, see *The Republic of China 1998 Yearbook* (Taipei: Government Information Office, 1998), chapter 3.

16. See Tse-han Lai, Ramon H. Myers, and Wou Wei, *A Tragic Beginning: The Taiwan Uprising of February 28, 1947* (Stanford, CA: Stanford University Press, 1991), 93–97.

17. See Anthony Kubek, *Modernizing China: A Comparative Analysis of the Two Chinas* (Washington, D.C.: Regnery Gateway, 1987), 187–189.

18. For details on the number of followers of the various religions in Taiwan, see *Taiwan Yearbook 2006,* 339.

19. *Taiwan Yearbook 2007,* 251–252.

20. Ibid., 248–251.

21. Ibid., 460.

22. Ibid., 252.

23. A Taiwanese national identity did not develop to any degree at this time because there was no central government and little communication between or among the Chinese on the

island. See, for example, Christopher Hughes, *Taiwan and Chinese Nationalism, National Identity and Status in International Society* (London: Routledge, 1997), chapters 1 and 2.

24. Land reform is also discussed in Chapter 5. For details on its impact on landowners and social change, see Thomas B. Gold, *State and Society in the Taiwan Miracle* (Armonk, NY: M. E. Sharpe, 1986), 37–38, 65–67. Also see Kubek, *Modernizing China*, chapter 3.

25. John C. H. Fei, Gustav Ranis, and Shirley W. Y. Kuo, *Growth with Equity: The Taiwan Case* (Washington, D.C.: International Bank for Reconstruction and Development, 1979), 38.

26. For some assessment on Taiwan's political leadership, see Wen-hui Tsai, *In Making China Modernized: Comparative Modernization Between Mainland China and Taiwan* (Baltimore: University of Maryland School of Law, 1993), 118.

27. For background and further details on this topic, see Hung-mao Tien, *The Great Transition: Political and Social Change in the Republic of China* (Stanford, CA: Hoover Institution Press, 1989), chapter 2, and Yu Tzong-shian, *The Story of Taiwan: Economy* (Taipei: Government Printing Office, 2001), 50. For recent per capita income data, see "Taiwan claims economy grew a robust 5.46 percent," *The Earth Times*, December 27, 2007 (online at earthtimes.org).

28. For details, see Fei, Ranis, and Kuo, *Growth with Equity*.

29. See Beatrice Liu, "Housing Crisis Grows Worse," *Free China Journal*, May 25, 1989, 7.

30. See Peter Chen-main Wang, "A Bastion Created, A Regime Reformed, An Economy Reengineered, 1949–1970," in Rubinstein, ed., *Taiwan: A New History*, 320–338.

31. For a comparison between Taiwan and other Asian countries, see chart in Yuan-li Wu and Kung-chia Yeh, eds., *Growth, Distribution, and Social Change: Essays on the Economy of the Republic of China* (Baltimore: University of Maryland School of Law, 1978), 42–43.

32. *Taiwan Yearbook 2007*, 27.

33. For details on women in the workforce, see Catherine Farris, Anru Lee, and Murray Rubinstein, eds., *Women in the New Taiwan: Gender Roles and Gender Consciousness in Changing Society* (Armonk, NY: M. E. Sharpe, 2004).

34. Ibid.

35. *Taiwan Yearbook 2007*, 171.

36. For details, see Yui-chun Yu and Peter Miller, "The generation gap and cultural influence—a Taiwan empirical investigation," *Cross Cultural Management: An International Journal* 10, issue 3 (2003): 23–41.

37. *Taiwan Yearbook 2007*, 82.

38. *The Republic of China on Taiwan: 2002 Statistics*, no page numbers listed.

39. For general background information on education in Taiwan, see *The Republic of China: Educational System* (Taipei: Kwang Hwa Publishing Co., 1980).

40. Mark Mancall, ed., *Formosa Today* (New York: Praeger, 1964), 2.

41. *The Republic of China 1998 Yearbook*, 297.

42. Ibid.

43. *Taiwan Yearbook 2007*, 200.

44. Ibid.

45. *The Republic of China Yearbook—Taiwan 2002*, 101. The literacy rate in Taiwan is 98.12 percent.

46. Ibid., 296. The rate was 49.41 per one thousand population in 2000.

47. Kubek, *Modernizing China*, 157.

48. Fei-yun Wang, "Solving Problems," *Free China Review* (January 1994): 42.

49. Chong-pin Lin, "China's Students from Abroad: Rates of Return," *The American Enterprise* (November–December 1994): 14.

50. See "The Combative Cabinet," *Taipei Review* (April 2002): 4–9. Sixty-two percent of cabinet members currently have foreign degrees and 42 percent have Ph.D. degrees.

51. Kelly Hu, "In Pursuit of Excellence," *Taiwan Review*, December 1, 2002.

52. *The Republic of China 1998 Yearbook*, 298.

53. *The Republic of China Yearbook—Taiwan 2002*, 296.

54. See Hu, "In Pursuit of Excellence."

55. *Asiaweek* has rated the universities, and Taiwan does not make the top ten list. See asiaweek.com/features/universities2000/. Recently, more than 80 percent of high school graduates taking their college/university entrance examinations passed. See "465 Places Still Vacant in Taiwan's Universities," *China Post*, August 10, 2002, 4.

56. See Jenny W. Hsu, "College presidents back PRC students: poll," *Taipei Times*, May 15, 2008 (online at taipeitimes.com).

57. For details, see Yeun-wen Ku, *Welfare Capitalism in Taiwan: State, Economy and Social Policy* (New York: St. Martin's Press, 1997).

58. Ibid., 36–37.

59. Ibid., 41.

60. *Taiwan Yearbook 2007*, 171.

61. For details, see Chi Pang Wen, Shan Pou Tsai, and Wen-Shen Isabella Chung, "A 10-Year Experience with Universal Health Insurance in Taiwan: Measuring Changes in Health and Health Disparity," *Annals of Internal Medicine* (February 2008): 258–267.

62. Ibid. Also see Pat Gao, "The State of Welfare," *Taipei Review*, March 2001, 6.

63. See Chien-Hsun Chen, "Taiwan's Burgeoning Budget Deficit: A Crisis in the Making," *Asian Survey*, May/June 2005, 383–396.

64. "VAC chief Hu Chen-pu vows to safeguard veterans' interests," *China Post*, October 4, 2007 (online at chinapost.com.tw).

65. Ibid., 142–143. Also see "It's Time to Face the Crime Problem," *China Post*, July 22, 2002, 2.

66. "It's Time to Face the Crime Problem."

67. *The Republic of China 1994 Yearbook* (Taipei: Government Information Office, 1994), 350; *The Republic of China 1998 Yearbook*, 320. See also "War Against Drugs Posts Some Success," *Free China Journal*, March 3, 1995, 7. This article was based on a speech by Minister of Justice Ma Ying-jeou.

68. *The Republic of China Yearbook—Taiwan 2002*, 325. The later figure is in *Taiwan Yearbook 2007*, 27.

69. Lena Feng Warmack, "Women in Taiwan find marriage no fairy tale," *Mercury News*, February 22, 2004 (online at internationaldivorce.com).

70. *The Republic of China 1998 Yearbook*, 319. The number of child abuse cases rose from 1,400 in 1993 to 3,000 in 1996. This figure is still very low compared to many Western countries. For recent measures taken to deal with the problem, see *Taiwan Yearbook 2007*, 170–171.

71. See "Who's Afraid of Marriage," *Taipei Review* (February 2002): 14.

72. Linda Chang, "Suicide Becomes 10th Biggest Killer," *Free China Journal*, May 22, 1998, 4. Also see *The Republic of China Yearbook—Taiwan 2002*, 255. For the latest data, see "Suicide Rate Rises Further," *Taipei Times*, July 2, 2006.

73. See *Taipei News*, May 18, 2002, 2, and "A Man-O-Jack or Devil's Advocate," *China Post*, September 24, 2007 (online at lexis-nexis.com).

4

POLITICAL SYSTEM

TAIWAN'S POLITICAL HISTORY is a complex one. Its political culture finds its origins primarily in local family rule, Western colonialism, China's bureaucratic system, and Japanese feudalism, with one or another prevailing during certain periods. Rule of the island changed several times in the past. After a brief period as a Dutch colony in the seventeenth century, Taiwan enjoyed a short interval of self-government before two centuries of Chinese rule. The island had no effective central government, however, until it was colonized by Japan in 1895. After World War II, Taiwan's political system, which was transplanted from China by Chiang Kai-shek, was based on Sun Yat-sen's writings and his goal of establishing republicanism in China. It was outwardly democratic in form and was constitutional. In practice, the system was authoritarian, based on one-party rule, with a strong executive, pervasive police control, and the frequent use of military courts. In the 1950s, local elections produced the basis for "democracy from the bottom up." Beginning in the 1960s, Taiwan saw the growth of a free-market economic system, political reform in both local and national politics, and the beginnings of democratic change. In the 1970s and 1980s, more Taiwanese taking positions in government, the rise of new political parties, competitive elections, the expansion of political and civil liberties, and a concern for Taiwan's image in the international community produced a budding democracy. Some even referred to Taiwan's rapid and peaceful democratization as a "political miracle." In 2000, Taiwan experienced what was said to be its "democratic consolidation," when Chen Shui-bian of the opposition Democratic Progressive Party was elected president. But Chen's poor leadership, an economic slowdown, and corruption engendered serious public disappointment with his administration. As a consequence, the KMT won several elections, culminating in a big legislative victory in January 2008 and Ma Ying-jeou winning the presidency in March. Taiwan's political system is still evolving as regards interest groups, the party system, and much more, including even its political structure—whether presidential, parliamentary, or neither.

Political Culture and Tradition

The political culture that evolved in China over many centuries—transported to Taiwan by early immigrants and later by officials who were sent to govern the island from the late 1600s to 1895—was elitist: It did not assume or favor mass participation. Yet it was comparatively egalitarian, since class was not a barrier to attaining a high position in government as it was in most places in the world at the time, although lack of education was (and attaining education required leisure time and money). Chinese political tradition was authoritarian, even though individualism was part of the culture, and it was highly humanistic and moralistic (political decision-making being seen as involving ethical choices).[1]

Both China's political culture and its political system were strongly influenced by the need to control water and maintain roads and other public projects. The construction and maintenance of public works required sophisticated levels of political organization and administration, which developed early in Chinese history. When public works were not kept in repair, flooding and crop failure resulted, and often thousands—even millions—of people died. Thus, the bureaucracy wielded considerable power; arms and money were not the main sources of authority in China as they were in most political systems. An emperor and a scholar-official class that was synonymous with a powerful ruling bureaucracy governed China.[2]

In theory, China had a unitary political system; in fact, however, political power was decentralized. Local government officials, nominally responsible to the emperor, were in reality largely autonomous. Officials sent by the emperor to govern provinces and lower units of government checked on local administrators and advised them; but because these emissaries usually did not know the language (dialect) of the regions they served and were rotated at regular intervals, they seldom became entrenched or powerful. Thus, a kind of balance of authority between the central and local governments was perpetuated by physical distance and the lack of modern transportation and communications as well as other limits on centralizing political control, with centrifugal tendencies being dampened or contained by the cohesive force of Chinese culture.

China's bureaucratic tradition was taken to Taiwan, though in many ways it did not fit. The control of water and the maintenance of public works were not critically important in Taiwan. Taiwan was much more geographically fragmented, and the livelihood of its population depended more on fishing, hunting, and, later, trading, than on farming. In addition, owing to Taiwan's good soil, moderate climate, and more regular and predictable rainfall, working the land was less risky than in China. Therefore, peasants on the island did not need government-built public works, as was the case in China. Finally, Taiwan's early cosmopolitanism and foreign influences affected its political tradition. Thus, Chinese political culture could not be totally transplanted to Taiwan, and it took root there only partially.[3]

Throughout most of its history, there was not much government at the top in Taiwan, even in theory. Today, centralized political authority in Taiwan is quite feasible, given the small size of the island and the efficient means of transportation and political communications available to its rulers. But a free-market economic system, political party competition, constitutional limits on the authority of the national government, and strong local government all prevent the centralizing of political power. Also militating against the concentration of political authority are concerns about political freedoms, Chinese individualism and distrust of political authority, and the lessons afforded by Mao's radical efforts in China to concentrate political power at the center and control all aspects of life. In contrast, geographic size and a huge population limit the effectiveness of a central government in China.[4]

Taiwan's political culture was affected, in some ways irreversibly, by Japanese rule from 1895 to 1945. In the Japanese political tradition, arms and money were the crucial ingredients of political power; the bureaucracy was less important. Japanese rule thus reinforced the feudal nature of Taiwan's political culture and its political system. Japanese control over Taiwan was also notable for its legalism since the establishment of a framework of laws and regulations facilitated its colonial rule. Finally, obedience and loyalty were esteemed in Japanese political thinking, while individualism was not.

Tokyo administered Taiwan efficiently and, in many ways, with fairness and justice, but, as noted earlier, it never treated its subjects as equals. Exclusionist and racially discriminatory policies—notwithstanding economic and social gains—led to the creation of an identity among the Chinese in Taiwan not unlike that fostered by colonial subjects in other parts of the world; indeed, Japanese rule marked the beginning, however weak, of a sense of community and nationalism in Taiwan. Toward the end of the period of Japanese colonialism, in a last-ditch effort to prevent defeat in war, Tokyo promised self-rule to many of the territories under its control, including Taiwan. But this effort was not very sincere and the population was not prepared for it, although it did create expectations.

Taiwan's political culture naturally bears the imprint of Nationalist China. Sun Yat-sen (1866–1925), the first president of China and founder of the Nationalist

Party, or Kuomintang (KMT), spent some time in Taiwan, where he discussed politics and China's future. Loyal supporters spread his political ideals in ensuing years, even after the Japanese colonized the island in 1895. Many in Taiwan also knew of Sun through their relatives and contacts in China. In 1945, when the Nationalist Chinese government assumed political control over Taiwan, Sun and his teachings were thus familiar to a significant segment of the local population. Sun's writings have provided Taiwan with a political philosophy and a formula for political development.[5]

Although there was a rebirth of Chinese political culture after World War II, economic development strategies implemented in Taiwan in the 1950s and thereafter diluted its elitist nature, as did democratic reforms. Education and success in business, meanwhile, afforded political careers to newcomers. Authoritarianism persisted because the ruling elite demanded it, the nation was at war (in a state of readiness and perceiving that a conflict with the People's Republic of China was likely), and the population of Taiwan felt a need for a strong leader (though in recent years democracy and the advent of party politics have weakened this facet of Chinese political culture). A strong concern for correct behavior in politics reflected the survival of Confucian ethics. Subsequently, democracy in some respects amplified concern about good government.

From the 1960s on, Taiwan became suffused with Western political ideas. Political rights as practiced in the West became idealized, especially by younger Chinese. As the free market expanded and foreign trade grew, democracy came to be seen as a necessity, especially because the free flow of information (which the authoritarian system impeded) came to be viewed as essential to the acquisition of technology and to sustain economic growth. Thus, Taiwan's political culture absorbed new democratic components.

In the 1970s and after, as Taiwan became diplomatically isolated, the desire of both the government and the population to protect Taiwan's (or the Republic of China's) national sovereignty inspired both national unity and democratization. Threats from Beijing and the need for Taiwan to impress the international community with its political modernization also impacted Taiwan's political culture and political system. Taiwan's economic accomplishments, societal change, and growing cosmopolitanism, all of which stimulated feelings of national pride and uniqueness, have also had consequences.

In sum, Taiwan's political culture has been shaped by a rich diversity of influences, most recently democratization.[6] The culture differs, however, from that of Western systems in being more conservative and favoring the society over the individual. The term "Asian democracy" may describe this kind of polity: a democracy (though some Western observers hesitate to use that word) that sees a danger in permissiveness, that puts a high value on hard work and social stability, that views the family as the basic social institution, that pays deference to the elderly, and that is less bureaucratic and less costly than Western democratic systems. Asian democracy seems to be what most people in Taiwan want.

The Constitution

Another place to begin an assessment of Taiwan's political system is its Constitution. Chiang Kai-shek brought the Republic of China's Constitution to Taiwan after World War II. This document evolved from a draft constitution written in May 1936 that became moot (or nearly so) when Japan invaded China the next year. Another effort was made to write a constitution at the end of World War II, even though civil war between the Nationalists and the Communists followed on the heels of peace with Japan. A final document was approved in late 1946. After elections in 1947 and 1948 (held in only part of the country because of widespread fighting between Communist and Nationalist forces), the document became the basis of constitutional government in areas controlled by the Nationalists, including Taiwan.[7]

The framers of the Constitution designed a republican-style representative democracy. The system was mixed, though, and included cabinet, presidential, and parliamentary features. Based on neither executive nor legislative supremacy (though in practice it favored strong executive authority), the political system was unitary, though it still had many characteristics of a federal system, such as allowing local government special prerogatives.[8] The Constitution guaranteed citizens a broad range of political and civil rights. It contained broader provisions for the separation of powers and checks and balances than are in most Western nations' constitutions.

The Constitution, in fact, was unique in that it established five branches (*Yuan*) of government rather than three, as is typical of Western systems. In addition to the executive, legislative, and judicial branches, there were the examination and control branches. The former three were accorded powers and functions similar to those in most Western democracies, while the latter two reflected the importance given to the recruitment of government officials and the need to keep a check on the bureaucracy to ensure its competence and honesty (as the Censorate did in the traditional Chinese political system). Designed to rule a very big country, the president and the vice president were elected by the National Assembly rather than directly by the electorate. The framers of the Constitution anticipated that political parties would perform many of the responsibilities relating to the functioning of democratic government, such as measuring and reacting to public opinion, responding to special interests, recruiting administrators and political leaders, and designing alternative policies. However—as in the US Constitution—political parties are not mentioned in the document.

Because of the war with the Communists and the ethnic tension that accompanied the rebellion that broke out in Taiwan in 1947, the Constitution was amended (or its implementation delayed, depending on one's interpretation) by the "Temporary Provisions Effective During the Period of National Mobilization for Suppression of the Communist Rebellion" in 1948. The Temporary Provisions gave the president emergency powers to deal with threats to national security as well as financial and economic crises. Based on this authority, in 1949, the executive branch of government pushed through the legislature a bill called *chieh yen fa* (literally "vigilance measures law," but generally translated as "emergency decree" in Taiwan and "martial law" by the Western media), which remained in effect until July 1987.

The emergency decree (or martial law) gave the military and intelligence agencies a special role in politics, making it legal for Chiang Kai-shek to continue to head an authoritarian political regime notwithstanding the democratic Constitution. The Temporary Provisions, in addition, banned the formation of new competing political parties, nullified the two-term limit on the president (Article 47 of the Constitution), and empowered the president to set up ad hoc organizations to mobilize and control the population and to appoint delegates to the elected organs of government. The National Assembly, which was controlled by the ruling Nationalist Party, was authorized to amend or abrogate the Temporary Provisions. However, it took no steps to do so until President Chiang Ching-kuo ordered it to do so.

Those who argued that the process of democratization in Taiwan was too slow condemned the Temporary Provisions. Others, however, contended that Taiwan successfully attained democracy precisely because the Temporary Provisions held back the democratization process until social and economic conditions were right (that is, until there was a large middle class and the population was sufficiently educated and otherwise able to participate intelligently in democratic government). The public in Taiwan was certainly aware of the failure of premature democratization in many developing countries during the 1950s and 1960s.[9] But Taiwan's populace also believed that the country had to democratize to accommodate to Taiwan's rapid economic development, the rise of a middle class, and its rapid social change. Moreover, after 1971, the year Taipei lost its seat in the United Nations and Taiwan was forced to engage in a struggle to win international support for its sovereignty (which China sought to undermine), it was widely thought that the rapid implementation of democracy would help that cause.

The Constitution contains provisions guaranteeing citizens basic rights similar to those found in Western countries: freedom of speech, belief, residence, publication, assembly, association, and the right to privacy. Arrest, trial, and punishment must be carried out according to constitutional provisions. In the past, critics charged that the Temporary Provisions undermined or seriously weakened these basic freedoms, especially guarantees of political and civil rights. In particular, they cited the role intelligence organizations played in censorship, the use of military courts to try civilian cases, and restrictions on forming political organizations. In response, the government lifted many of the restrictions in these areas in the 1970s and early 1980s. In 1986, President Chiang Ching-kuo announced he would lift martial law and did so in 1987. This went far to change the authoritarian nature of Taiwan's political system.

However, sentiments still ran deep among opposition politicians for more change. Though pleased by the progress democratization was making, they complained about obstacles to competitive elections, such as the practice of retaining old members of the government's elected bodies or their replacements (called the senior parliamentarians), who had been chosen when the government was on the Mainland; the advantages possessed by the Nationalist Party in elections because of its ownership or control of much of the media; and the KMT's close links with the government.

Compared with Western democracies, constitutional guarantees of freedom of assembly, speech, and press in Taiwan have been somewhat weaker (though the press is more representative of the populace in age, gender, political views, and place of birth generally than its counterparts in many Western countries). Many in Taiwan, however, note that the expression of civil and political liberties is conditioned by the political culture and, given the greater respect for political leaders in Chinese political culture and the values placed on stability, freedom of speech has not necessarily been more limited than in Western democracies. For example, most people in Taiwan do not consider it proper to criticize officials directly, or in vulgar language. In any event, in recent years, there seems to be little difference in the practice of basic rights by citizens of Taiwan as compared to most Western democracies. Meanwhile, the political culture has changed: Citizens and the media assail and castigate political leaders with a verve that equals or even surpasses that in the most contentious of Western polities.

Religious freedom is considered broader in Taiwan than in most Western nations because few religious organizations (other than the Presbyterian Church) have become involved in politics, and social problems seldom provoke religious debate. Also, few people discriminate against others for reasons of religion. Taiwan's lower crime rate affords greater freedom of movement. Freedom of association and privacy are guaranteed at about the same level as in Western nations. Taiwan's respect for basic rights and political and other freedoms are ranked high by various organizations, in marked contrast to the authoritarian tendencies of the People's Republic of China and many Third World countries.[10]

The Constitution provides citizens with the right to vote and the powers of recall, initiative, and referendum. Elections are held in Taiwan more often than in Western countries; indeed, political elites as well as many citizens complain about too many elections. Campaigns, however, are shorter than those in the West, and campaigning is more limited by election rules than in most Western countries (though the trend is toward fewer campaign restrictions).

Written with the intent to legitimate rule over a heterogeneous nation when the Nationalists ruled China (or all of China), the Constitution contains protections for the rights of the various minorities. These provisions are so strong and specific that government officials sometimes dub them "affirmative action" provisions. For example, if they are not elected in sufficient numbers, the Constitution allocates seats in the elective bodies of government to racial and ethnic minorities, women, labor, and other groups. Few Western constitutions have gone this far in helping minorities or the underprivileged.[11] The Constitution also specifies certain policies and goals in the areas of national economy, defense, foreign policy, social security, and education not usually found in Western constitutions. Some say these provisions have facilitated government planning, especially long-range planning, in these areas. Critics say it is unnecessary to have these things in the Constitution.

The Constitution makes reference to Sun Yat-sen's Three People's Principles—democracy, nationalism, and people's livelihood—suggesting that Sun's writings constitute an official ideology. However, Sun's teachings, sweeping in scope and designed for the masses to read and understand, do not readily lend themselves to political discourse of the kind that might become tenets of an ideology. Thus, the Constitution's deference to Sun's teachings has not caused much political controversy. In fact, opposition politicians have long preferred to take the position that Sun's ideals as espoused in the Constitution were not being fulfilled rather than suggest that they be scrapped or disregarded. On the other hand, one of Sun's unique but controversial ideas, which appears in the Constitution, was his plan to realize democracy in steps or stages. For a long time, this gradual approach was chided as an excuse for the government to perpetuate authoritarianism. Many now believe it served to implement democracy carefully and thus made it work.

In early 1991, in an extraordinary session, the National Assembly abolished the Temporary Provisions and adopted ten amendments, or "additional articles," to the Constitution. Observers said that these articles created genuine constitutional rule in Taiwan. The amendments ended the representation in Taiwan's elected bodies of government—the National Assembly, the Legislative Yuan, and the Control Yuan—of delegates representing areas on the Mainland. The political system was also changed to include the election of a national constituency in the National Assembly and the Legislative Yuan based on proportional representation, with at-large seats granted to the political parties (including a provision for a small number of delegates to represent "Chinese who reside abroad"). Constitutional revisions also provided for laws to handle matters arising from the increasing contacts between Taiwan and China. Finally, provisions were made for the election of a new National Assembly in December 1991 that would enact further amendments.

In May 1992, the second National Assembly met as a kind of constitutional convention and added eight more amendments to the Constitution. These articles provided for the following changes in Taiwan's political system: the election of the National Assembly every four years; the direct election of the president (though the details were to be worked out later) every four years; the appointment of members of the Control Yuan (instead of their being chosen by indirect election); the implementation of reforms in provincial and local government; guarantees of state support for science and technology; environmental protection; the equivalent of an equal rights amendment for women; and safeguards for the handicapped, disabled, and the Aborigines.

In July 1994, the National Assembly revised and consolidated the eighteen amendments, reducing them to ten. Some new provisions were added. One of these set forth the details for the direct election of the president and vice president, beginning in 1996. Another one restricted—and nearly canceled—the power of the premier to countersign presidential appointments and dismissals. The National Assembly was also given more political power through provisions added for a speaker and yearly meetings. Other minor changes were made.

In the summer of 1997, the Constitution was amended once again with eleven more "additional articles." Important provisions in these articles, made necessary by democratization and multiparty politics, changed the nature of the relationship among the branches of the national government. As a result, the president now appoints the premier without approval of the Legislative Yuan and can dissolve the latter. The Legislative Yuan, however, can render a vote of no confidence in the premier. The Legislative Yuan was also given the power of impeachment. One amendment all but eliminated the provincial government, which, to add efficiency in government, was subsequently downsized dramatically. Various local government offices were turned into appointed positions in order to reduce the impact of vote buying and corruption.[12]

In September 1999, the National Assembly passed several more amendments, which, among other things, lengthened its own term in office and canceled future elections for the National Assembly; thus the body became one comprised of delegates picked by proportional representation based on the last parliamentary election. However, just after the 2001 presidential election, the Grand Council of Justices ruled these changes invalid.[13]

In 2003, the Legislative Yuan passed the Referendum Act, which defined this term (used in the Constitution). Two referendums were put on the ballot for the presidential election in 2004. The Act did not allow referendums to be called to decide the national territory, and thus referendums could not be used to deal with the matter of independence. It did, however, allow the electorate to decide issues relating to national defense, and President Chen used this to add two referendums to the ballot during the 2004 presidential election that related to Taiwan's status as part of China or not. In 2005, the Constitution was amended to abolish the National Assembly and transfer its power to ratify the Constitution to the Legislative Yuan and the people. Another amendment changed the electoral system from a single, nontransferable vote to a single constituency, two-ballot system.[14]

Notwithstanding numerous constitutional amendments, Taiwan's political system remains a mixed one. Many officials and scholars believe the Constitution should be amended further in order to create either a presidential or parliamentary structure. In the past, this did not matter, since the Nationalist Party controlled both the executive and legislative branches of government. But divided government after May 2000 showed the political system was patently in need of repair. Nationalist Party election victories in a legislative election in January 2008 and a presidential election that March made this a mute point. Still, there is debate about whether presidentialism or parliamentarianism is best for Taiwan.

The National Assembly and the Presidency

The Constitution (before it was amended) provided for an elected National Assembly, members of which were chosen for six-year terms to represent counties, municipalities, and areas of equivalent status. The National Assembly's most important functions were to (1) elect the president and vice president, (2) recall the same if necessary, (3) amend the Constitution, (4) make provisions to exercise initiatives and referendums, and (5) approve appointments made by the president. The first National Assembly was elected in 1947, before the Nationalists fled to Taiwan. Until 1991, no full election of the National Assembly was held. The official reason for this was that the "Communist rebellion" on the Mainland precluded a nationwide election. Cynics, however, charge the Assembly was "frozen in time" in order to impede both democratization and Taiwanization.

Critics of the National Assembly voiced several other complaints: that it met only once every six years (therefore its members did not earn their pay); that it was too large to deliberate effectively; and that it was composed largely of delegates without significant political experience or qualifications, most of whom were too old to do much work. In addition, opposition politicians charged that the National Assembly was little more than a rubber-stamp body for approving decisions made by the ruling Nationalist Party. In short, it didn't do anything important. Thus, as political change proceeded apace, there was strong pressure to reform or abolish the National Assembly.

In fact, as democratization gained speed and momentum in the 1980s, pressure grew to reform the National Assembly. In January 1989, the Legislative Yuan passed the Law on Voluntary Retirement of Senior Parliamentarians in the hope of persuading the elder members of the National Assembly and Legislative Yuan to step down. But only a few resigned. The Nationalist Party then tried to induce its older members to quit, but with little effect. In June 1990, the Council of Grand Justices made a constitutional ruling that they had to retire before December 1991. This measure succeeded.

In December 1991, a second National Assembly was elected to a four-year term. The new National Assembly, democratically chosen and representing the population of Taiwan almost exclusively, became a democratic body of government. In 1994, the National Assembly's powers were expanded through changes in the Constitution noted above. However, because the president and vice president were now to be elected directly, the Assembly lost its most important function. At the time, it was uncertain whether it would become a second "chamber" (together with the Legislative Yuan) in a bicameral system, whether it would be abolished, or whether it would become simply an electoral college.[15]

As the 2000 presidential election approached, the future status of the National Assembly became the subject of considerable and often intense debate. The Democratic Progressive Party, which had long advocated abolishing the Assembly, made issue of its providing high-salaried sinecures for its members, thus constituting, it said, a form of political corruption. Court decisions regarding its future elections, and James Soong forming the People First Party after the election (and the prospect of his drawing KMT members of the National Assembly away), paved the way for a KMT-DPP deal to settle the National Assembly issue once and for all. In April, its members voted to reduce the National Assembly to an ad hoc body. As a result, it virtually ceased to function. However, it retained its powers to ratify constitutional amendments and to vote on a presidential impeachment. To do either, though, a new National Assembly would have to be constituted when called upon, and that would no doubt complicate both functions and probably make forming a National Assembly infrequent. In 2005, an ad hoc National Assembly ratified an additional article of the Constitution that included a provision to abolish itself.[16]

Unlike the National Assembly, the Office of the President has considerable authority that derives both specifically from the Constitution and has evolved through practice. As chief of state, the president is formally responsible for state functions such as promulgating laws, declaring martial law, appointing officials, granting amnesty and commutations, and conducting foreign relations including making treaties and executive agreements. He or she also commands the armed forces and can declare war or peace. Finally, the president is responsible for resolving disputes among the five branches of government and for exercising emergency powers.

The president, in addition, has powers that derive from his or her leadership position in the ruling party (if the president is of the ruling party), though this authority has not been institutionalized. (Yen Chia-kan, who became president when Chiang Kai-shek died, was not a strong president because he did not lead the party. Chen Shui-bian gave up his party posts after he became president because his presidency was weak due to the fact that his party did not have a majority in the Legislative Yuan.) This "derivative power," when the president has it, strengthens the authority of the presidential office considerably and it is in this instance not unlike similar powers enjoyed by presidents in Western democracies. The presidency has been bolstered further as a result of the perceived need for strong leadership and also because Taiwan's past presidents have been a major force behind successful economic and political reform. Symbolic duties and the president's role in representing the nation in the international community have similarly enhanced the power of the office.

The Office of the President consists of a secretary-general, senior advisers, national policy and military strategy advisers, and military aides. The secretary-general to the president manages the general affairs of the Office of the President, supervises staff members, and controls the president's time in a manner similar to that of the White House chief of staff in the United States. Bureaus under the president perform or oversee functions in three general areas: The First Bureau is responsible for the executive functions of the president, including promulgating laws and orders and also keeping confidential and secret documents; the Second Bureau transmits military orders and maintains the liaison with the military; and the Third Bureau handles protocol and administrative duties.[17]

In 1967, the National Security Council was established within the Office of the President to coordinate national strategy. In 1990, the National Unification Council was founded to bring various groups and individuals together to discuss the unification of China. Academia Sinica, the nation's foremost think tank—or association of scholars—and Academia Historica, a historical research center and document-preservation organization, were already under presidential administration.

In 1994, the details were worked out, following the passage of a relevant constitutional amendment, for the direct election of the president and vice president. The first such election was held in 1996. Lee Teng-hui won reelection, and, because of it being a direct election, it gave him a stronger mandate and enhanced his political power. Meanwhile, a constitutional provision reduced the authority of the premier, thereby making Taiwan's political system, according to many observers, more clearly presidential. Other constitutional provisions, however, such as the Legislative Yuan's expanded powers—especially its power to initiate impeachment of the president and the vice president—suggested otherwise. In any event, the lines of authority between the president and the legislature were in some important respects still unclear and needed to be clarified.[18]

Chiang Kai-shek was president from 1950 until his death in 1975, having been elected in 1972 to a fifth six-year term that he did not complete. The Temporary

Provisions enhanced Chiang's presidential powers as did martial law and the fact that he held undisputed control over the ruling party, the military, and the police. He was thus an "authoritarian president." When Chiang died, Vice President Yen Chia-kan, a former governor of Taiwan Province and vice president from 1966 to 1975, succeeded him. Yen, however, was not a strong president. Premier Chiang Ching-kuo, Chiang Kai-shek's son, controlled the ruling Nationalist Party and wielded considerable political influence elsewhere, notably in the police, the military, and the intelligence community. Yen announced in advance that he would not be a candidate for president in the next election, thus making himself an interim president. This did not create an untenable situation because Yen and Chiang Ching-kuo were not political opponents and because the Constitution was at this time ambiguous about whether the system was presidential, parliamentary, or cabinet.

Chiang Ching-kuo was elected president in 1978 and inherited many of the powers of his father. But he sought strenuously to make Taiwan a democracy and did not rule in an authoritarian way; in so doing, he weakened the powers of the presidency somewhat. Still, his will was seldom questioned. He was reelected in March 1984 for a second six-year term. Shieh Tung-min, the first Taiwanese to attain such a high office, was Chiang's first vice president. Chiang chose Lee Teng-hui, the former governor of Taiwan Province and also Taiwanese, as his second vice president and heir apparent in 1984. In January 1988, Chiang died in office.

Upon Chiang Ching-kuo's death, Lee Teng-hui became president. For a time, there was talk that Lee might be a figurehead president because he did not have the power base or popularity of Chiang. It was also widely speculated, because of the hold on power by Taiwan's Mainland Chinese, that Lee's powers would be circumscribed. But Lee had earned respect both in the Nationalist Party and among the populace because of his foreign education (in Japan and the United States, including a Ph.D. from Cornell University), his years of outstanding government service, and his many years of association with Chiang Ching-kuo. Lee also possessed considerable political acumen. Democratization, which many said required a Taiwan-born leader, also favored Lee, as did his election in a direct vote in 1996. Lee was nevertheless confronted by manifold challenges—many of which stemmed from Taiwan's rapid democratization and the transition to Taiwanese majority rule. He also had to deal with changes in the political system and the political culture, not to mention opposition politics and splits in his party. Still, he proved to be a strong, able, and generally popular leader.

In May 2000, Chen Shui-bian, a member of the opposition Democratic Progressive Party, became Taiwan's fifth president. He had been a legislator and was mayor of Taipei from 1994 to 1998. Almost immediately after his inauguration, the now-opposition Nationalist Party, in cooperation with James Soong's newly formed

People First Party, through their control of the legislature, engaged in a power struggle with President Chen that in part focused on the authority of the president. The gridlock that followed showed that presidential and legislative prerogatives should have been delineated more clearly and that constitutional amendments were needed to do this. The problem of divided government persisted throughout Chen's presidency, explaining in large measure why President Chen accomplished very little, though Chen also showed a lack of leadership at times, did not manage the economy well, and became seriously corrupt. He also exacerbated ethnic ill will to enhance his governance, which sullied his presidency. For most of his presidency, his public approval numbers were low.

In 2008, Ma Ying-jeou, a former Minister of Justice and Taipei mayor was elected president, representing the Nationalist Party, winning the largest number of votes and the biggest percentage of the popular vote ever. The KMT having won a solid victory in the legislature two months earlier, Ma did not face a divided government and he seemed destined to be a stronger president than Chen had been. Vincent Siew, an economic expert, was his vice president.

The Five-Branch Government

As noted earlier, Taiwan's central government is patterned after the US three-branch system, with the addition of two more branches. It was thought that a five-branch government would ensure greater division of power and more effective checks and balances. It had other advantages as well (though also some disadvantages), and at the time, its design was considered by officials and citizens of the Republic of China to be a uniquely Chinese system.

Of the five branches (*Yuan*) of government, the Executive Yuan has always been the most powerful. The reason, of course, is that the President controls this branch of the government. The Executive Yuan nevertheless was efficient early on and was responsive to public opinion, taking a major stride in that direction after Chiang Ching-kuo took measures to reform the government in the late 1970s. In fact, before the retirement of the "elder parliamentarians," the Executive Yuan was regarded as more sensitive to the public pulse than the Legislative Yuan and, in some respect, it still is.[19]

The premier is chosen by the President to head the Executive Yuan. Under the premier are a vice premier and eight ministers (Interior, Foreign Affairs, Defense, Finance, Education, Justice, Economic Affairs, and Transportation and Communications) appointed by the President. The ministries perform functions similar to those of their counterparts in other political systems.

Attached to the Executive Yuan are other important ministerial-level organs, such as the Mainland Affairs Council; the Department of Health; the Council for

Cultural Planning and Development; the Government Information Office; the Council for Economic Planning and Development; the National Youth Commission; the Research, Development, and Evaluation Commission; the National Science Council; the Atomic Energy Council; the Council of Agriculture; the Fair Trade Commission; the Environmental Protection Administration; the Council for Labor Affairs; the National Palace Museum; the Central Bank; the Central Election Commission; the Vocational Assistance Commission; the Directorate General of Budget Accounting and Statistics; and the Central Personnel Administration. Recent additions include the Public Construction Commission, the Council for Aboriginal Affairs, the National Sports Council, the Coast Guard, and the Council for Hakka Affairs. In 2006, the National Communications Commission was created to regulate telecommunications and the broadcast and the print media, taking many of these functions away from the Government Information Office.

The numerous government organs that are part of the Executive Yuan reflect its broad responsibility for policy formulation as well as its host of administrative duties. This is where most bills or laws are drafted and political decisions implemented. In both realms, officials of the Executive Yuan work closely with the President and top leaders of the ruling party who, as a matter of practice, take the initiative to formulate policy and exercise strong influence on the political agenda.

Actions of the Executive Yuan are checked by the Legislative Yuan, which has the power to interpret, reject, or alter them. In the past, these checks were rather feeble owing to a weak legislature and the fact that the Nationalist Party dominated the setting of policy goals. The Legislative Yuan gained power as it became more representative of the population and more active coinciding with Taiwan's rapid democratization in the 1980s and 1990s. After Chen Shui-bian was elected president in 2000 for eight years, the Legislative Yuan aggressively impeded many of his actions and policies and put forth its own agenda. Often this caused gridlock and political paralysis, as happens when there is divided government.

When Chiang Ching-kuo became premier in 1972, that office became more powerful. When he was elected president in 1978, Sun Yun-suan became premier and served until May 1984. Sun had a technical background, and though his critics claimed he did not have a sufficiently broad political base, he was highly respected and considered a superb leader. Before he suffered a stroke, many considered him the likely successor to Chiang Ching-kuo. Yu Kuo-hua, who had been head of the Central Bank, succeeded Sun. Yu was an effective—though not popular—premier.

In 1989, President Lee Teng-hui appointed Lee Huan, then secretary-general of the Nationalist Party and a popular political figure, as premier. However, a year later, in 1990, President Lee called on Hau Pei-tsun, then Minister of Defense, to be premier. Some said Lee sought to win the support of the military, where he had little influence, and needed Hau. Others noted that President Lee and Premier Lee

Huan had serious disagreements on policy as well as personal differences. Both were probably true.

In any event, relations between the president and Premier Hau also turned sour after a short time. Many said their difficulties reflected ethnic politics in Taiwan, since President Lee was Taiwanese and Premier Hau was Mainland Chinese (the same having been said also of the relationship between President Lee and Lee Huan). There were also disagreements between the two about policies and party issues. A systemic crisis then resulted because of the ill-defined relationship between the premier—who was appointed by the President but who could not be fired by him or her—and the President. The crisis was, in practice, resolved after the 1992 Legislative Yuan election, when Premier Hau resigned. The Constitution has since been amended, as noted earlier, to clarify the authority of the president and the premier in favor of the former.

President Lee appointed Lien Chan (a Taiwanese) as the nation's fourteenth premier in February 1993. Lien was elected vice president in 1996 and served concurrently in the two positions until August 1997. The Legislative Yuan questioned the constitutionality of this arrangement before President Lee appointed Vincent Siew (also a Taiwanese) premier in September 1997.

President Chen Shui-bian appointed General Tang Fei (a Mainland Chinese, a member of the Nationalist Party and a former Minister of Defense) premier in early 2000. Tang suffered physical problems and then resigned that fall over the issue of the fourth nuclear power plant, having served only five months in office. Chen replaced Tang with Chang Chun-hsiung—a Taiwanese and a member of the Democratic Progressive Party. After the 2001 legislative election, Chen formed a new cabinet and picked Yu Shyi-kun, also a Taiwanese and member of the DPP, to be premier. In 2005, President Chen named Frank Hsieh premier and in 2006, Su Tseng-chang. Both served only brief terms. In May 2007, Chang Chun-hsiung was again appointed to that office. All were handicapped in performing their duties by tension between the president and the legislature, corruption in the Chen administration, and President Chen's low popularity.

The unicameral Legislative Yuan is the law-enacting body of the national government, often called the parliament or senate. In addition to its legislative functions, it confirms emergency orders, approves budgets (submitted by the Executive Yuan), and proposes amendments to the Constitution. The Legislative Yuan approves Executive Yuan policy statements and reports, and serves as a check on the Judicial Yuan, the Control Yuan, and the Examination Yuan. It may, as noted earlier, also initiate impeachment proceedings against the president and vice president. It has some lesser powers as well, such as providing grants-in-aid to provincial government organs and settling disputes between the national government and units of local government.

Legislative Yuan members elect a president or speaker and vice president and endorse his or her appointment of a secretary-general to run the Secretariat. Members of the legislature make their own rules regarding procedures for debating and passing laws and bills as well as for dealing with members who misbehave or violate ethical standards, although such responsibilities also belong to the Control Yuan. Much of the work of the Legislative Yuan is done in its standing committees: Home and Border Affairs; Foreign and Overseas Chinese Affairs; Technology and Information; National Defense; Economics; Finance; Budget and Fiscal Accounts; Education and Cultural Affairs; Transportation and Communications; Judiciary; Organic Laws; and Health, Environment and Social Welfare. In addition, there are five special committees: Credentials, Discipline, Rules, Accounts, and Publications. As originally designed, committees were composed of not more than twenty-one members, and no member could serve on more than one important committee.

Members of the Legislative Yuan originally served three-year terms. In the recent past, the body had 225 members (enlarged by 61 seats before the December 1998 election); it was made up of 176 delegates that represent electoral districts (mostly multimember districts of varying size), and 49 at-large senators (41 of whom represent a national constituency and 8 of whom represent Chinese overseas). Currently, the Legislative Yuan convenes two sessions each year: one from February to the end of May, the other from September to the end of the year. It may hold extraordinary sessions, called by its president, at any time. A quorum consists of one-third of the body, though this is not sufficient for recommending a constitutional amendment, in which case three-fourths of members must be present. A simple majority passes resolutions, with some exceptions specified in the Constitution. Legislative Yuan members have immunity from being sued or indicted for most crimes while in office, though the scope of this exemption has been narrowed in recent years due to abuse.

Like the National Assembly, the Legislative Yuan, when first formed, represented all of China, or the Mainland as well as Taiwan, and continued to do so after the government moved to Taiwan in 1949. It became more representative of Taiwan after 1969, when new members were elected. Subsequently, as elections brought in more new blood and Mainland representatives grew older, younger members elected to represent Taiwan, who were mainly Taiwanese, dominated work in the Legislative Yuan. Still, critics protested that not all members of the Legislative Yuan were elected and that it unrealistically claimed to represent China. As in the case of the National Assembly, defenders pointed out that if the Legislative Yuan stopped representing districts in China, Taiwan would be de facto adopting a two-China policy, and Beijing's leaders had promised to use military force against Taiwan to prevent Taiwan's legal independence. This issue became moot after the "elder parliamentarians" stepped down and a plenary election was held in 1992.

The Legislative Yuan traditionally had much less decision-making authority than the Executive Yuan. This changed with the nation's democratization. Nevertheless, antics that go on in legislative sessions and the bad behavior of some of its members have aroused public ridicule and satire in the press at home and abroad. Known—indeed famous—criminals winning election to the legislature and the underworld ties of many other members, not to mention frequent cases of corruption, have brought dishonor to the body.[20]

There have consequently been a number of reforms enacted that have enhanced the prestige and effectiveness of the Legislative Yuan. In 1993, the legislature enhanced its image somewhat when it passed a "sunshine bill" that required members to disclose their personal wealth. In 1997, the Constitution was amended to give the president the authority to appoint the premier without the consent of the legislature, though legislators were given the power to force the premier out of office with a vote of no confidence. In 2004, the Legislative Yuan voted 217 to 1 (in the context of 70 percent public support) to halve the number of seats to 113, increase the terms of members to four years (so that elections would coincide with presidential elections), and change the electoral system for electing the legislature. The new legislature elected in January 2008 contained 73 directly elected members and 6 seats reserved for Aborigines, plus 34 seats filled by the parties, half of which must be women. There was considerable debate at the time concerning whether or not this would make the legislature more efficient and its members of higher quality and accorded greater respect.[21]

The Judicial Yuan functions much like the judicial branches of government in other nations, although structurally it is somewhat different. It is composed of a president, a vice president, and fifteen justices who serve six-year terms. All are appointed by the Office of the President, originally with the approval of the National Assembly but now the Legislative Yuan.[22] The Judicial Yuan is organized into a Council of Grand Justices, three levels of ordinary courts (the Supreme Court, high courts, and district courts), administrative courts, and a Committee on the Discipline of Public Functionaries. The Council of Grand Justices, which meets twice weekly and may hold extraordinary sessions, interprets the Constitution in a fashion that resembles the process of judicial review in Western systems. It also upholds laws, statutes, and government orders. An interpretation of the Constitution requires a three-fourths vote from the members present and a quorum of three-fourths of members; a simple majority can make other decisions. Government agencies and individuals can call for an interpretation of the Constitution. However, to do this, agencies of the government must be involved in performing their duties; be in dispute over their authority; or perceive that a law, regulation, or decree contravenes the Constitution. To institute such legal action, citizens must demonstrate that their constitutional rights have been infringed upon.

The Supreme Court is the highest court of the three levels of ordinary courts. It hears appeals in civil and criminal cases, motions to set aside decisions of the high courts, and special cases. The Supreme Court is divided into several civil and criminal "senates" (at present eight and twelve, respectively). Each senate includes a presiding judge and four associates. Because of this division of work, the Supreme Court can hear more cases than would otherwise be possible and thus avoids backlogs and delays. Since the Supreme Court decides only issues of law, not of fact, its proceedings are primarily documentary; also, because few of its proceedings are oral, the system is less adversarial than Western legal systems.

The high courts hear cases of appeal from district courts, criminal cases involving rebellion and treason, cases involving other nations, and election lawsuits. They have civil, criminal, and traffic sections and are divided into senates composed of a presiding judge and two associates. District courts hear original civil and criminal cases involving juvenile, family, traffic, financial cases, and other less contentious matters. Administrative courts handle cases involving violations of citizens' rights by administrative actions of the government and suits against the government. The Committee on the Discipline of Public Functionaries serves as a check on decisions of the Control Yuan involving impeachment, dismissal, and the like.

Critics of the Judicial Yuan have argued that it is not as strong as a judicial body of government should be and not sufficiently independent of ruling party influence. This charge was often leveled at the KMT when it was in power, but subsequently also about the DPP. Some observers complain that judges are government employees recruited through a government examination and are thus not impartial.[23] Defenders point out that the 1980 Separation of Trial from Prosecution Reform Act made the Judicial Yuan more independent and maintain that it should not be given excessive power because it is not an elected organ of government. Furthermore, they say that public distaste for instituting legal proceedings lessens the need for a strong judicial body. Taiwan is a less litigious society than the United States and other Western countries, though this has been changing in recent years.

Efforts have been made to change Taiwan's judicial system from a "judge-centered, inquisitorial system" (the German model) to a more "attorney-based, adversarial system" (like that of the United States) in view of the growing public interest in lawsuits and lawyers becoming more activist. It is also probable that the rules will be changed so that judges are chosen from among outstanding prosecutors and attorneys rather than from students trained early in their careers to be judges.[24]

Citizens' confidence in the judiciary suffered considerably during the Chen administration. The president promised judicial reform, but due to his administration's standoff with the Legislative Yuan and the paralysis that caused, plus corruption in the administration, little happened. Also, critics accused the Chen administration of making judicial appoints for purely political reasons. In fact, the street protest against President Chen and the DPP in 2006 was in part prompted by the fact that it was widely perceived that Chen controlled the judiciary and the prosecutors, and they protected a corrupt administration. Confidence was to some extent restored when prosecutors indicted Chen's son-in-law for insider trading and the president's wife for stealing government funds, forgery, and perjury.[25]

The Control Yuan was a special branch of government patterned after the Censorate in Imperial China, which functioned as a watchdog body similar to the Government Accountability Office in the United States. As originally comprised, provincial and municipal councils elected its twenty-nine members. Because of scandals that arose over the buying of seats and a decline in the number of important cases it heard, among other reasons, the status of the Control Yuan was changed dramatically. In February 1993, the Control Yuan became a body of government appointed by the president with the approval of the Legislative Yuan, and its basic functions were truncated. It is no longer a parliamentary (elected) body and has lost many of its supervisory functions.[26] The Control Yuan is now best described as a quasi-judicial oversight branch of government designed to check on officials.

The Control Yuan retained the powers of impeachment, censure, and audit—though the authority to impeach the president or vice president was taken away in 1997. It may investigate the Executive Yuan and its subordinate agencies. It may censure public officials. It oversees the Ministry of Audit—one of its main functions—and establishes various working committees. It approves presidential appointments (by a secret vote in a plenary session) and has the power to investigate and hear complaints from the public.

In 2004, President Chen submitted a list of Control Yuan appointees that the Legislative Yuan declined to approve. The legislature asked for a new list, but Chen did not submit one and the Control Yuan, for all intents and purposes, ceased to function. Some observers said it was simply a casualty in the power struggle between the president and the opposition. Critics said that the president did not want it to investigate corruption in his administration. It would certainly have played a role when President Chen's wife was indicted, and may have taken action against President Chen. The prosecutor said the president was probably guilty of the same crimes, though he could not be indicted while a sitting president.[27]

The Examination Yuan is responsible for writing and administering the equivalent of civil service examinations in Western political systems. In the Chinese political tradition, the examination function was of such importance that a special branch of government was created to conduct and oversee it. Today, the Examination Yuan administers four kinds of special examinations to recruit and screen applicants for government service. It also deals with job qualifications, job security, and retirement issues. The Examination Yuan is organized into a council, a secretariat, and two ministries: the Ministry of Examination and the Ministry of Personnel. The president appoints members of the Examination Yuan.

There has been considerable public debate about the structure of the government in Taiwan, and various individuals and leaders of the political parties have proposed abolishing the Control Yuan and the Examination Yuan and thereby establishing a three-branch system of government. If this were done, the functions of the two would be transferred to the Executive and Legislative Yuans. The relationship between the executive and legislative branches of government and the relationship of both to the president are also the subject of considerable talk about political reform.

Local Government

Taiwan's political system is basically a unitary one (meaning that the central government is the dominant political authority), though it has some of the characteristics of a federal system (signifying that local government has first or primary jurisdiction in certain realms).[28] There is also overlapping authority; this was particularly true in the past in the relationship between the provincial government and the central government. Advances in transportation and communications and also external threats in recent years have expanded the role of the central government, as have its quick responses to deal with problems associated with rapid economic and political change.[29] Finally, the ruling party and most top government officials both past and present have favored keeping power at the center.

Local government, on the other hand, gets much credit for political reform and democratization. Many argue that democracy evolved in Taiwan "from the bottom up," meaning that democratic change came first to local politics. Global trends also favor the decentralization of political authority, since the government must maintain cost-efficiency. Another factor that favors local government is that Taiwan's political system allows local politicians to gain experience and name recognition, thus providing them with an avenue by which they can move up to positions in the national government; indeed, local government remains strong and its various offices find talent more easily because of those opportunities. Local officials who rise to the top also favor keeping the functions and powers of local government intact. Finally, there has been and remains a strong interest in local politics on the part of the citizenry of Taiwan.

The organization of local government is based on provisions in the Constitution for local self-government that created provincial and county governments in addition to metropolitan, city, town, and village borough systems. Although units of local government report to officials or sections of government at a higher level, all are given some powers and responsibilities that do not relate to other units of government and do not depend on higher authority, as in federal systems.

The provincial government, the highest level of local government in Taiwan, was established in May 1947, following mass unrest and violence directed at the central government. It replaced the despised Office of Governor-General, but in 1949, after the Nationalists fled to Taiwan, Taiwan Province came almost totally under the control of the central government. Since it had jurisdiction over nearly all the land and population now constituting the Republic of China, many provincial government functions and duties overlapped with those of the central government. In these areas, the national government almost always dominated. In addition, most central government officials and Nationalist Party leaders did not want a strong or active provincial government.

Below the provincial government were sixteen counties, where most of the work of local government was performed. County governments were divided into urban or rural categories, the former being subdivided into boroughs and the latter into villages. Two metropolitan governments were established later: Taipei and Kaohsiung. In many ways, they became more important than the county governments and more powerful than even the provincial government (before it was downsized) because of the number of people under their jurisdiction, the many difficult but important tasks they performed, and their close relationship with the national organs of government.[30] There are now eighteen counties, sixteen of which are under the Taiwan Provincial Government.

Local government at the top originally was the popularly elected Provincial Assembly, composed of members who served four-year terms, and an appointed governor. The main policymaking body of the provincial government was the Provincial Government Council, which consisted of twenty-three of the seventy-nine members of the Provincial Assembly, especially selected by the Executive Yuan and the governor. The Provincial Government Council served as a cabinet. Though the powers of the Provincial Assembly were not broad, the body mirrored public opinion more accurately than elected bodies of the national government since the former was elected in full every four years and represented only Taiwan.[31]

For some years, many who demanded more democracy in Taiwan—especially those who rejected the ruling Nationalist Party's claim to represent China—advocated a greater role for the provincial government. In particular, they sought to give broader responsibilities and powers to the Provincial Assembly and grant it greater independence from the national government. However, after plenary elections democratized the National Assembly and the Legislative Yuan, this criticism subsided.

In 1992, the legalization of local autonomy was realized by constitutional amendment and had a major impact in strengthening local government.[32] In the process, Quemoy, Matsu, and the Pratas and Spratly Areas (the parts of these island groups that are under Taipei's control) were granted local autonomy. They had previously been under military jurisdiction. Quemoy and Matsu now have county governments. At this time, the provincial governor was made an elective office, and in 1994, Taiwan's voters elected James Soong governor.

As noted earlier, in 1996, President Lee Teng-hui convened a gathering of officials, scholars, and politicians (called the National Development Conference) to discuss political reforms and additional constitutional amendments. One of the main topics at the meeting was downsizing or eliminating the provincial and village levels of government. The considerable duplication of functions by the national and provincial governments was said to be expensive and made government less efficient. The opposition Democratic Progressive Party, as well as many scholars and government officials, supported Lee's proposals. The National Assembly subsequently acted, and, in 1997, made constitutional changes to shrink the provincial government drastically. In December 1998, the Provincial Assembly was virtually eliminated, along with the elected governorship and most other organs of the provincial government.

When the National Development Conference recommended that the provincial governor once again be made an appointed job, James Soong resigned. His resignation was not accepted, however, and he remained on the job until the end of 1998. In the meantime, his relationship with President Lee, which was once very close, deteriorated, and the two became quite bitter toward each other. Many disputes associated with downsizing the provincial government, such as where its assets and its personnel would go and who would control them, were aired in public.

In the meantime, Taipei was made a "special municipality" in 1967 and Kaohsiung in 1979. As a result, the mayors of Taiwan's two largest cities were thereafter appointed by the national government. The official reason given was that the size of these two cities made it necessary for their executive heads to coordinate policies and actions with the national government—a seemingly logical explanation given that Taipei was the seat of the national government and Kaohsiung was Taiwan's major port city. However, opposition politicians claimed that the national government sought to inhibit the development of democratic government in these cities and eliminate a political base for popular Taiwanese politicians. In any event, the mayorships of these two cities were made elective offices again, and, in December 1994, the two mayors were chosen by their respective electorates. The mayors of the two cities, but especially the mayor of Taipei, have been important and very visible political figures. President Chen was mayor of Taipei from 1994 to 1998, Ma Ying-jeou was mayor of Taipei from 1998 to 2006, and Frank Hsieh was mayor of Kaohsiung. Five other cities (Chiayi, Hsinchu, Keelung, Taichung, and Tainan) are organizationally under the Taiwan Provincial Government.

According to the Constitution before it was amended, below the provincial government (except for the two municipal governments just mentioned) were county, town, and village governments. These units of local government operated with considerable autonomy and authority. This was true even though, as noted earlier, the political system of Taiwan is designed to be a unitary one. Local leaders had considerable say over budget matters and other decisions that do not relate directly to national policy. They also coordinated other policies with the national government.

The National Development Conference, in addition to proposing that the provisional government be scrapped, recommended the elimination of another level of government: village government. Again, efficiency was the main consideration, but vote buying had also become a serious public concern, which was especially rampant in local government. The solution was to make more positions in local government appointive rather than elective. In fact, the National Development Conference's suggestion was made into another constitutional amendment, and village government was virtually eliminated. Some say it came at the expense of local democracy; others contend it made for better, more efficient, and more honest government.

Shortly after the Nationalists arrived in Taiwan, they held provincial and local elections. Contrary to expectations, the Kuomintang did not try to suppress democracy locally; rather, KMT officials encouraged it. Because of strong opposing factions in local politics and potent centrifugal forces, the KMT could play a mediator role and control or effectively play off local factions against one another while bringing many local leaders into the ruling party, thereby stemming the growth of a political opposition. On the other hand, many KMT leaders genuinely wanted to create a democratic system in accordance with Sun Yat-sen's teachings and felt that the existing local government was not sufficiently democratic.[33]

Many local officials did not share the KMT's view about local politics and believed that they could build the foundations for democracy locally, and later they said they did. Their view was that democracy came from "the bottom up." They argued that because democracy had been practiced locally for thirty years in the form of regular elections, the first competitive election in national politics in 1980 and national elections after that were successful. Interestingly, voter turnout has been higher in local elections than in national elections, which suggests that the electorate sees more—or at least more meaningful—democracy locally than it does at the national level. Part of the explanation, however, is that the electorate, like that in Japan and France (but unlike the United States and most other Western democracies), tends to identify with local issues. Voters also perceive that their votes are more important in deciding local matters than national ones, and they are generally better informed about candidates for positions in local government.

When it was founded in 1986, the Democratic Progressive Party attracted leaders and even candidates for high office that, for the most part, made their mark in local politics. In the 1990s, especially after the DPP won a major victory in local elections in 1997, there was talk that the DPP may come to control local politics and the KMT would continue to run the national government. This, of course, did not happen. Nevertheless, the DPP's success in ensuing years indicates how important local politics are in Taiwan. Finally, many of those who suggest Taiwan is a model for democracy in China note that democratization in the latter has begun with reform and elections in local governments.

Political Parties

To grasp how political power is exercised in Taiwan, one must understand the functions and roles of political parties, how they are organized, and how their leadership works, especially in the Nationalist Party and the Democratic Progressive Party. It is likewise essential to grasp the nature of Taiwan's party structure, how it has changed in some important respects in recent years, and what kind of system is evolving.

The Temporary Provisions, discussed earlier in this chapter, made it unlawful to form new political parties in Taiwan. Thus, until 1986, in addition to the KMT, only two other parties, the Young China Party and the China Democratic Socialist Party, campaigned and/or sponsored candidates in elections. Because these parties were small and were in large measure controlled (even financed) by the KMT, they had little real political power or influence. Taiwan thus had a one-party system. In fact, for many years, the Nationalist Party almost alone carried out the functions of recruitment and training, interest articulation, and interest aggregation. It also made decisions and policies that the government adopted, typical of one-party states.[34]

The Nationalist Party traces its origins to several political organizations founded by Sun Yat-sen, the first being the *Hsing Chung Hui,* or the Society for Regenerating China, set up in Hawaii in 1894. In August 1912, the *Tung Meng Hui,* or the Revolutionary Alliance, which Sun had established in Japan in 1905, merged with other groups to form the Nationalist Party or Kuomintang (KMT). In February of the next year, the KMT won a victory in China's first parliamentary elections. Meanwhile, however, Yuan Shih-kai, an advisor to the former imperial government, seized the reins of power in Peking and threatened battle with Sun's supporters in the south. The standoff seemed likely to start a civil war, so Sun abdicated. Yuan subsequently suppressed KMT activities and established himself as a virtual dictator. But the KMT survived, and after Yuan's death in 1916, Sun made several unsuccessful attempts to establish a democratic form of government, with the KMT serving as his power base.

Sun died in 1925. After a brief power struggle, Chiang Kai-shek, with the military as his base of support, took over leadership of the KMT. Chiang, mainly through the military and the KMT, ruled China until 1949, when the Communists defeated his armies. The Nationalist Party, along with the government and the military, fled to Taiwan. Chiang headed the Nationalist Party until his death in 1975 and retains the posthumous title of director-general of the party.

Chiang's son, Chiang Ching-kuo, was unanimously elected Chairman of the Central Committee of the party—and thereby head of the Nationalist Party—in an extraordinary party session held after his father's death. He remained chairman of the party until he died in January 1988. Vice President Lee Teng-hui then became acting chairman of the KMT; he was formally elected chairman at the Thirteenth Party Congress in July 1988. Lee was pressured to resign as head of the party after its defeat in the presidential election of 2000 and did step down. Lien Chan replaced him. Ma Ying-jeou was elected party chairman in 2005 and held that office until 2007.

Owing to the influence of Soviet advisors and because of Sun's perception that the West had not adequately supported him and his calls for democracy in China, plus due to the need for strong organization, the Nationalist Party took its organizational structure from the Communist Party of the Soviet Union. Thus, many refer to it as a "Leninist party," which is an accurate description of the KMT's structure. The National Party Congress is theoretically the highest decision-making body in the KMT, but, it is too large to deliberate on issues efficiently and was, until recent years, generally a rubber-stamp body. To a large extent, it still is. When not in session, the KMT delegates authority to its Central Committee as well as its thirty-some member Central Standing Committee, which analysts have long regarded as the center of political power (before 2000). As with other Leninist parties, the secretary-general of the party, in concert with the chairman and other top-ranking members, make policies, and even specific decisions. The Central Committee then confirm their decisions.

The KMT differs, however, from Leninist parties in some important ways. For example, unlike the ruling parties in Communist countries (including China), the KMT is more a mass party than an elite party. In the 1990s, the KMT claimed a membership of 2.1 million, or about 10 percent of the population.[35] Also, in contrast to the Chinese Communist Party, it did not create a centrally planned economy or attempt to completely mobilize and control the population. Furthermore, it never gave much importance to ideology. Finally, the KMT changed its organizational structure and decision-making process to keep up with the nation's political modernization. Successful efforts to democratize the KMT were undertaken at the Thirteenth Party Congress as well as subsequent congresses.[36]

Various departments in the KMT carry out party work: Organization Affairs, Mainland Operations, Overseas Affairs, Cultural Affairs, Social Affairs, Youth Activities, Women's Activities, and commissions dealing with financial affairs, party history, and discipline. Party activities are broad and involve such things as welfare, recruitment for government jobs, and guiding or dictating government policies. Thus, the Nationalist Party is much more a Western-style political party than other Leninist parties.

In the past, the KMT operated numerous profit-making business enterprises, including several in the media and cultural fields. Critics long contended that the KMT monopolized many areas of business and controlled the media. Its past influence over the news, publishing, and movie industries did, in many respects, amount to media control, but that changed with democratization and the increasingly pluralistic nature of the society. In recent years, the KMT has sold various businesses and has cut its ties with certain media organizations. It still owns some businesses, but so does the DPP.

The KMT was long financially well off. With assets of at least US$2 billion (some say it is much more), it has been labeled the richest political party in the world.[37] Its assets naturally have been an advantage for the party in running campaigns and in many other respects. But its wealth has also been a handicap in the context of the evolution of popular democracy, especially when the opposition claims that the KMT buys elections and this undermines good government. When running as the KMT's nominee for president in the 2000 election, Lien Chan pledged to put the party's assets in trust. But the DPP and President Chen continued to talk about the KMT's money and how it got it, suggesting it did so by illegal means and repeatedly called for investigations into the matter. The DPP even put the issue before the voters in a referendum in January 2008, but it failed to win sufficient votes. In the meantime, DPP corruption became a more serious issue, and this and the depletion of the KMT's financial resources has resulted in a different view about whether or not the KMT is a rich party that thrives on money politics.

In the past, most important political decisions in the Republic of China were made by and within the party, and for that reason, the Nationalist Party to a large extent controlled or manipulated the government. In the minds of most citizens, the KMT was the government or was synonymous with it. Others described Taiwan as a "corporate state" because of these connections.[38] However, beginning in the 1980s, party leaders sought to change the party's image by breaking ties between it and the government—a necessary process if the KMT was to avoid being blamed for mistakes made by government officials and if the country was to evolve into a two-party or multiparty system.[39]

Meanwhile, beginning in the 1960s, as Nationalist Party leaders began to change their attitude about the need for party competition, a number of opposition politicians ran in elections as independents. In the 1970s, a loose political organization called the *tangwai*, or "outside the party" (meaning the KMT since it was the only party), began to become active. It "sponsored" candidates in various local elections and began to recruit and train political leaders. In the national election in 1980—a watershed election for the growth of party competition and contested elections in Taiwan—the *tangwai* supported candidates who openly opposed those of the Nationalist Party.[40]

After 1980, Taiwan witnessed the rapid growth of opposition politics. In the 1983 national election, the *tangwai* developed "party goals" and campaigned as an organization. It had a platform that included issues upon which the opposition generally agreed: placing more seats up for election in the National Assembly, the Legislative Yuan, and the Control Yuan; holding popular elections for the governor of Taiwan and the mayors of Taipei and Kaohsiung; appointing more Taiwanese to high government posts; allowing new political parties to form legally; expanding the scope of freedom of the press, speech, and assembly; lessening restrictions on campaigning for elections; abolishing the Temporary Provisions; reviewing trials that had resulted in the jailing of political prisoners; and demanding that the KMT relinquish powers and prerogatives that should belong to the government, not to a political party.

However, the *tangwai* suffered from factionalism and did not immediately mature into a viable, competitive political party. In particular, it was plagued by differences between radicals and moderates and by personality disputes among its leaders. Many of its members also made unrealistic demands for more extensive reforms of the political system than the public wanted or were feasible at the time. Thus, it did not perform as well as hoped at the polls or in recruiting new members.

In early 1986, President Chiang Ching-kuo appointed a twelve-member committee made up of party leaders and government officials, among others, to discuss the termination of martial law, ending the ban on forming new political parties, and making other reforms in government. In September, in a unilateral (and technically illegal) move, a number of *tangwai* politicians met and announced the formation of the Democratic Progressive Party (DPP). Chiang Ching-kuo ordered the government not to take any legal or administrative actions to block this move because the restriction on forming new parties was going to be lifted.[41]

The newly formed DPP announced a platform that closely resembled that of the *tangwai*, and a slate of candidates campaigned in the December election with a party flag and party slogans. Meanwhile, most *tangwai* members and many independents joined the DPP. The electorate, as well as most observers, viewed the 1986 campaign and election as a two-party contest.

The DPP won support among Taiwanese, workers, city dwellers, the poor, and people who did not like the KMT and/or the government (some say from 10 to 15 percent of the population—that some called the protest vote). Because Taiwanese generally reside more in rural areas where the KMT was well organized and had strong support (stemming from its successful efforts in land reform), building a rural base of support was problematic. A platform to attract workers with its welfare or socialist agenda also failed. For the same reasons, the DPP alienated many Taiwanese businesspeople that might otherwise have provided money and talent for the DPP. The DPP's frequent use of street demonstrations, disruptive tactics, and violence in Legislative Yuan sessions meanwhile hurt its image. These tactics conflicted with the basic Chinese desire for stability.[42]

The DPP, like the *tangwai,* also suffered from factionalism and from fundamental differences in views on some important political questions. One of the most divisive issues was support of Taiwan's independence. Many DPP members supported independence or permanent separation from China, while many considered it premature and/or dangerous. Another controversial matter was the party's relationship with the KMT. Some argued that the DPP had little chance of carrying out its agenda unless it cooperated with the KMT, at least at times. Others regarded the KMT as "the enemy" and found any compromise objectionable. Still another issue was whether to welcome Chinese residents of other countries to return to Taiwan and whether nonresidents of Taiwan should be allowed to vote or run for political office.[43]

The DPP succeeded nonetheless in attracting new members and running well-known, popular, and qualified people for office and winning at the polls. It adopted a host of fresh issues, many of which it promoted successfully between elections and during campaigns, and won broad public support on many of them. In addition, it exploited KMT weaknesses and capitalized on the public's desire for democratization, which translated, it said, into the need for party competition. It also used its underdog status and what some called the Taiwanese feeling of victimhood to win votes. And, last but not least, it learned quickly and became experienced in democratic politics.[44]

The DPP performed well in national elections in 1989 and 1992 as well as in local elections in 1997. (See section on elections below.) After election victories, pundits regularly voiced the opinion that the DPP was the only real opposition party, and some said it would not be long before it was in power. This prediction indeed proved accurate. In 2000, the DPP's candidate, Chen Shui-bian, was elected president. Subsequently, the DPP was designated the "ruling party," even though it controlled only a third of the seats in the Legislative Yuan. In 2001, the DPP became the largest party in the Legislative Yuan, and at that point, the term "ruling party" seemed undeniable.

Interestingly, the DPP is organized in much the same way as the KMT, and for that reason, may also be called a Leninist party. It holds party congresses and its delegates pick a central committee, which then selects a core leadership—just as the KMT does. Its leadership, however, has not been very stable, especially during the several years immediately after its formation. Party leaders said this made the party's decision-making process more democratic. The DPP is a mass party, like the KMT, which it intended to be from the beginning. Thus it has engaged in energetic recruitment efforts (though new members do have to be recommended by current members, and there are some other requirements to attain membership). After Chen Shui-bian was elected president in March 2000, the DPP was much more successful in attracting members.[45]

The DPP, on the other hand, was not the only opposition party to arrive on the political scene during the 1980s and 1990s. Six new political parties appeared in 1987, and several more in 1988. In February 1989, when the formation of new political parties became legal, sixteen parties registered. Leading up to the 1991 election, Taiwan had sixty-seven registered political parties, though only seventeen ran candidates and only two besides the KMT and the DPP supported enough candidates to qualify for television time. Before the 1992 election, there were seventeen political parties, but only fourteen fielded candidates, and only two other than the KMT and the DPP met the requirements for television time.[46] Because it is easy to form a political party in Taiwan, and because typically several parties register and run candidates in election contests, until very recently some observers described Taiwan's party system as a multiparty one.[47] On the other hand, there were few serious contending political parties. There are other reasons—including election laws that favor big parties and the US model, which has an attraction in Taiwan—to believe Taiwan was, in fact, a two-party system or was evolving in that direction.

In 1992, the KMT became badly divided between "mainstream" (pro–Lee Teng-hui) and "non-mainstream" factions (mostly Mainland Chinese who supported Premier Hau Pei-tsun). In 1993, a number of members of the nonmainstream faction left the KMT to form the New China Party, which later changed its name to the New Party (NP). Supporters of the New Party charged that the DPP was a party composed only of ethnic Taiwanese and separatists, or champions of Taiwan's independence. They further complained that the KMT under Lee Teng-hui had moved to the left to co-opt many of the tenets of the DPP and, like the DPP, did not support the reunification of China. Interestingly, many members of the New Party and the nonmainstream faction of the KMT (not all of its members joined the New Party) had been hard-line anti-Communists, but now supported better relations with the People's Republic of China and the idea of "Greater China." The New Party performed well in two elections, but experienced a disaster in the 2001 Legislative Yuan election.

The DPP has experienced similar problems with party splits, though the results have been very different. Perceiving the DPP had "surrendered" to the KMT on the issue of independence, a number of DPP members and some top leaders left the party. The party's 1996 presidential candidate, Peng Min-ming, called the DPP's independence view weak and, after losing the election, he formed the Taiwan Independence Party (or "nation-building party" in Chinese). Some other DPP members and former heads of the party, departed for other reasons, including some that opposed independence, and some formed new parties. This, however, has not fatally hurt the DPP because these parties have had serious problems in recruiting and raising funds and have not performed well in elections. Also, most voters believed the DPP stands for an independent Taiwan, even though it has moderated its stance on this issue.

In 2000, immediately after the presidential election, James Soong formed the People First Party (PFP). Though he had little money and not much grassroots organization, he was able to attract some KMT members into his party, including members of the Legislative Yuan. Being a political star, Soong gave the party broad appeal. Those who questioned whether the PFP would grow and survive called it a "one man" party (meaning it was Soong's personal party). The party performed very well in the 2001 legislative election and was subsequently considered a viable and active party.

During the 2001 Legislative Yuan election campaign, former Interior Minister Huang Chu-wen formed the Taiwan Solidarity Union (TSU) with former president Lee Teng-hui's blessing and backing. Lee was angry about being removed from the chairmanship of the KMT and was upset that the KMT was going in a pro-unification direction under Lien Chan. He also opposed Lien's cooperation with James Soong to block President Chen Shui-bian's legislative agenda. Lee hoped to entice some members of the KMT into the TSU and win over some independents; he found some success in this effort. On the issue of independence, the TSU took a noticeably stronger position than the DPP. The TSU performed well in the election that year, especially for a new party, and was subsequently considered an important political party and a force in Taiwan politics.

After the 2001 election, Taiwan had what many called a "two-bloc" party system. The KMT, PFP, and the New Party jointly opposed the Chen administration, and through their control of the legislature, blocked Chen's policies and set forth their own agenda. Observers called them jointly the "blue team" or "pan-blue." The TSU supported President Chen and the DPP's agenda, and the two were referred to as the "green team" or "pan-green."

Some speculated at the time that pan-green would become the dominant force in Taiwan politics as the KMT had been in the past and that the system was evolving toward a new dominant one-party (or bloc) system. Following the 2004 Legislative Yuan election and subsequent elections, this view was rarely heard. In fact, during 2006 and 2007, when the Chen Administration and the DPP suffered from falling public support due to poor governance and especially from the view the Chen administration and the party were woefully corrupt, this view ceased to be heard. Following big election defeats in January 2008 in the legislative election and in March in the presidential election, many pundits predicted the KMT would be the majority for some time.

After changing the electoral system in 2004, pundits speculated that the two blocs of parties would likely be transformed into two parties as a result of the new voting process that greatly advantaged large parties. In the January 2008 legislative election, the smaller parties and independents fared very poorly, indicating that this view was true. This opinion was heard again in the presidential election that followed. Taiwan's political party system seems now be evolving into a two-party one.

Elections

Elections have played a vital role in Taiwan politics locally since 1950 and nationally since 1980. They were instrumental in bringing about the country's successful political modernization and democratization. They have also assumed great importance in bolstering the political parties, helping formulating policy, and in democratizing the workings of the polity. Thus, grasping how elections have evolved to become a central part of the political process is essential to understanding politics in Taiwan.

Under Japanese rule, but only after 1935, elections were held for some town, county, and prefectural offices. Although these elections were unprecedented, they were of limited significance since the number of officials elected had to be balanced by an equal or larger number of appointed Japanese and elected officials. There was no island-wide election in Taiwan during the Japanese colonial period.

This situation changed little in the years immediately after 1945 because the Nationalist Chinese government was at war with the Communists and considered Taiwan's affairs to be a low priority.[48] On the other hand, after 1949, when the Nationalist government moved to Taiwan—realizing that its failure to implement democracy on the Mainland was an important reason for its defeat by the Communists—the attitude of ruling party leaders changed. In particular, it shifted after the United States extended to Taiwan military protection in 1950, thus affording a secure environment in which to hold elections. That year, local election contests were held for county and city councils and for magistrates and mayors in sixteen counties and five cities. Smaller townships and villages elected councils and village or town chiefs. Voter turnout was high, and the electorate was knowledgeable about the qualifications and the views of candidates.[49]

Since then, local elections have been held regularly. Owing to the nature of Taiwan's political system as noted earlier, many locally elected officials were able to move to higher positions, including top offices in the central government. Voter turnout in local elections was high and has remained so—rarely below 70 percent of eligible voters and, in some elections, above 85 percent. For the most part, qualified individuals ran for office, and the electorate was aware of issues and enthusiastic about the process. In short, local elections made a major contribution to Taiwan's democratization.

In December 1951, an election was held for the Taiwan Provincial Assembly—the first island-wide election ever. However, the Provincial Assembly was not an important organ of government because it was subordinate to the Legislative Yuan and many of its functions overlapped with those of the central government. Nevertheless, it operated democratically and was the locus of considerable political debate. Subsequently, Provincial Assembly elections were held regularly.[50]

There were no meaningful elections at the national level at this time. The stated reason was that the central government represented the population of "all of China," and elections could not be held on the Mainland since it was under Communist control. Government leaders, of course, feared that democratizing too quickly would create political instability. Most government officials also thought that a too-hasty approach was not in keeping with Sun Yat-sen's plan to institute democracy in stages. The government, comprised primarily of Mainland Chinese, was also concerned that democratization done too fast would engender ethnic tensions and would threaten their political power and status.

A competitive national election, to be Taiwan's first, was scheduled for December 1978, but it was canceled when the United States broke diplomatic relations with Taipei. The election was subsequently rescheduled for December 1980. In the meantime, under President Chiang Ching-kuo's leadership, agreements were worked out with *tangwai* leaders, independents, and other opposition politicians so that they could genuinely compete with KMT candidates for parliamentary seats.

Thus, 1980 became a turning point: Taiwan held its first competitive national election. The campaign was the most lively and interesting one to date; in fact, it was more exciting than any subsequent campaign. In a milieu of freedom and openness, opposition candidates said things publicly they had never enunciated before. The public was, to say the least, surprised—flabbergasted or amazed would be better words.[51] Cynics said the election was for show and that such free and open campaigns would not be allowed again. But another open and competitive election was held in 1983 and this skepticism faded. In both of these elections, the KMT performed well against competition it had never seen before. This success gave party leaders confidence.

In December 1986, after *tangwai* politicians organized the Democratic Progressive Party, Taiwan witnessed its first two-party election. Because no Chinese nation had ever had a two-party election contest, this election was another watershed event. Even though it faced formal competition, and despite the doubts of some, the KMT performed well. Opposition politicians, however, said the KMT still controlled the government and the media and enjoyed too many advantages. Others noted that the ruling party had changed and that concessions made to the opposition were meaningful; this meant that the KMT had true support from the electorate.[52]

The Democratic Progressive Party learned from its defeats, and at the same time, the KMT became too self-confident. In the 1989 election, the DPP performed much better than it had in 1986. Major newspapers called the DPP's performance a "victory" and a "breakthrough." Many spoke of Taiwan as now having a true two-party system. DPP leaders, while celebrating the victory, were quick to point out that, because the election was only supplemental and because so many delegates representing the Mainland were still in office, the opposition could not win control of the parliamentary body of government even if it won a majority of the popular vote. Some declared with confidence that if a plenary election were held, the DPP would rule the nation.[53]

Before the 1991 National Assembly election, the "elder parliamentarians" resigned and a non-supplemental, or plenary, election was held. Deploying their superior organizational skills and benefiting from the DPP's unwise strategy of making Taiwan's independence a major issue, and also having learned from an election setback in 1989, the KMT won a big victory on what many said was a "level playing field."[54] The KMT could now claim a popular mandate it had not enjoyed before. Significantly, it won three-fourths of the seats, thus ensuring its ability to amend the Constitution without interference by the opposition. Last but not least, with countries throughout the world tossing out ruling parties in the context of global changes that seemed to make parties in power almost by definition unpopular, the KMT win seemed even more impressive.

However, the KMT did not repeat its stellar performance in what was, in 1992, a more important Legislative Yuan election. DPP candidates learned from their defeat the previous year, and more talented DPP candidates entered this race. (Many had refused to run in the National Assembly election because they had argued that this body of government was superfluous and should be abolished.) Though the KMT won a comfortable majority in seats and the popular vote, it was accustomed to winning by wider margins; the tallies therefore represented gains and a "victory" for the DPP. Its leaders spoke of ruling the country in three to five years.[55]

Subsequent local elections, though, did not see the DPP's upward trend continue. The first election for the governor of Taiwan and the revived elections for the mayors of Taipei and Kaohsiung in late 1994 made for a "split decision." The DPP won the mayorship of Taipei but lost the other two offices, and it performed only marginally better in the Taiwan Provincial Assembly, Taipei City Council, and Kaohsiung City Council contests.[56]

In the 1995 Legislative Yuan election, in the context of charges of corruption that stuck, a weak economy (for Taiwan), and other problems, the KMT performed poorly. However, the DPP's internal difficulties, along with the Beijing government's intimidation (conducting missile tests in the Taiwan Strait during the summer and just before the election threatening to invade Taiwan if it declared independence), minimized the DPP's gains. The New Party, in contrast, more than tripled its seats. After the election, Taiwan heard talk of an evolving three-party system and/or future party coalitions.[57]

In 1996, the Republic of China held its first direct election for its president and vice president. Incumbent President Lee Teng-hui and his vice presidential running mate, Lien Chan, won handily, getting over 54 percent of the popular vote against three other sets of candidates: the Democratic Progressive Party's candidates and two sets of independents (although one set tacitly stood for the New Party). The election was lauded by the Western media and was seen by many observers as a defining event in Taiwan's democratization. Even Taiwan's critics acknowledged that Taiwan was now a genuine democracy. Not only was the election the first of its kind in Chinese history, but it was also held amid threatening missile tests conducted by the Chinese People's Liberation Army. (See Chapter 6 for further details.) The Nationalist Party emerged with a big victory, though the DPP and the NP made marginal gains in the concurrent National Assembly election.[58]

Offsetting this KMT win, the Democratic Progressive Party scored a momentous victory in local elections in November 1997: It captured county and city executive offices that put the main opposition party in a position of running local governments with jurisdiction over more than 70 percent of the population. In subsequent local elections, however, the DPP did not do so well, and in the 1998 Legislative Yuan and metropolitan mayor and city council races, the Nationalist Party won significant victories, including taking back the Taipei mayorship with Ma Ying-jeou defeating incumbent mayor Chen Shui-bian.

Taiwan's second direct presidential election in March 2000 was an earthshaking event. Several months before the voting, the KMT split when President Lee supported his vice president, Lien Chan, to be the party's presidential candidate. Lien was eminently qualified, but former governor James Soong enjoyed higher poll ratings and had strong support in the party. There was hope that Soong might join the ticket, but apparently Lee nixed that. Thus, Soong decided to run on his own as an independent. A few months before the voting, a KMT legislator released documents suggesting that Soong, when he was secretary-general of the party, had diverted party money to his own and relatives' accounts. Lee even called Soong a thief. Although Soong was later exonerated, he had difficulty answering to the charges, and his popularity—which had been double Lien and Chen Shui-bian's in many polls—dropped precipitously. Meanwhile, Chen ran an astute campaign. He played down his pro-independence views while painting the KMT as a corrupt party with ties to criminal elements. Chen convinced voters he could manage the economy and, because of increasing interest in the environment and other issues, the KMT did not find promoting economic growth as good a campaign issue as in the past. With the help of Lee Yuan-tseh, the Nobel Prize winner and head of Academia Sinica, and several important business leaders, Chen peaked just days before the voting. China's Premier Zhu Rongji's warning to Taiwan's voters not to vote for Chen evoked a backlash that also helped him.[59]

Although Chen did not get a majority of the vote and won just over 2 percent more of the popular vote than James Soong, many observers said his election marked the "consolidation" of Taiwan's democracy. The KMT had ruled the country for more than half a century, but now the opposition was in office after a peaceful transition of power. Chen proved an astute leader and was as charismatic as president as he was as a candidate, at least among the Fukien Taiwanese who voted for him (the other ethnic groups did not).

In the subsequent December 2001 Legislative Yuan election, not only did the KMT lose its majority, but the DPP also made big gains and became the largest party in the legislature. Former President Lee's TSU performed fairly well and helped Chen gain a near majority. James Soong's PFP, however, also turned in a stellar performance and, together with the KMT, kept a slim majority for the "blue team." While this election helped President Chen and gave him a better environment in which to govern after the election, it did not reflect a shift in voter preference. Moreover, the DPP's election victory was tainted by ethnic appeals and by the undemocratic practice of voter allocation.[60]

President Chen and Vice President Lu were reelected in the spring of 2004 in a very close election that Chen's critics charged they stole. Chen and Lu were both shot the day before the voting, and President Chen used this as justification for ordering the military and police, who would have voted mostly pan-blue, to stay at their posts. There was also a sympathy vote from pan-green's base. In view of the fact that the polls, gamblers' odds on the election, and the stock market all predicted a pan-blue win, this assessment seems correct.[61]

The DPP, however, lost the next several elections. It lost the legislative election in late 2004 and two subsequent local elections. The KMT won the metropolitan mayoral and city council races in 2006, except for the mayorship of Kaohsiung.[62] The DPP suffered a serious setback in the January 2008 legislative election; the KMT won two-thirds of the seats (controlling three-fourths with party allies). The Chen administration's poor management of the economy and its and the DPP's rampant corruption were the reasons. The KMT's Ma Ying-jeou won the March 2008 presidential election by a large margin—capturing more of the popular vote than any candidate ever. This put the KMT strongly back in power.[63]

Ideology, Modernization, and the Future

To understand Taiwan's politics, it is essential to comprehend its philosophical and ideological underpinnings and how they have evolved. Both have been impacted by the nation's search for a national identity, about which there are conflicting views, and many other core issues that are often the subject of debate. Before looking at these matters, it is necessary to explain where Taiwan came from ideologically and the basic political thinking of its population.

There was historically virtually no systematic "Taiwanese" political philosophy espoused by the local population (other than certain ancient tenets of political philosophy taught by Confucius, Mencius, and others, and some elements of Japanese political philosophy), when the Nationalists moved to Taiwan. Thus their political ideology—Sun Yat-sen's Three People's Principles (nationalism, democracy, and people's livelihood)—were easily transplanted. This process was facilitated by Sun's earlier visits to Taiwan that had given him a following on the island and the fact that people knew about his teachings and writings. Finally, his ideas were not generally at odds with those of the ancient sages (though Sun's philosophy was in some ways antitraditional). On the other hand, ethnic enmity created some reluctance on the part of Taiwanese to accept what they considered a Mainland Chinese ideology.

Sun's Three People's Principles emphasized nation building (because China was traditionally more a culture than a nation), democracy (mass participation in politics to emulate what many—certainly Sun—saw as successful Western democratic systems), and economic development (to make the nation rich and powerful and the people prosperous). Sun, however, taught that democracy would have to develop in stages because the people were not yet trained or ready to accept their responsibilities as citizen-participants. Hence, there would be a period of "political tutelage" before full democracy could be realized. Sun's political ideals provided the KMT with an ideology and a basic blueprint for government, and his teachings and writings were widely propagated in Taiwan after 1945.[64]

Political opposition groups in Taiwan for the most part did not offer alternative ideologies; rather, most embraced Sun's teachings. Some actively promoted them—especially the second and third principles—and argued for some time that the KMT was not trying hard enough to carry out Sun's ideals for democratic government. In particular, the *tangwai* and the DPP called for increased spending for welfare and other programs based on Sun's concept of "people's livelihood."

Sun also advocated the notion of an intimate relationship between economic and political development; indeed, some say he was the first political theorist to see a causal link between the two.[65] He believed that economic growth would spur social change and political modernization and thus lead to democracy. In other words, economic development should precede political change. Most people in Taiwan accepted this premise. In the 1970s and 1980s, however, critics warned that the lag between economic development and political modernization in Taiwan created an explosive or revolutionary situation. But the gap closed, and observers now speak of Taiwan's combined approach to economic and political moderniza- tion as a model. Some have used the term "Taiwan political miracle" to describe this.[66] Clearly, other countries, including China (though not usually openly), have emulated Taiwan's political experience.

In the early days, the KMT promoted anticommunism as one of its core ideo- logical tenets, along with the cause of returning to the Mainland, liberating it from communism, and establishing Sun's teachings and a republican system of government there under Nationalist rule. Taiwan's populace never found commu- nism appealing, but neither were most Taiwanese enthralled with the govern- ment's anti-Communist propaganda. The masses in Taiwan, likewise, never enthusiastically accepted the government's policy of reconquering the Mainland. Most—particularly the young—instead identified with the West when they thought about Taiwan's future. During the 1960s and 1970s, the KMT appeared to be giving up hope of liberating China, even though returning to the Mainland remained its official policy until the 1990s.

Early on, opposition politicians paid lip service to the return to the Mainland policy and the government's anticommunism, or didn't talk about either. More outspoken oppositionists chided the policy of liberating China as being unrealistic and even silly, while labeling it a pretext for the "Chiang clique" to maintain its dic- tatorship and resist democratic reform. Some opposition stalwarts in private advo- cated a Taiwan legally separate from China, but did not express this openly because advocating independence was regarded by the government as treason. Many in- stead called for self-determination and argued that the people of Taiwan should decide Taiwan's future. Thus, although the assumption was that Taiwan should be- come a democracy, there was little debate about its philosophical underpinnings.

The Kuomintang embraced free-market capitalism and free trade as important ideological tenets, though they were not an important part of the party's political lexicon during the early years. Taiwan had a large public-sector (some say socialist) economy until the late 1950s, when the private sector grew in importance. Thus, free-market capitalism evolved under Nationalist rule, and so did free trade. KMT leaders linked free-market capitalism to democracy, while most party members identified with the Western bloc and its political cum economic ideology.

Opposition politicians, though they opposed neither capitalism nor free trade, advocated more welfare, better pay for workers, and what would be described in the West as a liberal agenda. Some DPP leaders called for Taiwan to adopt policies that resembled European social democracy, though this did not become a "DPP ideology." Moreover, because the KMT instituted rather broad social and other welfare programs in the 1980s and 1990s, and because most of the population remained supportive of capitalism and a free market, the opposition's liberal and socialist ideas did not appeal broadly to the populace. Opposition leaders pushed environmental protection, but so did the KMT. Opposition politicians advocated unemployment insurance and national health care, and the KMT adopted these policies in large measure. The government and the opposition advocated similar policies regarding such problems as traffic, public transportation, land use, water control, and crime. Some opposition politicians appealed to ethnic identity (namely Taiwanese) and class issues (pushing causes of the poor) during election campaigns. Though ethnicity and economic status were important influences on voting, these appeals were only at times effective.[67]

The ideological gap between the KMT and the opposition began to narrow in the 1970s. This was especially noticeable as both tried to appeal to a bigger segment of the voting population. The *tangwai* also became more moderate as it participated seriously in elections. From its inception in 1986, the DPP took pragmatic positions on many issues that public opinion polls showed to be concerns among the electorate. It gradually abandoned its more radical positions as its candidates won office and had to make policy decisions and manage government offices and programs. The DPP's "ideology" (if one can call it that) focused mainly on rapid democratization and other political reform and the idea of a Taiwanese consciousness. Hence, many observers said the basic philosophical principle of the KMT and the DPP, as well as the PFP and the TSU, was pragmatism.[68]

In power after 2000, the Democratic Progressive Party made no serious effort to develop a new political philosophy or ideology for Taiwan. Sun's teachings and other tenets of the KMT's ideology were played down and sometimes criticized, and, some might say, they were even discarded. But nothing was substituted for them. For a time, President Chen's adulation of British sociologist Anthony Gidden's "third way"—which offers a moderate leftist perspective but is supportive of global capitalism—seemed like an effort to construct an ideology. But it never developed into anything more than a few headlines.[69] Some DPP leaders referred to their party as a liberal party, some even making comparisons with the Democratic Party in the United States. The problem with this was that the DPP took an aggressive stance on Taiwan's independence that often provoked China, and because of this, needed military support from the United States; but the US Republican Party favored using military force to defend Taiwan much more than the Democratic Party.

The blue and green blocs differed, and still do, on the issue of Taiwan's national identity (whether Taiwan is part of China) and whether Taiwan's history, culture, etc. should be more locally focused, and this may be said to constitute a philosophical divide. Pan-green favored localization. The blue camp advocated more links with China and favored the idea of "Greater China." Yet both sides generally saw independence versus unification as a future problem more than an issue to be immediately resolved. The two camps espoused other differences concerning foreign policy, Asian democracy versus Western democracy, taxes, welfare, and a number of other issues. But these differences in view can hardly be called ideological, and it has been noted that both parties have implemented policies that were not "ideologically based." One might conclude that Taiwan's political culture and the pragmatism of its people preclude the success of any ideology.

When Ma Ying-jeou was elected president in March 2008, there appeared to be a revival of the KMT's political ideas, but Ma has exhibited little concern over ideology and has rather shown that his is pragmatic.

Notes

1. For a discussion of China's political culture, see June Teufel Dreyer, *China's Political System: Modernization and Transformation* (Boston: Allyn and Bacon, 1996), chapter 2; Kenneth Lieberthal, *Governing China: From Revolution Through Reform* (New York: W. W. Norton, 1995), chapter 1; James R. Townsend and Brantley Womack, *Politics in China* (Boston: Little, Brown and Company, 1986), chapters 1 and 2; James C. F. Wang, *Contemporary Chinese Politics: An Introduction* (Upper Saddle River, NJ: Prentice-Hall, 1999), chapter 1.

2. See Karl Wittfogel, *Oriental Despotism: A Comparative Study of Total Power* (New Haven: Yale University Press, 1957).

3. Little has been written in detail on the subject of Taiwan's political culture. For some discussion on this topic, see *Area Handbook for the Republic of China* (Washington, D.C.: US Government Printing Office, 1982), chapter 16; Christopher Hughes, *Taiwan and Chinese Nationalism: National Identity and Status in International Society* (London: Routledge, 1997), chapter 1; Gary Klintworth, *New Taiwan, New China: Taiwan's Changing Role in the Asia-Pacific Region* (New York: St. Martin's Press, 1995), chapter 1; Alan M. Wachman, *Taiwan: National Identity and Democratization* (Armonk, NY: M. E. Sharpe, 1994), chapter 1.

4. For details, see John F. Copper, with George P. Chen, *Taiwan's Elections: Political Development and Democratization in the Republic of China* (Baltimore: University of Maryland School of Law, 1984), chapter 2.

5. For details, see A. James Gregor, with Maria Hsia Chang and Andrew B. Zimmerman, *Ideology and Development: Sun Yat-sen and the Economic History of Taiwan* (Berkeley: University of California Center for Chinese Studies, 1981).

6. See Lucian W. Pye, *Asian Power and Politics: The Cultural Dimensions of Authority* (Cambridge: Harvard University Press, 1985), 228–236.

7. For details on Taiwan's constitution, see Zhao Suisheng, *Power by Design: Constitution-Making in Nationalist China* (Honolulu: University of Hawaii Press, 1996).

8. For details, see Ray S. Cline and Hungdah Chiu, eds., *The United States Constitution and Constitutionalism in China* (Washington, D.C.: US Global Strategy Council, 1988).

9. For details, see John F. Copper, *A Quiet Revolution: Political Development in the Republic of China* (Lanham, MD: University Press of America, 1988), chapter 2.

10. Amnesty International ranks Taiwan one (the highest possible rating in political rights) and two in civil liberties—the same rating as France, Germany, Italy, and Japan. It is

called a "free" nation. China is ranked seven (the lowest number possible in the two categories) and is labeled "not free." The US Department of State and several other organizations paint a similar picture (see www.worldaudit.org for further details).

11. In allocating seats in the elected bodies of government for women if they are not elected, the Republic of China's Constitution is unique.

12. Yeong-kuang Ger, *The Story of Taiwan: Politics* (Taipei: Government Information Office, 1998), 45–48.

13. Yun-han Chu, "Democratic Consolidation in the Post-KMT Era: The Challenge of Governance," in Muthiah Alagappa, ed., *Taiwan's Presidential Politics: Democratization and Cross-Strait Relations in the Twenty-First Century* (Armonk, NY: M. E. Sharpe, 2001), 100.

14. *Taiwan Yearbook 2006*, 68–69.

15. Jaushieh Joseph Wu, *Taiwan's Democratization: Forces Behind the New Momentum* (Hong Kong: Oxford University Press, 1995), 129–132.

16. *Taiwan Yearbook 2007*, 66.

17. See *The Republic of China 1994 Yearbook* (Taipei: Government Information Office, 1994), 101–102.

18. For the background of this situation, see Harvey J. Feldman, ed., *Constitutional Reform and the Future of the Republic of China* (Armonk, NY: M. E. Sharpe, 1991).

19. Polls have been taken periodically by the Research, Development, and Evaluation Commission on this issue and confirm this observation.

20. See John F. Copper, "Taiwan in Gridlock," in John F. Copper, ed., *Taiwan in Troubled Times: Essays on the Chen Shui-bian Presidency* (Singapore: World Scientific, 2002).

21. See Steve Chan, "Taiwan in 2005: Strategic Interaction in Two-Level Games," *Asian Survey* (January–February 2006): 67.

22. For background on Taiwan's judicial and legal system, see Hungdah Chiu, "Legal Development in the Republic of China, 1949–1981," in Hungdah Chiu and Shao-chuan Leng, eds., *China: Seventy Years After the 1911 Hsia-Hai Revolution* (Charlottesville: University of Virginia Press, 1984), 287–331.

23. This is also the practice in some other democracies, such as France.

24. Brian Kennedy, "Modified Adversarial System Proposed," *Taipei Journal*, November 30, 2001, 6. Also see Brian Kennedy, "Rules for Judicial Selection, Discipline Will Bring Needed Quality to the Bench," *Taipei Journal*, April 12, 2002, 6.

25. See John F. Copper, *Taiwan's 2006 Metropolitan Mayoral and City Council Elections and the Politics of Corruption* (Baltimore: University of Maryland School of Law, 2006), 28–34. For details on problems in the judiciary, see Brian Kennedy and Elizabeth Guo, "The Verdict on Judicial Reforms," *Topics*, October 2006, 21–28.

26. See Hung-mao Tien, *The Great Transition: Political and Social Change in the Republic of China* (Stanford: Hoover Institution Press, 1989), 152–153, regarding the decline in cases heard by the Control Yuan.

27. "'Defunct' Control Yuan," *China Post*, February 20, 2008 (online at chianpost.com.tw).

28. Much less has been written on local government in Taiwan than on other aspects of its politics. For a brief discussion of the topic, see *Area Handbook for the Republic of China*, 188–190, and Tien, *The Great Transition*, 128–132. The workings of local government and various changes made are described in various editions of *The Republic of China Yearbook*.

29. See Tien, *The Great Transition*, 131.

30. The population of these two cities is about one-fifth of the nation's population. The two mayors are members of the Executive Yuan. A host of other reasons can be cited for the importance of these metropolitan governments.

31. For a thorough, though now somewhat outdated, study on the Provincial Assembly, see Arthur J. Lerman, *Taiwan's Politics: The Provincial Assemblyman's World* (Washington, D.C.: University Press of America, 1973).

32. Yung-mao Chao and Michael Y. M. Kau, "Local Government and Political Development in Taiwan," *In Depth* (Winter 1993): 17.

33. See Copper, with Chen, *Taiwan's Elections*, 40–46.

34. For background and details on the history and organization of the Nationalist Party and its rule of Taiwan, see Peter R. Moody, Jr., *Political Change in Taiwan: A Study of Ruling Party Adaptability* (New York: Praeger, 1992), and Stephen J. Hood, *The Kuomintang and the Democratization of Taiwan* (Boulder, CO: Westview Press, 1977).

35. *The Republic of China 1998 Yearbook* (Taipei: Government Information Office, 1998), 109.

36. For details, see John F. Copper, "The KMT's 13th Party Congress: Reform, Democratization, New Blood," in Cynthia Chenault, ed., *Modernizing East Asia: Economic and Cultural Dimensions of Political Change* (New York: St. John's University Press, 1989); John F. Copper, "The KMT's 14th Party Congress: Toward Unity or Disunity?" *Journal of Chinese Studies* (October 1994); and John F. Copper, *The KMT's 15th Party Congress: The Ruling Party at a Crossroads* (Baltimore: University of Maryland School of Law, 1997).

37. See Julian Baum, "The Money Machine," *Far Eastern Economic Review*, August 11, 1994, 62–64.

38. For further details, see Edwin A. Winckler and Susan Greenhalgh, eds., *Contending Approaches to the Political Economy of Taiwan* (Armonk, NY: M. E. Sharpe, 1988).

39. See Tien, *The Great Transition*, 90.

40. See Copper, with Chen, *Taiwan's Elections*, chapter 5.

41. Shelley Rigger, *Politics in Taiwan* (London: Routledge, 1999), 126.

42. For details, see Jaushieh Joseph Wu, *Taiwan's Democratization: Forces Behind the New Momentum* (Hong Kong: Oxford University Press, 1995), especially chapter 4.

43. See Alexander Ya-li Lu, "Political Opposition in Taiwan: The Development of the Democratic Progressive Party," in Tun-jen Cheng and Stephen Haggard, eds., *Political Change in Taiwan* (Boulder, CO: Lynne Rienner, 1992). The DPP currently has a membership of around 400,000, compared to the KMT's nearly 1 million.

44. See Shelley Rigger, *From Opposition to Power: Taiwan's Democratic Progressive Party* (Boulder, CO: Lynne Rienner, 2001).

45. See Rigger, *From Opposition to Power*, 61–66.

46. See John F. Copper, "The Role of Minor Parties in Taiwan," *World Affairs* (Winter 1993).

47. John F. Copper, "The Evolution of Political Parties in Taiwan," *Asian Affairs* (Spring 1989).

48. See Copper, with Chen, *Taiwan's Elections*, chapter 4.

49. Ibid.

50. Ibid.

51. Fifteen were added to the National Assembly, eleven to the Legislative Yuan, and two to the Control Yuan. For further details, see ibid., 50, and chapter 5.

52. See John F. Copper, *Taiwan's Recent Elections: Fulfilling the Democratic Promise* (Baltimore: University of Maryland School of Law, 1990), chapter 3.

53. Ibid., chapter 4.

54. John F. Copper, *Taiwan's 1991 and 1992 Non-Supplemental Elections: Reaching a Higher State of Democracy* (Lanham, MD: University Press of America, 1994), chapter 2.

55. Ibid., chapter 3.

56. John F. Copper, *Taiwan's Mid-1990s Elections: Taking the Final Steps to Democracy* (Westport, CT: Praeger, 1998), chapter 2.

57. Ibid., chapter 3.

58. Ibid., chapter 4.

59. John F. Copper, *Taiwan's 2000 Presidential and Vice Presidential Election: Consolidating Democracy and Creating a New Era of Politics* (Baltimore: University of Maryland School of Law, 2000).

60. See John F. Copper, *Taiwan's 2001 Legislative, Magistrates and Mayors Election: Further Consolidating Democracy* (Singapore: World Scientific/Singapore University Press, 2002).

61. *Taiwan's 2004 Presidential and Vice Presidential Election: Democracy's Consolidation or Devolution* (Baltimore: University of Maryland School of Law, 2004).

62. John F. Copper, *Taiwan's 2006 Metropolitan Mayoral and City Council Elections and the Politics of Corruption* (Baltimore: University of Maryland School of Law, 2006).

63. John F. Copper, *Taiwan's 2008 Presidential and Vice Presidential Election: Maturing Democracy* (Baltimore: University of Maryland School of Law, 2008).

64. See Paul M. A. Linebarger, *The Political Doctrines of Sun Yat-sen* (Westport, CT: Hyperion Press, 1973).

65. See Gregor, with Chang and Zimmerman, *Ideology and Development,* chapter 1.

66. This writer has used this term. See John F. Copper, *The Taiwan Political Miracle: Essays on Political Development, Elections and Foreign Relations* (Lanham, MD: University Press of America, 1997).

67. Although more Taiwanese than Mainland Chinese support the DPP, in all national elections in Taiwan, the KMT has won more than half the Taiwanese vote.

68. See Wachman, *Taiwan: National Identity and Democratization,* 65–68.

69. Su Lin Chieh-yu, "Chen Greets the British Sociologist Who Inspired His Election Success," *Taipei Times,* April 16, 2002 (online at www.taipeitimes.com).

A farmer drying rice in a courtyard.

Rice-harvesting time. Machines relieve backbreaking work.

Fourth- and fifth-grade students on a field day.

The computer is Taiwan's key to future economic growth and is an important tool in education.

Nuclear plants provide a large portion of Taiwan's electricity but nuclear power is controversial.

Soldier guarding Taiwan's outpost on Quemoy.

In Taiwan, athletic shoes of every kind and style are produced mostly for export.

The textile industry in Taiwan is large but its importance is declining.

A tollgate on an expressway. Such highways link all of Taiwan's major cities.

Commuting to work.

Religion and scenic vistas meet in Taiwan.

Central Taipei—the heart of a modern city.

The Presidential Palace during Nationalist China's celebration of Double-Ten Day (October 10), similar to July 4 in the United States. On October 10, 1911, Sun Yat-sen's supporters overthrew the Manchu dynasty.

Minority groups in native dress.

The Peking Opera is popular in Taiwan, where the government tries to preserve Chinese culture.

Buddhist ceremony at the Temple of Guanyin.

The Presidential Palace in downtown Taipai—built by the Japanese.

Hsinchu Science Park—Taiwan's Silicon Valley.

President Ma Ying-jeou.

Vice President Vincent Siew.

Photos courtesy of the Government Information Office of the Republic of China (Taiwan).

5

THE ECONOMY

IN ITS RECENT HISTORY, Taiwan experienced several periods of economic boom and decline. Several centuries ago, Taiwan was for a time a center of trade and commerce in East Asia. Then this ended. In the late 1800s, as a part of China, for a brief time, Taiwan witnessed impressive economic progress. Under Japanese control from 1895 to 1945, Taiwan thrived economically, surpassing by most standards all of East Asia except for Japan. Immediately after World War II, Taiwan's economy deteriorated. In the 1950s, and even into the 1960s, Taiwan did not appear to have good prospects for economic development. Predictions at that time were pessimistic because of the island's lack of resources, an unfavorable land-to-population ratio, a shortage of capital, and a discredited political leadership. Some even called Taiwan a "basket case"—meaning that it had little or no hope of developing economically. In the mid-1960s, however, Taiwan's economy took off and its rapid growth soon became the envy of the world. Many used the term "miracle" to describe Taiwan's economic success. Its economic boom engendered vast social and political change, producing a large middle class, consumerism, Westernization, democratization, and more. It also created a huge economic gulf between the island and China, dampening the desire on the part of its political leadership, not to mention its citizens, for uniting with China. In the 1990s, growth slowed, the economy having matured; but Taiwan continued to do well economically—even through the so-called Asian economic meltdown in 1997. In 2001, Taiwan experienced a severe recession caused partly by the US and global economic slowdown and partly by political gridlock as well as President Chen and his administration's poor economic management. Subsequently, Taiwan's economic performance improved, but was still viewed by most citizens as mediocre or less when compared to the other "Asian dragons" (South Korea, Hong Kong, and Singapore) or China—which are the benchmarks for most people in Taiwan. China's booming economy attracted Taiwan's investment and entrepreneurs and changed a significant portion of the population's view about China, making it now an attractive partner for Taiwan commercially. With the portion of Taiwan's exports to the United States and Japan declining and exports to China increasing fast, many even perceived that links with China were the only way for Taiwan's economy to grow and remain dynamic.

The Economy to 1950

Centuries ago, although Taiwan's economy was defined as one in a primitive state of development, the Aborigines engaged in commerce with other areas in the region, and Taiwan was more prosperous than most of East Asia. By the 1500s, however, Taiwan's external trade had all but disappeared, and, at the time of meaningful Chinese immigration to the island, the economic activities of the Aborigines were generally limited to hunting, fishing, berry picking, and some farming. The mountain Aborigines mainly engaged in the former three pursuits, while the lowland Aborigines cultivated some of the level land on the island. Taiwan subsequently became the base of operations for Chinese and Japanese pirates who engaged in various forms of trade in the area before and during the time of the arrival of the Europeans.[1]

In the seventeenth century, the Dutch introduced oxen and farm implements to the island, created a cash economy, and launched modern forms of commerce and trade. The Dutch East India Company, which managed the economy, promoted the exports of rice, sugar, and deerskins, and imports of silk, porcelain, and other goods from China for re-export. The Company also encouraged the immigration of Chinese, who came in large numbers. They revolutionized farming by bringing new crops as well as the more advanced cultivation and irrigation techniques used in South China.

Under Chinese rule from the late 1600s to 1895, Taiwan's economy experienced some economic modernization. Owing to an increase in the Chinese population of the island, agricultural production expanded markedly as the land under cultivation grew from a very small area to nearly all the island's flatlands. Trade also increased, and significant quantities of rice and sugar were shipped to China. The mining of coal and other minerals also became a part of the economy—coal primarily because it was exported and because Taiwan became a coaling station for steamship traffic in the region in the nineteenth century. Still, the island's economy was largely agricultural. Improvements in the economic infrastructure and the growth of business enterprises saw only modest progress.

In the late 1800s, significantly more economic advances were made as a result of Peking's appointing better governors, who adopted new policies to improve the economy of the island. As noted in Chapter 2, the best was Liu Ming-ch'uan, whom Peking made governor of Fukien Province (of which Taiwan was a part) in 1884. Liu, a close friend of China's modernizer, Li Hung-chang, was given a mandate to extend to Taiwan the "self-strengthening" movement popular in China at this time so as to improve economic conditions there. The island at this time lacked modern transportation and communications facilities, and its industries were few and mostly small and inefficient. Education was poor and not standardized. Finally, wealthy families controlled the economy and resisted being displaced from their inherited rights.[2]

Liu moved the capital from Taiwan City in the south to Taipei and renamed the former Tainan. Liu expanded telegraph lines, built by a former governor, and oversaw the construction of harbors and railroads. He conducted an extensive land survey and improved the island's transportation system. Liu also adopted specific policies to improve the production of camphor, which quickly became a major export product. He then made tea production a priority. Rice and sugar production were increased. Liu built new harbors, opened new mines, and modernized existing ones. In a few years, he transformed Taiwan from one of China's most backward provinces into an advanced one. Although much of what Liu did, particularly at first, was aimed at strengthening Taiwan militarily in order to fend off foreign encroachments, his efforts had a positive effect on the economy overall.

But Liu's efforts were short-lived. Because the powerful families in Taiwan felt threatened by Liu's modernization efforts, they used various means to undercut him. Liu then contracted malaria. Finally, his support in Peking waned. As a result, in 1891, Liu left Taiwan without accomplishing nearly all he had hoped for. Moreover, most of Liu's economic improvements would have had little lasting effect had Taiwan not soon become part of the Japanese empire. Many projects had to be completed later by the Japanese.[3]

While Taiwan experienced impressive economic progress before the Japanese colonized the island, its economic structure remained quite similar in many ways to that of the provinces of coastal southern China in 1895. There were vast discrepancies in income and wealth, and most people were poor. Yet Taiwan differed economically from China in some significant ways. Taiwan did not have a history of frequent famine caused by floods and crop failures. Fishing provided a more important food source than it did in China, especially inland China. Crop yields were better than China's because of Taiwan's richer volcanic soil and its heavier and more even rainfall. The island's economy was also much more heavily involved in trade. Finally, capitalism, which was brought to Taiwan earlier by the European colonial powers, was more in evidence.

Serious economic modernization in Taiwan began early in the twentieth century, shortly after the island became a Japanese colony. Important progress in four areas laid the foundation for Taiwan's later growth: (1) the building of an economic infrastructure, including roads, railroads, port facilities, and electrification; (2) the establishment of local industries (such as food processing) and an export-oriented economy; (3) the organization and training of the labor force; and (4) the opening of banking and other economic institutions.

Japan's colonial leaders concentrated first on agriculture. Tokyo provided capital investment, technology, and management skills and also established farmers' associations. Crops were improved by the introduction of new farming techniques, irrigation, and fertilizers. Rice and sugar were given the highest priority, and both were shipped to Japan in significant quantities. From 1910 until World War II, agriculture spearheaded Taiwan's economic development, and economic productivity overall exceeded population growth by about threefold. Agriculture also made a major contribution to capital formation throughout this period and aided the subsequent growth of other sectors of the economy.[4]

A decade or so later, Japan started building factories in Taiwan in significant numbers, marking the beginning of Taiwan's industrial revolution. The decline of European trade during World War I and Japanese policies aimed at making Taiwan's economy more industrial, along with the infusion of large amounts of Japanese capital into the island's economy, contributed to the process. World War II, which started in Asia in the 1930s, further stimulated Taiwan's industrialization and contributed to even faster economic growth.

Japan's management of Taiwan's economy during the fifty years before the end of World War II contributed immensely to its economic development and growth, but the island and its population were also exploited. Although the Chinese population's standard of living saw unprecedented increases, it lagged far behind rises in productivity and economic growth. As evidence of its colonial status, Taiwan exported considerably more to Japan than it imported.[5]

Before and during World War II, Japan used Taiwan as a base of operations and invested in industries there, including some heavy industry. Taiwan's economy thus thrived. Because US bombing during the war was generally restricted to military targets and oil storage depots, Taiwan sustained less damage to its economy than other parts of the Japanese empire, or even other Japanese-controlled areas of some East Asian countries. Meanwhile, Japan and China suffered considerable war damage. Hence, Taiwan was in much better shape economically when the war ended than either Japan or China.

From 1945 to 1949, however, Taiwan's economy suffered from several severe shocks and from general mismanagement. The first was caused by the sudden withdrawal of Japanese administrators and businesses. Lack of attention to the economy by the Nationalist Chinese government in the immediate postwar period made the situation worse. Then, ruinous economic policies resulting from Nationalist leaders' preoccupation with the war against the Communists on the Mainland caused even more serious economic harm. Finally, Ch'en Yi's efforts to create a state-managed socialist economy on the island were disastrous. In short, for several years after World War II, Taiwan suffered economically almost as if it were a country at war.

Economic activity declined precipitously during this period, as measured by the output of nearly all goods and services. By 1946, just a year after Taiwan was turned over to Nationalist China, economic production had fallen to less than half of what it had been.[6] Subsequently, the economy declined even further. Many consumer products became scarce or unaffordable. Poverty and disease followed. The education system and public services deteriorated commensurately. Because China's monetary system was used in Taiwan, inflation decimated many commercial enterprises. In a period of just one year (from November 1945 to the beginning of 1947), the price of food rose 700 percent, fuel and construction materials 1,400 percent, and fertilizer 25,000 percent.[7] In short, Taiwan's economy was severely traumatized by the Nationalist government's policies—or, in many cases, a lack of them—and its bad economic oversight.

An additional economic shock came in 1949 in the form of approximately 1.5 million Chinese immigrants arriving from the Mainland. This influx of people caused severe dislocations in housing, employment, and the already heavily taxed infrastructure. On top of this, preparations to defend the island against an invasion from the Mainland diverted precious resources that might have been used to revive the economy. As a result, at this time most citizens in Taiwan, as well as Western observers, were extremely pessimistic about Taiwan's economic future.

Economic Recovery and Boom: 1950–2000

In the 1950s, Taiwan's economy began to recover. At the onset of the Korean War and a consequent shift in US policy favoring Chiang Kai-shek and his government, the US Navy provided Taiwan a secure environment for economic planning. US economic and military aid helped Taipei make up for a serious foreign exchange shortfall and allowed it to divert funds from defense spending to economic rebuilding. The huge pool of administrative and other human talent that came from China in 1949 with Chiang Kai-shek and also the desire of the population for economic growth coincided with the implementation of good economic development ideas.

Because of concern over feeding Taiwan's rapidly growing population and the realization that peasant support had been a major factor in the Communists' success on the Mainland, economic planners in Taipei decided to focus first on the agricultural sector, a choice that comported with advice they received from US aid personnel. It turned out to be a very wise decision.

Land reform was the first important measure taken to foster growth in the agricultural sector.[8] It was carried out in three stages: (1) rent reduction in 1949 (from around 50 percent to 37.5 percent of the main crop); (2) the sale of public lands in 1951 to tenant farmers at 2.5 times the value of one year's crop (resulting in 96,000 hectares of public land going to 156,000 tenant farm families); and (3) the "land-to-the-tiller" program, which forced landlords to sell land they did not farm themselves, except for 2.1 hectares of paddy field and double that amount for dry land.

The Joint Commission on Rural Reconstruction (JCRR), composed of two US and three Chinese commissioners, planned and carried out these decisions. After land reform was completed, the JCRR created farmers' associations, initiated a government program to exchange fertilizer for rice, and sponsored other activities that helped farmers. Nearly all the commission's efforts were successful—so much so that Taiwan's land reform program is emulated today by economists in developing countries.

Individual initiative and hard work on the part of the farmers, who could now realize profits from their efforts, and also flexible government planning that encouraged the planting of new crops and innovative farming techniques were critical to increasing agricultural productivity. Taiwan's agricultural sector also responded to markets abroad. In the early 1950s, when Japan lifted restrictions on banana imports, Taiwan's farmers doubled their yield in two years and took most of the Japanese market. Farmers began asparagus cultivation and canning in 1954, increasing production almost one hundredfold in the next fifteen years. Mushroom growing and canning became major enterprises in the 1960s. By 1971, asparagus and mushroom exports had earned US$82 million in foreign exchange.[9]

Taiwan's average annual real growth rate in agricultural production during the 1950s was an impressive 14 percent. But by the 1960s, farming had nearly reached its full potential. Growth in the agricultural sector of the economy dropped to 4.5 percent annually at this time. Forestry was the slowest, while livestock, fish raising, and fruit production surpassed the average. Expansion of the agricultural sector overall was around 3 percent in the 1970s and 2 percent from the mid-1980s to the early 1990s.[10]

In short, although agriculture's contribution to Taiwan's economic development occurred mainly in the early years, it was a significant contribution. During the 1950s and early 1960s, agricultural exports supplied half the nation's foreign exchange earnings. Taxes collected from rural Taiwan, farmers' savings (40 percent of capital formation in the 1950s), and their purchases of goods from Taiwan's fledgling factories greatly facilitated Taiwan's industrialization. Even more important, rural Taiwan, because of rapid increases in agricultural productivity, was able to supply nearly half the new labor in nonagricultural production from the 1950s to the 1970s. Meanwhile, by the mid-1960s, Taiwan's farmers had provided the population a level of food consumption superior to that of any country in Asia except Japan; in caloric content, Taiwan even eclipsed Japan a few years later.

Though farmers continued to enjoy an improved standard of living, they suffered from relatively declining incomes—down to about 70 percent of nonfarm income by 1992. Farmers' buying power fell, and, in turn, agricultural work became less attractive. In addition, soaring labor and land prices, an aging workforce, foreign competition, and environmentalism beset farming. The result was that the agricultural sector's contribution to the nation's gross national product (GNP) fell from over 32 percent in 1952 to just 1.7 percent in 2000, while the farm population has fallen from more than one-third of the total population to 15 percent during the period from 1975 to 2005.[11] Taiwan joining the World Trade Organization in January 2002 had a further negative impact on agriculture in Taiwan, forcing the country to cut tariffs on food products that had protected farmers.[12]

Meanwhile, Taiwan's farmers began to adjust to a changing economic situation by reducing the production of some crops and increasing others. Production of sugar, sweet potatoes, rice, and other grains was cut; production of soybeans, tea, fruits, and vegetables was expanded. Hog and chicken raising increased. When fishing was affected by fewer catches in proximate waters, fishermen shifted to other endeavors: deep-sea fishing (farther and farther away from Taiwan's shore), marine aquaculture, and on-land fish farming. Recently, Taiwan's farmers have increased the production of flowers, fruits, tea, and aquaculture.

Farmers also became more politically active: In 1988, they engaged in a mass street demonstration to draw the government's attention to their plight.[13] In response, the government rezoned farmland so that it could be sold for other uses. This decision pleased many farmers, but did not help agriculture overall. The government helped farmers mechanize and diversify, but this had limited effect. Because of participation in international agreements on free trade and, in particular, joining the World Trade Organization, the government cannot subsidize agriculture (except to help it adjust to different situations). Thus the future of agriculture in Taiwan is not promising. The latest statistics on agricultural imports and exports show that Taiwan imported US$9 billion worth of farm products while it exported just over US$3 billion.[14]

After the late 1950s, industry was the engine driving Taiwan's economic growth. In the late 1950s, annual growth in the industrial sector of the economy was around 12 percent; it exceeded 17 percent during the 1960s, and rose even faster in the 1970s. Factories, especially around Taiwan's cities, proliferated so rapidly that, by 1977, the industrial index had increased more than twenty-eight times the level in 1950. In fact, Taiwan's industrial sector grew at a rate seldom equaled anywhere in history.[15] Comparisons with other countries are instructive: During the 1960s and early 1970s, industry's share of Taiwan's gross national product grew by 18 percent, double the pace of Britain and Japan during their industrial takeoff. Even compared to other booming East Asian countries, Taiwan's industrialization was considerably faster. As a result, Taiwan was more industrialized by the mid-1970s than any other country in Asia except Japan.[16]

What accounted for this lighting pace of industrialization? The key factors were: (1) the expansion of industrial employment; (2) increases in labor productivity; (3) US economic assistance; (4) privatization; (5) a high rate of local savings and considerable foreign investment; (6) a solid economic infrastructure, including transportation and port facilities; and (7) excellent planning by the government and the business community. The contribution of each needs some elaboration.

The industrial labor force in Taiwan grew from virtually nothing in 1950 to 850,000 by the mid-1960s and to more than 2 million by the mid-1970s. The increases were especially large in manufacturing and construction. Taiwan's rapid population growth and the movement of workers out of the agricultural sector owing to mechanization and other increases in farming efficiency were the main reasons for the large numbers of new entrants into the industrial labor force. From 1952 to 1968, workers employed in industry increased from 16.9 percent to 41.5 percent of the total workforce.[17]

Labor productivity in industry, though not initially high, began to increase rapidly in the early 1950s and continued to rise sharply thereafter. Initially, Taiwan's industrial sector benefited from a low cost of labor, a relatively high level of skills and education among workers (particularly compared to labor costs), and a strong work ethic. Later, rising labor productivity came from the efficient organization of labor, laborsaving devices, and the rapid capitalization of production.

In the early years, US economic aid and advice were as important to Taiwan's industrial progress as they were to its agricultural growth. From 1951 to 1964, the United States injected nearly US$100 million annually into Taiwan's economy, capital critically needed to build Taiwan's new factories. As a matter of record, from the early 1950s to 1960, US aid provided 40 percent of Taiwan's capital formation, most of it helping the industrial sector. Few underdeveloped nations at that time or since have benefited as much from economic growth generated by foreign aid. Although US help ended in 1964, it had by then stimulated Taiwan's industrial progress enough that the island's economy was able to sustain its rapid growth. In short, Taiwan's economy had "taken off." Taiwan later was applauded for being the only country in the world to experience increasing economic growth after the termination of US aid.[18]

Privatization also spurred Taiwan's industrial growth. In 1945, the government assumed management over most of the large manufacturing enterprises left by the

Japanese. It also created or kept in place (those it had created on the Mainland) government monopolies to provide sources of needed tax revenues. Top government leaders at that time believed that large industries must be government-owned because of their size and importance to the economy and for reasons relating to national security. In 1954, only 43.4 percent of industrial production was privately owned. Subsequently, government economic planners changed their view, and the government sold many public enterprises. By the early 1960s, industrial production in the private sector was over 50 percent and growing fast. It reached 80 percent by 1972, and nearly 90 percent by the mid-1980s.[19] Subsequently, even compared with the other successful capitalist, free-market countries in Asia, a larger portion of Taiwan's enterprises were privately owned—due both to government privatization and the proliferation of small family-owned businesses, a hallmark of Taiwan's economy.[20]

A high rate of domestic savings and large inputs of foreign investment also helped Taiwan's economic development. During the 1950s and 1960s, growth in the agricultural sector and US economic assistance were the primary sources of capital accumulation. In the mid-1950s, new investment laws made it possible for foreign firms to import plants and equipment and sell their products in the domestic market to make profits and generate additional capital. Tax incentives were added in 1959 to attract foreign capital. Special laws were passed that included a maximum tax rate of 18 percent and a tax-exempt "holiday" lasting as long as five years for some new investors. In the mid-1960s, export processing zones (EPZ)—a Taiwan invention according to some economic historians—were established, giving foreign companies special set-aside zones to build factories where they enjoyed free-port status for imports and exports, relief from government red tape, and access to good harbors. Taiwan's EPZ's were considered extremely successful because they attracted foreign companies that invested and created jobs while also training workers and upgrading labor skills. Interestingly, the People's Republic of China later copied this concept.

These policies resulted in a marked increase in foreign capital input in Taiwan: from a total of US$20 million from 1952 to 1959 to more than US$950 million between 1966 and 1973. Amazingly, foreign investment in Taiwan's economy increased by almost fifty fold during the 1960s and the early 1970s. Most of it came from the United States, Japan, and Overseas Chinese (especially from Southeast Asia); most was private investment. By the mid-1980s, Taiwan was absorbing more than US$500 million in foreign capital annually.[21] Meanwhile, by the 1970s, the rate of individual and company savings had risen rapidly—to about 25 percent annually—providing further funds for investment. Personal savings were also increasing. In 1987, individual savings stood at 40 percent—the highest of any nation in the world. The main reasons for this high rate of savings were favorable interest rates, individual frugality, and optimism about future economic growth.[22]

Taiwan's high savings rate was a boon to economic growth at a critical time. However, in the 1990s, the rate of savings in Taiwan fell to the high 20 percent range for private savings and company investment. The main reason for the decline was that Taiwan now had a capital surplus. Also, because of high labor costs, environmental problems, and a host of other factors, Taiwanese entrepreneurs and industries began to invest elsewhere. Still, a high level of capital accumulation helped Taiwan to continue to transform the economy to one based on capital- and knowledge-intensive industries. Foreign investment in Taiwan remained high, and though it was not now as vital as it had been in fostering economic growth, it did aid the development of new industries and the inward transfer of technology, and it bolstered commitments to Taiwan among countries that were economically and politically important to Taipei.

A good economic infrastructure also helped Taiwan's economic growth. In the early years, the government offered help in the form of cheap electricity and easy access to ports, good roads, and a well-trained labor force to domestic businesses and foreign enterprises. Later, transportation, energy, and banking were improved to further upgrade the economic infrastructure.

In 1973, the government launched ten projects at a cost of US$5 billion. Beginning in 1975 and for the next ten years, it spent US$2.7 billion on transportation projects, including an island-long freeway, railroads, airports, harbors, and ports. More projects were begun even before these were completed. In addition to these transportation projects, a steel mill, a shipyard, a petrochemical facility, and a nuclear power plant were built. In 1978, 14 more large projects were started, including housing construction and farm mechanization. In 1985, an additional 14 were added at a cost of US$3 billion. Finally, in 1991, more than 700 other projects were approved as part of a six-year development plan. The cost of this last group of projects was projected to be more than US$300 billion. The government boasted at the time that these infrastructure improvements would ensure continued economic growth and make Taiwan one of the top twenty countries in the world in per capita income by the year 2000. Meanwhile, the government helped finance the Asia-Pacific Regional Operations Center, to make Taiwan a "hub" for business in the region, a US$16 billion-plus high-speed railroad, and energy development and other infrastructure projects.[23]

Finally, astute planning lay behind Taiwan's economic success. This included research, forecasting, and planning done by the Ministry of Economic Affairs; the Research, Development, and Evaluation Commission; the Economic Planning Council (now the Council for Economic Planning and Development); and other organs of government coordinated by the premier. Although Taiwan does not have a planned or command economy and business is less regulated than in other similar free-market nations—including Japan, South Korea, and Singapore—the government has consistently given direction to the economy. The business community, farmers, and others have benefited greatly from government forecasts about the economic climate (including opportunities and difficulties). Government policy, in fact, has played such an important role in Taiwan's economic miracle that it warrants further attention.[24]

Economic Growth Strategies

Taiwan's economic system is a capitalist one and ranks as one of the freest economic systems in the world by many key yardsticks: trade policies, taxation, monetary policy, wage and price controls, property rights and regulations, foreign investment, and banking. For some time, Taiwan has also been one of the most successful economies in the world.[25]

Before the period of Taiwan's miraculous economic growth, the government advocated—and created—an open market economy. The reasons behind favoring capitalist development were many, though four deserve special mention: (1) Japan had bequeathed the Nationalist government a capitalist economy; (2) the February 28 Incident in 1947 engendered public hostility to government monopolies; (3) socialist planning and a socialist economy were associated with former Governor Ch'en Yi; and (4) the world had split into two camps—communism and capitalism—and Taiwan was in the latter, aligned with the United States.[26]

Nevertheless, as noted above, the government has guided, and in some respects designed, economic growth. Government planners have been careful and astute in managing the economy: They altered development strategies several times (radically at one point), and fine-tuned the nation's development strategies periodically. An examination of the work of these planners and their designs for promoting economic growth is essential in any assessment of Taiwan's economy, as is an understanding of their attitudes about a free-market economy and the limited, yet critical, role of government.

The first task of Taiwan's economic planners, going back to the late 1940s, was to stabilize the economy and reduce inflation, which was around 500 percent annually at that time. In early 1949, because of the defeat of the Nationalist regime on the Mainland, it was a horrendous 3,000 percent. The government, in response, legislated and enforced currency reform. Specifically, government officials imposed regulations on the financial system to control the money supply to prevent a resurgence of inflationary pressures. Finally, economic planners adopted conservative fiscal policies that required balanced budgets, reduced government spending, and controlled interest rates.[27]

These policies worked. Skyrocketing inflation was curtailed. The inflation index fell from 300 percent in 1950 to 30 percent in 1951–1952, and subsequently dropped to a reasonable 10 percent annually. In addition to stabilizing the economy, anti-inflationary policies benefited industrialization in two important ways: It encouraged labor-intensive production and, at the same time, made small factories and businesses compete. Reduced inflation meanwhile made economic planning easier and facilitated growth in general.[28]

Next, the government turned to land reform. Several aspects of Taiwan's successful land reform program have already been discussed. In its official involvement in the economy, land reform was the first important example of keen government economic planning that went beyond emergency efforts to foster economic stability. It also reflected more than just reactive planning. Sun Yat-sen had discussed and advocated land reform, including specifics; thus, Taiwan's land reform was well conceived from the outset. Launched in early 1948 by Ch'en Ch'eng, who was governor of Taiwan at the time and later became premier and vice president, rural land tenure policy was discussed, debated, and planned by several government agencies and departments for many months before laws were enacted. For Ch'en and other government planners, the primary economic goals of land reform were: (1) privatizing (to promote higher productivity in the agricultural sector, thereby enhancing the diet of the people); (2) increasing savings (to provide capital for new industrial enterprises); and (3) later increasing the availability of labor to the newly opened factories (to lay the groundwork for industrialization).

In 1953, the government expanded its role in economic planning when it launched a four-year plan, setting goals and guidelines for overall economic development. The objectives were stated in general terms, but planners were also specific about the government's role, thereby giving the business community clear signals concerning the economy's direction. The Ministry of Economic Affairs and the Ministry of Finance, under the general supervision of the premier, provided the leadership; other government organs and agencies followed. The business community gave the government high marks for its efforts and, in ensuing years, increasingly looked to government planners for guidance. Concrete government development plans lasting four or six years followed regularly.

With respect to generating economic growth in the industrial sector, in the early 1950s, Taiwan's development strategy was based on a policy of import-substitution. Several conditions dictated this choice: Taiwan's Japanese market for food products had been cut off, capital and technology were in short supply, the currency was overvalued, and the bureaucracy was an obstacle to implementing a policy of promoting exports. Thus, the best economic growth strategy available was to aid the development of local industries by guaranteeing them special access to the domestic market. This approach, it was perceived, would help absorb excess labor, stabilize prices, and conserve foreign exchange. Industries such as textiles, food processing, fertilizers, and chemicals benefited from this policy. Finally, the import-substitution policy helped support Taiwan's continued efforts at controlling inflation and stabilizing the economy.[29]

In adopting an import-substitution strategy, government policies in the next several years kept Taiwan's currency overvalued, tariffs high (doubling from 20 percent in 1948 to 40 percent in 1955), and import quotas and other controls severe—all measures that blocked or discouraged the purchase of foreign goods. Imports of flour and yarn, for example, fell from 70 and 80 percent, respectively, to less than 5 percent of local consumption, while synthetic yarn and bicycles fell from 100 percent to 1 percent. Selected businesses or producers, of course, quickly grasped the opportunity to produce and market these items. In 1951, a system of multiple exchange rates was established that discriminated in favor of certain industries. Also, special laws and regulations provided selected producers with favored treatment in acquiring credit.

Taiwan's import-substitution policy was quite successful. Between 1952 and 1959, various chosen industries grew at a rapid rate—sufficient to increase by 6 percent industry's share overall of the gross national product. Over 70 percent of the industrial sector's new production came from food (including tobacco), cotton and wool textiles, leather goods, and chemicals (including rubber goods, plastics, and petroleum)—all favored industries. Government policies also helped other industries. Factories making sheet glass, nonmetal mineral products, machinery, equipment, and rayon also managed to gain a foothold and grew at this time.

Although the government deserves high marks for adopting an import-substitution policy at the proper time and for making it work, thus promoting economic growth, it probably warrants even more applause for realizing that it had to be a temporary strategy. Otherwise, many industries would have become accustomed to protection and thus grown weak and noncompetitive. Certainly, rapid growth in the industrial sector could not have been sustained. Taiwan's leaders thus resisted long-term reliance on the import-substitution policy—unlike planners in most developing countries then and now.

During the late 1950s, the government made a major shift in economic strategy when, for several reasons, it decided to scrap the import-substitution policy in favor of an export-promotion policy: First, the domestic market for the protected industries had become saturated, and there was little room for expansion. Second, some of Taiwan's industries had gained sufficient experience and efficiency to be internationally competitive. Third, the workforce had improved. Finally, Taiwan now enjoyed a competitive advantage over Japan in some industries because of the rising labor costs there.

Thus, in 1959, to transform Taiwan's economy into one that was export-led, the government abolished its dual exchange-rate system and devalued the currency. It reduced tariffs and established laws and regulations favoring export companies.

Taxes, interest rates on loans, and regulations on the importation of raw materials were altered, as were laws regulating foreign investment. Later, as noted above, export-processing zones were established.

The industries picked as "leading" export industries were chiefly those that produced consumer goods: textiles, processed food products (mostly canned), leather goods, wood products, and paper products. These industries, almost exclusively labor-intensive ones using small-scale production facilities, accounted for nearly 60 percent of the increase in exports during the early 1960s.

Taiwan's export policy was a big success. The industries slated to sell abroad did so. During the first half of the 1960s, the value of exports rose nearly 20 percent a year. Export companies absorbed considerable excess labor, generated needed foreign exchange, and attracted more foreign investment. Companies that aimed at specific foreign markets, in particular, contributed to growth, propelling the gross national product to record double-digit annual increases. As a result, by the 1970s, Taiwan had become a "newly industrializing country," or NIC.

Continued growth required more policy adjustments. The decade of the 1970s saw Taiwan's economic development strategy shift dramatically again in the use of labor and capital. The nation's labor surplus had become a labor shortage, and labor costs rose dramatically. This situation, and the availability of large quantities of investment capital, made it logical to promote capital-intensive industries such as electronics, electrical products, chemicals, machinery, instruments, and metal products. Textiles continued to do well only because the industry turned to high fashion and a better grade of textiles; but cheap textiles soon became only a memory. In other words, the export-oriented policy of the 1960s continued, but the quality, sophistication, and price of Taiwan's exports changed.

Taiwan's economy continued to boom. Though it suffered a severe shock during the 1973–1974 oil crisis, economic planners quickly adjusted to higher energy costs. They diversified energy sources, encouraged conservation, and tried to promote less energy-intensive industries. Taiwan also needed to store more energy—and did so. To justify keeping large stores of petroleum, planners facilitated the start up and, later, the growth of Taiwan's petrochemical industry, which soon became one of Taiwan's largest industries.

During the first half of the 1980s, Taiwan's economy encountered even higher domestic labor costs and faced more intense international trade competition. But, with high standards of education, which enhanced the quality of Taiwan's human resources, and a quick start in such areas as computers and electronics, Taiwan had—or appeared to have—a comparative advantage internationally in knowledge-intensive industries.[30] Government planners, therefore, favored the computer and other knowledge-intensive businesses.

Meanwhile, Taiwan had accumulated valuable experience in selling in the global marketplace. The quality of Taiwan-made products rose quickly. In the late 1980s and early 1990s, the government began to promote Taiwan's best companies in order to build an international reputation for high-quality goods. Taiwan became increasingly conscious of standards for export products, even prohibiting the export of certain inferior goods. Innovation was also crucial, and government policies shifted accordingly. The government meanwhile encouraged the growth of financial services companies and sought to make Taiwan a regional distribution hub.

Government planners, working with business and labor, continued to attract foreign capital and expertise, put more money into education as well as research and development (double-digit or near double-digit increases), kept taxes low (13 percent of gross domestic product, compared to 30 percent in the United States and much higher figures in Europe), helped build a good infrastructure (especially roads and railroads), wisely regulated banking and financial institutions, and maintained social and political stability. Together, these efforts earned Taiwan a favored position among analysts who rank countries for investment potential and risk.[31]

Key Industries and the Taiwan "Economic Miracle"

A brief survey of Taiwan's successful industries—including several that played a major role during the import-substitution policy period, then in Taiwan's export-led economic growth policy, and later during its efforts to move up-market and to capital- and knowledge-intensive industries—sheds considerable light on the origins and nature of Taiwan's economic miracle. Some industries were important only in the past, while others have become, and remain, world leaders.

For a number of years, the textile industry was Taiwan's largest when measured by the value of production. Taiwan got its start with two textile mills at the end of World War II. By 1980, 200 cotton and wool mills were operating on the island. The industry was helped both by import-substitution and export promotion policies and became Taiwan's biggest export commodity and its largest source of employment. At first, Taiwan's textile industry took advantage of cheap labor, but when labor costs increased, the industry turned to synthetic fabrics and specialty products since natural fabrics could be produced more cheaply in poorer countries. This strategy worked. Taiwan's textile industry remains an important part of the economy. The value of output in 2006 was US$11.8 billion, or 5.3 percent of Taiwan's manufacturing sector, and exports totaled US$9.1 billion. Helping the industry is the fact that Taiwan is the second largest producer of synthetic fibers in the world.[32] Automation and going up-market, plus moving low-end production to China and elsewhere, have saved the industry.

Beginning in the 1960s, the electrical equipment and electronics industries seemed to have a bright future. In fact, these industries soon blossomed, beginning with electric fans, integrated circuits, and other labor-intensive products. As labor costs escalated, these industries became capital-intensive and attracted more foreign investment than most other industries in Taiwan. Factories went upscale to produce household appliances, communications equipment, and consumer electronics. In a few years, Taiwan became a major producer of radios, tape recorders, televisions, videocassette recorders, stereo equipment, calculators, and video games, not to mention parts and accessories and also electrical equipment.

Information products (mostly computer products) followed and have seen the biggest growth of any sector of Taiwan's economy in recent years; in fact, computers and related products "put Taiwan on the map" in the global business community. Taiwan ranks number one in global market share for the production of liquid crystal monitors, motherboards, and notebook computers. In 2006, sales amounted to US$88.6 billion. And although a large share of Taiwan's production is for foreign companies, Taiwan's own brands, such as Acer, are growing in market share (especially in Third World countries), even though they are not yet widely known elsewhere. Related to the success of computer production is the semiconductor industry. Taiwan has the world's two largest contract semiconductor companies—Taiwan Semiconductor Manufacturing Company Ltd and United Microelectronics Corporation. The value of chips and related products produced in 2006 was US$37.2 billion.[33]

But many of Taiwan's computer hardware and chip factories have moved elsewhere, especially to China, due to high labor costs in Taiwan. The size of China's market is also an attraction. Thus, some see Taiwan's computer industry as well as its semiconductor industry as under threat. Others say moving to China is simply a factor in globalization. In any case, these industries would not survive otherwise. The future of these industries, many say, hinges on Taiwan's economic—and perhaps political—relations with China.[34]

The petrochemical industry in Taiwan is new but is large. Beginning in the 1970s, government planners foresaw Taiwan's comparative advantage in petrochemical products. Twenty years later Taiwan became one of the world's largest producers of petrochemicals and the world leader in ethylene production. In 2006, the total value of production of its petrochemical factories was US$39.1 billion.[35] Although Taiwan's petrochemical companies export, they also produce for domestic use, including the ingredients for plastics, synthetic rubber, and textiles. Plastics, in fact, for some time as been one of Taiwan's strongest industries. Domestically produced plastic products went into many of the goods Taiwan exported, not to mention that plastics themselves are exported. Rising labor costs and environmental problems, as well as public protest movements opposing new factories, however, have confronted the plastics industry with some serious problems.

In the late 1970s, Taiwan got into the production of metals, especially steel, and opened a blast furnace in 1977. The decision seemed questionable for a time because of tough competition in the world market, especially from much larger Japanese steel plants. Initially, the only major customer of any importance was China Shipbuilding Corporation, which itself was not a growth company. But Taiwan's China Steel Corporation also built offshore drilling platforms (though this market did not expand at the time) and moved into ship breaking (which did grow). Both aided the steel industry, as did the rise of the yen and the consequent declining cost competitiveness of Japan's steel industry. Subsequently, the auto industry and ship-building saw better growth, providing markets for the steel industry. Recently, however, China Steel has suffered losses and, like some other heavy industries in Taiwan, has not been doing well.

Meanwhile, the production of aluminum, copper, and other metals grew, spurred by the growth of an aviation industry and extensive building construction. Today, though Taiwan's metal industry is healthy, in large part because it has gone upscale and has diversified, it is also suffering from higher labor costs, a more ex-pensive Taiwan dollar, foreign competition, and environmental concerns.

Taiwan also launched a shipbuilding industry in the 1970s. In 1973, it completed a dockyard that had a capacity of 1.6 million tons of construction and 2.5 million tons in repairs. But the timing was bad because of the surplus of tankers and other ships on the world market at the time. Beginning in the 1980s, Taiwan's shipbuild-ing industry was hit by a global decline in fishing fleets and foreign competition. As a result, China Shipbuilding Corporation was not profitable for some years. Consequently, it diverted a considerable amount of its productive capacity to off-shore drilling rigs, nuclear power plant equipment, steel structures, and the like. Meanwhile, Taiwan developed a world-class yacht industry. But in the 1980s, the yacht industry fell on hard times because the US market contracted.

Taiwan's vehicle industry was and is an important one in the value of its produc-tion and the number of employees, though production has been declining in re-cent years. In 2006, the value of production was US$14.5 billion. An automobile industry was launched in 1953, but overprotection prevented it from becoming competitive enough to export. Beginning in the mid-1980s, with a local buying boom, auto production increased markedly, although most of this came from for-eign companies operating factories in Taiwan. Meanwhile, Taiwan became a world leader in car parts, motorcycles, and bicycles. The island even became the world's largest manufacturer of bicycles in the 1980s.[36]

A number of other industries are worth mentioning for their role in the Taiwan economic miracle or have promise to grow in the future. In the 1980s, Taiwan expe-rienced quite impressive growth in telecommunication equipment, precision tools, optical machines and supplies, and sporting and fitness goods. The construction business has and is doing well because of higher standards of living, which led many people to seek better housing, and because of the nation's ambitious public works projects. Less strong are food processing, tobacco, alcoholic beverages, fertilizers, pharmaceuticals, rubber products, cement, glass products, nonferrous metals, wood products, and paper products. Tourism is a major industry, though a decade or more ago its halcyon days seemed to be over because of high prices in Taiwan. Tourists from China may revive the tourist industry.

Taiwan produces some state-of-the-art weapons, including a jet fighter plane and missiles. (For further details, see Chapter 6.) However, while the arms industry may contribute to modernizing the economy due to a certain amount of spin-off, it is doubtful that it will become globally competitive because Taiwan is a small country and will not likely be able to develop markets abroad. It got into the weapons business because of concerns about its lack of sources for buying arms, because it helped the United States argue (when dealing with China) that Taiwan could build its own weapons if the United States refused sales, and because Taiwan was able to acquire US weapons technology. As will be noted in Chapter 6, it is difficult to say whether Taiwan will remain in the business of producing arms and, if it does, to what degree.

Currently, the most dynamic sector of Taiwan's economy is the services sector. Now services accounts for over 71.7 percent of the gross domestic product, up from 50 percent in 1988 and 64.5 percent in 1996. Service industries employ around 57.9 percent of the workforce, and are growing at a healthy rate. Recently, the total value of services reached US$261.1 billion. The main categories are wholesale and retail trade, finance, and insurance.[37]

The government and the private sector have been and are investing heavily in research in certain areas that may indicate commercial trends in Taiwan or the makeup of its economic future. Biotechnology, space technology, optoelectronics, biomedical, and pharmaceuticals are among these. All are perceived to involve opportunities to specialize and to link up with companies in foreign countries, especially the United States. Taiwan's planners hope to move into research substantially in coming years and create many new and advanced high-tech companies.[38] Taiwan's leaders also want to make the island a "commercial hub" for business in East Asia, in particular for foreign companies going to China. However, Hong Kong and Shanghai will compete, and much depends on Taipei's relations with Beijing.

The Labor Force

Labor deserves special attention for its role in the Taiwan economic miracle; after all, Taiwan has almost no natural resources of commercial value. Its only resource of any importance is its human talent.

The expansion of the workforce was, in the early years after World War II, an especially important factor in the country's economic growth. Because of Taiwan's rapid population growth between the early 1950s and the early 1970s, the labor pool more than doubled. Employment rose from 2.89 million in 1953 to 5.5 million in 1974. By 1987, it had reached 8 million. Today, it is more than 10.5 million. The percentage of the population in the workforce—57.9 percent of those over age fifteen—is high by international standards. In this category, Taiwan is on par with Western nations.[39]

The skill and education levels of Taiwan's workers have also been high, particularly relative to labor costs—another critical factor in the nation's competitiveness and its rapid economic growth. Even more important, labor skills and the education of workers have increased at rapid rates and developed according to the changing needs of the economy. Worker flexibility—willingness to change jobs or acquire new skills—has also been high.

As a result of the success of Taiwan's industrialization and the upscaling and maturing of the economy, there has naturally been a huge shift of employment from agriculture to industry and services. In 1952, the mix was 52.1 percent agriculture, 20.8 percent industry, and 27.7 percent services; in 1962, the percentages were 45.9, 22.5, and 31.6, respectively; and in 1972, 33.0, 32.1, and 34.8 percent. By 1988, the number of employees in agriculture had shrunk to a quarter of what it was in 1952. Meanwhile, industry's portion had increased to 41.5 percent and services to 40.9 percent. Now the labor force is approximately 1.5 percent agriculture, 26.8 percent industry, and 71.7 percent services.[40] Most of new jobs are now being generated in the service sector.

Unemployment, in double-digit figures in the 1950s, dropped markedly from the 1960s on. During the economic crisis of the early 1970s, Taiwan boasted the lowest unemployment rate in the world.[41] During the 1980s and early 1990s; the rate hovered below 2 percent and was among the lowest in the world. The Asian economic crisis, which started in mid-1997, caused it to increase a bit, though it remained below 3 percent. In fact, many companies complained of difficulties in hiring and retaining workers and sought to solve the problem by increasing automation, transplanting factories to other countries, and hiring foreign workers.[42] However, as a result of the 2001 recession, the rate of unemployment exceeded 5 percent the next year and remained above 4 percent for the next three years.[43]

Wages increased with economic growth, especially for unskilled workers, who earned around US$5 to US$10 monthly in the 1950s. Salaries rose quickly, especially in the mid-1960s and after. In 1985, the average monthly income for workers in eight primary industries was US$368 per month. In 1999, the average wage was US$1,263 and US$1,421 for service workers.[44] Meanwhile, laborsaving methods and equipment, increased specialization, and better labor organization helped increase productivity, which offset some of the rapid increases in labor costs. In addition, labor and management both realized that labor costs would have to be kept from increasing too quickly if many of Taiwan's products were to remain competitive in the international marketplace. In order to adjust to rising labor costs, the government pressured businesses to invest in research and development and to phase out labor-intensive production.

Now the days of cheap labor are long gone and Taiwan's business community must adjust to even higher labor costs in the future. The quality of labor, however, remains high in Taiwan, and the labor force is hardworking. The average worker puts in nearly 200 hours per month (196.8 hours in the industrial sector and 183.7 in the service sector)—which is high even compared to other East Asian countries.[45] Many economists say the Confucian ethic of "work hard and don't complain" has made labor a major positive contributor to Taiwan's economic miracle and still explains why Taiwan's labor force is considered one of the finest in the world.[46]

There are a host of other reasons for labor's contribution to the country's economic success other than the quality of labor. A look back is instructive. So, too, is an examination of labor laws and organizations. During the period of Taiwan's rapid industrialization, workers were generally not organized. The formation of labor unions was discouraged—actually preempted—by the government and the ruling Nationalist Party. Strikes were forbidden under martial law. Although much has changed over the past few years, labor unions in Taiwan still do not wield much clout compared to their counterparts in most Western countries. The reason is that a large portion of the labor force is employed in small or family businesses. Also, many workers are employed in factories that sell to large foreign companies that can easily buy elsewhere. Workers in these factories have little bargaining power.

After martial law was lifted in 1987, however, labor became more active. Within a year, new unions began to form and compete with the government-controlled Chinese Federation of Labor. Soon, nearly 1,200 industrial unions and 2,400 craft guilds had formed.[47] Subsequently, new laws were written to cover bargaining, strikes, and other issues. Meanwhile, in late 1987, the Labor Party formed in order to represent workers in the political arena. And, in March 1989, the Workers Party was founded. The Democratic Progressive Party, even though it made numerous appeals to labor organizations and took up workers' causes, was seen by labor as too preoccupied with Taiwanese nationalism and other issues. The KMT was seen as probusiness, though it had and continued to seek labor support. Thus Labor's political affiliation has been uncertain. It seems likely to remain uncommitted to any political party.

Though labor is not considered as active or as militant as it is in most other countries, the rate of union membership is high. Unionized workers constitute 39 percent of union-qualified labor. This percentage is much higher than it is in the

United States (13.5 percent), Japan (22 percent), and other East Asian countries. If labor organization is defined broadly to include all kinds of workers' groups, such as craft guilds and other such organizations, over half of Taiwan's labor force is organized. However, the reason for the high rate of union participants is legislation that requires factories employing more than thirty workers to organize an industrial union. Trade union membership is also mandatory where there are thirty workers with specialized skills. Only civil servants, teachers, and workers in munitions plants cannot join unions. There are 4,534 regulated labor unions in Taiwan and 8 island-wide labor federations. Most workers consider the union membership pro forma and the main benefit of membership to be labor insurance rather than bargaining strength through organization.[48]

The government of the Republic of China brought with it to Taiwan laws and regulations that affected labor. These laws generally favored management and sought to maintain a passive labor force by banning strikes and discouraging labor from organizing or engaging in collective bargaining. Nevertheless, in 1958, the Labor Insurance Act was passed and, in 1994, the Labor Safety and Health Law. The most important piece of legislation, however, went into effect in 1984: the Labor Standards Law. It provided comprehensive guarantees and rights to workers and defined many unclear provisions in labor-management relations. This law now covers 40 percent of the labor force, including agricultural workers.[49]

In 1992, the Employment Services Act legalized the employment of foreign workers in Taiwan. This law was passed in the context of a shrinking labor force caused by a slowdown in the birthrate for more than two decades. Also, more people were pursuing advanced education and thus staying out of the labor force for extended periods. Meanwhile, the increasing participation of women in the workforce had set off some controversy: Many women did not want to work, and, as mentioned earlier, there was a growing perception that an increase in the number of working women would further weaken the family and result in high social costs due to increases in juvenile delinquency and crime. Thus, the number of female workers did not increase. Finally, effective January 2001, Taiwan shortened the workweek to forty-four hours per week and no more than eighty-four hours in a two-week period.

Hence, the number of foreign workers recruited by employers in Taiwan soared; by 2001, it had reached 325,000, or 3.3 percent of the workforce. Some 54 percent were employed in manufacturing and 11 percent in construction. There were many foreign workers in the nursing and caretaking fields, and many more worked as maids. Most of Taiwan's foreign workers came from Thailand (43 percent), Indonesia (27 percent), the Philippines (26 percent), and Vietnam (3 percent). A significant number of foreign workers came from several other countries, notably China, and were employed in Taiwan illegally.[50]

Most labor organizations oppose foreign workers for fear they will depress wages. Members of the Democratic Progressive Party have long expressed concern that workers from China might alter the ethnic balance in Taiwan. The Council of Labor Affairs, the organ of government responsible for labor issues, has tried to balance labor and management interests. Safety, working hours and conditions, and workers' rights have also been major concerns of foreign workers and their employers. Fringe benefits and workers' rights have similarly attracted the attention of labor, business, and government. During the 2000 election, presidential candidate Chen Shui-bian promised to cut the number of foreign workers if elected. The following year, the Chen administration reduced the number by 15,000 immediately and promised cuts by 5 percent yearly after that. Subsequently, though, foreign workers increased in numbers, reaching 367,119 by April 2008, up 5.75 percent from a year earlier. The largest portions were from Indonesia. Most were employed in industry, followed by caregiving and construction.[51]

Trade, Investment, and Energy

Foreign trade, foreign investment, and imported energy are three special factors that help explain not only the nature of Taiwan's economy but also its economic success. Although Taiwan has traditionally engaged in foreign commerce, the growth of trade over the past four or more decades has been momentous by any standard. In 1953, Taiwan's imports and exports totaled only US$320 million. Trade began to increase rapidly in the late 1950s and, especially, in the early 1960s, with the launching of Taiwan's export-oriented growth policy. In fact, trade grew at the astounding rate of more than 22 percent a year from 1959 to 1965, and it reached an annual value of more than US$1 billion and continued to grow to US$3 billion by 1970.[52] Not only did Taiwan's industrialization and its upscaling production further accelerate exports, but also both caused the value of exports to continue to skyrocket. By 1984, two-way trade totaled US$52.4 billion, making Taiwan the tenth largest exporting nation in the world and the fifteenth largest trading nation. And the boom continued: In 2006, the value of Taiwan's trade exceeded US$426 billion.[53]

Clearly, Taiwan's trade growth was by design. Having almost no resources and facing a serious population-to-land disadvantage, the government early on calculated that Taiwan had to trade to survive. When the nation's import-substitution policy of the 1950s was abandoned in favor of an export-led growth strategy, exports became particularly crucial. There was a surplus of well-educated and properly trained laborers, meaning that the economy could grow by exporting Taiwan-produced goods. Taiwan was burdened by foreign debt, yet the country needed more foreign capital to improve the infrastructure and build new factories. Finally, Taiwan's economic planners anticipated economic benefits by specializing and selling in the global marketplace and perceived that certain of Taiwan's industries were globally competitive and that more such enterprises could be built.[54]

Being a small nation with a small domestic market, Taiwan was soon trading more than Japan relative to the size of its economy. By the 1980s, its imports and exports amounted to more than 85 percent of its gross national product compared to Japan's 30 percent. Taiwan exported well over half of what it produced. Moreover, because most of its exports—over 75 percent—went to developed Western countries, Taiwan became very sensitive to the economic health and trade policies of the capitalist industrial nations, particularly of the United States and Japan, which, in the late 1980s, accounted for more than 40 and 30 percent, respectively, of Taiwan's foreign trade.[55]

The scope and the direction of Taiwan's trade by the 1970s, and even more clearly by the 1980s, might have set off alarm bells had economic planners in Taipei feared the possible dangers of linking the economy through trade to the capitalist West, or had they believed in "dependency theory." Planners in many other nations were apprehensive about tying their economies to the Western nations, thinking they would lose control over their economies and that the Western countries would impede their nations' economic development. But Taiwan's planners did not. Instead they calculated that participating in international trade was much more of an advantage than a disadvantage; so, they did almost precisely what critics said was potentially ruinous. Some writers subsequently argued that Taiwan, by directing such a large portion of its exports to Western countries and benefiting from doing so, disproved dependency theory.[56]

In fact, Taiwan experienced quite a different set of problems. Its exports found so many receptive customers in the United States that Taiwan soon developed a large trade surplus with the United States. This surplus grew throughout the 1970s and 1980s—peaking at US$16 billion in 1987. Instead of becoming dependent, Taiwan became the target of US government criticism and possible retaliation. The United States then ended special tariffs for Taiwan under the Generalized System of Preferences (GSP). In a few cases, the United States took legal actions against Taiwan for dumping. In response, Taipei adopted measures to cut its trade surplus with the United States: sending buying missions, banning the purchase of certain goods from other countries, and giving US exporters various kinds of preferences. These measures reduced the surplus markedly.

On the other hand, Taiwan had a big deficit in its trade with Japan—its second largest trading partner. Taiwan took various steps to increase its exports to and cut imports from Japan, but these measures had only marginal success. The imbalance remained a concern for Taipei, and still is.

Other Asian countries, excluding Japan, accounted for about 15 percent of Taiwan's foreign trade in the 1970s and 1980s, with neither surpluses nor deficits constituting serious problems. Western Europe accounted for 10 percent of Taiwan's foreign commerce, and the Middle East another 10 percent, largely from oil purchases. Taiwan carried a trade surplus with most West European countries and a deficit with Middle Eastern countries. These patterns largely retain today.

In the 1980s, Taiwan began trading with East European Communist countries and the Soviet Union, though this trade did not become economically significant. Taiwan also began trading with China, indirectly (through Hong Kong). Taiwan's China trade skyrocketed, and, with exports leading imports by a huge margin, the Mainland became an important market for Taiwan in the early 1990s. Soon, China was competing with the United States as a market, and, by 2000, it was receiving 21.9 percent of Taiwan's exports (compared to 22.5 percent for the United States).[57] Some saw this development as natural; others expressed concern that it would tie Taiwan to China economically and politically. Still others said that, if it wanted to remain economically healthy, there was nothing Taiwan could do.

Several factors accounted for the rapid growth of trade across the Taiwan Strait. First, Taiwan's products built a particularly good reputation in China for their quality and style. Second, beginning in the early 1980s, Beijing encouraged the purchase of Taiwan-made products and exempted them from tariffs by labeling them "domestic," though this policy was later revised because of the excessive demand for Taiwan-made goods and a shortage of foreign exchange in China. Third, Chinese economic planners noted that Taiwan's trade surplus with China provided Taiwan's companies with profits, which they invested in China; thus, the trade deficit did not really matter. Fourth, Taipei took the position that although trade with China was illegal, it was not practical to try to control where its products were sold. Still, trade remained primarily indirect—mostly through Hong Kong. Taipei, meanwhile, allowed imports from China, but also only through third countries.

By 2002, China had become Taiwan's largest export market and, by 2006, overall trade exceeded that with any other country. Trade with Japan, the United States, the Association of Southeast Asian Nations (ASEAN), and the European Union followed and, combined, totaled 80 percent of Taiwan's external commerce. Its trade continued to increase—in 2006 by 12 percent with the value reaching over US$426 billion. This meant Taiwan was one of the top twenty trading nations in the world (sixteenth for exports).[58]

Over the years, the kinds of products Taiwan exported has changed, often dramatically. In 1952, industrial goods accounted for only 8 percent of Taiwan's foreign sales; agricultural products were Taiwan's main export items. Within just a decade, manufactured goods accounted for 94 percent of Taiwan's total foreign sales. Agricultural exports, meanwhile, became insignificant. During this period, the portion of capital-intensive, high-tech, and knowledge-intensive products in the manufactured goods category increased as Taiwan's exporters went "up-market" and favored value-added products in their exports. Currently, Taiwan's main exports are computers and electronics (20 percent of total), optical instruments, iron and steel articles, machinery, and electrical equipment. Its leading imports are electronics, oil, machinery, metal products, iron, and steel items.[59]

In part engendering the rapid growth of foreign trade from the 1960s to the 1980s were extensive capital inputs, mostly from large quantities of foreign investment. In the 1950s, Taiwan's main source of foreign capital was US economic assistance. Later, Taiwan attracted foreign firms and private investors that provided large sums of needed capital. Most foreign funds went into manufacturing; indeed, close to 10 percent of investment in companies in the manufacturing sector came from foreign sources during the 1960s and 1970s—a very high figure when compared to the percentages in other developing countries. And this made a mark: In 1979, 795 foreign firms accounted for over 8 percent of Taiwan's gross national product. At this time, the exports of foreign firms accounted for 20 percent of the nation's exports.[60]

Foreign investors contributed to Taiwan's economic growth in still another important way, namely, by facilitating technology imports. Nonlocal firms brought new production techniques to Taiwan while stimulating research and providing training for workers. Because Taiwan's educational system was geared toward training young people to learn new technologies, the rate of technology absorption and use was high and accounted in considerable measure for Taiwan's rapid growth. Among less-developed nations, for some years, Taiwan enjoyed the world's highest proportion of growth through the addition of new technologies.[61]

Government policies were in large part responsible for the large inputs of foreign investment. Legislation provided for start-up periods when foreign companies were exempt from most taxation. Government agencies also recruited and trained workers, especially for foreign investors. Foreign firms benefited in particular from Taiwan's export processing zones, which, as noted earlier, afforded foreign companies freedom from taxes and many regulations. Finally, private businesses often sought foreign partners and usually worked well with them.

Although foreign investment is not crucial to Taiwan's economic health now, it nevertheless remains quite substantial. In 1995, when foreigners were allowed to invest in Taiwan's stock market, considerable funds flowed in from abroad. As a result of the Asian economic crisis that began in 1997, Taiwan, having a stable economic situation, attracted capital from other countries in the region. In 2006, foreign investment in Taiwan was almost US$14 billion, and it reached US$15 billion in 2007. Most of it came from offshore banking sources, the Netherlands, the United States, Singapore, Japan, and the United Kingdom. The favorite areas attracting foreign capital were electronics, financial services, and venture capital.[62]

As a result of Taiwan's favorable balance of trade beginning in the 1970s and its continued high rate of savings, Taiwan accumulated large amounts of capital, which it began to invest in other countries. During the Lee Teng-hui years, most of this went to the United States, Southeast Asian countries, and Japan. It also started going to China in sizeable amounts, though Lee discouraged it. It went in even larger amounts during the Chen Shui-bian administration, in some measure because of concern in the business community and among investors about his economic policies. It was also driven by China's economic boom and the opportunity to make money. President Chen became concerned about this causing the "hollowing out" of local industries and the loss of technology, but he could do little to stop it. The industries Taiwan has invested in include electronics and computers, communication and audio equipment, and electrical machinery—industries that are among Taiwan's best. It is commonly reported that Taiwan has invested more than US$100 billion in China, but some say it is much more than that. When Ma Ying-jeou campaigned for president in early 2008, he proposed a cross-strait market, indicating that inhibiting trade and investment ties between Taiwan and China was futile and that they should, in fact, be encouraged as part of the process of globalization that had been key to Taiwan's economic miracle in the past.[63]

As might be deduced from Taiwan's economic success and the types of industries that have facilitated it, as well as the rapid rise of living standards, Taiwan has been a rapidly growing energy user. From 1954 through 1985, energy consumption increased at an average rate of 9.2 percent per year—faster toward the end of the period. In contrast to the situation in the 1960s and 1970s, increases in energy use have recently fallen behind growth in the gross national product, but are still skyrocketing nonetheless. As a consequence of the growing consumption of energy, combined with limited indigenous supplies, Taiwan became a major importer of energy. In the mid-1950s, Taiwan produced more than 80 percent of the energy it used, and cheap hydroelectric power helped the growth of industry. By the late 1960s, only half of Taiwan's energy was derived locally. In 1972, that amount fell to 34 percent. Today it is 1.8 percent.[64] Consequently, Taiwan has become extremely dependent on foreign energy sources.

Although cheap foreign energy early on was a boon to Taiwan's economic development, this situation obviously did not last. After the oil crisis in 1973, and again in 1978, energy costs soared, and uncertainty about supplies caused anxiety for economic planners as well as the business community. Nevertheless, Taiwan could not do much about the quantity of energy it imported, nor could it reduce its reliance on foreign supplies. Its coal mines could not increase production and were closed. Taiwan has some natural gas and petroleum, but exploration has yielded disappointing commercial results. Petroleum and natural gas were found offshore, but not in significant quantities. Thus, the situation of energy import-dependency persists, and there seems to be no solution in sight.

On the other hand, the government has been quite successful in diversification. In the early 1970s, Taiwan imported oil, its main source of energy, mainly from Saudi Arabia and Kuwait. Those countries remained the main suppliers for Taiwan, and 80 percent of the nation's petroleum still comes from the Middle East. But after the oil crisis, Taiwan began buying petroleum from Indonesia, Malaysia, Brunei, several Latin American countries, the United States (Alaska), and some other countries. It also began buying coal. During the 1950s and until the mid-1960s, the use of coal had declined rapidly for environmental and cost reasons, accounting for only 13 percent of the total energy used in 1979. Now, however, owing to better burning techniques, Taiwan is importing a considerable amount of coal, and suppliers are not generally the same countries from which Taiwan buys oil: the United States, Australia, Canada, South Africa, and China. Taiwan has also begun importing liquid natural gas, mostly from Indonesia.

Currently, petroleum accounts for 51 percent and coal for 31 percent of total energy production. The Republic of China has also experimented with solar and thermal power, and has even used biogas produced on hog farms. Also, conservation has helped reduce consumption. Still, Taiwan's dependence on imported energy is not likely to change in the foreseeable future, nor is its reliance on nonrenewable energy sources. Only 5 percent of the island's energy comes from renewable sources, though it is expected to increase to 8 percent of total energy use by 2025.[65]

Taiwan meanwhile became a user of nuclear power. The first plant was opened in 1978, and, with the building of more nuclear plants, Taiwan became a major consumer of nuclear power. Today, Taiwan has six nuclear units (in three plants) producing 17 percent of the nation's electricity.[66] A fourth nuclear plant is under construction, but, as noted in Chapter 2, this plant became controversial after Chen Shui-bian was elected president because he and his party had adopted an antinuclear power stance. Chen cancelled the plant's construction in 2000, but then reinstated it. It now appears that nuclear power will contribute more to the energy mix in the future.

Taiwan's energy use has changed markedly over the years. As the industrial sector became a major part of Taiwan's economy, it accounted for the lion's share of energy use. In 1972, it took 61 percent of the nation's energy. This proportion has declined with Taiwan's economy shifting to less energy-intensive and more knowledge-intensive production and to a service economy. Industry's share of energy use is now around 58.7 percent. Meanwhile, transportation's share rose from 8 percent in 1972 to 15.5 percent today. Agriculture dropped from 4 percent to 1 percent during that same period, while residential use rose from 9 percent to 12 percent, and commercial use from 2 to 11.1 percent.[67]

A Model of Economic Development

Taiwan's economic development has been so successful that referring to it as an "economic miracle" is hardly an overstatement. This being so, what Taiwan has accomplished in the realm of economic development and, in particular, the nature of its economic planning, that made it a model for both economists and leaders of developing nations, warrants further discussion.[68]

First, it is necessary to recapitulate a bit and look at Taiwan's economic growth over the past four decades. During the 1950s, the island's economy grew at a healthy rate of 8.2 percent annually; expansion in the 1960s averaged 9.2 percent annually. Taiwan was hit hard by the oil crisis in the early 1970s, but it quickly adjusted and turned slow growth back into "miracle" growth after a two-year hiatus. After the adjustment, Taiwan's economy grew even faster than it had before the oil crisis—notwithstanding much higher energy prices. During the 1970s, Taiwan's GNP grew at an average annual rate of 10.2 percent. In the 1980s, the rate was 8.2 percent. Taiwan's economy slowed down a bit more in the 1990s; after all, Taiwan was now a developed—or mature—economy. But, in 1997, when the "Asian meltdown" saw many Asian countries experience economic bad times, Taiwan was virtually unaffected.

For three decades, Taiwan had more years of double-digit growth than any nation in the history of the world. For a decade and a half, its growth was approximately double Japan's and triple that of the United States. Taiwan's per capita income, which was nearly the same as China's in the 1950s, by the 1980s was twenty times that on the Mainland. When economists rank nations' growth records, they usually mean increases in the gross national product over two or three decades. By that criterion, at the end of the twentieth century, Taiwan could claim to be number one in the world.[69]

To explain Taiwan's success, looking back is instructive. In the 1950s Taiwan was a very poor place. Many experts considered its economic prospects dismal and even called Taiwan hopeless. In short, Taiwan succeeded against what seemed to be long odds. To repeat, these were: an unfavorable land-to-population ratio, almost no natural resources, little capital, the loss of its markets in Japan and China, a discredited government, the influx of 1.5 million people, and the need for high defense spending owing to the threat of invasion from the People's Republic of China.

Moreover, Taiwan's leap into prosperity was mostly free of the side effects that attend rapid growth. It had low inflation, no price instability, and no increase in income disparity; in fact, income disparity decreased during Taiwan's period of rapid growth to become one of the lowest of any nation in the world. Taiwan has also avoided some of the other pitfalls of high growth rates: a large external debt, serious dislocation of certain sectors of the economy, and political instability.

What Taiwan accomplished was indeed a miracle. No wonder its economic success has attracted the attention not only of economists and political leaders in other countries but also of political scientists, risk analysts, and others. Indeed, those who view Taiwan's accomplishments as instructive and worthy of the label "economic miracle" span a large gamut. Yet, most important among those who admire Taiwan's economic development are the many leaders of developing countries who see Taiwan as a country to study in planning their own economies. Some have even come to believe that what Taiwan did simply needs to be copied wholesale. Others point to specific lessons: that the capitalist model of growth does not necessarily mean income disparity, as many have thought, or that the Confucian work ethic is the way to go. Most have been convinced that a free-market economy and an emphasis on exports is the formula for economic success.

Here are some of the more specific lessons gleaned by development economists from Taiwan's economic success: agriculture first; import substitution, but only for a short period; export-led economic growth based on comparative advantages in international trade; and a free market. Government planning, forecasting, and advice to guide the economy and to help the decisions of farmers, owners of small companies, and business leaders were also important. In addition, foreign investment in the initial phases of growth is crucial; a high savings rate is to be encouraged or forced; productivity must exceed wage increases; noncompetitive sectors of the economy must be pressured to restructure or close; the populace must be made aware of economic goals and plans and must support them; economic planning decisions must reflect changes in the world economy; taxes must be kept low; political and social stability are crucial; and welfare dependency and crime must be minimized.

Some less noticed points can also be taken from Taiwan's economic success. One is that foreign aid can promote economic development—if both donor and recipient sincerely regard growth as their goal and work together to accomplish it. Taiwan's US aid had a major positive impact at a critical stage in the island's economic development. Most nations failed to use aid well because of poor planning, corruption, a lack of cooperation between recipient and donor, and the absence of a commitment on the part of the citizenry. Taiwan has also been adept at going upmarket as labor costs increased and at building a reputation for quality control. It has also invested a large portion of the governments' (at all levels) budgets in education, which it has tailored to meet the needs of business, and in training workers.

Comparing Taiwan's style of capitalism with other successful East Asian nations is also instructive. Japan and South Korea have enjoyed exemplary economic development and, along with Hong Kong and Singapore, are considered among the world's shining examples of economic modernization. Japan and Korea, however, have far more large companies and more heavy industries than Taiwan. Hong Kong and Singapore, also high-growth countries, have almost none. In short, the role of big business and heavy industry varies considerably among these countries, as does the closeness of ties between government and business (greater in Japan and Korea, less in Hong Kong and Singapore). Nevertheless, all four "little dragons" and Japan are major trading nations and have adopted strategies that emphasize exports and the use of comparative advantage in the world market. A strong work ethic can be found in all five, while a free market has encouraged innovation and initiative and kept government small and efficient. Social and political stability are important goals. Unlike Japan, which has protected its manufacturing sector from foreign competition, and because of that has experienced recession in the 1990s that lasted into the new millennium, Taiwan let industries move out and encouraged the service sector to grow.

Taiwan is usually considered a better model for Third World developing economies than Hong Kong and Singapore, which are little more than cities. Some also consider Taiwan a more relevant prototype than Japan, which industrialized before World War II and benefits from economies of scale and low defense spending—strategies most developing nations cannot adopt. Finally, Taiwan is more highly regarded than South Korea because the latter's economic system is modeled after Japan's. Like most developing countries, Taiwan is small and comparable to them in population, climate, and so on. Taiwan's growth has also been more recent than that of the Western industrial nations and Japan, and it started from a lower base. Finally, most of Taiwan's planning and economic development strategies have been assessed by foreign and local economists and can be used by developing nations (and they are using them—even China). Although an exact duplication may not be possible, most developing countries can in large part replicate Taiwan's success. Perhaps Taiwan is the best economic model in the world.

The Economy Under Chen Shui-bian

In 2001, Taiwan's economy fell into recession. The proximate cause was the Chen administration's fight with the opposition parties in the legislature over the construction of Taiwan's fourth nuclear plant. President Chen and the DPP had long opposed nuclear power. The opposition won the fight and President Chen's image was hurt in the business community, which worried about future energy supplies and began to perceive his administration as antibusiness. The opposition charged Chen with poor leadership and mismanagement of economic affairs. The recession was caused, Chen said, by the world recession that had adversely affected high-tech industries and the opposition's stubbornly blocking his economic agenda.[70]

In any case, by the end of the year, the stock market had lost 50 percent of its value, defaults on loans reached new highs, and private investment fell dramatically as capital fled to China (triple the amount a year earlier). The Council for

Economic Planning and Development reported that Taiwan's "economic fitness index" had fallen ten points to the lowest point since it had begun keeping records.[71] By mid-year, the stock market had fallen by another 40 percent and unemployment topped 400,000, or 4 percent of the workforce (both forty-year highs). The media reported that the business community had almost no confidence in the Chen administration, and this was reflected in local industries closing down and going to China. It was said that "China fever" in Taiwan was fifty to eighty times what it was in Japan and the United States. By year-end unemployment went up to 5 percent and the gross national product contracted 2 percent.[72]

In response, the government took funds from the National Stabilization Fund and labor insurance and pension reserves to prop up the stock market, adding NT$350 billion to the national debt. The Chen administration pressured banks to help companies facing bankruptcy, which diverted funds that otherwise would have been available to help start-up companies and finance growth by healthy enterprises. The stock market and Taiwan's currency fell further. According to a poll conducted at this juncture, 60 percent of the population lacked confidence in Chen's economic policies. The president then established the Economic Development Advisory Council to give him recommendations on fixing the economy, but many business leaders refused to participate, citing the poisonous political atmosphere and fearing that Chen was seeking to pass blame for his situation.[73]

In 2002, the economy showed signs of recovering from the recession. But it did not perform up to the expectations of most citizens. The gross national product grew by 3.5 percent, but unemployment remained a high (for Taiwan) 4 percent. The Chen administration tried various other means to stimulate growth and employment. It cut taxes, which meant programs to help the poor had to be pared. The government sold state assets and increased fees and fines, sometimes to very high levels. Chen proposed making Taiwan a "gateway to China" for foreign business, but this idea failed to materialize. This is because there were two obstacles. First, many in his party opposed the idea as it would mean expanding commercial relations with China and make Taiwan dependent; former president Lee Teng-hui and Vice President Annette Lu both warned about dependency. Second, China was not cooperative and most foreign companies saw Shanghai as the place to operate from in doing business in China.

The economy continued to grow, but at what citizens in Taiwan considered an anemic rate, while other economic signs, such as unemployment, foreign investment, and the stock market didn't look good. The Chen administration continued borrowing to the point that public debt by the end of President Chen's second term was 45 percent of the gross national product—if hidden debt were counted, it was perhaps 90 percent. During 2006 and 2007, the media and the Chen administration critics cited bad economic news with regularity. For example, in 2002, Taiwan's economy measured by the gross national product was the sixteenth largest in the world, but in 2006, it ranked twenty-second—dropping six places. During that period Taiwan dropped from 30 percent of China's economy to 18 percent. When Chen Shui-bian became president, South Korea's per-capita income was two-thirds of Taiwan's; in 2006, South Korea's was higher. In 2000, Kaohsiung was the second busiest port in Asia, and six years later it ranked seventh.[74]

In early 2007, Bloomberg reported that Taiwan's stock exchange had devalued 18.5 percent in US dollars during President Chen's tenure—the worst among ninety indexes it tracked. Shortly thereafter, the World Competitiveness Report showed Taiwan fell one place in the past year while China rose three slots—to pass Taiwan for the first time ever. The Directorate General of Budget, Accounting and Statistics announced that the wages of workers increased 1.77 percent in 2007; this was below the rate of inflation. In other words, workers' buying power had declined.[75]

When Ma Ying-jeou was elected president in March 2008, the stock market jumped up, as did Taiwan's currency, housing values, and other indicators. Many observers expected Taiwan to see better times again, but that presupposed better relations with China. Some thought that would lead to sacrificing Taiwan's sovereignty, while others said it was simply part of globalization, which Taiwan could not avoid, and that—its commercial relations with the United States and Japan being extensive—more ties with China did not matter.

Notes

1. For details about Taiwan's early economic history, see James W. Davidson, *The Island of Formosa: Past and Present* (New York: Oxford University Press, 1988).

2. For background on Taiwan's economy, see Samuel P. Ho, *Economic Development of Taiwan, 1860–1970* (New Haven, CT: Yale University Press, 1978). Also, see the introductory chapters of the books cited in the economy section of the bibliography of this book.

3. Samuel Chu, "Liu Ming-chuan and the Modernization of Taiwan," *Journal of Asian Studies* (November 1963): 37–53.

4. For details on capital formation during this period, see Teng-hui Lee, *Intersectoral Capital Flows in the Economic Development of Taiwan, 1895–1960* (Ithaca, NY: Cornell University Press, 1971), 19–20.

5. Cal Clark, *Taiwan's Development: Implications for Contending Political Economy Paradigms* (New York: Greenwood Press, 1989), 60.

6. Ho, *Economic Development of Taiwan*, 104.

7. See Anthony Y. C. Koo, "Economic Development of Taiwan," in Paul K. T. Sih, ed., *Taiwan in Modern Times* (New York: St. John's University Press, 1973), 402–406.

8. See Anthony Y. C. Koo, *The Role of Land Reform in Economic Development: A Case Study of Taiwan* (New York: Praeger, 1968), and Ho, *Economic Development of Taiwan*, for further details.

9. Walter P. Falcon, "Lessons and Issues in Taiwan's Development," in T. H. Shen, ed., *Agriculture's Place in the Strategy of Development: The Taiwan Experience* (Taipei: Joint Commission on Rural Reconstruction, 1974), 275.

10. *The Republic of China 1998 Yearbook* (Taipei: Government Information Office, 1998), 164, 199.

11. Tzong-shian Yu, *The Story of Taiwan: Economy* (Taipei: Government Information Office, 2001), 7. *Taiwan Statistical Yearbook 2007* (Taipei: Council for Economic Planning and Development, 2007), 84.

12. *Taiwan Yearbook 2007* (Taipei: Government Information Office, 2007), 102–103.

13. Ibid., 138.

14. Currently, the tariff rate on agricultural goods in Taiwan is 20.6 percent. It will drop to 14.1 percent when Taiwan joins the WTO; after six years, it will drop again, to 12 percent. This fall will likely hurt agriculture in Taiwan. The demonstration, on May 20, 1988, was the largest one in several decades and resulted in several hundred injuries. Farmers were joined by opposition supporters and students and were supported by some labor groups. At the time it was difficult to say whether this kind of political protest would be repeated.

15. See Yuan-li Wu, *Becoming an Industrialized Country: ROC's Development on Taiwan* (New York: Praeger, 1985), for further details on this subject.

16. Ibid. Moreover, Taiwan's agricultural sector did not experience the adverse effects that Britain's did during its industrial revolution.

17. "Farming Population Declines," *Free China Journal*, August 14, 1998, 4.

18. See Neil H. Jacoby, *U.S. Aid to Taiwan: A Study of Foreign Aid, Self-Help, and Development* (New York: Praeger, 1966), for details.

19. The data cited above are from Anthony Kubek, *Modernizing China: A Comparative Analysis of the Two Chinas* (Washington, D.C.: Regency Gateway, 1987), 94.

20. More than 95 percent of registered companies in Taiwan are privately owned. See Chen Chien-jen, "ROC Looks to Future with a Vision," *Free China Journal*, April 10, 1998, 7.

21. See Wu, *Becoming an Industrialized Country*, 12, 48–49.

22. See *The Taiwan Development Experience and Its Relevance to Other Countries* (Taipei: Kwang Hwa Publishing Company, 1988), 25. This study was prepared by Stanford Research Institute International.

23. See *The Republic of China Yearbook—Taiwan 2001* (Taipei: Government Information Office, 2001), 216.

24. For details, see Wu, *Becoming an Industrialized Nation*, chapter 2.

25. See various issues of *The Index of Economic Freedom*, published by the Heritage Foundation and the Wall Street Journal.

26. See Wou Wei, *Capitalism: A Chinese Version* (Columbus: Ohio State University Asian Studies Center, 1992), 55.

27. See Clark, *Taiwan's Development*, 168.

28. Ibid.

29. See Wei, *Capitalism*, chapter 7.

30. Ibid., 39–40, 45–46.

31. See Richard Dobson, "New Report Contradicts AmCham," *Taipei Times*, May 6, 2002 (online at www.taipeitimes.com); the author cites Switzerland's Business Environment Risk Intelligence (BERI).

32. *Taiwan Yearbook 2007*, 107.

33. Ibid., 105.

34. Many of Taiwan's factories that produce computers, chips, and other high-tech products have moved to China, and most expect many more to go soon.

35. *Taiwan Yearbook 2007*, 107.

36. Ibid. 107.

37. Ibid., 103. Also see Cindy Sui, "Service Sector Key to Long-term Growth," *Topics*, July 2008, 46–48.

38. Ibid., 105, 106, and 108.

39. *Taiwan Statistical Yearbook 2007* (Taipei: Executive Yuan, 2007), 19. This book is a collection of data prepared by the Council for Economic Planning and Development.

40. Ibid., 18.

41. See Jan Prybyla, "Economic Development in Taiwan," in Hungdah Chiu, ed., *China and the Taiwan Issue* (New York: Praeger, 1979), 106. See also *National Economic Statistics of the Republic of China* (Taipei: Department of Budgeting and Statistics, 1985), 34, cited in Wou Wei, *Capitalism: A Chinese Version* (Columbus: Ohio State University Press, 1992).

42. See Yu, *The Story of Taiwan: Economy,* 49–50.

43. *Taiwan Statistical Yearbook 2007,* 19.

44. *The Republic of China 2001 Yearbook,* 337.

45. Ibid., 336.

46. A recent survey rated Taiwan's labor number four in the world in work ethics and labor laws, sixth in productivity, and tenth in labor capability. See Dobson, "New Report Contradicts AmCham."

47. *The Republic of China 2001 Yearbook,* 343.

48. Jim Huang, "Behind the Numbers," *Taipei Review* (November 2001): 22–23; US Department of State, "Taiwan: Country Reports on Human Rights Practices, 2007," March 11, 2008, http://www.state.gov/g/drl/rls/hrrpt/2007/.

49. *The Republic of China 1998 Yearbook,* 338.

50. Pat Gao, "Adjusting Foreign Labor's Role," *Taipei Review* (November 2001): 10. Between 1990 and 1994, there were reportedly 73,000 foreign workers illegally in Taiwan. See *The Republic of China 1995 Yearbook* (Taipei: Government Information Office, 1995), 388.

51. "Council urged to control number of migrant workers," *China Post*, May 23, 2008 (online at chinapost.com).

52. See Shirley W. Y. Kuo, Gustav Ranis, and John C. H. Fei, *The Taiwan Success Story: Rapid Growth and Improved Distribution in the Republic of China, 1952–1979* (Boulder, CO: Westview Press, 1981), chapter 6.

53. *Taiwan Statistical Yearbook 2007,* 18.

54. See Wei, *Capitalism,* chapters 2 and 3, for further details.

55. The United States accounted for almost half of Taiwan's trade in the mid-1980s. New trade policies and efforts to expand trade elsewhere soon reduced this proportion to less than 40 percent.

56. For details, see Edwin A. Winckler and Susan Greenhalgh, "Analytical Issues and Historical Episodes," in Edwin A. Winckler and Susan Greenhalgh, eds., *Contending Approaches to the Political Economy of Taiwan* (Armonk, NY: M. E. Sharpe, 1988), 6–7.

57. *Republic of China on Taiwan: 2002 Statistics.*

58. *Taiwan Yearbook 2007,* 99.

59. Ibid., 99–100.

60. Chi Schive, *The Foreign Factor: The Multinational Corporations' Contribution to the Economic Modernization of the Republic of China* (Stanford, CA: Hoover Institution Press, 1990), 4.

61. Ibid.

62. "2000 Taiwan White Paper," *Topics*, May 2008, 10.

63. See Willy Lam, "Ma Ying-jeou and the Future of Cross-Strait Relations," Association for Asian Research, March 23, 2008 (online at asianresearch.org).

64. For background details on Taiwan's energy problems, see John F. Copper, "Taiwan's Energy Situation," in Kenneth R. Stunkel, ed., *National Energy Profiles* (New York: Praeger/Holt, Rinehart and Winston, 1979). For details on the current situation, see *Taiwan Yearbook 2007*, 104.

65. "Nuclear power listed as energy option," *Taipei Times*, June 6, 2008 (online at taipeitimes.com).

66. Ibid.

67. For the early figures, see *The Republic of China Yearbook—Taiwan 2001*, 166. For the recent data, see "Invest in Taiwan," Department of Investment Services. Data are for 2007 (online at investintaiwan.nat.gov.tw).

68. In this connection, see *The Taiwan Development Experience and Its Relevance to Other Countries* (Taipei: Kwang Hua Publishing Company, 1988).

69. See John M. Leger, "The Book: How Asians Started the 'Pacific Century' Early," *Far Eastern Economic Review*, November 24, 1994, 43. China, South Korea, Hong Kong, and Singapore rank in that order after Taiwan. The ranking is based on the period from 1975 to 1993. For the period 1968 to 1998, Taiwan ranks number one in the world in per capita growth in the gross national product, but it was surpassed by Botswana, Oman, and South Korea in overall GNP growth. See Herman Pan and Elizabeth Hsu, "ROC Long-term Economic Growth 4th Largest; GNP Growth Highest," *China Post*, April 26, 1998, 14. The first two being very small countries economically that export raw materials, they may be considered of little importance. Because of South Korea's recent economic problems, Taiwan has again surpassed South Korea in GNP growth.

70. Yu-shan Wu, "Taiwan in 2000: Managing the Aftershock of Power Transfer," *Asian Survey* (January-February 2001): 47.

71. "Taiwan economic outlook dim," *Economic News Daily*, March 20, 2001 (online at taiwanheadlines.com.

72. Ramon H. Myers and Jialin Zhang, *The Struggle Across the Taiwan Strait* (Stanford, CA: Hoover Institution Press, 2006), 70.

73. Yun-han Chu, "The Political Economy of Taiwan's Politics: Implications for Northeast Asia," (Paper presented at The London School of Economics and Politics, May 12, 2007).

74. See David DeVoss, "Tear Gas and Running Dogs," *Weekly Standard*, December 4, 2006, 18–19.

75. See "The State of the Nation," *CommonWealth*, March 28, 2007 (online at cw.com.tw).

6

FOREIGN AND MILITARY POLICIES

TAIWAN HAS LONG BEEN, AND STILL IS, a special player in international politics. It was the first ever Western colony to become independent. It was the launching pad for Japan's invasion of Southeast Asia at the onset of World War II. During the Cold War, on two or three occasions it was involved in conflicts with China that portended to explode into a global war. For twenty-two years, from 1949 to 1971, as the Republic of China, it represented China in the United Nations (and held a permanent seat on the Security Council). Then it was expelled and quickly lost formal diplomatic ties with most nations of the world. In 1979, Taipei suffered a break in formal ties with its most important friend and ally, the United States. Although weakened diplomatically, Taipei resisted Beijing's efforts to isolate and delegitimize its government and carried on diplomacy by way of commercial, cultural, and other contacts. Taipei also adopted a democratic foreign policy. In 1991, Taipei officially terminated its war with China (or the Beijing regime). This and the end of the Cold War should have given Taiwan greater security, but Beijing lost an enemy (the Soviet Union) and, as a consequence, moved more of its soldiers and weapons to areas close to the Taiwan Strait. Meanwhile, China's military power grew quickly as a product of its booming economy, making it a serious threat to Taiwan. In 1996, China intimidated Taiwan with missile tests close to Taiwan's shores; the United States sent aircraft carriers to protect Taiwan—precipitating a face-off between Washington and Beijing that by many accounts almost led to war. After 2000, President Chen Shui-bian made moves toward legal independence and, in doing so he angered both China and the United States (which was focused on the war on terrorism); as a consequence, US-Taiwan relations deteriorated badly. Chen's policies also contradicted Taiwan's growing economic integration with China and his administration's reduced defense spending. President Ma Ying-jeou, elected in 2008, rejected independence but also unification. Ma sought to expand economic relations with China, which may lead to a common market and eventually to a confederation or union. Alternatively, Ma will endeavor to preserve Taiwan's sovereignty, and the United States will continue to support Taiwan's separation.

Background

Before the era of Western colonialism, Taiwan engaged in interactions with several neighboring countries, though one would certainly not equate these contacts to the formal diplomatic relations that were being practiced in the West at the time. The island's merchants, meanwhile, maintained active commercial contacts with trading centers in East Asia, including some in China. In the sixteenth century, both the Chinese inhabitants of the island and the Aborigines began to engage in diplomacy of a sort with the Western powers and Japan.[1]

While Taiwan was under Dutch colonial rule, its foreign relations were managed by the mother country. When the island was subsequently governed by China, Peking handled Taiwan's external affairs. China, however, did not adhere to modern diplomatic practices and at times made disclaimers to the United States, Japan, and other foreign countries about its responsibilities over Taiwan, giving rise to doubts about whether China claimed sovereignty over the island.[2] Between 1895 and 1945, while a Japanese colony, Taiwan's external relations were handled by Tokyo. Relations with other nations varied during this period, but they were generally more restricted during the later years of Japanese rule. Contacts with China at any time during this period were limited.

In 1945, responsibility for Taiwan's external affairs passed to the Nationalist Chinese government in Nanking, even though the issue of Taiwan's sovereignty was not decided.[3] In 1949, after its defeat by the communists, the Nationalist government moved to Taiwan, at which time Taiwan and the Republic of China became virtually synonymous. The United States abandoned Chiang Kai-shek but changed its policy as a result of the Korean War and once again became Taiwan's protector.

Chiang contended Mao's government was illegitimate and would not last—a somewhat credible claim at the time because of internal instability in China, US antipathy toward the communist regime, and the UN-inspired boycott of the People's Republic of China after its entry into the Korean War. Most Western countries—with a few exceptions, such as the United Kingdom (because of Hong Kong)—accorded diplomatic relations to Taipei instead of Peking and supported Taipei's claim to represent the Chinese people in international affairs. The Republic of

China occupied the China seat in the United Nations, including a permanent seat on the Security Council, notwithstanding Soviet protests. Soviet-bloc countries, of course, accorded diplomatic recognition to the People's Republic of China and established embassies in Peking.

Both Nationalist China's foreign policy and its defense strategy were founded on the premise that its military would counterattack the Mainland and defeat Communist forces and again rule China. This objective, at least nominally, dominated Taiwan's external relations for some years. But carrying out this plan with any real hope of success depended on help from the United States and/or a global conflict between the communist and Western blocs. Neither happened.

The local population of Taiwan had little or no experience in making—or in even influencing—diplomatic decisions; thus, it would be conjecture to suggest to what extent public opinion supported the main tenets of the country's foreign policy. It seems fair to say a majority of the populace did not favor a policy of liberating the Mainland, yet they clearly opposed Peking ruling Taiwan. They supported aligning with the United States, but the Nationalist government already had such a policy. In sum, the population's views on foreign policy were unclear and seldom articulated; anyway, the masses had little influence on foreign policy decision makers.

Because the government of the Republic of China regarded Mao's communist regime its enemy, links between Taiwan and the Mainland that had been established after 1945 were severed. Two Chinas thus emerged: Nationalist China and Communist China, or the Republic of China and the People's Republic of China. The two contended for legitimacy, influence in the world community, and the allegiance of the Overseas Chinese. Because it espoused capitalism and aligned with the United States, Nationalist China enjoyed advantages that offset its much smaller size and population.

Owing to Nationalist China's new situation—that is, its move to Taiwan and its greater dependence on the West, especially the United States—its diplomatic practices and policies shifted. The vestiges of traditional Chinese-style diplomacy were displaced by Western practices. The island's external policies also reflected its government-in-exile status and its reliance on America for economic and security support. The Republic of China's foreign policy did not, in any meaningful way, reflect Taiwan's past practice of foreign relations.

In the late 1950s, Taipei began to play down its policy of "liberating" the Mainland. In his 1959 New Year's speech, Chiang Kai-shek defined the Mainland recovery policy as 70 percent political. Many thought this remark signaled a change of strategy and believed the plan to return to China would eventually be scrapped.[4] Chiang's decision probably stemmed from the perception that the United States no longer supported Taipei's desire to liberate China, as demonstrated by Washington's stance during the two Offshore Islands crises of 1954–1955 and 1958. In fact, the US

Department of State conveyed the message, especially after the second conflict, that it did not sanction efforts by Taipei to start a conflict with Peking and believed that two Chinese nation-states would become a permanent arrangement.[5]

Taipei also began to perceive the world differently as it became aware of détente between the superpowers and Sino-Soviet discord. In 1960, the rift between Moscow and Peking ended Soviet military support for China, a decision that reduced China's military capabilities and, thus, the likelihood that it would attack Taiwan. Taipei's underground and intelligence networks on the Mainland, meanwhile, no longer functioned as they had before; its personnel there had aged, some had defected, and many had been captured. The division of China, meanwhile, became less a concern to the rest of the world. Hence Taipei's leaders had to design policies based more narrowly on Taiwan's national interests.

Nationalist Chinese leaders similarly understood that world opinion was shifting toward Peking in the battle for diplomatic recognition; in other words, Taipei could not continue to garner global support to represent all of China in various international forums and organizations. In the United Nations, Peking each year won more support on the issue of whether it or Taipei should represent China. Still, leaders in Taipei did not formulate a new policy agenda. Some argued at the time that Taipei should quickly abandon its claim to represent China and adopt a foreign policy that represented the reality of governing only Taiwan. Had it not been for the Vietnam War and the Cultural Revolution in the People's Republic of China, both of which played into the hands of hard-liners in Taipei, a new foreign policy might have been forthcoming.

Some Western scholars have argued that, in the early 1960s, Taipei would have been successful in promoting a two-Chinas or a one-China, one-Taiwan policy, thereby avoiding the subsequent humiliation of being "expelled" (technically Taipei withdrew) from the United Nations in 1971 and the diplomatic isolation caused by the loss of recognition from a host of countries in the mid- and late 1970s. Others, however, doubt this. They said Taipei could not forsake the one-China ideal because of ethnic tensions between the ruling Mainland Chinese and the Taiwanese, since such a change would have evoked demands by Taiwanese for a bigger political role too soon. Indeed, abandoning the one-China policy might have engendered domestic political instability that would have made Taiwan vulnerable to Peking's efforts to subvert and weaken it, while giving Mao a pretext for attacking Taiwan, as he had planned to do in 1950.[6]

Diplomatic Decline and Partial Recovery

In 1968, US voters elected Richard M. Nixon president of the United States with a mandate to get out of the Vietnam War with honor. To do this, Nixon needed to improve US-China relations. In fact, he made this a central goal in American foreign policy. The US-China rapprochement and Peking's (now spelled Beijing) ending its self-imposed isolationism were to Taiwan's detriment.

In 1971, Taiwan lost the China seat in the United Nations and, with it, membership in that important world body. Henceforth, Taiwan could no longer claim to represent the Chinese people in international affairs. This was a major foreign policy setback for Taipei. It resulted in the loss of diplomatic ties with a host of nations. By 1970, the number of countries recognizing each had already tipped in Beijing's favor, 68 countries to 53. Three years later, Beijing had more than twice as many: 85 to 39. In 1977, Beijing had 111 compared to Taipei's 23.[7] Fearing that diplomatic seclusion would make it vulnerable to Beijing's claim that Taiwan belonged to China and had to be returned, Taipei adopted a policy called "substantive diplomacy," in which it sought to substitute commercial and other ties for formal diplomatic links.[8]

Taipei suffered still another shock in December 1978, when President Jimmy Carter announced the end of US diplomatic recognition effective on January 1, 1979 and the termination of the US–Republic of China defense treaty a year after that. Taipei reacted stoically. President Chiang Ching-kuo reiterated Taiwan's earlier declared "three no's policy": no contact, no negotiations, and no compromise (with China). But he also took important steps to democratize the political system and construct a "democratic foreign policy." This meant Taiwan could promote the view that it was democratic and China was not and that it, therefore, deserved to be considered sovereign and independent.

Beijing broached reunification (unification from Taipei's point of view since Taiwan had never been governed by the People's Republic of China) proposals to Taipei. On the surface, its offers seemed generous, but the bottom line was that Chinese leaders called on Taipei to surrender its sovereignty.[9] Thus, neither Taiwan's leaders nor its population considered China's proposals seriously. Nevertheless, the Western media often treated Beijing's gestures as benevolent while labeling Taipei's responses stubborn. Taiwan thus adopted new stratagems: making counter-offers that Beijing could not accept, publicizing Taiwan's wish (and its moral and legal right) to determine its own future, and, at least for the time being, as long as China was communist and poor, stating its citizens' desire to remain separate.

In ensuing years, Taipei sought more energetically to cement as many contacts as possible of any kind with willing nations and global organizations to avoid being isolated. Taipei went a step further with its substantive diplomacy; it began to speak also about its "informal diplomacy," which emphasized various new kinds of ties. Though the number of countries having official relations with Taiwan remained low, few nations formally recognized Beijing's claim that Taiwan was a province of the People's Republic of China. Even fewer cooperated with Beijing in its efforts to prevent Taipei from participating in international affairs.

As a result, Taiwan's global status became in some new ways *sui generius*. Beijing denied that Taiwan was a nation-state or had sovereignty. Although most nations of the world agreed (when establishing diplomatic relations with the People's Re-public of China) that there was only one China, few concurred that the island was legally a part of China—or, at least, few expressed such a view.[10] Nor did interna-tional law support Beijing's claim; Taiwan was self-governing, had a territory base, and enjoyed the support of the population. The paucity of nations with whom Taipei maintained formal diplomatic ties, however, was a problem.

The 1980s saw another shift in Taiwan's diplomatic strategy. Taipei began to pursue economic and other ties with China and a general lowering of cross-strait tensions. Although Taiwan's leaders coveted the nation's sovereignty, they per-ceived that they needed to pursue amicable relations with Beijing. Some thought that, ultimately, unification was likely and desirable. The People's Republic of China had in many ways become a new and different country following the death of Mao in 1976. Deng Xiaoping's economic policies brought prosperity, which gave rise to manifold political change in China. More important, China was on the way to becoming a global economic power that no one, especially Taiwan, could ignore.

The end of the Cold War and the rise of a New World Order from 1989 to 1991 presented Taiwan with not only bigger diplomatic opportunities, but also more challenges.[11] The Tiananmen Massacre in June 1989 made the People's Republic of China a pariah nation in the eyes of many Western countries. Yet Taipei could not, or at least perceived it should not, try to isolate China or even eschew contacts with Beijing. The People's Republic of China and Taiwan were in the same economic bloc in what many in Taiwan perceived was an evolving tripolar (the European Union, the North American Free Trade Association, and the Pacific Basin bloc) world.[12] China-Taiwan trade and investment ties would likely continue to expand.

In January 1988, Lee Teng-hui became Taiwan's first Taiwanese president. He coined the term "pragmatic diplomacy" to describe Taiwan's approach to foreign affairs. Lee accelerated Taiwan's efforts to reestablish or maintain contacts with as many nations as possible—even those having formal diplomatic ties with the People's Republic of China. This included dual recognition, which Taipei had hereto-fore rejected. Taipei at this time adopted still another term—"flexible diplomacy"—or a multidirectional or omnidirectional approach to diplomacy. Accordingly, Taiwan sought trade and other relations with various former and current Commu-nist nations. Taipei also made renewed efforts to adapt to the New World Order and to take advantage of new rules and ideals in global politics, including the notion that no country or political entity should be barred from participating in the world community. In short, Taiwan's foreign policy makers quickly adjusted to a new global structure and became more assertive and dynamic.

In 1991, Lee ended Taiwan's so-called "period of mobilization," officially termi-nating the state of war with Beijing. In 1993, Taiwan "negotiated" (labeled talks) with Beijing for the first time. The meetings were predicated on Taiwan accepting the doctrine of one-China, though Taipei could have its own interpretation of the meaning of "China." There was a significant thaw in cross-strait relations. But soon President Lee perceived China was closing Taiwan's "international space" and undermining its diplomatic status. He visited the United States in 1995, and this soured relations with China seriously. In 1999, President Lee announced a "two-state theory," again provoking China and causing his tenure to end on a low note in terms of cross-strait relations.

When Chen Shui-bian became president in 2000, he promised to improve relations with both the United States and China. He made no headway in dealing with China. Early in the Bush administration, US-Taiwan relations were better than they had been in a long time, but soon deteriorated badly. The United States perceived that Chen sought to provoke China for his own political gain while disregarding America's preoccupation with the war on terror; thus, the Bush administration questioned whether Taiwan under the Chen administration was a faithful ally. Washington subsequently responded with anger to Chen's push for independence.[13]

Taiwan's relations with China also worsened. Taipei lost diplomatic relations with several countries, even though Chen had boasted he could improve Taiwan's diplomatic situation. Efforts to win representation in the United Nations turned into embarrassment. The Chen administration's localism prompted many Overseas Chinese communities to switch their loyalty to China. In short, under Chen, Taiwan became more isolated and its foreign policy less successful.

In 2008, Ma Ying-jeou was elected president. Ma sought to lessen tension with China and improve relations with the United States. To some degree he succeeded in doing both. But Ma had to consider the reality that the population of the island wanted to preserve Taiwan's sovereignty, that China and the United States were competing countries, and that Taiwan was a point of contention between the two—a difficult situation to manage.

Domestic Affairs and Foreign Policy

The influence of domestic politics on Taiwan's foreign policy has increased markedly in recent years for a host of reasons. Most relevant to this change, of course, was, and is, the democratization of Taiwan's political system. But even before this, domestic politics influenced foreign policy to a degree not usual for a small, underdeveloped country. In the 1950s, Taiwan was a focal point in the bipolar global struggle. Its center-stage role in world politics and its permanent membership in the United Nations Security Council drew public attention to Taiwan's importance and to foreign policy matters. The KMT also proclaimed it represented "Free China" as opposed to the communist regime on the Mainland. Hence officials in Taipei felt compelled to demonstrate that they had public support for the major tenets of Taiwan's foreign policy.

Public opinion thus influenced, or at least limited, some of the major tenets of foreign policy. The return-to-the-Mainland policy lacked the enthusiastic support of the people, particularly Taiwanese. Most citizens felt that the government should be more concerned about domestic problems, especially economic development, than with overthrowing Mao's regime in China. This may explain why the leadership started playing down this policy. Subsequently, the government rationalized, proclaiming that Taiwan had to develop a strong economy (which had strong public support) if it were to defeat communism.

The public strongly supported relations with the developed Western countries because they, especially the leader of the Western bloc, the United States, guaranteed Taiwan's security and extended economic aid. Later, the United States and other Western countries (including Japan) provided capital investment for Taiwan's economic expansion. For these reasons and the popularity of the United States in Taiwan, neither the populace nor important government officials ever seriously considered questioning the US lead in international affairs. Likewise, they never regarded isolationism as an option, even as Taipei's global status declined.

During the 1960s, when Taiwan's economy began to boom (but when its diplomatic ties with most of the world began to look tenuous), foreign policy makers started to seek greater domestic support for their main external goals. Taiwan's leaders realized that time was not on their side in the struggle with Beijing for diplomatic recognition. Yet economic ties could be translated into support for Taiwan's sovereignty. Policymakers won broad public approval for their economic diplomacy and got it—a situation that prevailed into the 1970s and 1980s.

In the early 1970s, public input into foreign policy making increased markedly. Taipei's expulsion from the United Nations in 1971 engendered widespread public anxiety that the Republic of China was doomed to delegitimization and isolation. For the first time, serious public debate ensued over foreign policy. When Chiang Ching-kuo became premier in 1972, he ordered the Nationalist Party and the government to heed public opinion in making both domestic and foreign policy. Foreign policy decision makers often suggested that Taiwan's future should be determined in a democratic way, the implication being that Taiwan sought to remain sovereign and independent because the population wanted this. Taiwan's Mainland Chinese leaders had by this time become increasingly comfortable with the idea of remaining on Taiwan and, with the exception of a few hard-liners, they abandoned any hope of returning to China. The others, because of their bad experience negotiating with the Chinese Communists in the 1930s and 1940s and the bright economic prospects at home, saw little advantage in trying to reach an agreement with Beijing. The Taiwanese mostly favored separation anyway.

The 1970s marked the formalization of a policy that Taipei called "economics first," motivated largely by Taiwan's losing formal diplomatic ties.[14] Japan had made this kind of policy work; why not Taiwan? Taipei thus combined commercial contacts with a new public relations diplomacy. Its officials began to set up trade offices wherever they could. Taiwan even allowed trade and other business contacts with Communist countries—with the exception, of course, of the People's Republic of China.

With Taiwan's first national competitive election in 1980, a two-party election in 1986, and the termination of martial law the following year, opposition politicians became much more active and their influence on foreign policy increased. Their dissatisfaction with foreign policy was often expressed in public. The Ministry of Foreign Affairs became sensitive to public views: In fact, some say this gave rise to the term "public diplomacy." In one important respect, the public debate worked to the advantage of foreign policy decision makers: Because of democratization, they could say the reason they resisted negotiating with Beijing about reunification was that the people did not want it, at least not now. They also pointed out that because the Nationalist Party was no longer the only political party in Taiwan, party-to-party talks were inappropriate (which Beijing called for to avoid government-to-government contacts that would, China feared, give Taipei the status of a sovereign nation-state.)

In 1979, after the United States broke diplomatic relations with Taipei, widespread debate regarding foreign relations again ensued. Many citizens questioned the wisdom of certain tenets of the government's foreign policy, especially its claim to represent China in world affairs. Opposition politicians became particularly vocal at this time.[15] They advocated a more "democratically based" foreign policy lest the nation not survive. In the 1980s, the issue of Taiwan's independence was thrust into the foreign policy debate. Government officials faced a dilemma: Advocacy of legally separating Taiwan from China was sedition according to the law, yet the government had abandoned, in all but name, its policy of liberating China. Proclaiming an independent Taiwan was also unnecessarily risky because it could provoke Beijing into using military force against Taiwan. In addition, the United States opposed it. Yet because of democratization, the advocacy of independence could not be stopped.[16]

The government, or at least the ruling Nationalist Party, found it best to argue that its policy was "moderate," since Beijing demanded reunification and Taiwanese independence advocates asked for separation and no ties with China. In fact, the KMT's status quo or "wait and see" policy looked reasonable and found broad support. Opinion polls showed that the population strongly supported the status quo. In the early 1990s, the independence issue seemed in large part resolved, or at least defused, when, in 1991, the Democratic Progressive Party placed the issue of independence in its campaign platform and voters rebuffed it. The issue of independence arose again after China conducted missile tests to intimidate

Taiwan in 1995 and 1996—gaining considerably in popularity, according to various opinion polls. But with the resumption of talks between Taipei and Beijing begun in 1993, the issue receded a bit. Supporters of independence did poorly in the December 1998 election. Thus it seemed that the public had considerable input on this issue.

Meanwhile, with so many citizens traveling to China and with trade and investment increasing rapidly beginning in the late 1980s, attitudes regarding contacts with China began to change. Many people in Taiwan, especially businesspeople (including many Taiwanese), not only began to advocate ties with China but also opposed government restrictions preventing more extensive contacts. Many feared being left out of the "China boom." With the advent of a New World Order, many citizens in Taiwan started to think about belonging to the same economic bloc as China and even began to favor the idea of a "Greater China."

In 1989, after the massacre of students and other protesters in Tiananmen Square in Beijing, Taiwan's pariah image evaporated; the People's Republic of China was now *the* pariah nation. These developments and an election victory by the opposition Democratic Progressive Party that year caused the Western media to treat Taiwan as a democracy worthy of self-determination. Beijing's overtures and its pressure on Taipei to negotiate reunification lost credibility. At the same time, support from the population and the media gave the government more confidence and prompted it to take domestic public opinion more seriously.

Although the opposition regularly enunciated its own foreign policy goals and positions, by this time it was less at odds with the government's foreign policy. Thus, officials often welcomed opposition views on foreign policy, perhaps as much as or more than their counterparts in Western democracies. Clearly, foreign policy decision makers found it convenient, at times at least, to defer to public opinion or to acknowledge opposition views on various issues. Claims of being a democratic nation and mention of public influence in the formulation of foreign policy justified Taipei's stance on unification and confused Beijing's negotiators.

Concern for public opinion has also been widely cited in Taipei's efforts to participate in various international organizations after it lost membership in the United Nations and subsequently other world organizations at Beijing's behest.[17] Although Taiwan did not win support from many important nations in this effort, it embarrassed various organizations for excluding Taiwan by citing its successful democratization and the wishes of Taiwan's citizens. DPP leaders even said the ruling party had adopted a "preemptive policy" regarding participation in the United Nations after the Democratic Progressive Party articulated a position on the issue and won public acclaim.

Public opinion also began to have an impact through the legislature in Taiwan. Lawmakers were sensitive to public views, especially organized groups. The legislature put pressure on foreign policy decision makers in a number of ways. The most noteworthy was the influence it used to push for larger business investments in China and easier contacts across the Taiwan Strait. The public sometimes exerted more influence at election time. It was given a new venue for doing this when the Referendum Act was passed in 2003, though its use has not proven helpful to augment the effect of public opinion on foreign policy decision-making.[18]

The government's promotion of its democratic foreign policy has also been reflected in its publication of treatises on defense and foreign policy. In 1992, the Ministry of Defense published its first "white paper" explaining in layman's language the nation's strategic and defense problems and policies.[19] In early 1993, the Ministry of Foreign Affairs published its first-ever foreign relations white paper, presenting an easy-to-read but detailed statement of foreign policy. Meanwhile, high officials who had been in the academic world wrote books and contributed articles on Taiwan's foreign relations and foreign policy.[20] More recently, reports and statements on defense and foreign policy have been issued with considerable frequency. It seemed clear that in the future, the media, opposition groups, political parties, lobbying and public interest organizations, and the public would have even more influence on foreign policy.

When Chen Shui-bian campaigned for president, he built the tenets of his foreign policy on public opinion surveys and the notion of public diplomacy. As president, Chen found that he could improve his image by making foreign policy pronouncements and personally taking charge of diplomacy while drawing public attention with foreign trips; some even said that Chen was Taiwan's first "foreign policy president." But as his popularity waned, this did not work well and, in fact, created a disconnect between public sentiment and the conduct of foreign relations.

President Ma Ying-jeou has heeded (or used) the views of the public on various issues in making foreign policy decisions. His diplomacy with China, especially on the issue of unification, has been based on the public's view that trade ties should go forward quickly but that political change should proceed slowly, if at all.

Taiwan's National Security Policy

As is true with most nations, national security is the driving force that, to a large extent, molds Taiwan's foreign policy.[21] In fact, this is true of Taiwan more than other nations. Almost without peers, Taiwan has been and is a nation under threat by a much bigger power—in fact, now a truly global power. Taiwan's strategic thinking is thus dominated by how to deal with the China threat.

This of course, has a background that helps put it in perspective. Shortly after the Nationalists fled to Taiwan in 1949, Mao laid claim to Taiwan and made plans to "liberate" the island using thousands of small boats carrying soldiers who would swim ashore to engage and defeat Nationalist forces defending the beaches. US intervention—President Truman dispatching the Seventh Fleet to the Taiwan Strait—saved Taiwan from an invasion that would have been horrendously bloody but doubtless would have succeeded.

Because of the Korean War, the United States not only stopped a People's Liberation Army (PLA) invasion, but America also became the guarantor of Taiwan's security. In 1954, this relationship was made a formal one when Taipei and Washington signed a mutual defense pact. In ensuing years, Chiang Kai-shek hoped to use the treaty to enlist US help to invade the Mainland and free it from the Communists. But, as noted earlier, Washington feared Chiang might drag the United States into a war with both China and the Soviet Union (the two had a mutual defense treaty in force); the United States did not want this. Thus, Washington sought to limit Taiwan's offensive military capabilities by supplying it with defensive arms only. American advisors also tried to persuade Taipei to reduce its forces on Quemoy and Matsu—the site of two crises in the 1950s. The United States reasoned that they were a tinderbox and also vulnerable to being cut off and destroyed by Mao's PLA forces. But Chiang Kai-shek was unwilling to do this since the Offshore Islands symbolized Taipei's links with the Mainland and its claim to be the legitimate government of China. Thus, Chiang kept approximately one-third of Taiwan's military manpower on these islands.[22]

Eventually realizing the size of its military in terms of manpower was too small to attack China while gradually abandoning a military strategy in favor of a political one to liberate China, President Chiang bowed to US pressure and cut the size of Taiwan's military (which was large and costly for a small country) while he also upgraded its professionalism and its quality of weapons. From a peak of more than 600,000 troops, Chiang cut the standing army to below 500,000. Currently Taiwan's military is just over 300,000 and is slated to be comprised of only volunteers by 2013.[23]

Related to improving Taiwan's military capabilities, a serious problem in the past was that Taiwan could not obtain all of the weapons it wanted or raise the level of sophistication of its most important weapons systems. In particular, it needed state-of-the-art fighter planes and antisubmarine warfare capabilities. The United States was Taiwan's only meaningful supplier of weapons, but it refused to sell Taipei all it wanted or needed. So Taiwan looked for other sources. The government did manage to purchase two submarines from Holland (delivered in 1988), but Beijing put such pressure on the Dutch government that it promised to not make any more weapons sales to Taiwan. Taiwan purchased weapons from other European countries, but nothing significant. Israel was willing to sell weapons to Taiwan, but Taipei, with a few exceptions, eschewed buying weapons from Israel because of Taiwan's good relations with Saudi Arabia and its dependence on several Middle Eastern countries for oil.

Taipei was able, in part, to overcome this problem to some degree by obtaining US weapons technology, which was not covered in Washington's 1982 pledge to Beijing to cut arms sales to Taiwan. Such technology transfers made it possible for Taiwan to build a new high-performance jet aircraft called the Indigenous Defense Fighter or Ching Kuo (after the late president), a prototype of which was put into service in 1994. Then there was a breakthrough: In 1992, the United States offered to sell F-16 fighter planes to Taiwan. At almost the same time, France proposed selling Taipei its Mirage fighters. The government bought both. This change in policy by two major arms producers seemed to reflect a consensus abroad, or in the United States at least, that Beijing's increased defense spending and its purchasing more sophisticated weapons from Moscow after the breakup of the Soviet Union and in the context of Russia's economic travails and China's economic boom, needed to be balanced.[24] Clearly, Taiwan's security was weakened, not enhanced, by the end of the Cold War.

Subsequently, Taiwan's biggest concern became the short-range missiles Beijing placed in areas adjacent to Taiwan across the Strait. In 1995, and again in 1996, Beijing conducted intimidating missile tests in the Taiwan Strait that exposed Taiwan's vulnerability. Soon China had more than a thousand missiles aimed at Taiwan and was reportedly increasing the number by fifty to one hundred per year. In addition to the damage that a missile attack would do to military facilities and/or population centers, Taiwan also has to worry that Beijing will quarantine the island through verbal threats and military maneuvers (with missiles to back them up), a situation that would disturb links with Taiwan's trading partners. In response, and coinciding with a continuing willingness on the part of the United States to sell arms to Taiwan, Taipei has purchased antimissile defense systems (including the patriot missile system), ships, and other weapons.[25]

This situation prompted the Chen administration to move toward a new strategy in dealing with the China threat. President Chen suggested an offensive policy to replace what had long been a defensive posture, when he announced a strategy of "decisive offshore campaign." Chen's premier even spoke publicly of bombing Shanghai and Hong Kong in retaliation if China were to attack Taiwan. But President Chen had his detractors. Many felt that such "wild talk" would make Taiwan less secure. The United States and some other countries did not view Chen's proposed shift of policy with approval, and it was never formally adopted.[26]

Another way to assess Taiwan's strategic thinking is too look at its options. Clearly Taiwan cannot match China's military buildup with one of its own and must rely on the United States' military to deter China from attacking the island. But what else can it do?

One option for Taipei is to look for other allies. One possibility in the past was the Soviet Union. During the 1960s and 1970s, because of strained relations between Moscow and Beijing, there was reason to believe that Soviet leaders wanted to see Taiwan remain outside Beijing's control. The Soviet Union's Pacific Fleet indeed benefited from the Taiwan Strait being an open international waterway. Moscow gave some signals, including making references to Taiwan as a "nation" and giving Taipei information on Soviet naval maneuvers, that it wished to see the status quo in the area preserved.[27] But with the collapse of the Soviet Union and the fact that Russia now is pursuing good relations with China, this situation no longer prevails.

Japan has also been considered a possible ally, and still is. Many, probably most, policymakers in Tokyo prefer a separate Taiwan to one that is part of the People's Republic of China. One reason for such a view, or policy (if it may be called that), is Japan's trade and investment ties with Taiwan. Some also cite historical links and Japan's interest in eventually extending its naval power farther south. In a joint communiqué with the United States in 1969, Tokyo referred to Taiwan as being "within its defense perimeter." It has never repudiated (or clarified) this statement. In fact, recently, in the context of US-Japan military cooperation, Tokyo has talked of "assuming responsibilities" for the defense of areas south of Japan that include Taiwan. Meanwhile, Japan's military spending is increasing, and its military power is growing. Some say Japan and the People's Republic of China are, or soon will be, locked in an arms race, an eventuality that might well provide opportunities for Taipei.

On the other hand, Tokyo is restrained by pacifism at home. Also, the Japanese government faces the problem of apprehension and even fear among nations in the region about its growing military strength. Thus, even though Japan may have designs on Taiwan, and certainly wishes it to remain independent, Tokyo is reluctant to translate this into overt policies to fulfill its wishes. Japan is also highly unlikely to pursue a Taiwan policy that is at odds with that of the United States. Finally, Japan does not seek to challenge the People's Republic of China directly by establishing military ties with Taiwan.

On the other hand, Tokyo has some influence on Beijing's foreign policy that is to Taiwan's advantage because of the importance of Japanese trade and investment to China. Beijing, furthermore, does not want to give cause for Japan to alter its defense policies. China's brandishing its military forces against Taiwan would, indirectly at least, threaten Japan and might serve as a catalyst for Japan to rearm quickly and even abandon its antinuclear weapons policy. Chinese leaders obviously do not want that.

Also, there is the issue of theater missile defense (TMD). The United States and Japan are working on such a system for Northeast Asia, nominally aimed at the

North Korean missile (and nuclear weapons) threat. Some say, however, that TMD is also (primarily perhaps) directed at China, and Taiwan may join this project. Its leaders have hinted strongly that Taiwan would like to. If Taipei were to participate, Taiwan could better defend itself against the threat (and use of) Chinese missiles. In addition, Taiwan would benefit from an important psychological boost because its security would be linked to Japan's and the US commitment to defend Taiwan would be enlarged. For these reasons, China is adamantly opposed to TMD and is very hostile to the idea of Taiwan's joining.

Another option for Taiwan is to build nuclear weapons. Since Beijing has them—and has never ceased to threaten military force against Taiwan—Taipei would seem to be justified in making its own. Taipei has done research on nuclear power and has the technology, the money, and the scientists to build nuclear bombs, probably within less than a year if it decided to do so. As noted earlier, in the 1970s, the United States pressured Taiwan to stop its nuclear weapons program and Taipei obliged. It could, however, reinstate its programs, or it could purchase nuclear weapons. Perhaps, even worse, it could produce or buy chemical and biological weapons. Incidentally, Beijing claims that Taiwan could produce nuclear weapons easily and speculates that it already has chemical and biological weapons (although Taipei denies it).[28]

Taipei has no defense against Beijing's nuclear weapons, but this handicap may not be exactly that; in fact, a defense against China's nuclear weapons might not be necessary. The 1968 Nuclear Nonproliferation Treaty signed by the United States and the Soviet Union guarantees non-nuclear nations protection from those with nuclear weapons. Although the signatories do not recognize Taipei diplomatically, Taiwan may still be protected from nuclear attack under the broad terms of the agreement. Beijing is also constrained by world opinion from using nuclear weapons against a non-nuclear country (or a province of China, in its view). Anyway, Chinese leaders have publicly stated that they will never use nuclear weapons on their own people. Finally, it has been rumored that Taipei concluded a secret agreement with the United States that affords Taiwan certain military guarantees in return for Taiwan's not developing nuclear weapons. In the late 1970s, Taiwan was close to nuclear capability, but it discontinued that effort at Washington's behest.[29]

Taipei's strategic planners have shown an interest in an East Asian security system or collective security organization—with or without Beijing. If an "Asian NATO" were to evolve, Taiwan might use it to bolster its security. Such an alliance system, however, seems distant, if a possibility at all.

Other options are available to Taipei in the event of a conflict with Beijing. Taipei could cause considerable dislocation to trade and travel in the area by declaring a state of war or by delineating military zones and warning ships and planes to stay away. It might surrender islands it controls in the South China Sea to Vietnam or some other country in the region, thereby creating a diversion. It might allow or encourage citizens to flee to the United States and other countries, generating a refugee problem and thereby making the problem one of US and/or international concern. Taiwan might even threaten to bomb cities in China or dams (including the Three Gorges dam, which would cause tremendous losses in lives and property if hit properly). There are, of course, other possibilities.

Taiwan and the United States

Of all the nations in the world, the United States is the most important to Taiwan; indeed, it is probably fair to say that it may be more important than all of the others combined. This has a history going back to World War II. The United States was Nationalist China's ally before the war (unofficially). During the Chinese civil war that followed, the United States continued to support the Nationalists with arms and money. With the onset of the Korean War, US aid, which had been briefly terminated, was resumed. Up to 1965, it totaled US$1.5 billion—more than the United States had given to any country not at war.[30] In ensuing years, the United States was Taiwan's leading trading partner and source of investment capital. The United States concluded a defense treaty with Taipei that afforded Taiwan US protection while Washington gave Taiwan political backing so that it could remain in the United Nations and represent China in the global community for more than two decades after the Nationalists moved to Taiwan.

Accordingly, Taipei cultivated good relations with the United States. During the early years, it maintained intimate ties with the so-called China lobby in the United States, which supported closer US relations with Taiwan and opposed any US dealings with "Red China."[31] The China lobby's influence in Washington, however, began to wane in the late 1950s, and by the 1960s, foreign policy makers in Taipei realized that close ties with friends in the US Congress were not enough, were too partisan, and could not be sustained in the face of America's need and desire to establish contacts with the People's Republic of China.[32] Taipei thus sought other means of influence, which initially included sending outstanding diplomats to Washington, making efforts to impress US tourists visiting Taiwan, and expanding contacts with US military personnel stationed in Taiwan. Taiwan also hired public relations firms and cultivated various kinds of informal ties in America.

In the 1950s and early 1960s, a two-China policy began to evolve in the United States. Following the two Offshore Islands crises, the Eisenhower administration began seriously to consider such a policy in an effort to preclude the outbreak of hostilities between Chiang Kai-shek and Mao Tse-tung that might ensnare the United States. Scholars and policy wonks recommended a policy either of a separate Taiwan or one-China and one-Taiwan.[33] After 1960, as the foreign policy elite in the United States became aware of Sino-Soviet differences, pressure mounted to end the US policy of trying to isolate China. A vocal minority of intellectuals and others meanwhile advanced the idea of granting China diplomatic recognition. But events intervened: The Great Proletarian Cultural Revolution resulted in China's self-imposed isolation, and escalation of the war in Vietnam again increased hostilities between the United States and China. Washington's view of China, and Taiwan, were affected by the lunacy in China. Taiwan served as a rear base of operations for the United States during the Vietnam War and as a result, Washington viewed Taiwan once again as an important ally.[34]

Under President Richard Nixon, US policy toward China/Taiwan changed dramatically. Nixon was determined to get out of Vietnam and avoid involvement in another land war in Asia and to establish better relations with China to realize these goals. President Nixon faced another serious foreign policy problem. Because of diminishing public support for military spending at home and larger military outlays by the USSR, the United States was losing the arms race. Nixon thus sought to establish strategic ties with the People's Republic of China as a way to avoid having to continue to engage in a weapons-building contest with the Kremlin that the United States probably could not win, at least not in the short run. To Nixon's advantage China's relations with the Soviet Union had deteriorated markedly following a war on their border in the spring of 1969. President Nixon thus employed what became known in the West as the "China card" (using closer ties with China to hold the Soviet Union in check), and, in the process, relations between Washington and Beijing improved dramatically.

The "Taiwan issue" could not be allowed to block a US-China rapprochement. US relations with Taiwan had to be downgraded, and Taipei had to accommodate. Taipei had no alternatives to its vital US ties and reliance on Washington as its protector. Moscow was not a feasible option because economic ties to the United States were too important. And Taiwan was already evolving into a democracy solidly in the Western camp, both economically and politically. Although Taipei knew it could not prevent US-China relations from improving, it felt it could maintain good enough relations with the United States that Washington would not completely abandon Taiwan.

Taipei adjusted by democratizing its political system along lines suggested by Washington, and, as it did so, it let Washington know. It paid more attention to human rights. As noted earlier, Taipei, also at the request of the United States, terminated its plans to build nuclear weapons and promised never to go nuclear. In short, Taiwan still sought to keep its friends in the United States and impress the US government—and did so.

Taiwan survived the trauma when the United States severed diplomatic relations in January 1979 and terminated the US–Republic of China defense treaty a year later. The shock was softened by actions taken by the US Congress, which reacted with anger to President Jimmy Carter's one-China policy and his "abandonment" of Taiwan by enacting the Taiwan Relations Act (TRA). This, the first-ever US law establishing guidelines for Washington's relations with another country, was signed reluctantly by President Carter in April 1979. In essence, the TRA reestablished Taiwan's status as a sovereign nation-state according to US law and, in considerable measure, in US foreign policy. It allowed Taipei to post foreign affairs representatives in the United States, have access to US courts, and retain diplomatic privileges and most of the other perquisites restricted to sovereign nation-states. Finally, it provided Taiwan with security guarantees.[35]

Some in Taiwan did not like the TRA. Throughout the document, the term "Taiwan" or "the people of Taiwan" rather than "Republic of China" was used. This, some people said, was demeaning. Others said it supported independence. Still, most government officials supported the Taiwan Relations Act since it preserved the role of the United States as Taiwan's protector and put Taipei-Washington ties on a stable—albeit less formal—basis. In most respects, the TRA treated Taiwan as a nation-state; it certainly did not acknowledge that Taiwan is part of China—as Beijing contended and as was stated in President Carter's Normalization Agreement with China.[36]

The TRA also guaranteed normal economic relations between Taiwan and the United States. Trade and US investment in Taiwan increased considerably in ensuing years. Indeed, a serious problem soon developed in US-Taiwan relations (for the United States): a trade imbalance. In the 1950s, Taiwan purchased much more from the United States than the United States bought from Taiwan. But, as trade increased by large amounts in the 1960s and 1970s, this trend reversed, and by the mid-1980s, Taiwan was exporting so successfully that its large trade surplus became an irritant in the US. In 1987, Taiwan's surplus reached US$16 billion, making Taiwan second only to Japan as a cause of the US trade deficit (and, incidentally, four times Japan's surplus on a per capita basis). Congress and US labor unions began criticizing Taiwan for causing unemployment in the United States and hurting certain US industries.[37]

Taipei responded with quick and drastic action: It sent buying missions to the United States, lowered tariffs, and underwent several currency revaluations. All these things helped, and so did export diversification. Thus, the US market, which took nearly 50 percent of Taiwan's exports in 1985, absorbed just over 35 percent in 1988. The United States remained Taiwan's most important market, but it declined in relative importance due to Taipei's successful search for new markets. The trade imbalance also became a less serious political issue as Taiwan bought more and more from the United States—at times discriminating against products from other countries to do so.[38]

In 1989, the US public and the American media began seriously to reassess US-Taiwan relations as a result of the Tiananmen Massacre in Beijing and an election in Taiwan that reflected its rapid democratization (when the opposition Democratic Progressive Party scored well at the polls and began to have a serious impact on policymaking). An even more important event to policymakers occurred at this time: The Soviet bloc began to disintegrate and the Cold War drew to an end. This was evident in 1989, though the process finally culminated only in January 1991. US policy did not shift immediately or formally, but it gradually changed to the benefit of Taiwan. After all, US-China relations had been built on common strategic interests—which no longer existed. Taiwan did not exploit the situation immediately because it wanted to maintain good relations with China; but it certainly benefited later.

In 1992, as noted above, US policy toward Taiwan made a turnabout in the realm of strategic cooperation when President George H. W. Bush approved the sale of F-16 fighter planes to Taiwan. The move reflected US concern that Beijing, by markedly increasing its defense spending and buying sophisticated weapons from Russia, had undermined the balance of forces in the Taiwan Strait. (Though the media in the United States said Bush made the sale to win voters in Texas, where the plane was made, in view of the coming fall election.) Washington also questioned why Beijing was expanding its military budget when other powers throughout the world were cutting theirs in response to the end of the Cold War. In any event, Taiwan's most serious strategic problem, air superiority over the island and part of the Taiwan Strait, was resolved in its favor.

President Bill Clinton at first seemed favorably disposed toward Taiwan. Clinton had made four trips to Taiwan when he was the governor of Arkansas, with his main purpose being to sell the state's products. He had not visited China and was critical of Beijing for its human rights abuses during the campaign and after. In 1994, the Clinton administration reviewed US policy toward Taiwan and made adjustments that included allowing senior officials to visit Taiwan, permitting Taiwan's leaders to make stopovers in the United States, and sanctioning changing the title of Taiwan's diplomatic offices in the United States (from the Coordination Council for North American Affairs to Taipei Economic and Cultural Representative Office—the latter indicating who the office represented). He also promised support for Taipei's entrance into international organizations where statehood was not at issue.[39]

But this came after considerable congressional pressure; Clinton was otherwise tilting toward China. As Clinton became more pro-China, Congress became more pro-Taiwan. Following open disagreements between the White House and the legislative branch of government on US-Taiwan policy, Congress attached a provision to an appropriations bill stating that the Taiwan Relations Act had precedence over the communiqués negotiated with Beijing. President Clinton signed it. Congress also pressured the president to allow President Lee Teng-hui to visit the United States—which he did in June 1995—and began work on a bill called the "Taiwan Security Enhancement Act" to upgrade the defense provisions of the Taiwan Relations Act.

The United States came to Taiwan's assistance when Beijing conducted threatening missile tests in 1995 and 1996. President Clinton ordered an aircraft carrier to the Taiwan Strait in December 1995, though only after the crisis had passed. In 1996, he dispatched two carrier groups to the Taiwan Strait in a move to constrain Beijing and brandish US power (though some say he did this in anticipation of intense pressure from Congress if he failed to act). This action constituted the largest display of US military power in Asia since the Vietnam War. Some said later that the United States and China nearly went to war.[40]

In the aftermath of the crisis, the White House spoke of ending America's policy of "strategic ambiguity" in US–China/Taiwan policy. Clinton administration people also expressed concern that Taiwan's major opposition party, the Democratic Progressive Party, and its leaders, especially after a major election victory in November 1997, might seek to push Taiwan further along the road toward formal separation from China in defiance of America's one-China policy. President Clinton sent officials to Taipei to "send a message" and head off serious advocacy of independence. This is when Washington seemed to change its Taiwan policy: No longer did it believe that the Taiwan issue was "a matter for the Chinese themselves to resolve" (as many US leaders had said). Rather, the crisis warranted US concern and intercession.[41]

In 1998, President Clinton traveled to China. There, he formally stated what became known as the "three no's" policy: no to two Chinas, no to one China and one Taiwan, and no to Taiwan's joining international organizations that required statehood for membership. This had been US policy, but no president had ever stated it in public, much less in China. The president also described the relationship of the United States with the People's Republic of China as a "strategic partnership." Both statements upset Taiwan as well as the US Congress. Congress passed several resolutions repudiating Clinton's notion of strategic ties with China and his ill treatment of Taiwan. Clinton subsequently decided to pursue theater missile defense (TMD) in Northeast Asia (part of his national missile defense program), with Japan as a major partner. This incensed Chinese leaders and contradicted Clinton's statement that China was a strategic partner. There was talk of Taiwan's participating in the TMD project because it would enlarge the area covered and be more effective, and Taiwan could help pay for it. Taiwan's willingness to do so greatly upset Chinese officials in Beijing.

President Clinton left these matters to his successor, George W. Bush. President Bush had taken a decidedly more friendly line toward Taiwan during the campaign, and he put that into policy as president. He repudiated the strategic partnership idea (with China). After a crisis in April 2001 that resulted from a mid-air crash involving a US reconnaissance plane, which was gathering information on China's new weapons that threatened Taiwan, and a Chinese air force fighter, called the EP-3 Incident, he spoke of doing "whatever it took" to defend Taiwan. He subsequently approved the largest arms sales purchase ever for Taiwan, save his father's F-16 sales. He also let high officials from Taiwan visit or travel through the United States—and they did. Pundits in Taiwan reported that US-Taiwan relations had not been better in many years. President Bush gave the impression that the United States feels Taiwan is strategically important. The Bush administration appeared to want to preserve close ties with Taiwan rather than allow it to become part of China.[42]

But, Bush did not alter America's one-China policy or announce support for Taiwan's independence. These mainstays of US-Taiwan policy remained unchanged. Moreover, after 9/11, the Bush administration's relationship with Taipei changed dramatically. This was partially due to the fact that China signed on as a partner in the war on terrorism, but it was more that Washington became convinced that President Chen was taking the United States for granted and that he disregarded US concerns when, for his own political reasons, he provoked China. Bush policymakers concluded that Chen was dangerous, a view that some in the Eisenhower administration took of Chiang Kai-shek. As a result, the United States labeled Chen a loose cannon and took various measures to express America's dislike of him and his policies. These included even questioning Taiwan's sovereignty (though this was a warning, not a shift in US policy) while limiting Chen and people in his administration from visiting the United States while openly opposing his efforts to push for Taiwan's legal independence in the form of a referendum to join the United Nations as Taiwan.[43]

When Ma Ying-jeou was elected president, the United States sent its congratulations and expressed a feeling of relief. It appeared that US-Taiwan relations were headed toward greater normalcy.

Taiwan and the People's Republic of China

When Chiang Kai-shek and the Chinese Nationalist army and government fled to Taiwan in 1949, their stated policy was to counterattack, destroy the Communist "bandit" regime on the Mainland, and reunite China. Chiang asserted that his defeat by Mao was the product of international communism and Soviet assistance to the Chinese Communists. He rationalized his Mainland policy by what he called the Soviet Union's efforts to "enslave China." This perspective fit with the bipolar nature of the global system at the time and the fact that the People's Republic of China was a member of the Soviet bloc.

This policy, of course, meant that political, economic, cultural, and all other ties with China were cut. The government did not allow citizens from Taiwan to go to China or to communicate with relatives or others there by mail, telephone, or other means. The two were at war.

However, Chiang's policy of liberating the Mainland could not be carried out given the size of Taiwan's military compared to China's. In fact, it depended on the international situation and, in particular, US-China policy. In other words, Chiang's real hope was that he could defeat Mao and return and rule China on the coattails of a broader East-West war. Chiang thought the Korean War might provide him an opportunity, but it didn't. Worse, after the war in Korea stalemated, the United States came to view Taipei's policy of liberating the Mainland as dangerous. Washington, therefore, sought to preclude any confrontation between the Nationalists and the Communists, and took appropriate actions such as pressuring Taipei not to provoke the People's Republic of China.[44] Still Taiwan served as a base of operations for American forces that "contained" China and kept intact its intelligence operations against China.

In the early 1960s, as noted earlier, Taipei lost of a good portion of its network of agents on the Mainland. Détente between the superpowers further dimmed Chiang's hopes for "liberating" China. The economic downturn in China and the Sino-Soviet dispute, which became serious at this time, offered the Nationalist government some hope. But generally conditions in China, the international situation, and US-China policy did not give Chiang any serious expectation for overthrowing Mao and returning to China.

Taipei's policy of liberating Mainland China might have been abandoned or may even have evolved into a two-China policy in the mid-1960s had it not been for the Vietnam War, which repolarized the world and gave Taipei renewed hope, however small, of once again ruling all of China. The Great Proletarian Cultural Revolution (when Mao promoted radical egalitarian communism in the People's Republic of China and pushed the nation into self-imposed isolationism) also gave Taipei reason to think its policies could be sustained. But as it turned out, Taipei espoused false hopes.

In the 1970s, after the Cultural Revolution ended (the violent phase coming to a close in 1969) and the Vietnam War became unpopular in the United States, Taipei lost two diplomatic battles with Beijing: one over representing China in the United Nations and the other in maintaining formal diplomatic ties with the United States. Subsequently, Beijing pressured Taiwan to reunify with China on its terms. Taipei adopted a policy called the "three no's" (no contact, no negotiations, and no compromise) to show its determination not to succumb. Nevertheless, Taipei's harsh rhetoric changed; for example, it stopped using the term "Communist bandits" to describe the government in China. Taipei sought to make a good impression on the United States and the world community and to deal with Beijing peacefully.[45]

In the early 1980s, China proposed to Taiwan what it called the "three links"—mail, trade, and transportation ties. Taiwan's response was cautious, but not hostile. In 1986, a plane belonging to Taiwan's flag carrier, China Airlines (CAL), was hijacked and flown to China. In an unexpected move, CAL officials (with the approval of the government) offered to negotiate with officials from Beijing (in Hong Kong) to get the plane back. This was the first time the two sides openly talked.[46] Not long after this incident, Taipei announced that its citizens could participate in conferences and its athletes go to games in Communist countries—including the People's Republic of China. Taipei's change of stance toward Beijing happened largely because economic and political reforms launched by Deng Xiaoping in 1978 had dramatically changed China. But Taipei was also influenced by criticism abroad and by suggestions that its policies were too hard-line in view of the vast changes going on in the world.

In 1987, Taipei enacted a new policy allowing its citizens to travel to the Mainland. Contacts with China, including trade and investment relations, mushroomed as a result. The next year, at its Thirteenth Party Congress, the Kuomintang adopted a new "Mainland policy," formally scrapping Taiwan's harsh anti-Communist posture.[47] To manage its new policies, which some labeled "détente," the government created the Mainland Affairs Council to coordinate efforts of government agencies and regulate exchanges across the Taiwan Strait. The council became an official organ of government in 1990, at which time the National Unification Council was established in the Office of the President and empowered with similar functions. Still another organization (this one private or semiprivate), the Straits Exchange Foundation, was created to manage unofficial relations.[48]

In the meantime, in the early 1980s, Beijing proffered the "one country, two systems" formula for resolving the "Taiwan issue" and unifying the country. Taiwan replied that the idea, which was the blueprint for Hong Kong's return to China, did not apply to Taiwan, as Taiwan had sovereignty and could defend itself. The opposition in Taiwan spoke about self-determination and the right of Taiwan's citizens to determine their future. In 1989, a member of the Legislative Yuan offered the idea of "one nation, two equal governments" as a framework for pursuing a more positive relationship with China. According to this formula, Beijing and Taipei both had sovereignty, but the latter espoused hope they might unite to become one nation in the future. The government in Taiwan realized it had to formulate new policies on its relations with China, formal and otherwise.[49]

Cross-strait détente was put on hold when Beijing blamed Taiwan for instigating the student protests that led to the Tiananmen Massacre in June 1989. Citizens in Taiwan were taken aback by the accusations and appalled by the brutal massacre that was followed by a sudden turn to the left politically (and to some degree economically as well) in China. Notwithstanding, Taipei took the view that, though the People's Republic of China had become a global pariah and was hostile toward Taiwan, Beijing would not likely adopt a self-imposed isolationist policy, as it had in the mid-1960s, and would continue to boom economically. Thus, Taipei still had to deal with Beijing.

In 1991, the National Unification Council adopted the "Guidelines for National Unification," which amounted, some said, to a formal statement of Taiwan's China policy. The document said unification would have to be attained in three stages: first, establishing exchanges and reciprocity; second, building trust and confidence; and third, promoting consultations and unification. The timing for moving from stage one to stages two and three, it said, should "respect the rights and interests of the people in the Taiwan area, and protect their security and welfare." Whether President Lee Teng-hui genuinely sought unification is uncertain; clearly government leaders held differences of opinion. The opposition espoused its own views—which were less supportive of cross-strait ties. The bottom line appeared to be: Taipei's policy was a wait-and-see position and to meanwhile maintain the status quo.

That same year, Taipei also proclaimed an end to the war with the People's Republic of China and pledged that it would not use force to achieve China's unification. Although war between Taiwan and China was not really at issue, formally ending this policy had some salience. It seemed a friendly gesture toward China, though oddly Taipei's terminating its claim that the Beijing government was not legitimate and formally ending the policy of liberating China was construed as rejecting Taiwan's one-China policy and was seen as another step in separating Taiwan from China. Taipei also announced its opposition to political negotiations until the "second stage" of relations had been reached. Additionally, it stated that direct trade, postal, and transportation links would have to wait until Beijing ceased denying Taipei's existence and dropped its threats to use force to resolve the Taiwan question.

In April 1993, unprecedented "negotiations" were held between representatives from Taipei and Beijing in Singapore. The "Koo-Wang (Wang-Gu in Beijing) talks," named after the heads of the unofficial organizations they represented (the Straits Exchange Foundation in Taiwan and the Association for Relations Across the Taiwan Strait in China), led to agreements on legalizing documents and establishing formal channels for communications between China and Taiwan. Though the agreements were not of great substance, the talks that produced them marked a significant breakthrough in cross-strait relations. In addition, both sides promised more significant talks in the future.[50] The meeting was thus called historic. Trade and investment contacts continued to flourish at this time: Taiwan soon became the People's Republic of China's second largest source of investment capital (after Hong Kong), and China became one of Taiwan's biggest export markets.

But President Lee also announced a "Go South" policy in order to encourage Taiwan's business community to look for trade and investment opportunities in Southeast Asia instead of China because, Lee thought, Taiwan was becoming too economically dependent on the Mainland. He reiterated this policy in stronger language in 1995 in another policy called the "no haste" policy. The government formalized this policy with "guidelines," stating that no enterprise in Taiwan should invest more than US$50 million in the Mainland or put money into infrastructure projects.

Better relations between Taipei and Beijing were subsequently hampered by the latter's hostile reaction to Taipei's attempt to rejoin various governmental and international organizations, including the United Nations, and actions Taipei regarded as part of Beijing's "scheme" to isolate Taiwan. A white paper on reunification, released in late 1993 by the People's Republic of China, contributed to further ill feeling, as did an incident at the time in which some tourists from Taiwan were murdered in China, following which Beijing engaged in a cover-up.[51] Relations were even further strained by Lee Teng-hui visiting the United States in 1995 in an effort to "break out" of the isolationism China had imposed on Taiwan after which Beijing conducted missile tests in the Taiwan Strait in response and also by even more provocative tests and military exercises in the spring of 1996 during Taiwan's first direct presidential election. Taiwan's voters expressed their displeasure with Beijing by reelecting President Lee with more votes and a stronger mandate than he would have won otherwise.

Two years later, cross-strait relations witnessed improvements, with the United States encouraging and apparently pressuring both sides to resolve their differences through talks. In October 1998, the Koo-Wang talks were put back on track. Koo Chen-fu, head of the Straits Exchange Foundation, traveled to China to meet with his counterpart and, at the same time, talked with President Jiang Zemin. The meetings were cordial and seemingly productive. But in July 1999, President Lee Teng-hui, during an interview with a German radio station, announced that hereafter cross-strait relations must be considered state-to-state. Chinese leaders were incensed and castigated Lee in numerous public statements. Some observers said that Lee's pronouncement was a response to President Clinton's "three no's" statement made in China in 1998 that many considered hostile toward Taiwan. In any event, cross-strait relations again turned sour.

During the 2000 presidential election campaign in Taiwan, all of the major candidates adopted policies of pursuing better cross-strait relations. Chen Shui-bian, who had been a staunch advocate of independence, softened his views dramatically—many observers said for the purpose of winning the election

since voters viewed him and his party as too radical on this issue. In his inauguration address, President Chen pledged that, as long as China does not use military
force against Taiwan, he would not declare independence, change the national title,
put former president Lee Teng-hui's state-to-state relationship idea in the Constitution, or promote a referendum to change the status quo regarding the question
of independence or unification. He also promised not to abolish the National
Reunification Council or the National Reunification Guidelines. This statement
was labeled Chen's "five no's" policy.[52]

But not long after this, President Chen strongly rejected Beijing's one-country,
two-systems formula (except as a talking point) and repudiated the so-called "1992
consensus" (both sides would espouse a one-China policy, though each could interpret this as they wished), which had made possible the Koo-Wang talks. This
and Chen's previous advocacy of Taiwan's independence, his not so subtle pro-
independence actions, and the view that Chen was a weak president prompted
Chinese leaders in Beijing to eschew dealing with him.[53]

In August 2002, President Chen, in the context of failed efforts to improve cross-
strait relations and Beijing's continuing to shun him, announced that perhaps Taiwan's future should be decided by a referendum. He also spoke of two sovereign
states, one on each side of the Taiwan Strait. Beijing's reaction was hostile. In 2004,
Chen had certain referendums put on the presidential election ballot that again
provoke China. After his reelection, he said he had a mandate to push for Taiwan's
independence. In 2006, Chen declared the National Unification Council ceased to
function and the unification guidelines were defunct. Meanwhile, President Chen
stated his intent to rewrite Taiwan's constitution (not keeping the provision that
Taiwan was a part of China) while advocating a referendum on participation in the
United Nations as Taiwan. Beijing's response was to request the United States to
"handle" Chen, promote expanded commercial relations with Taiwan, and ignore
Chen's provocations so as to avoid helping him politically.

Meanwhile, in 2005, in response to President Chen's provocations, China's
parliament enacted the Anti-Succession Law that read that China would employ
nonpeaceful means to prevent Taiwan from implementing legal independence.
Taiwan's response understandably was negative. But soon Beijing invited leaders of
the opposition in Taiwan to China, took a more friendly line on trade and some
other issues, and, in 2006, offered pandas to the Taipei Zoo.

However, it was said that Chinese leaders personally hated Chen Shui-bian. He
was a serious distraction to Beijing's policy of advancing its economic growth
(which was advantaged by good relations with the United States and tranquility in
East Asia). President Chen also caused discord between China's civilian and military leaders. But there was another view on this issue: that Chinese leaders liked
Chen because he mismanaged Taiwan's economy (making Taiwan economically

dependent on China), ruined its democratic image (with his policies of ethnic discrimination and declining press freedom and civil rights), and destroyed relations with the United States (thereby strengthening Sino-US ties). In other words, Beijing viewed the Chen administration as having done more to bring Taiwan "into the fold" and make unification more likely than any leader in Taiwan's recent past.[54]

When Ma Ying-jeou was elected president in 2008, Ma promised to promote better relations with China. Indeed, tensions subsided. There was considerable hope that economic ties would increase, though Ma could not do much to improve political relations in view of the fact that most of Taiwan's citizens preferred the status quo regarding unification and independence, and most wanted Taiwan to keep its sovereignty. In addition, while the United States did not want Taiwan to provoke China, it appeared to want Taiwan to remain separate from China.

Taiwan and the Rest of the World

In Asia, Japan is by far the most important country to Taiwan.[55] Even though the two countries have not had formal diplomatic ties since 1972, relations at various levels are extensive and meaningful. When Japan broke relations with Taipei, its government opened the Japan Interchange Association in Taipei, and Taiwan set up the Association of East Asian Relations in Tokyo. Both were designed to handle business formerly done by their embassies. Japan continued to trade with Taiwan and maintained other contacts almost as before, though most Japanese businesses renamed their operations in Taiwan. Japan's strategy—ending formal diplomatic ties while keeping other relations, especially commercial ties, otherwise undisturbed—became known as the "Japan Formula," and many other nations used it as a model when they shifted formal diplomatic ties to Beijing.

In 1992, Tokyo "upgraded" Taiwan's representative office in Japan, renaming it the Taipei Economic and Cultural Representative Offices. The word "Taipei" made the title seem more official and eliminated the confusion the old title had caused by not using any word that suggested the organization represented Taiwan. Neither the term "Republic of China" nor "Taiwan" was used in the new name, however, so as to avoid implying a two-Chinas policy. Many nations have followed Japan's lead on this name change.

Japan was Taiwan's second largest trading partner after the United States, and this trade relationship was important to Taiwan, though leaders in Taiwan have been concerned, and still are, about a large and persistent trade deficit with Japan. In addition, Japan is Taiwan's largest foreign investor. Finally, Taiwan's leaders believe Japan has a security interest in Taiwan and that Tokyo therefore favors Taiwan's continued sovereignty (though neither side says this openly). However, Taipei realizes Japan is not in a position to challenge China militarily or in other ways, and Tokyo's Taiwan policy will not depart from US policy in any meaningful way.

Taiwan long shared a bond with South Korea based on their strongly anti-Communist foreign policies (though now relaxed considerably in both countries). South Korea was one of the last important countries (and the last in Asia) with whom Taipei retained formal diplomatic ties, relations having been broken in 1992. Though the two are economic competitors, political and other relations are friendly. With the change in the bipolar world, Taipei has made some contacts with North Korea; however, this has not affected relations with South Korea. In pursuing relations with nations who have formal ties with Beijing, Taiwan's diplomats have often cited the fact that China has formal relations with both North and South Korea (or a two Koreas policy).

Taiwan's contacts with Hong Kong are important, though they have presented Taipei with unique challenges. The Nationalist Chinese cause once found many supporters (both anti-Communist and admirers of the Republic of China) among Hong Kong Chinese, and trade with the British colony was significant. Thus, the 1984 agreement between Beijing and London on Hong Kong's reunification with China presented Taipei with a serious dilemma: whether to try to continue contacts with Hong Kong after July 1, 1997 (the date Hong Kong would revert to China), and if so, in what fashion. Taiwan chose to maintain commercial and other links with Hong Kong. In fact, much of Taiwan's extensive trade with the People's Republic of China transited Hong Kong. Ironically, better relations between Taipei (especially direct trade links) and Beijing will hurt Hong Kong economically.

On the other hand, the government in Taiwan was, and is, careful to point out that Taiwan's situation is different from that of Hong Kong previous to its reversion to China. For example, President Lee noted that Taiwan is some distance away from China, that Taiwan has its own military, that Taiwan is not dependent on China economically, and, most important, that Taiwan (or the Republic of China) is a sovereign nation-state, not a colony. Therefore, he said, the "one country, two systems" used by Beijing to incorporate Hong Kong cannot apply to Taiwan. President Chen Shui-bian also made this argument.

Taipei maintains trade and other ties with nearly every country in Southeast Asia, though it has diplomatic ties with none. Singapore and Indonesia for some time diplomatically recognized neither Beijing nor Taipei, but in 1990, both established formal ties with the People's Republic of China. The other pro-Western, capitalist Southeast Asian nations (the Philippines, Brunei, Malaysia, and Thailand) have long been friendly toward Taipei, and Taiwan has significant commercial contacts with businesses there as well as ties with their Overseas Chinese communities. These countries at times have defied Beijing's efforts to isolate Taiwan diplomatically by sending high officials to Taipei and receiving Taiwan's top leaders on what have appeared to be state visits.

In the 1980s, Taipei sought to balance its trade and other ties with Beijing by what it called a "Go South" strategy aimed at forging closer economic ties with the countries of Southeast Asia. Taiwan became (if it wasn't already) a major trading partner with most of the countries in the region and a critical capital investor in several. It is now the leading investor in many countries in the area and an important source of foreign capital for the area as a whole. Taiwan imports natural resources from the area, including sizable quantities of oil from Indonesia. Foreign laborers from the area work in Taiwan, most of them from Thailand, the Philippines, Vietnam, and Indonesia. However, President Chen Shui-bian's support of local nationalism and his anti-Chinese (as opposed to Taiwanese) policies undermined Taiwan's relations with the Overseas Chinese communities in Southeast Asia while he needlessly (in the eyes of most Southeast Asian leaders) provoked Beijing and thereby hurt Taiwan's diplomatic efforts in the region.

Until the 1990s, relations with the former Communist Indochina countries—Vietnam, Cambodia, and Laos—were all but nonexistent. As Taipei changed its policy of not dealing with Communist countries, relations also changed with these countries—especially Vietnam, where Taiwan became a major investor. As a result of the 1997 East Asia economic crisis, Taiwan became an even bigger economic and political player in Southeast Asia. Relations with Myanmar (formerly Burma) have been poor, however, because of the disruptive presence of Nationalist soldiers there after World War II (a problem not completely resolved to this day) and its government's close ties with Beijing.

Ties with the countries of South Asia have not been very meaningful to Taiwan, either politically or economically. On the other hand, Taiwan has a representative office in India, and trade between the two countries and investment ties are growing. Taiwan does not perceive the region as one where it has vital interests, though Taipei does realize that India plays a "balancing role" against China, and this may become more meaningful in the future, especially if US-Indian relations (particularly at the strategic level) improve. In other words, India may become part of an Asian balance of power that will have relevance to Taiwan.

Taiwan for some years had meaningful ties with several Middle Eastern countries, especially those that were most strongly anti-Communist, but over time, it lost formal diplomatic relations with all of the countries in the area. In 1991, Taipei ended its diplomatic ties with Saudi Arabia—the most important nation in the world with which Taipei still had formal relations at the time and the last country in the region to diplomatically support Taipei. Yet relations remained cordial with Saudi Arabia, and it is still Taiwan's largest supplier of petroleum. Kuwait is also a major source of oil for Taiwan, and relations between the two countries are good.

Taipei, in addition, maintains very friendly relations with several other Middle Eastern countries. Taiwan's Middle East policy concentrates on maintaining reliable sources of petroleum (getting a large portion of its imports from the area), encouraging trade, and maintaining cultural contacts.

Taipei maintains informal—but in some ways important—ties with Israel. In 1949, Israel granted diplomatic recognition to the People's Republic of China (though the latter did not reciprocate). Taipei did not openly try to promote better relations because it did not want to endanger its relationship with Saudi Arabia and other Arab countries. This situation generally persists. Taiwan for some time saw its own situation as similar to that of Israel: Israel's geographic location in the midst of enemies that have support from the Third World; its status as a pariah nation; and its role as a successful, albeit controversial, regional actor (although Taiwan is certainly no longer a pariah nation). Taipei still views its geopolitical status as similar to Israel's in some respects.

In Western Europe, Taipei maintains formal diplomatic ties with only one nation—the Vatican. The good relationship with the Vatican has hinged mainly on strained relations between the Catholic Church and Beijing, which may or may not last. Taipei's contacts with other European nations are primarily commercial. Several Western European countries are important trading partners for Taiwan, the largest being Germany. Trade between Taiwan and the European Union has increased appreciably in the last two decades. Taipei's major objectives vis-à-vis Europe are to increase and diversify its trade relations and also to maintain and enhance nonpolitical ties that can bolster support for its sovereignty. It likewise seeks to increase its global political ties and win European support for its participation in various international organizations. The European Union has often supported Taipei's efforts to gain global status, especially in international economic organizations.

Taiwan has no diplomatic ties with any of the nations of Eastern Europe. Taipei established formal diplomatic relations with Macedonia when it became independent after the breakup of the former Yugoslavia, but subsequently those ties were broken. After the collapse of the Soviet bloc in 1991, Taipei initiated informal contacts with several Eastern European countries that led to establishing trade and cultural ties in the region. In fact, links with East European nations have helped Taiwan diversify its imports and exports and also establish relations with Communist (now former Communist) countries so as to bolster its flexible diplomacy and its efforts to avoid being isolated by Beijing. Taiwan's "dollar diplomacy" (giving economic aid for increased political ties) has also had some results in the region. Taiwan's leaders have made some high-level visits to Eastern European countries.

Before 1990, Taiwan had few formal contacts with the Soviet Union, though there were some reports of behind-the-scenes meetings in the 1960s as Sino-Soviet relations deteriorated. In April 1990, Taiwan ended many restrictions on links with the Soviet Union as part of its flexible diplomacy; trade, which was minimal, increased very quickly. Until recently, though, decision makers in Taipei have had little hope of establishing more meaningful relations with Russia, particularly political ties, because of closer relations between Moscow and Beijing.

After the breakup of the Soviet Union, Taipei sought to develop various contacts with members of the new Commonwealth of Independent States, though it did not think seriously of establishing formal diplomatic relations with any of them. In 1991, Taipei's China External Trade Development Council opened an office in Moscow, and in 1992, Taipei negotiated establishing a representative office there called the Taipei Moscow Economic and Cultural Coordination Commission, which it opened in 1993. In 1996, Russia established a similar office in Taipei. Taipei has placed special emphasis on relations with Russia, Belarus, Ukraine, and Kazakhstan, with its diplomatic efforts emphasizing aid, investment, and trade.

In Africa, Taipei established and maintained formal diplomatic ties with a number of countries, notwithstanding its close relations with South Africa. Relations with South Africa were the most meaningful of any countries on the continent, and South Africa was, when it severed formal ties with Taipei in 1996, the most important nation in the world with which Taipei maintained formal diplomatic relations at that time. Informal relations have been retained, and Taiwan still purchases uranium from South Africa; other trade between the two is also significant. Investment from Taiwan has diminished with the break in diplomatic relations, however, and does not seem likely to be restored.

Although Taipei lost its diplomatic relations with most other African states in the competition with Beijing for recognition in the 1960s and 1970s, many of these states established ties with Beijing for symbolic reasons only or to support what was then considered a Third World cause. Few broke diplomatic relations with Taiwan for other reasons, and few were hostile toward Taipei when severing relations. Some retained formal diplomatic ties with Taipei even after establishing them with Beijing; Taipei accepted dual recognition, but Beijing did not. Taipei maintained a good image in Africa—generally because of its economic successes and because Beijing, with its new cordial relations with the West, in many ways disappointed African countries. China's diminished foreign aid was also a factor, especially since Beijing, from the 1980s on, began taking the lion's share of loans and grants from various international financial organizations to the detriment of many African countries. Taipei has also won sympathy from African countries because it is a small nation bullied by a larger one—a familiar situation for many African nations. Its enlarged economic assistance program, called the International Economic and Cooperation Development Fund, established in 1988, enabled Taiwan to reestablish ties with several African nations and restore formal diplomatic relations with some of them.

In recent years, however, Taiwan has suffered repeated diplomatic setbacks in Africa due to China's increased interest in the area as a source of energy and raw materials needed to keep its economy booming and the fact that it has money to spend on aid and investment, which African nations sorely need. Taiwan has not been able to compete.

Taiwan maintains formal diplomatic ties with more nations in Latin America than anywhere else—mostly Central American and Caribbean countries. The reason for this is that most of these countries simply lack any motive for establishing relations with Beijing. Taipei's efforts to rejoin the United Nations (since 1993) and other international organizations have been supported by some of these nations. However, like Africa, Taiwan's relations with nations in the region have recently been undermined by China's increased trade, investments, and aid.

In lieu of formal diplomatic relations, Taiwan has trade and cultural ties with Australia, New Zealand, and Canada. Relations have improved with all three in recent years, most noticeably with Canada, whose government was cool toward Taiwan for some years after it established diplomatic relations with Beijing in the 1960s. Australia is a major source of natural resources for Taiwan, and Taiwan has made sizable investments there. However, it is unlikely Taiwan can count on any of these nations for support for its separation from China.

Taipei maintains formal diplomatic ties with several South Pacific countries. Though there is aid competition with China in this region, Taipei may be able to keep its ties with some of these nations because it can concentrate aid in smaller countries. On the other hand, these countries do not have much global influence and certainly won't impact Taiwan's status as a nation or not.

When the Chen administration left office in May 2008, only twenty-three countries, all minor ones, maintained formal diplomatic relations with Taiwan. This is half a dozen fewer than in 2000 when President Chen assumed office. He had promised to expand Taipei's formal relations when he campaigned for president, saying that he would establish ties as Taiwan. In this effort, he failed. Whether he damaged Taiwan's bid to be a sovereign nation because of this is difficult to say. Taipei's status as a nation-state had already diminished considerably before 2000. In any case, there is no set number of nations with which a country has to have diplomatic ties in order to keep its sovereignty.

Ties with International Organizations

The Republic of China was a founding member of the United Nations in 1945 and was one of the five big powers given a permanent seat on the Security Council.[56] When the Nationalist government fled to Taiwan in 1949, it retained the China seat mainly for two reasons: (1) The government of the Republic of China had survived, and (2) the newly founded People's Republic of China expressed hostility toward the Western rules of diplomatic practice as well as toward most international organizations, including the United Nations. After China became an active participant in the Korean War, sending troops that battled UN forces, China's relations with global organizations (which China regarded as controlled by imperialist forces) worsened. In ensuing years, Taipei and many of its supporters in the United Nations contended that the Communist regime in China did not meet the UN Charter's requirement that member nations be "peace-loving." Meanwhile, Mao and other Chinese leaders made no serious efforts to counter this view and expressed no serious interest in joining the United Nations.

Given Peking's strongly anti–status-quo foreign policy that lasted for the next two decades, it was obvious that China had no desire to join the world body and occupy the China seat on the UN Security Council. Moscow likewise did not appear to want the People's Republic of China admitted, though it consistently said it did. Taipei, on the other hand, wished to remain a member and continue to represent China, and the United States and many other Western countries supported Taipei's position.

As memories of the Korean War faded, global politics evolved away from a rigidly bipolar structure, and as the People's Republic of China established diplomatic ties with a significant number of non-Communist nations around the world, Taipei gradually lost support for its efforts to continue to represent China in the international community. As early as 1960, Taipei encountered some problems with the United Nations and other international organizations. For example, in 1961, it was put in an awkward position in the United Nations when the Soviet Union proposed that Outer Mongolia be admitted. Taipei claimed Outer Mongolia was Chinese territory; furthermore, it did not want to see another Communist country admitted to the UN for fear of setting a precedent that might lead to the seating of the People's Republic of China. But the proposal was to admit Outer Mongolia and Mauritania simultaneously, and Taipei did not want to anger African nations by invoking the veto.[57] Taiwan, therefore, acquiesced. More such situations followed.

Likewise, the charge that the People's Republic of China was not a peace-loving nation began to lose credibility as there occurred frequent examples of less than peace-loving acts committed by UN members. Moreover, because universality was considered important, many nations felt it was wrong to isolate the People's Republic of China, the largest nation in the world in population, by keeping it out of the United Nations. Hence, Taipei's supporters, rather than continuing to condemn the People's Republic of China, switched approaches, arguing that the issue of China's representation in the United Nations was an "important matter" that required a two-thirds vote. China was unlikely, Taipei reckoned, to get two-thirds of UN members to support its admission, which presumably meant also expelling Taiwan.

During the 1960s, Beijing's unsuccessful efforts to create its own "revolution-ary" United Nations (in cooperation with Indonesia) and China's self-imposed isolationism, caused by the Cultural Revolution, gave Taipei a brief respite. Never-theless, throughout the decade, the UN vote on the issue of Chinese representa-tion increasingly favored Beijing. In 1965, it was a tie: forty-seven for the People's Republic of China, forty-seven against, and twenty abstentions. China seemed destined to win the China representation battle. In 1970, Beijing got two more votes than Taipei when the issue of the China seat was considered. This margin was not sufficient, though; the "important" issue of membership required a two-thirds majority. In 1971, after US National Security Adviser Henry Kissinger flew to Beijing and arranged for President Nixon's visit there to take place in February of the following year (a highly publicized event), a vote was taken on the two-thirds rule. The United States, which tacitly supported the rule (though it put little pressure on its allies to vote with the United States), lost.[58] The United Nations thereupon seated Beijing.

In the wake of losing the UN fight (actually withdrawing rather than proposing two China seats or a new seat for Taiwan, or creating a crisis by claiming the right to veto), Taipei lost its representation in other international organizations; indeed, in the wake of its UN victory, Beijing actively sought Taipei's expulsion from all in-ternational public or governmental institutions, even demanding the exclusion of statistics on Taiwan from the United Nations and its affiliated agencies' publica-tions. Its objective was to completely isolate Taiwan from the international com-munity and thereby compel Taipei to negotiate reunification with Beijing. Taipei, of course, resisted.

Taiwan remained in the World Bank and the International Monetary Fund until the early 1980s, but was eventually forced out of these organizations at Beijing's behest. By 1984, Taiwan belonged to only ten governmental international organi-zations, the most important of these being the Asian Development Bank (ADB). Taipei retained its membership in the ADB because it had different rules for mem-bership; in addition, the United States supported Taipei's inclusion. Still, pressure mounted to admit the People's Republic of China, and a compromise in 1985 al-lowed representation of both regimes in the bank. Meanwhile, in 1981, Taipei re-joined the International Olympic Committee under the name "Taipei, China." While this term was humiliating to Taiwan (and was used also by the Asian Devel-opment Bank after Beijing joined), it reflected Taipei's flexible diplomacy and pre-vented Taiwan from being excluded from these two important international organizations.

During this period, Taipei remained active in many other international bodies that were less important and not overtly political. Additionally, from 1979 to 1982, it increased its representation in nonpolitical or nongovernmental international organizations from 254 to 630. By the middle of the 1980s, Taiwan was represented in a host of nonpolitical (not requiring statehood for membership) organizations that Beijing also participated in. It currently belongs to more than 1,000 international organizations.[59] It sends representatives to several hundred international meetings each year and hosts many conferences and gatherings in Taipei. Taiwan also continues to participate in sports, cultural, and other gatherings sponsored by other countries and international bodies. In short, Taiwan has been excluded only from the larger, more important global political organizations (with the exception of those just mentioned).

In the late 1980s, Taipei launched some new and creative efforts to rejoin some important international organizations, chiefly financial or trade groups. In 1990, when Taipei formally applied for membership in the General Agreement on Tariffs and Trade (GATT), it was given observer status. The next year, it attained membership (together with the People's Republic of China and Hong Kong) in the Asia Pacific Economic Cooperation (APEC) group, using the appellation "Chinese, Taipei," agreeing to be represented by its minister of economic affairs rather than its foreign minister. In 1992, Taipei was admitted to the South Pacific Forum using the name "Taiwan/Republic of China."

Meanwhile, in 1991, the Legislative Yuan passed a motion saying that Taiwan should be allowed to rejoin the United Nations. Two years later, President Lee Teng-hui announced that Taipei would seek participation in the world body, after which the Foreign Ministry declared this a major goal of the Republic of China's foreign policy. Subsequently, seven Central American countries put this issue on the agenda of the General Assembly's fall meeting. Though the proposal did not succeed, supporters continued to speak for Taiwan's representation in the United Nations and UN-affiliated organizations. In ensuing years, Taipei failed in annual bids to "participate" in the United Nations, but the number of supporters increased from the previous year: from three in 1993 to seventeen in 1996. In 1996, the European Parliament passed a resolution stating that Taiwan deserved a seat in all major international organizations. Subsequently, the US Congress passed a resolution supporting the European Parliament's position.

In 1997, Taipei changed its strategy a bit and asked its supporters to request that the UN General Assembly reassess Resolution 2758 (which, in 1971, unseated Taipei and seated Beijing) and revoke it. The efficacy of such a tactic—or, for that matter, any other—however, was doubtful. Beijing remained adamantly opposed to Taipei's presence in the United Nations in any form and held veto power over its admission; it also has had the support of the United States and many other countries for this position. On the other hand, the United Nations allows representation of non–nation-state representatives and is endeavoring to be more universal, positions that favor Taiwan.

In January 2002, Taiwan gained membership in the World Trade Organization (WTO). Because the WTO is a prominent international organization, membership was an important event for Taipei—even though it had to wait many years to enter due to an agreement whereby China would enter first, and Taiwan had to accept the title "Customs Territory of Taiwan, Penghu, Kinmen, and Matsu." Some in Taipei said that Taiwan's membership would facilitate its efforts to negotiate with Beijing, though China rejected this idea. In any case, this did not prove true.

Taipei charges that not being allowed a voice in the United Nations and other bodies is based on a "myth" (reminding one of the argument used by supporters of Beijing's application in the 1960s) that Taiwan does not exist. It says that its exclusion is a violation of the human rights of its 23 million people and further claims that its being (the only "nation" in the world) denied membership is not consonant with the inclusive and nondiscriminating ideals of these organizations. Finally, Taipei notes that it is a democratic nation and an upstanding member of the international community and does not deserve the treatment it has received from the world body. Reason would suggest Taiwan be allowed membership in some global regulatory organizations, such as the World Health Organization, the International Atomic Energy Agency (since Taiwan is a major user of nuclear energy), as well as environmental, law enforcement (such as INTERPOL), and other such agencies.

In 2008, the Chen administration made a bid for Taiwan to participate in the United Nations as "Taiwan"—it having been expelled as the Republic of China and having failed to obtain admission to global institutions using that name. But the United Nations rejected its bid and many nations, including the United States, saw the effort as an effort by President Chen to provoke China for his own partisan political reasons. The DPP presented the bid to the electorate in the form of a referendum, but it failed to pass in large part because this is not easy to do according to provisions in Taiwan's Referendum Law. This to some degree discredited Taiwan's effort to gain greater global recognition.

Notes

1. See W. G. Goddard, *Formosa: A Study in Chinese History* (East Lansing: Michigan State University Press, 1966), 25. The author notes that in the year 1000, sugar, rice, tea, and dyes were exported to China in meaningful amounts.

2. See Denny Roy, *Taiwan: A Political History* (Ithaca, NY: Cornell University Press, 2003), 29–30.

3. For a detailed study of Taiwan's external relations for the three decades after 1949, see Chiao Chiao Hsieh, *Strategy for Survival: The Foreign Policy and External Relations of the Republic of China on Taiwan, 1959–79* (London: Sherwood Press, 1985). For a more recent analysis, see Yu San Wang, ed., *Foreign Policy of the Republic of China on Taiwan* (New York: Praeger, 1990).

4. Chiang's speech can be found in *The China 1959–1960 Yearbook* (Taipei: China Publishing Company, 1960), 947.

5. Thomas E. Stolper, *China, Taiwan and the Offshore Islands* (Armonk, NY: M. E. Sharpe, 1985), 88–90. Also see David M. Finkelstein, *Washington's Taiwan Dilemma: From Abandonment to Salvation* (Fairfax, VA: George Mason University Press, 1993). This agreement was formalized in a communiqué between Washington and Taipei. See "ROC-US Joint Communiqué, October 23, 1958," in *American Foreign Policy Documents* (Washington, D.C.: US Government Printing Office, 1962), 1184–1185.

6. This point is further argued in John F. Copper, "Taiwan's Strategy and U.S. Recognition of China," *Orbis* (Summer 1977): 261–276.

7. Ralph N. Clough, *Island China* (Cambridge, MA: Harvard University Press, 1978), 153–154.

8. See John F. Copper, *China Diplomacy: The Washington-Taipei-Beijing Triangle* (Boulder, CO: Westview Press, 1992), chapter 4.

9. For details, see Robert L. Downen, *To Bridge the Taiwan Strait* (Washington, D.C.: Council for Social and Economic Studies, 1984).

10. See Vernon V. Aspaturian, "International Reactions and Responses to PRC Uses of Force Against Taiwan," in Parris H. Chang and Martin L. Lasater, eds., *If China Crosses the Taiwan Strait: The International Response* (Lanham, MD: University Press of America, 1993), 126.

11. See John F. Copper, "Taiwan and the New World Order," *Journal of East Asian Affairs* (Winter/Spring 1995), for further details.

12. See John Fuh-sheng Hsieh, "Chiefs, Staffers, Indians, and Others: How Was Taiwan's Mainland China Policy Made?" in Tun-jen Cheng, Chi Huang, and Samuel S. G. Wu, eds., *Inherited Rivalry: Conflict Across the Taiwan Strait* (Boulder, CO: Lynn Rienner, 1995).

13. John F. Copper, "Why the Bush Administration Soured on Taiwan," in Suisheng Zhao, ed., *U.S.-China Relations: Cooperation and Competition in Northeast Asia* (London: Palgrave/Macmillan, 2008).

14. For details on Taiwan's security problems, see Dennis Van Vranken Hickey, *United States-Taiwan Security Ties: From Cold War to Beyond Containment* (New York: Praeger, 1994), and Martin L. Lasater, *The Taiwan Issue in Sino-American Strategic Relations* (Boulder, CO: Westview Press, 1984).

15. Chiang Kai-shek increased Nationalist forces on Quemoy and Matsu after the second Offshore Islands crisis in 1958. See Hsieh, *Strategy for Survival*, 87.

16. See "The Republic of China," *Wikipedia* (online at wikipedia.com). In addition, Taiwan had reserves totaling US$3.87 million.

17. Clough, *Island China*, 118–120.

18. See Dennis Hickey, *Foreign Policy Making in Taiwan: From Principles to Pragmatism* (London: Routledge, 2007), 66–67.

19. See John W. Garver, "Taiwan's Russian Option: Image and Reality," *Asian Survey* (July 1978): 752.

20. Various authors and publications have listed Taiwan as a potential nuclear power. There seems little question that Taiwan could build a nuclear weapon if it chose to do so.

21. See Dennis Van Vranken Hickey, *United States–Taiwan Security Ties: From Cold War to Beyond Containment* (New York: Praeger, 1994), 79–81.

22. See Clough, *Island China*, 64–66.

23. "Phasing out conscription readies army for a new era," *Taiwan Journal*, August 29, 2008 (online at taiwanjournal.nat.gov.tw).

24. See Ralph N. Clough, *Reaching Across the Taiwan Strait: People-to-People Diplomacy* (Boulder, CO: Westview Press, 1993), 156–157, for further discussion of domestic politics and foreign policy. Also see Chapter 8 of this book.

25. See Jonathan D. Pollack, "Short-range ballistic missile capabilities," in Steve Tsang, ed., *If China Attacks Taiwan: Military Strategy, Politics and Economics* (London: Routledge, 2006) 57–72.

26. Michael D. Swaine, "Taiwan's Defense Reforms and Military Modernization Program: Objectives, Achievements, and Obstacles," in Nancy Bernkopf Tucker, ed., *Dangerous Strait: The U.S.-Taiwan Crisis* (New York: Columbia University Press, 2005) 156.

27. See Dennis Hickey, "Coming in from the Cold," *Issues and Studies* (October 1994): 101–102.

28. See *1992 National Defense Report: Republic of China* (Taipei: Li Ming Cultural Enterprise Co., 1992).

29. See *ROC Foreign Affairs Report* (Taipei: Government Information Office, 1993). Some other examples are King-yuh Chang, *A Framework for China's Unification* (Taipei: Kwang Hwa Publishing Company, 1987); Parris H. Chang, "China's Relations with Hong Kong and Taiwan," *The Annals* (January 1992); Parris H. Chang, "Beijing's Relations with Taiwan," in Chang and Lasater, *If China Crosses the Taiwan Strait*; Frederick Chien, "A View from Taipei," *Foreign Affairs* (Winter 1991–1992); Bih-jaw Lin, "Taipei's Search for a New Foreign Policy Approach," in Stephen W. Mosher, ed., *The United States and the Republic of China: Democratic Friends, Strategic Allies, and Economic Partners* (New Brunswick, NJ: Transaction Publishers, 1992); Yu-ming Shaw, "Taiwan: A View from Taipei," *Foreign Affairs* (Summer 1985).

30. For background details, see Jerome Alan Cohen, Edward Friedman, Harold C. Hinton, and Allen S. Whiting, *Taiwan and American Policy: The Dilemma in U.S. China Relations* (New York: Praeger, 1981).

31. See Nancy Bernkopf Tucker, *Taiwan, Hong Kong and the United States, 1945–1992: Uncertain Friendships* (New York: Twayne Publisher, 1994), 45–47.

32. Ibid., 122.

33. See Roderick MacFarquhar, *Sino-American Relations: 1949–1971* (New York: Praeger, 1972), 183–184.

34. A. James Gregor and Maria Hsia Chang, "Taiwan: The 'Wild Card' in U.S. Defense Policy in the Far Pacific," in James C. Hsiung and Winberg Chai, eds., *Asia and U.S. Foreign Policy* (New York: Praeger, 1981).

35. See Copper, *China Diplomacy,* chapter 2.

36. Ibid., 88–95.

37. See Jan Prybyla, "Economic Relations," in Stephen P. Gilbert and William M. Carpenter, eds., *America and Island China: A Documentary History* (Lanham, MD: University Press of America, 1989), 66–67.

38. For details on the US-Taiwan trade issue, see Jimmy W. Wheeler and Perry L. Wood, *Beyond Recrimination: Perspectives on U.S.-Taiwan Trade Tensions* (Indianapolis, IN: The Hudson Institute, 1987).

39. For further details, see Robert G. Sutter, "Taiwan: Recent Developments and U.S. Policy Choices," CRS Issue Brief (Congressional Research Service, Library of Congress), January 23, 1995.

40. See Copper, *Playing With Fire,* chapter 13.

41. See John F. Copper, "A U.S. Negotiating Role in Resolving Beijing-Taipei Differences," *Journal of East Asian Affairs* (Summer/Fall 1998).

42. See Nancy Bernkopf Tucker, "If Taiwan Chooses Unification, Should the United States Care?" *Washington Quarterly* (Summer 2002).

43. Hickey, *Foreign Policy Making in Taiwan*, 38–39.

44. See Hsieh, *Strategy for Survival*, chapter 4.

45. Premier Sun made this statement in a speech titled "The China Issue and China's Re-unification" in June 1982. The Government Information Office in Taipei subsequently published this speech.

46. Taipei was represented by officials of China Airlines, but since CAL is the Republic of China's national carrier, talks were considered official.

47. See John F. Copper, "The KMT's 13th Party Congress: Reform, Democratization, New Blood," in Cynthia Chenault, ed., *Modernizing East Asia: Economic and Cultural Dimensions of Political Change* (New York: St. John's University Press, 1989).

48. For details on these organizations, see Copper, *Historical Dictionary on Taiwan*.

49. See Clough, *Reaching Across the Taiwan Strait*, 16.

50. For details, see Hungdah Chiu, *The Koo-Wang Talks and the Prospect of Building Constructive and Stable Relations Across the Taiwan Straits* (Baltimore: University of Maryland School of Law, 1993).

.51. For details on Beijing's "White Paper" and its policies toward Taiwan, see John F. Copper, *Words Across the Taiwan Strait: A Critique of Beijing's "White Paper" on China's Unification* (Lanham, MD: University Press of America, 1995).

52. Hickey, *Foreign Policy Making in Taiwan*, 100–101.

53. For details, see Lijun Sheng, *China and Taiwan: Cross-Strait Relations Under Chen Shui-bian* (London: ZED Books, 2002), chapter 4.

54. See John F. Copper, "China's Choice for Taiwan's Next Leader," *Taipei Times*, July 15, 2007 (online at taipeitimes.com).

55. For details on Taiwan's relations with various countries, see *The Republic of China Yearbook—Taiwan 2002* (Taipei: Government Information Office, 2002), 130–138.

56. For background, see Jerome Alan Cohen, "U.S. Policy Options: The United Nations, Diplomatic Relations, and the Status of Taiwan," in Cohen et al., *Taiwan and American Policy*, 156–166.

57. See Samuel S. Kim, *China, the United Nations and World Order* (Princeton, NJ: Princeton University Press, 1979), 189.

58. Ibid., 101–105.

59. *Taiwan Yearbook 2007*, 127.

7

THE FUTURE

THROUGHOUT THIS BOOK, the reader has learned that few nations face a future more fraught with uncertainty than Taiwan. The People's Republic of China claims Taiwan is not a nation; rather, Taiwan is its territory—a province of China. And Beijing promises to use military force to resolve the matter. This has brought China into conflict with the United States, the last time in 1996. The two—the world's only superpower and the world's fastest rising power and challenger—are not able to resolve the "Taiwan issue." That is why the Taiwan Strait is the world's number one flashpoint—or the place that might ignite a global war. Yet some Chinese leaders seem to think the problem should not and/or cannot be resolved soon. They don't see it as an urgent matter—economic development is China's first priority. The virulence of Chinese nationalism and irredentism and the Chinese military say otherwise. Some in Taiwan see its future as part of China or a Chinese federation; most do not. The Chen administration espoused a policy of independence, but that failed. Most citizens in Taiwan prefer the status quo: they want separation from China for now, but they also favor cordial cross-strait relations and want the government to promote economic ties and avoid war. But that is no answer to the question. In deciding Taiwan's future, US policy is more important than what either Beijing or Taipei does or says. If Beijing decides to invade Taiwan and the United States does not intervene, Taiwan will not survive; if the United States intervenes on Taiwan's side, it will. But how long can the United States be responsible for Taiwan's fate? Perhaps twenty years, or a bit longer. The international community may help resolve the "Taiwan issue," but its role will be a marginal one. Taiwan's destiny in the meantime will be affected by its changing social, economic, and political conditions—though they will be important mainly because they change the milieu in which Taiwan's status will be determined by the United States and/or China. Following is some further analysis that may shed some light on where Taiwan is going, what its future ultimately is, and what of that is important.

Beginning Assumptions

Taiwan's historical records are not very useful in ascertaining whether or not it is or should be part of China. In any case, historical arguments are generally not effective in resolving territorial claims. In the twentieth century, Taiwan was part of China for only four years. However, for a number of years, Taipei, representing the Republic of China, claimed legal jurisdiction over all of China, saying that the government in Beijing was illegitimate. Taipei formally and officially espoused a one-China policy, meaning that it considered Taiwan part of China, but it showed that it meant this less and less over time. President Lee Teng-hui spoke of unification, but acted for independence. The 2000 election appeared to change Taiwan's national identity and its future: President Chen Shui-bian had long been an ardent advocate of Taiwan's permanent separation from China, or in other words, its legal independence. But the Chen government was inconsistent about this; indeed, some of its statements and actions suggested its policy was independence, while others did not. In the end, President Chen hurt the cause of independence more than he helped it.

Taiwan is regarded by its population as well as most of the international community as sovereign. Under traditional international law, there were four qualifications for nationhood: territory, population, government, and diplomatic ties. As noted in Chapter 1, Taiwan is as large in territory as nearly half the world's nations. The territory under its control has remained unchanged for more than a generation. Its population is larger than more than two-thirds of the member states of the United Nations. Its government is stable. Taiwan, in the view of the Western media and most other observers, is a democracy. Its diplomatic status is weak, but, in most respects, is on a par with that of most Third World countries.

Meanwhile, according to modern practice, the qualifications for nationhood have been weakened so that former colonies, trust territories, and numerous small and Third World countries can qualify. There was, and is, a popular expectation that all the land territory in the world will become or join sovereign nation-states—most likely the former. In the wake of the Cold War, international institutions were supposed to be universal and past feuds ended—peacefully. The proliferation of nation-states in recent years, based on the idea of self-determination, is also a poignant fact. All of these trends appear to advantage Taiwan if it wants to remain a nation-state.

On the other hand, Beijing has successfully pressured most nations not to maintain diplomatic relations with Taiwan and has blocked Taipei from entering international organizations where statehood is a qualification for membership. Thus, the international community does not view Taiwan as fully sovereign, or at least it perceives it should not make an issue of this so as to avoid war. This situation is unlikely to change, but if it does, it will not favor Taiwan. The reality is that China is now a great power. For three decades, its economy has boomed. Its economic growth has literally eclipsed that of any other important power. For nearly two decades, its military spending increases have outpaced all competitors. The rise of China is unprecedented in modern history, and this will inevitably impact how others view Taiwan's status and how Taiwan views itself.

Chinese leaders in Beijing contest Taiwan's claim to nationhood and threaten to deploy their military against Taiwan under certain circumstances. Beijing says it will use the force of arms if Taipei (1) allows foreign bases on or foreign control of any or all of its territory, (2) builds nuclear weapons, (3) experiences internal turmoil, (4) declares independence, or (5) refuses to negotiate reunification over a long period. This casts further doubt on Taiwan's sovereignty. Who is to challenge China on this matter now or in the future?

But how serious are Chinese leaders in Beijing about this threat? Is there a perceived need to resort to force? Finally, what about the United States? What will it do? (The latter question will be considered in the next section.)

In the years immediately after 1949, the People's Republic of China feared that some other nation or nations might have territorial designs on Taiwan. The United States was first on the list. American imperialism explained why Taiwan was yet to be incorporated. But this may have been more a propaganda play rising out of the status of Sino-American relations than a genuine concern. The Soviet Union was thought, after about 1960, to have ill intentions toward Taiwan; although this may have been true at that time and perhaps was during the 1970s and 1980s, it is no longer the case. Japanese leaders may well covet Taiwan and may want to govern it, but this will not happen under foreseeable circumstances. The United States forswears any territorial interest in Taiwan. Beijing probably does not need not worry seriously that Taiwan will become the property of another nation, even though it was for extended periods in the past. Given these circumstances, any recourse to using force against Taiwan seems unlikely.

What about a foreign nation acquiring bases on Taiwan? It also seems unlikely. The United States closed its bases in Taiwan after President Nixon's rapprochement with China, and it is not Washington's policy to reestablish them. Yet the possibility of stationing troops on Taiwan, at least temporarily, was broached during the 1996 missile crisis. If there is a conflict in the Taiwan Strait or an attack on Taiwan, the United States may well exercise this option. But in this event, the conflict will have already started, so if the United States acquired or built bases on Taiwan in this context, they would probably be little more than a minor irritant or a small issue in a broad war that would have other more serious consequences.

What about Taiwan going nuclear? As noted in Chapter 6, at one time Taiwan considered the "nuclear option." Top government officials, including President Chiang Ching-kuo, even broached this possibility. Washington's "abandoning" Taiwan under Nixon, Ford, and Carter caused the issue to gain resonance. The United States, however, took overt (brazen and illegal) actions to stop it, and nothing much has been heard of it since. Taiwan cannot engage in a nuclear arms race with China. So why try? It would lose US and global support if it did. Both presidential candidates in the 2008 election forswore seeking nuclear weapons. Thus, the likelihood is that Taiwan won't go nuclear and the People's Republic of China has no "nuclear reason" to attack Taiwan.

Internal stability, or the lack of it, in Taiwan cannot be easily defined, much less predicted. One can say with a great deal of certitude, however, that Taiwan (as was noted in Chapter 4) has a good record of political and social stability, particularly given the vast economic, political, social, and other changes it has undergone in recent years. It has democratized smoothly and without bloodshed (though there have been frequent highly publicized fistfights in its legislature and threats of violence and political gridlock during the Chen years). Taiwan made a peaceful transition of executive power from the KMT to the opposition party in 2000. This produced less turmoil and uncertainty than a similar change of governments in most developing nations. In 2008, Taiwan's democracy was "consolidated again" when the KMT returned to power. Therefore, there is little reason to anticipate serious chaos in Taiwan in the future.

Taiwan does have a potential for ethnic conflict. Notwithstanding equitable economic and social opportunities, considerable intermarriage, and other indicators, ethnic discord is still a problem, as has been evident in the ethnic tendencies in voting and candidates playing the "ethnic card" during recent election campaigns. Tensions were particularly evident after Chen Shui-bian became president in 2000. Ethnic friction might erupt as a byproduct of future debates about reunification with the People's Republic of China. It is a problem. But exacerbating ethnic ill will was part of the reason the DPP was removed from power in 2008. Citizens voted for better ethnic relations, and ethnic tension subsided.

Other potential causes of political instability are crime, corruption, and possibly some (perceived at least) critical social problems. Crime has increased markedly in recent years, along with the public's apprehension about it. Corruption is a major concern to Taiwan's populace. Because corruption is viewed as bad for its democratization and is related in the public's mind to crime (inasmuch as politicians and gangs have been associated), it is viewed as a more serious problem than it really is—at least comparing Taiwan to other countries. But corruption was a cause of the ruling party's fall from power in 2008 and may be the cause for any party or government that succumbs to it in the future to be voted out. Taiwan has other social problems, but they are probably not of such magnitude as to cause the kind of serious instability that might justify Beijing's intervening militarily.

A declaration of independence by a political party or a top politician has long been considered a distinct possibility. Depending on how "declaration" is defined, it may be considered very likely or not likely at all. That is, what constitutes a declaration of independence is unclear. Politicians, especially opposition politicians, for years discussed the issue of self-determination. They spoke in favor of it and even advocated it. They cited provisions in the Atlantic Charter and the UN Charter that support self-determination and, thus, legitimated their bid for a government free from Nationalist rule and now an independent Taiwan separate from China. With democratization, self-determination came to mean, almost exclusively, separation from the People's Republic of China. In the last decade or so, independence, a more provocative term has been discussed in public, advocated by the main opposition party and even put into the ruling party's campaign platform, after 2000, and its party charter. Taiwanese politicians, while railing for independence, burned the flags of the People's Republic of China in public before television cameras and cursed Chinese leaders in Beijing while calling them cowards for not invading Taiwan as they promised. One might thus ask: What more could they do that might provoke Beijing?

What then might constitute an "official" declaration, or one provocative enough to cause Beijing to attack Taiwan? If the ruling party were to issue a formal proclamation of independence or amend the Constitution to this effect, this might be viewed in Beijing as an "official declaration." President Chen and the DPP broached policies like this. They, however, are no longer in power. In fact, these ideas went out with their election defeat, one might say. Alternatively, a joint declaration of independence by two or more political parties might be a possibility if Taipei becomes too isolated, feels excessively threatened, or becomes desperate for some other reason; certainly, this could provoke hard-liners in Beijing. A statement by the president or a future president unequivocally suggesting the permanent separation of Taiwan from China might be enough for the People's Liberation Army to call for military action. But these things do not seem likely. Moreover, any number of statements or actions, if made only by individual politicians, would not indicate broad support in Taiwan for independence and could easily be ignored in Beijing.

Finally, what constitutes refusing to negotiate over an extended period is very unclear. Chou En-lai (Zhou Enlai) once talked about Taiwan's "returning to the fold" after 50, 100, or 1,000 years. Mao said something similar. Deng Xiaoping spoke of Taiwan as being a "back burner" issue that could wait until later— perhaps much later—to be resolved. Yet Deng also made quite different statements about Taiwan, no doubt under pressure from the military and because of nationalist sentiment that enveloped China during his rule. Jiang Zemin was subject to even greater pressure and spoke of resolving the "Taiwan question" earlier rather than later. It seemed he was taking action in 1995 and 1996 when he ordered missile tests near Taiwan, though it is likely the tests were more the military's idea than his own. Whether future leaders will be compelled to do something aggressive is difficult to say.

One might query: As long as Taiwan does not declare independence and does not allow its territory to be used or taken by another nation, why should there be a deadline? Also, are deadlines ultimatums? Regardless, deadlines have been discussed—even set—and they have come and gone. Clearly, a long time may be, or become, acceptable. Chinese are known for their patience. Beijing's leaders are obviously more concerned about economic growth than anything else, as is the population of China. Finally, if Beijing were to govern Taiwan, the island's economy would likely decline, and an invasion would certainly precipitate a full-blown economic disaster, including the flight of Taiwan's valuable human capital. Taiwan, at the same time, would become a human rights case. For good reason, then, Chinese officials may find it to their advantage not to hurry the process of unification. Thus, some say seriously that Beijing does not want Taiwan—not now at least.

However, there are some assumptions that cannot be assessed so easily. One is how Taiwan's new president will deal with the issue of its sovereignty. Ma Ying-jeou has engineered a rapprochement with China. Although he has made war less likely, whether he can resolve the political issue of Taiwan's status is another question. It seems fair to say that he cannot advocate unification and also remain, with the KMT, in power. He instead has to emphasize better economic relations and expectations for a peaceful settlement of other problems without pushing for resolution of the ultimate one. Can he succeed at this? Another matter is the rapid growth of China's military power. The United States can fend off China's military for some years. But will China's generals become more confident in dealing with Taiwan and less patient? This is uncertain.

Last but not least: for some time, Taiwan assumed that time was on its side. In other words, the longer it remained separate from China, the more likely it was to stay that way. China has also assumed that time favors it, and increasingly sees the Taiwan issue in that way. It is probably a good thing that both sides feel that waiting accords with their respective goals. Yet it now seems that China has the advantage. Will that destabilize an otherwise difficult situation?

External or Global Variables

Having considered certain basic assumptions that relate to Taiwan's future, in particular its legal status and its relationship with China, it is necessary to assess how other external (or global) variables may affect Taiwan's destiny, as these forces may be the most important determinants affecting Taiwan's future, especially if there is a stalemate or long delay in resolving Taiwan's status.

As already noted, the United States is Taiwan's most important external or foreign influence. Concerning US-Taiwan relations as they relate to Taiwan's future, there are three salient questions that need to be addressed: What exactly is US policy toward Taiwan? Will it change? And what might those changes be? A brief review of US-China policy in this context is in order.

US policy toward both Beijing and Taipei, as suggested in Chapter 6, has been ambiguous for some time, some say by necessity. When President Richard Nixon visited Beijing in 1972, it was obvious that the United States could no longer ignore the People's Republic of China, nor could it contain or isolate China. It did so in the past with Beijing's help, but that would not be possible any longer. Given the realities of international politics—in particular, the Soviet military buildup, which the United States could not alone counter—it was in Washington's interest to improve relations with China. Furthermore, Nixon perceived that the United States had to get out of the Vietnam War. China could facilitate—or impede—this effort. Beijing and Washington thus ended two decades of enmity and became friends, perhaps even allies. Taiwan could not be allowed to interfere in forging this new relationship.

Yet President Nixon did not abandon Taiwan. (Recently declassified documents about US negotiations with China at this time confirm this.) He did not declare that Taiwan was a part of China, but rather he said that the United States "does not challenge" Beijing's view—likely meaning that the United States did not really agree. The issue of Taiwan was not (and ostensibly could not be) resolved at this time, and, as a consequence, US policy toward Taiwan became, in some critical ways, more ambiguous.

In concluding the Normalization Agreement of 1979, the Carter administration concurred with China, as Deng Xiaoping demanded, that Taiwan is part of China. Washington broke diplomatic relations with Taipei, and it gave notification of canceling the US–Republic of China mutual defense treaty. At this juncture, it appeared that the United States had decided to forsake Taiwan. But Carter's policy was reversed a few months later when Congress passed the Taiwan Relations Act (TRA). Some say President Carter anticipated this, perhaps even wanted it. In any event, the TRA, for all intents and purposes, restored Taiwan's sovereignty in the eyes of the United States. It also pledged US security guarantees. After that, the

United States had, many said, two China policies: one made by the White House and the Department of State, the other made by Congress (the latter being pro-Taiwan). This dichotomy, a new form of ambiguity or more of it, seemed often-times convenient.

In 1982, the Reagan administration promised to end arms sales to Taiwan, but President Reagan said this agreement was predicated on a "peaceful solution only" of the "Taiwan issue," supposedly pledged by Beijing. Deng Xiaoping said he had made no such promise. The communiqué was not signed, and later the State Department said it "lacks status" in international law. More important, Reagan did not restrict military technology transfers, and he rejected Beijing's requests to pressure Taipei to negotiate with Beijing on reunification and other matters. Reagan's "six assurances" to Taiwan, given at this time, also seemed to directly contradict the communiqué.

The first Bush administration seemed to favor Beijing, but with the breakup of the Soviet Union and the end of the Cold War, Washington no longer needed the "China card" as leverage against the Soviet Union. Almost coinciding with this sea change in international politics was the Tiananmen Massacre in June 1989, which caused China to become a pariah nation in the eyes of most Americans. Thus, Congress and Democrats bashed Bush's pro-Beijing policy. In 1992, Bush suddenly adopted what seemed to be a pro-Taiwan policy, or at least a policy much more favorable to Taipei in the security realm. He broke Reagan's promise to cut arms sales to Taiwan and sold 150 F-16 fighter planes to Taipei. With these planes, Taiwan could protect its air space. Moreover, Taipei didn't need to negotiate with China and could remain separate and sovereign.

The Clinton administration was hostile toward China early on. President Clinton called Chinese leaders "butchers." He allowed the planes promised to Taiwan by the Bush administration to be delivered, even though he could have blocked the sale. He even sold more weapons to Taiwan. In 1994, President Clinton "upgraded" relations with Taiwan (as a part of a "Taiwan policy review"), making it possible for high US government officials to have contacts with government officials from Taiwan. President Clinton also accepted the position that the Taiwan Relations Act has precedence over communiqués signed with Beijing. In 1995, President Lee Teng-hui, with White House approval, was given a visa to visit the United States.

But all these decisions came in the face of congressional pressure. Then, in 1998, President Clinton traveled to China. There he talked of a "strategic partnership" with the People's Republic of China and announced a "three no's" policy. Clinton said: "We don't support independence for Taiwan, or two Chinas or one Taiwan, one China. And we don't believe that Taiwan should be a member in any organization for which statehood is a requirement." Clinton subsequently denied that he changed US–China/Taiwan policy or that he in any way had hurt Taiwan. Still, his pronouncements deeply troubled Taipei. Congress acted to override Clinton's anti-Taiwan policy change by voting overwhelmingly on resolutions favorable to Taiwan while expressing America's support for Taipei. The gap between executive and legislative branch views toward US-China policy, and especially toward Taiwan, widened. This confused onlookers and officials in both China and Taiwan.

President George W. Bush was much more friendly toward Taiwan and tougher toward China than his predecessor. He denied that China, as President Clinton had said, was a strategic partner. He called China instead a challenge and a competitor and said he would do "whatever it took" to defend Taiwan. He increased arms sales to Taipei, including offensive weapons (submarines), even though the Taiwan Relations Act specified defensive weapons. Yet President Bush did not alter the US one-China policy, nor did he hint that he supported Taiwan's independence— other than by allowing Taiwan's leaders to visit the United States.

Also, as presidents before him, except faster, Bush moved away from a pro-Taiwan stance. He was influenced by America's preoccupation with the war on terrorism. China "signed on" and became an important US ally in that "war." The Chen Shui-bian administration came to be viewed as a provocateur that would risk a war between the United States and China for its own domestic political benefit. President Bush ceased to view Taiwan as a loyal ally and even displayed anger and hostility toward President Chen.

US-Taiwan policy, in short, has shifted a number of times. It has been affected by the triangular relationship of Washington, Taipei, and Beijing, as well as the vagaries of world politics. It has been subjected to differences of viewpoints among foreign policymakers and power struggles between two branches of government, based on different perspectives espoused by the White House and the Department of State on the one hand and the Congress on the other. Washington's vague and inconsistent China policy, in fact, seems well ensconced and unlikely to budge for a long while.

History suggests the United States will intervene if China threatens Taiwan. It did in the past, during two Offshore Island crises in the 1950s, and Washington appeared prepared to do so again in the 1960s and 1970s. Furthermore, the Taiwan Relations Act seemed to legally obligate the United States to protect Taiwan. Finally, the Clinton Administration acted with resolve during the 1996 missile tests in the Taiwan Strait. The record shows that the United States has consistently used military force when necessary to protect Taiwan.

But have conditions changed? Has China become too big a power to face down? Is China too important an ally? Is Taiwan too much trouble? Is the war on terror too important? Is the antiwar sentiment in the United States too strong?

Before considering these questions, it is necessary to point out that US military threats or posturing before a crisis breaks out (and there would no doubt be some warning) would likely dissuade forces in the People's Republic of China from attacking. This happened during the crises in the 1950s and perhaps in 1962. Even if a conflict were to start, it might be dampened and de-escalated by US military action, as seems to have happened in 1996. If there were a conflict now, the United States would win. But it might be a pyrrhic victory. If China's rulers were to fall, those who replaced them might be irreversibly hostile to the United States.

Thus (it seems), in the event of a declaration of independence by Taipei, Washington might do as follows: Inform the government in Taipei that it will withdraw its support by canceling all deals or promises to protect Taiwan and not reinstate them if Taipei does not retract its proclamation; put economic and other pressure on the government in Taiwan and split the military from the government; and use even more extreme means if necessary to force the government to change its policy, or overthrow it.

The fear of such US threats and actions would be a powerful deterrent to Taipei's declaring independence. Although decision makers in Washington have not formally announced a policy about this kind of contingency, some officials have stated publicly that the United States will not come to Taiwan's rescue if a declaration of independence provokes the People's Republic of China. Washington clearly sees this as a serious and dangerous matter to be avoided at all costs.

What if Taiwan does not declare legal independence, but otherwise provokes China? Many say the Taiwan Relations Act obligates the United States to protect Taiwan; indeed, the US Congress believes this is so. Reason suggests that the US military would align with Congress. Allowing Taiwan to be made part of China by force would permanently sully America's reputation and its credibility as an ally or protector of other East Asian countries, and the US military cannot allow that. Yet circumstances do matter, including other foreign policy problems Washington faces at the time. Last but not least, the reader is reminded that the executive and legislative branches of government in the United States have at times espoused quite disparate views about US policy toward both Taiwan and China, and the nature of the White House–Congress relationship at the critical juncture when a crisis breaks out may prove decisive.

Since the role of the United States is so critical to Taiwan, Taipei knows it must maintain its friends and sources of influence there. In the past, Taiwan's diplomats have done a very good job in the United States. They, along with those from Israel and Japan, were the best in Washington. Their diplomatic skills, combined with Taiwan's democratization, seemed to assure Taiwan would remain in good graces. Favorable public opinion in the United States toward Taiwan has also helped.

But some things have changed. The view in Washington that China is a big and important nation, that United States–China relations are more and more critical to America, and, further, that good relations will ensure world peace is widespread and is growing. In addition, China now has strong support in the US business community that, to some degree, makes up a new "China lobby." In recent years, Beijing has also come to realize more and more that it needs influence in the United States, and its diplomacy in the United States in the last few years has, as a result, become more effective. Meanwhile, Taiwan's astute diplomacy declined during the Chen administration due to Taiwan's foreign service personnel becoming politicized, the DPP having too few good diplomats and not keeping the friends the KMT had cultivated, and President Chen taking the United States for granted. Taiwan has since fixed this, but it will probably never have the edge it once had over China in the eyes of the United States.

Then there are the vicissitudes of American politics to consider. In 2004, Senator John Kerry, when campaigning for the presidency, said that he would not spill the blood of American soldiers to protect Taiwan. There was a sizeable segment of the American public that concurred. Furthermore, in the context of the Iraq War, many Americans felt that coming to Taiwan's rescue was not something that they wanted to consider. This feeling may persist.

As observed in Chapter 6, two other regional powers might also play a role in determining Taiwan's future: Russia and Japan. Both have given signals that they desire a separate Taiwan. One may speculate as well that the Association of Southeast Asian Nations (ASEAN) countries prefer a separate Taiwan. However, it seems unlikely that any one of these actors alone can or will affect Taiwan's future very much.

Could there evolve an alliance, informal or otherwise, between Japan and ASEAN that includes the United States to counterbalance China's growing military power? That may be Taiwan's best hope. In late 1993, the United States seemed to enunciate such a policy. Japan and ASEAN want the US military presence to remain in the region even though the Cold War has ended, and they frequently say this. Both supported US military actions in March 1996 in response to Beijing's missile tests in the Taiwan Strait. Japan supports theater missile defense and is providing funding for it. There are other signs, not to mention a logical argument (i.e., about the need for a balance of power to maintain stability and peace in the area) for an alignment, though tentative, of these powers against China. This being so, Taiwan gains in leverage if it chooses not to be part of China or if it wants more time to decide.

Yet Japan fears China, as does ASEAN. Both see economic relations with China as being critical to their prosperity. Furthemore, Beijing may develop a strategy to counter such an alignment of forces against it.

The international community will also play a role in determining Taiwan's future. World public opinion, UN policies and actions (especially in support of self-determination), and efforts to make the United Nations and other international organizations genuinely universal all favor Taiwan. That the world community is made up mostly of small nations seems to be to Taiwan's advantage because Taiwan is more like them than China is. The support of the international community to some extent offsets Taiwan's diplomatic defeats and lack of representation in most foreign capitals and major international organizations. And there are also collateral effects: Taiwan's good image in the international community will indirectly—if not directly—influence US-Taiwan policy in a positive way for Taipei.

Furthermore, China is reluctant to violate international public opinion. Its leaders understand the connection between good relations with the international community and its successful economic growth. China has in recent years become trade-dependent. Globalism, which has provided for the expansion of world trade and commerce, has greatly benefited China. Chinese leaders are well aware of this, so it is no wonder that they say their first foreign policy objective is a peaceful world.

Yet one should not make too much of all this. Beijing is represented in the United Nations and the other most visible global political organizations; Taipei is not. Beijing also has the veto in the UN Security Council. It sees giving legitimacy to a separate Taiwan as dangerous in terms of encouraging separatism in Tibet, Xinjiang Province, and elsewhere in China. Thus, it is unlikely that Taipei will be able to gain membership in the UN—or even UN or UN-affiliated organizations (Taiwan is presently seeking only some form of participation in the latter) for the foreseeable future, if ever. Most nations are afraid to challenge China on the Taiwan issue.

Internal or Domestic Variables

Taiwan has developed its own identity. This process is sometimes called Taiwanization or localization. The Mainland Chinese who came to the island after World War II promoted the island's Chinese heritage and its links with the Mainland, but with democratization, the Taiwanese majority began playing a new and much greater role in education, social policy, the economy, and politics. From the growing influence of the locally born Chinese there came a "revisionist" history of the island. Most historians now emphasize the island's uniqueness rather than its likeness to China. Likewise, Taiwan's culture has become more Taiwanese. Taiwanese "things," such as books, dance, songs, and much more, are now more visible than Chinese "things."

Most Mainland Chinese accepted this reality and came to identify with Taiwan. In fact, a merging of Mainland Chinese and Taiwanese culture has affected all ethnic groups' perspectives about Taiwan's place in the world and its future—hence the popular notion of a "new Taiwanese" that encompasses the whole population.

Assuming good relations among the ethnic groups in Taiwan, the notion of the "new Taiwanese" (defined broadly as anyone who loves Taiwan and identifies with it) will contribute even more in the future to a new and different (from China) national identity.

In the last two decades, these trends have been balanced or even offset by an increasing interest in China. Many people are looking for their roots. Many share a desire to see China restored to its once-dominant role in the world. Many recognize that Taiwan is too small to make an impact on world history. Many believe that if Taiwan were to become part of China, it would make a difference. Finally, if Taiwan is, as many in Taiwan and elsewhere suggest, a model that the People's Republic of China is applying in its economic and political development (which seems to be happening), there will doubtless be convergence and eventually the foundation laid for a smooth, peaceful joining at some levels—maybe many.

Which of these trends will prevail? In the short run, probably the separate Taiwan identity, although it seems much less likely to dominate in the long run. What are the variables that will be decisive?

Taiwan's consumer culture, cosmopolitanism, Westernization, and growing middle class define Taiwan's present, though the middle class has shrunk in recent years due to economic stagnation. Socially, Taiwan will continue to be highly penetrated by Western countries and Japan, evolving even further in the direction of pluralism, capitalism, and democracy. More and more of Taiwan's citizens travel to foreign countries each year, and most have become cosmopolitan and internationalist in their outlook. The United States and Japan are very much in Taiwan's future.

But there has also grown a noticeable resistance in Taiwan to the wholesale imitation of the United States and Europe. Unlike two or three decades ago, many in Taiwan today see much in the United States that is undesirable: crime, mistreatment of the aged, child abuse, juvenile delinquency, pornography, drugs, a decline in the quality of education, excessive freedom, and the like. Most people oppose allowing these problems to "infect" Taiwan's society. Many also observe racial discrimination against Asians, notably in America's best academic institutions, but also in America's immigration policies, which keep Asians out while ignoring millions of illegal immigrants from Latin America.

There is a general feeling in Taiwan that its experiment with American-style democracy went too far. They associate it with the Chen Shui-bian era. Instead, they are thinking more of Asian democracy, and this change in outlook seemed to be the lesson of the KMT victories in the 2008 elections. Many of Taiwan's citizens have the feeling that too much democracy has hurt economic development.

Taiwanese also harbor some similar if less impassioned feelings about contemporary Europe. They see Europeans as lazy—the product of the nanny state. They perceive Europe as increasingly uncompetitive, protectionist, and irrelevant in world affairs. One hardly hears the word "model" together with the name of a European country anymore. Fewer students want to study in Europe, and there is less interest in learning European languages, with the exception of English. Few in Taiwan read or cite European authors or scholars.

Meanwhile, Taiwanese have also been visiting China in significant numbers—more than four and a half million in 2007. Early on, such visits reinforced the belief in Taiwan's superior economic and political system and its living standards and lifestyle. Clearly, China was not a country that the people of Taiwan emulated. But recently that has changed. Now 5 percent of Taiwan's population resides in China, and a much higher percent of its work force and an even bigger portion of its entrepreneurs are in China. There is a brain drain moving toward China. Fifteen percent of college students consider a career in China. China fever has struck Taiwan.

Being pulled in two directions or accepting neither the West or China as determining Taiwan's future, many speak of Taiwan as having its own identity, like Singapore—a Chinese nation, but not part of China. Some local scholars refer to Taiwan as "the Switzerland of the East," thinking Taiwan should be culturally unique, politically neutral, yet active and independent. But are these realistic alternatives for Taiwan? They are heard less often in recent years.

Residents of Taiwan realize the world is evolving into economic blocs and that Taiwan is part of the Pacific Rim bloc, along with Japan and China. They see the United States to some degree as having retreated from East Asia economically, militarily, and politically. They perceive protectionist and isolationist forces growing in the United States.

Most see China and Japan increasingly playing a role in Taiwan's future. The big question is this: Will Taiwan choose China or Japan if competition for leadership of the Pacific Rim bloc escalates or the region splits into two blocs? Japan appears to be a declining power judging from its economy, its demography, and even its culture. But a US-managed balance of power system in Asia designed to offset China's rising power makes Japan still appealing. Some see Taiwan's future in the US-Japan alliance.

Let us return again to the basics: the trends. What are the relevant trends that influence citizens of Taiwan when they think of their future?

There are now visible trends in Taiwan's demographics that will affect its future. Will these changes in the makeup of the population impact Taiwan's relationship with China? After 1949, Taiwan accepted few immigrants. But this changed as the birthrate fell and the cost of labor rose, and Taiwan attracted foreign workers. In addition, a high standard of living attracted immigrants as did the imbalance in the gender ratio. Taiwan will likely continue to experience a decline in its birthrate, which will require policies in favor of immigration. The source of immigrants will be China and Southeast Asia, which could upset the ethnic balance. Furthermore, this immigration will dilute support for independence. More immigrants favor linking up with China than either the United States or Japan.

On the other hand, Taiwan is crowded, and an influx of people could easily cause a backlash—as it did in 1949. Thus, Taiwan's demographic situation seems only to facilitate closer ties with China—gradually, if managed well.

Economic trends? Taiwan was still being called a "miracle economy" up until 2001, when it was hit by recession. Can it return to high growth? Given the ingredients that made Taiwan successful—planning, technology, research and development, and, perhaps most of all, human resources—one can logically anticipate solid, sustainable economic growth in the future. This, together with Taiwan's high levels of savings and investment and its quality of labor, management, and innovation, will no doubt help preserve the island's economic vitality for some years to come—assuming a healthy global economy. Yet, the double-digit annual gross national product (GNP) growth of the 1960s through the 1980s is likely a thing of the past. GNP increases of the 1990s—from 5 to 7 percent—must be considered a benchmark. In short, one should expect that growth rates higher than the world's average can be sustained for some time, but there will be no return to "miracle" growth.

In the future, more and more of Taiwan's gross national product will be generated by services than by producing goods, especially from the manufacturing sector. Meanwhile, industry will become increasingly capital- and knowledge-intensive. Research and development will play a bigger role in production, and Taiwan-made goods will continue to move up-market and increase in quality and price. These trends will promote further economic integration with China. The United States, and to a lesser extent Japan, have been moving toward a service economy for some time, which explains in part why Taiwan's trade with China has recently surpassed both.

Another variable is the integration of Taiwan's economy into China's. This has gone a considerable way already. Many of Taiwan's companies are linked in terms of division of labor, research and development, and in a host of other ways to the companies they have built or helped build in China and to Chinese companies. This will no doubt continue; it will probably continue to accelerate fast. It will likely be further advanced by China's investment in companies in Taiwan, which is now a growing trend.

There is a caveat: Rapid economic growth in the past thirty years has created a new and different Taiwan. Attention has shifted from high growth rates to a better environment, more leisure, and a higher quality of life. The population of Taiwan is now more interested in the good life than high GNP growth figures. Fewer are willing to sacrifice in the same way that their parents did or even as they themselves did in the past. Thus Taiwan may go the way of some other rich countries.

Will these antigrowth prodivities get out of hand? Most of Taiwan's citizens are very cognizant of the fact that the country must remain productive to survive. It must export. Although the work ethic has declined somewhat, it will not likely fade quickly or disappear, and it will probably decrease more slowly than in most other rapidly developing countries. Its lack of natural resources makes it necessary for Taiwan to export so that it can buy raw materials. Its population density makes its economic vitality more important than in other countries. Consequently, Taiwan will probably not witness public outcries for no growth or slow growth anytime soon. Workers' organizations are similarly not likely to become significantly stronger. Environmentalism will not become an ideology, as it has in some Western nations, but will rather be a call for cooperative action.

As mentioned in Chapter 5, Taiwan is seeking to be a business or commercial hub in Asia. But Shanghai and Hong Kong are winning the contest. Both are closer to the China market, and Beijing prefers them. Will Taiwan continue to pursue this objective? If it does, it will have to cement even closer economic bonds with China. Some say Taiwan is already dependent on China economically. This may be exaggerated, but the trends are fast making this true. The recent discussions in Taiwan to the effect that the island will be the "gateway to China" assumes that Taiwan's economy compliments China's. But some in Taiwan call China a "fatal attraction" that is causing Taiwan's industry to flee to the Mainland and to "hollow out." China's economy may prove to be too big and too dynamic for Taiwan to handle. Taiwan must think of ways to accommodate or to balance this attraction.

Then there is also the military equation. The rise of China's military power in recent years has not been met by Taiwan strengthening its military proportionally or in a way that might counter China's threat. During the Chen era, Taiwan's military budget decreased as a proportion of the gross national product, and as a result, troop levels were cut and military morale fell. Taiwan did not buy the weapons the United States allocated in 2001. Taiwan thus became very vulnerable to China's missile intimidation and became more dependent on the US military while relations with the United States plummeted.

Chen administration officials spoke of bombing Shanghai or Hong Kong. There was even talk off the record of employing missile strikes against the Three Gorges Dam, which would flood the largest expanses of populated areas of China, resulting in huge casualties. This was labeled deterrence. Most observers thought this was wrong thinking and would hurt Taiwan's image.

A more rational policy for Taiwan is to bolster its military strength and preparedness to be able to fend off the Chinese military for a few days or weeks until the US military arrives and also to take measures to limit the impact of a Chinese missile attack. Citizens of Taiwan are willing to pay for larger defense spending for this, especially if the economy is doing well, though they do not favor Taiwan going nuclear or building offensive weapons. They want to avoid provoking China and hope that China responds by reducing the level of its military that targets Taiwan.

Taiwan should assume, especially in the absence of other choices, that the United States will defend the island. This will be more assured if Taiwan acts like an ally. The United States needs Taiwan's military cooperation and its help in gathering intelligence information on China. Taiwan has to be concerned that China's growing emergence as a military power means that the United States needs more cooperation with Taiwan and may need to use Taiwan in the event of a conflict with China. This will put Taiwan more in contention with China if this happens.

Taiwan can endeavor to join an East Asian alliance system that includes—or doesn't include—China in the future. But the likelihood of this seems dim for the moment. Because they do realize Taiwan is at the center of strategic conflict in the area and there is no way to change that, Taiwan's citizens would probably approve if the option were available.

This brings us to the critical question: Where is Taiwan going politically? Taiwan has undergone profound change over the past two or three decades. Many observers say it is the only democratic Chinese nation in history. These are no small accomplishments, and the population of Taiwan is aware of this. But Taiwan's role as a model for China has been marginal at best. The Chen period made Taiwan a model not to follow. Most people in China equate a good political system as one that facilitates impressive economic development and saw Taiwan's political system under Chen as less one the emulate than in the past. The Overseas Chinese turned away from Taiwan because of President Chen's ethnic policies and his administration's promoting localism. The media in China played up Taiwan's chaotic politics, gridlock, and poor economic growth. Boasting of its democratic system will probably do little for cross-strait relations at the present or in the future, and using it as a negotiation tool won't work.

The crux of the problem anyway will be whether a political solution can be found to Taiwan's relationship with China. Chinese leaders in Beijing have already debated this. After passing the Anti-Succession Law in 2005, Beijing made some concessions to Taiwan—inviting leaders from Taiwan to China, trying to work out transportation links, and so on. China even offered pandas to Taiwan's zoo. Thus, China seems receptive to a political solution or solutions; but the devil is in the details for China as well as Taiwan.

The idea of a federation or a commonwealth has been broached in both Taiwan and China. Greater China is certainly an idea that might become attractive on both sides for a host of reasons. Beijing does not want to risk serious reactions from the United States (even short of military action) and/or the international community for using force against Taiwan. Taiwan can resolve the matter of China's fatal attraction or the contradiction of having intense economic relations with China with few political ties. The sticky issue is sovereignty, and that means that political arrangements will be difficult and will probably be slow in coming. Hopefully, both sides will understand that and will not be disappointed by slow progress, or even none at all.

Alternative Futures

From the information and analysis presented throughout this book and summarized above, one can suggest several possible futures for Taiwan. The most extreme, and at the same time the most unlikely, will be presented first.

One possibility is that China will attack Taiwan and the United States does not intervene. In this scenario, it is assumed that the United States is seriously preoccupied with another conflict, has lost its will to fight for some reason, or has changed its policy toward Taiwan. These conditions are certainly all possible. If this were to occur, Taiwan would probably still assume that the United States would come to its aid and would fight for some time while waiting for the United States to enter the war. The result would likely be a bloody conflict resulting in a huge number of causalities on both sides—perhaps totaling a million or more. Civilian causalities could be large because the war would likely be carried to population centers in Taiwan, and Taiwan's military might retaliate against Chinese cities within range (such as Hong Kong, Shanghai, and Nanking), thereby engendering China's retaliation in kind. One cannot exclude the possibility of the use of nuclear, chemical, or biological weapons. If there were any warning before the conflict started, there would likely be a flow of people out of Taiwan to other places in Asia and North America. China would ultimately win the conflict and Taiwan would be absorbed by China.

A second possibility is that Taiwan will declare full or legal independence and elicit no response from China. This would assume that China is concerned with a war somewhere else or that it is suffering from serious internal strife, perhaps causing China to fragment or worse. A change in China's policy toward Taiwan—namely, giving up claim to sovereignty over Taiwan (which one could argue would be a logical decision given China's concern with its own survival)—would also be a situation wherein this would work. If this were to occur, Taiwan's nation-state status would be uncontested, the island would probably win recognition from many nations in the international community, and its future would be one separate from China's. China would probably experience increased internal political difficulties for some time if this were to occur, and its fragmentation would be more likely. The Chinese people would resent the leadership that allowed this to happen, and this could well give rise to more extreme politics—possibly fascism or a return to communism.

Both of these scenarios seem improbable. However, they are not impossible, so they do need to be considered and their attendant problems understood. They are also a useful frame of reference when looking at other possibilities and solutions.

In contrast to the above, one likely possibility is that neither side takes extreme measures and the status quo lasts for some time. In this scenario, both sides as well as other players assume that the "Taiwan issue" is a problem defying solution, or they simply like the present situation too much to change it. This would probably be a good thing since it keeps the peace. But it also offers no solution to eliminating what many consider the world's most serious flashpoint. Can one assume the status quo, if it lasts a long time, will result in a lowering of tensions? Probably not, and this is especially so if the United States and China remain a challenge to each other. One must thus assume that some solution has to be found.

A likely solution is for Taiwan to join China in some kind of federation based on economic ties, perhaps resembling in structure and organization the European Community in its early years or the current Association of Southeast Asian Nations or the British Commonwealth. Economic ties, it can be assumed, would precede political and legal ties, with the latter remaining weak for some time. The first steps in establishing such a federation might consist of an agreement or understanding to disagree politically but proceed with trade, investment, and other commercial interchange and to also consider establishing some kind of provisions for a union that does not infringe on Taiwan's sovereignty. In such a scenario, Taipei might promise not to allow foreign bases or influence on the island or to declare independence if, in turn, Beijing reduces its threat of military force against Taiwan.

The attractiveness of this model is based on the assumption of meaningful benefits from economic ties and the importance of cultural similarities between China and Taiwan. Greater China, in fact, already exists in the sense that there is considerable trade linking Chinese entities together. Hong Kong and Macao have been incorporated into the People's Republic of China, yet they also remain separate in important ways. Singapore, Taiwan, and the Overseas Chinese have not been incorporated, yet they are linked to China through trade, investments, networking, and many other ways. The end of the Cold War has seen the world gravitate into cultural groupings. As many Chinese as well as foreigners traveling to China note, going from Taiwan to China or vice versa is less a cultural leap than going from China to Hong Kong or Tibet (both part of China).

Another option, of course, is for Taiwan to join another bloc. Taipei might try to align with Japan, or it may try to join the Association of Southeast Asian Nations. Either seems farfetched, but not in the context of a US-constructed alliance system or a balance of power system. If given a choice, Taiwan might decide that it does not want to be part of Greater China. There is good reason to believe this could happen. The United States and China are foes, as one can witness by the widespread belief in the "China threat" and the fact that Washington will, in the future, have to compete with China's rapid military buildup by forging closer ties with Japan and ASEAN if it is to devote a good portion of its resources to policing the world and dealing with terrorism. Taiwan's close ties with the United States, both economic and military, may persuade Taiwan's leaders to choose this option. Both Japan and ASEAN fear the rise of China and are looking for allies.

Gauging which way Taiwan is going to go is useful in order to examine what might be called "creeping independence" or "creeping unification." Maintaining the status quo, which seems like a good plan given the sensitivity of the Taiwan matter in both China and the United States, will dampen the possibility of extreme solutions, though it might eventually favor one trend or the other. Chinese leaders in Beijing might "surrender" to a balance of power against them that they cannot overcome, which would dilute China's claim to Taiwan, and Beijing might simply let Taiwan go. Some scholars of international politics argue that territory is not important to power status in the present era; China may come to accept this notion.

The array of scenarios or options just offered spans a large spectrum. To help rarify the possibilities and make the choices easier to understand, another matter needs to be addressed; that is, what specific approaches or models might Taiwan consider? Several models have been discussed in Chapter 6. They need to be re-examined here.

China's model for dealing with the "Taiwan issue" is the "one nation, two systems" model. Hong Kong was incorporated into the People's Republic of China in 1997 using this model. It was given the status of a special administrative zone and remains separate from China in important respects (currency, legal system, separate membership in the World Trade Organization, etc.). Hong Kong's situation, with a few exceptions, has proved to be workable and satisfactory to its residents. Beijing says the model will work for resolving the Taiwan problem and has even made its offer more generous. On the other hand, Taiwan does not see the Hong Kong model as attractive or appropriate. Taiwan's view is this: Unlike Taiwan, Hong Kong was never sovereign, economically self-sufficient, or able to defend itself. It was a colony, and its colonial status had to end; it didn't have the option of sovereignty. Over time, the differences between Hong Kong (before reunification with China) and Taiwan are likely to become more widely appreciated.

It is possible that Beijing will alter this approach. In fact, one can say it already has, depending upon one's interpretation of its words, and may change it even further to make it more attractive. At present, though, Beijing's approach isn't attractive. Taiwan considers it too close to the invasion scenario mentioned above or at least to a solution that is not acceptable in Taiwan, and it feels that Beijing neither sufficiently considers the desires of the government or the people of Taiwan nor the fact that Taiwan possesses sovereignty and is a democracy.

The Singapore model is another approach often cited as a possible model/ solution for resolving the Taiwan question. This "Chinese nation" (80-plus percent of the population is Chinese) is ostensibly destined to remain independent.

Notwithstanding its Chinese population, Beijing makes no claims to Singapore. (In the past, Beijing claimed jurisdiction over all Chinese, regardless of where they resided, but then it dropped this claim.) Although Taiwan is unlike Singapore in many ways, especially in its proximity to China, Taiwan resembles Singapore more than it does Hong Kong. Or, at least, so say most people in Taiwan. Meanwhile, China's relations with Singapore have improved, as has China's image in Singapore.

Some officials in the government in Taiwan suggest their own formula: "one country, two governments" or "one country, two areas." Some also call this the "Taiwan model." Those making this proposal say that China is one country, and Taiwan should not be independent or separate from cultural or historic China. But until the time is right, the two Chinese states—China and Taiwan—should remain apart, and Taiwan (or the Republic of China), like the People's Republic of China, should be regarded as sovereign. Although some say this simply confirms the status quo, it does, however, offer a solution for the future, presumably after a considerable period of convergence. It would be more feasible, they say, if Beijing should forswear using force and pledge to resolve the Taiwan question peacefully, although this is unlikely.

Another plan is the German formula. The two Germanys were granted diplomatic recognition jointly by various countries, and then both entered the United Nations and other international organizations as separate sovereign states. Subsequently, and presumably because of their equal and sovereign status, they were able to negotiate and merge into one country. The problem with this argument is that Beijing (or so it says) cannot negotiate because negotiations assume statehood and equality, and Beijing does not accept this status for Taiwan. If this were to change, meaningful talks might transpire and might eventually lead to unification, thereby fulfilling the German model. However, another obstacle is that China is a big power, and, in Beijing's eyes, there are many who do not want Taiwan unified (quite in contrast to the German situation) because it would make China stronger and a bigger threat; the German model, therefore, will not work.

The Korean model is another idea sometimes broached to resolve the Taiwan matter. It assumes that greater contacts and a lowering of tension, as has happened recently between the two Koreas, will result in unification. The end of the Cold War provided a favorable environment for a rapprochement. Like the two Germanys before unification, both Koreas were granted diplomatic recognition by a number of countries and, in the end, neither objected. The problem is that Korea is not yet unified, so there is really no model. Also, the two Koreas are almost the same size, which is not the case with China and Taiwan. Finally, both sides appear to want unification more than Taiwan. Regardless, China does not like this model and has not accepted it, and it probably will not do so in the future.

The critical variable affecting which model or formula gains favor probably is the extent of progressive economic and political change in China. Since 1979, China has done extremely well economically. It has boomed as no other large country in history has. A rational free market economic system seems to have become permanent. Economic growth, and its attendant prosperity, may also be the key to democratic political change. But maybe not. It is said that if political modernization in the direction of democracy continues, the barriers to reconciliation will, in time, diminish. Thus the recipe for reconciliation between Taiwan and China is one China, one system—democracy. But those who speak of this do not seem to realize that democracy is not well defined in China or Taiwan.

However, regarding political reform in the People's Republic, one must bear in mind that it has been set back several times. It is something people in Taiwan, and their supporters, have little trust in. Furthermore, many of China's leaders, especially Communist Party leftists and hard-line military leaders, see democracy as ultimately destabilizing and, therefore, highly undesirable. Even a little democracy, they think, could engender unmanageable centrifugal tendencies. Given these uncertainties, one cannot now be optimistic about basing Taiwan's future on assumptions about China's political modernization.

One must also recognize that Taiwan is far ahead of China in economic and political development. Therefore, even if present trends in the People's Republic of China continue and capitalism and democracy take root, it may take a decade or two—perhaps much longer—before China catches up with Taiwan. Meanwhile, trade and investment ties will likely continue to grow, and both Taiwan and China will increasingly benefit from their relationship. More extensive economic ties may be possible without a formal decision about Taiwan's sovereignty. Thus, an economic common market solution and/or a "Chinese" solution (meaning lots of patience) might be the best model and, in the long run, succeed.

Finally, the choice of scenarios depends on several global trends not yet discussed here, including a move toward smaller nations as large ones split up. Smaller nations can be governed more easily, world trade offsets the advantages of large national markets, and advances in computer and communications technology favor smaller countries, just as they favor smaller companies. More nation-states are thus more likely to remain independent than to merge with others by any of the various means possible. Yet the formation of loose political groupings by culture and function seems also to be the wave of the future. In addition, economic blocs have been forming, and these challenge the nation-state system. The two sets of trends seen together suggest that Taiwan and China have a future together, but probably a weak and tenuous one for some time—if not a long time.

Summing Up

In the near term, Taiwan seems most likely to remain separate from China, as it has been since 1949. However, ties with China, especially commercial and cultural ones, will increase. This will have significance.

In the future, connections with China may pave the way for political links that will eventually lead to unification. Yet they may not. Because of China's rise and its perceived threat to the United States, America will see a separate Taiwan as being in its national interest. Yet America also knows that although China is its foremost enemy, China is its most important friend. This dichotomy may not end soon. US policymakers know they cannot keep up with China's booming economy and its growing military power, but it can balance it if an equilibrium develops in Asia. This will give Taiwan a choice.

Legally, Taiwan will likely remain an anomaly for some time. Many say Taiwan is not a nation; but few can say convincingly what it should be called. Taiwan will remain diplomatically isolated, yet it will also remain an important player in international politics and economics. It will be an important "issue" in relations between Washington and Beijing, and the Taiwan Strait will remain a flashpoint.

Taiwan is, and will remain, special. Few political entities have ever been regarded simultaneously as a pariah and a role model, a sovereign nation-state and part of a major power. Few small entities have played such a key role in so many of the major dramas of modern history: at the center of the East-West struggle and the Cold War, as part of the dynamic western Pacific, and as an issue in the foreign policies of so many nations, including the world's most powerful.

Taiwan's future will certainly be an interesting and no doubt exciting one. The most important question, the one that relates to all the rest, is settling Taiwan's status: is it a nation-state or a province of China?

SELECTED BIBLIOGRAPHY

General

Area Handbook for the Republic of China. Washington, D.C.: US Government Printing Office, 1983.

Chai, Winberg, and May-lee Chai, eds. *Chinese Mainland and Taiwan: A Study of Historical, Cultural, Economic and Political Relations.* Dubuque, IA: Kendall/Hunt, 1996.

Chang, Cecilia S. T., ed. *The Republic of China on Taiwan, 1945–1988.* Jamaica, NY: St. John's University Press, 1991.

Chiu, Hungdah, ed. *China and the Taiwan Issue.* New York: Praeger, 1979.

Chiu, Hungdah, with Shao-chuan Leng, eds. *China: Seventy Years After the 1911 Hsin-Hai Revolution.* Charlottesville: University of Virginia Press, 1984.

Clough, Ralph N. *Island China.* Cambridge, MA: Harvard University Press, 1978.

Edmonds, Richard Lewis, and Steven M. Goldstein, eds. *Taiwan in the Twentieth Century: A Retrospective View.* Cambridge: Cambridge University Press, 2001.

Feldman, Harvey, and Ilpyong J. Kim, eds. *Taiwan in a Time of Transition.* New York: Paragon House, 1988.

Han, Lih-wu. *Taiwan Today.* Taipei: Institute of International Relations, 1986.

Hsieh, Chiao-min. *Taiwan–Ilha Formosa: A Geography in Perspective.* Washington, D.C.: Butterworths, 1964.

Hsiung, James C., ed. *Contemporary Republic of China: The Taiwan Experience 1950–1980.* New York: Praeger, 1981.

Jo, Yung-hwan, ed. *Taiwan's Future.* Tempe: Arizona State University, 1974.

Klintworth, Gary. *New Taiwan, New China: Taiwan's Changing Role in the Asia Pacific Region.* New York: St. Martins, 1995.

Kubek, Anthony. *Modernizing China: A Comparative Analysis of the Two Chinas.* Washington, D.C.: Regency Gateway, 1987.

Long, Simon. *Taiwan: China's Last Frontier.* New York: St. Martin's Press, 1991.

Mancall, Mark, ed. *Formosa Today.* New York: Praeger, 1964.

Shambaugh, David, ed. *Contemporary Taiwan.* Oxford: Clarendon Press, 1998.

Sih, Paul K. T., ed. *Taiwan in Modern Times.* New York: St. John's University Press, 1973.

Sutter, Robert G. *Taiwan: Entering the 21st Century.* Lanham, MD: University Press of America, 1988.

Taiwan Statistical Data Book 2007. Taipei: Executive Yuan, 2007.*

Taiwan Yearbook 2007. Taipei: Government Information Office, 2007.*

* These books are published annually. The *Taiwan Yearbook* has been published for several decades, earlier under the title *Republic of China Yearbook.*

History

Cline, Ray S. *Chiang Ching-kuo Remembered: The Man and His Political Legacy.* Washington, D.C.: US Global Strategy Council, 1989.

Copper, John F. *Historical Dictionary of Taiwan.* 3rd ed. Lanham, MD: Scarecrow Press, 2007.

Crozier, Ralph C. *Koxinga and Chinese Nationalism: History, Myth and the Hero.* Cambridge, MA: Harvard University Press, 1977.

Davidson, James W. *The Island of Formosa: Past and Present.* New York: AMS Press, 1977.

Davison, Gary Marvin. *A Short History of Taiwan: The Case for Independence.* Westport, CT: Praeger, 2003.

Edmonds, Richard L., et al. *Taiwan in the Twentieth Century: A Retrospective View.* Cambridge: Cambridge University Press, 2001.

Furuya, Keiji. *Chiang Kai-shek: His Life and Times.* New York: St. John's University Press, 1981.

Gilbert, Stephen P., and William M. Carpenter. *America and Island China: A Documentary History.* Lanham, MD: University Press of America, 1989.

Goddard, W. G. *Formosa: A Study in Chinese History.* East Lansing: Michigan State University Press, 1966.

Gordon, Leonard H. D., ed. *Taiwan: Studies in Chinese Local History.* New York: Columbia University Press, 1970.

Hung Chien-chao. *A History of Taiwan.* Rimini, Italy: Il Cerchio, 2000.

Kagan, Richard C. *Taiwan's Statesman: Lee Teng-hui and Democracy in Asia.* Annapolis, MD: Naval Institute Press, 2007.

Kerr, George H. *Formosa Betrayed.* Boston: Houghton Mifflin, 1965.

_____. *Formosa: Licensed Revolution and the Home Rule Movement, 1895–1945.* Honolulu: University of Hawaii Press, 1974.

Knapp, Ronald G., ed. *China's Island Frontier: Studies in the Historical Geography of Taiwan.* Honolulu: University of Hawaii Press, 1980.

Lai, Tse-han, Ramon H. Myers, and Wou Wei. *A Tragic Beginning: The Taiwan Uprising of February 28, 1947.* Stanford, CA: Stanford University Press, 1991.

Lee Wei-chin, and Y. T. Wang, eds. *Sayonara to the Lee Teng-hui Era.* Lanham, MD: University Press of America, 2003.

Leng, Shao-chuan, ed. *Chiang Ching-kuo's Leadership in the Development of the Republic of China on Taiwan.* Lanham, MD: University Press of America, 1993.

Li, Laura Tyson. *Madame Chiang Kai-shek: China's Eternal First Lady.* New York: Atlantic Monthly Press, 2006.

Lou, Tsu-kiang. *Personal Legends of Formosa.* Pasadena, CA: Oriental Book Store, 1975.

Lumley, F. A. *The Republic of China Under Chiang Kai-shek.* London: Barrie and Jenkins, 1978.

Manthorpe, Jonathan. *Forbidden Nation: A History of Taiwan.* New York: Palgrave-Macmillan, 2005.

Phillips, Steven E. *Between Assimilation and Independence: The Taiwanese Encounter Nationalist China, 1945–1950.* Stanford, CA: Stanford University Press, 2003.

Riggs, Fred W. *Formosa Under Chinese Nationalist Rule.* New York: Macmillan, 1952. Reprint, New York: Octagon Books, 1972.

Roy, Denny. *Taiwan: A Political History.* Ithaca, NY: Cornell University Press, 2003.

Rubinstein, Murray A. *Taiwan: A History.* Armonk, NY: M. E. Sharpe, 1998.

_____, ed. *The Other Taiwan: 1945 to the Present.* Armonk, NY: M. E. Sharpe, 1994.

_____, ed. *Taiwan: A New History.* Armonk, NY: M. E. Sharpe, 2007.

Takekoshi, Yosaburo. *Japanese Rule in Formosa.* 1907. Reprint, Pasadena, CA: Oriental Book Store, 1978.

Taylor, Jay. *The Generalissimo's Son: Chiang Ching-kuo and the Revolutions in China and Taiwan.* Cambridge, MA: Harvard University Press, 2000.

Wang, David Der-wei, and Carlos Rojas, eds. *Writing Taiwan: A Literary History.* Durham, NC: Duke University Press, 2007.

Society and Culture

Ahern, Emily Martin, and Hill Gates, eds. *The Anthropology of Taiwanese Society.* Stanford, CA: Stanford University Press, 1981.

Aspalter, Christian. *Democratization and Welfare State Development in Taiwan.* London: Ashgate, 2002.

Brown, Melissa J. *Is Taiwan Chinese?: The Impact of Culture, Power, and Migration on Changing Identities.* Berkeley: University of California Press, 2004.

Ching, Leo T. S. *Becoming Japanese: Colonial Taiwan and the Politics of Identity.* Berkeley: University of California Press, 2001.

Clart, Philip, and Charles B. Jones, eds. *Religion in Taiwan: Tradition and Innovation in a Changing Society.* Honolulu: University of Hawaii Press, 2003.

Cohen, Marc J. *Taiwan at the Crossroads: Human Rights, Political Development and Social Change on the Beautiful Island.* Washington, D.C.: Asia Resource Center, 1988.

Cohen, Myron L. *House United, House Divided: The Chinese Family in Taiwan.* New York: Columbia University Press, 1976.

Corcuff, Stephane, et al. *Memories of the Future: National Identity Issues and the Search for a New Taiwan.* Armonk, NY: M. E. Sharpe, 2002.

Eberhard, Wolfram. *Moral and Social Values of the Chinese: Collected Essays.* San Francisco and Taipei: Chinese Materials and Research Aids Service Center, 1974.

Gold, Thomas B. *State and Society in the Taiwan Miracle.* Armonk, NY: M. E. Sharpe, 1986.

Harrell, Steven, and Huang Chun-chieh, eds. *Cultural Change in Postwar Taiwan.* Boulder, CO: Westview Press, 1994.

Hsiao, Hsin-huang Michael, Wei-yuan Cheng, and Hou-sheng Chan, eds. *Taiwan: A Newly Industrialized State.* Taipei: Department of Sociology, National Taiwan University, 1989.

Kang, Peng-cheng. *The Story of Taiwan: Culture.* Taipei: Government Information Office, 2001.

Ku, Yeun-wen. *Welfare Capitalism in Taiwan: State, Economy and Social Policy.* New York: St. Martin's Press, 1997.

Lai Ming-yan. *Nativism and Modernity: Cultural Contestations in China and Taiwan Under Global Capitalism.* Albany: State University of New York Press, 2008.

Liao, Ping-hui, and David Der-wei Wang, eds. *Taiwan Under Japanese Rule 1895–1945: History, Culture, Memory.* New York: Columbia University Press, 2006.

Liu, Alan P. L. *Social Change on Mainland China and Taiwan.* Baltimore: University of Maryland School of Law, 1982.

Marsh, Robert M. *The Great Transformation: Social Change in Taipei, Taiwan Since the 1960s.* Armonk, NY: M. E. Sharpe, 1996.

Moser, Michael J. *Law and Social Change in a Chinese Community: A Case Study from Rural Taiwan.* Dobbs Ferry, NY: Oceana Publications, 1983.

Myers, Ramon H., ed. *Two Societies in Opposition: The Republic of China and the People's Republic of China After Forty Years.* Stanford, CA: Hoover Institution Press, 1990.

Rubinstein, Murray A., ed. *The Protestant Community on Modern Taiwan: Mission, Seminary and Church.* Armonk, NY: M. E. Sharpe, 1991.

The Story of Taiwan. Taipei: Government Information Office, 2000.

Thornton, Arland, and Hui-sheng Lin. *Social Change and the Family in Taiwan.* Chicago: University of Chicago Press, 1994.

Tien, Hung-mao. *The Great Transition: Political and Social Change in the Republic of China.* Stanford, CA: Hoover Institution Press, 1989.

Tsai, Wen-hui. *In Making China Modernized: Comparative Modernization Between Mainland China and Taiwan.* Baltimore: University of Maryland School of Law, 1993.

Weller, Robert P. *Alternate Civilities: Democracy and Culture in China and Taiwan.* Boulder, CO: Westview Press, 2001.

Wilson, Richard W. *Learning to Be Chinese: The Political Socialization of Children in Taiwan.* Cambridge, MA: The M.I.T. Press, 1970.

Wu, Tsong-shien. *Taiwan's Changing Rural Society.* Pasadena, CA: Oriental Book Store, 1973.

Yip, June. *Envisioning Taiwan: Fiction, Cinema, and the Nation in the Cultural Imaginary.* Durham, NC: Duke University Press, 2004.

Government and Politics

Alagappa, Muthiah, ed. *Taiwan's Presidential Politics: Democratization and Cross-Strait Relations in the Twenty-First Century.* Armonk, NY: M. E. Sharpe, 2001.

Chao, Linda, and Ramon H. Myers. *The First Chinese Democracy: Political Life in the Republic of China on Taiwan.* Baltimore, MD: Johns Hopkins University Press, 1998.

Cheng, Chu-yuan, ed. *Sun Yat-sen's Doctrine in the Modern World.* Boulder, CO: Westview Press, 1989.

Cheng, Tun-jen, and Stephen Haggard, eds. *Political Change in Taiwan.* Boulder, CO: Lynne Rienner, 1992.

Chin, Ko-lin. *Heijin: Organized Crime, Business, and Politics in Taiwan.* Armonk. NY: M. E. Sharpe, 2003.

Ching Cheong. *Will Taiwan Break Away? The Rise of Taiwanese Nationalism.* Singapore: World Scientific, 2001.

Copper, John F. *A Quiet Revolution: Political Development in the Republic of China.* Lanham, MD: University Press of America, 1988.

_____. *Consolidating Taiwan's Democracy.* Lanham, MD: University Press of America, 2005.

_____. *Taiwan's Recent Elections: Fulfilling the Democratic Promise.* Baltimore: University of Maryland School of Law, 1990.

_____. *Taiwan's 1991 and 1992 Non-Supplemental Elections: Reaching a Higher State of Democracy.* Lanham, MD: University Press of America, 1994.

_____. *The Taiwan Political Miracle: Essays on Political Development, Elections and Foreign Relations.* Lanham, MD: University Press of America, 1996.

_____. *Taiwan's Mid-1990s Elections: Taking the Final Steps to Democracy.* Westport, CT: Praeger, 1998.

_____. *Taiwan Approaches the New Millennium: Essays on Politics and Foreign Affairs.* Lanham, MD: University Press of America, 1999.

_____, ed. *Taiwan in Troubled Times: Essays on the Chen Shui-bian Presidency.* Singapore: World Scientific, 2002.

Copper, John F., with George P. Chen. *Taiwan's Elections: Political Development and Democratization in the Republic of China.* Baltimore: University of Maryland School of Law, 1985.

Dickson, Bruce J., and Chien-min Chao, eds. *Assessing the Lee Teng-hui Legacy in Taiwan Politics: Democratic Consolidation and External Relations.* Armonk, NY: M. E. Sharpe, 2002.

Feldman, Harvey J., ed. *Constitutional Reform and the Future of the Republic of China.* Armonk, NY: M. E. Sharpe, 1991.

Ger, Yeong-kuang, *The Story of Taiwan: Politics.* Taipei: Government Information Office, 1998.

Gregor, A. James. *Ideology and Development: Sun Yat-sen and the Economic History of Taiwan.* Berkeley, CA: Institute of Asian Studies, 1981.

Hood, Steven J. *The Kuomintang and the Democratization of Taiwan.* Boulder, CO: Westview Press, 1997.

Hughes, Christopher. *Taiwan and Chinese Nationalism.* London: Routledge, 1997.

Lerman, Arthur J. *Taiwan's Politics: The Provincial Assemblyman's World.* Lanham, MD: University Press of America, 1978.

Liu, Alan P. L. *Phoenix and the Lame Lion: Modernization in Taiwan and Mainland China, 1950–1980.* Stanford, CA: Hoover Institution Press, 1985.

Mendel, Douglas. *The Politics of Formosan Nationalism.* Berkeley: University of California Press, 1970.

Moody, Peter R. *Political Change on Taiwan.* New York: Praeger, 1991.

Rigger, Shelley. *From Opposition to Power: Taiwan's Democratic Progressive Party.* Boulder, CO: Lynne Rienner, 2001.

_____. *Politics in Taiwan: Voting for Democracy.* London: Routledge, 1999.

Shaw, Yu-ming. *Beyond the Economic Miracle: Reflections on the Developmental Experience of the Republic of China on Taiwan.* Taipei: Kwang Hwa Publishing Company, 1988.

Tsai, Henry Shih-shan. *Lee Teng-hui and Taiwan's Quest for Identity.* New York: Palgrave/Macmillan, 2005.

Wachman, Alan M. *Taiwan: National Identity and Democratization.* Armonk, NY: M. E. Sharpe, 1994.

Wei, Jennifer M. *Virtual Missiles: Metaphors and Allusions in Taiwanese Political Discourse.* Boston: Lexington Books, 2001.

Wu, Joseph Jaushieh. *Taiwan's Democratization: Forces Behind the New Momentum.* Hong Kong: Oxford University Press, 1995.

Zhao, Suisheng. *Power by Design: Constitution-Making in Nationalist China.* Honolulu: University of Hawaii Press, 1996.

Economy

Berger, Suzanne, and Richard K. Lester, eds. *Global Taiwan: Building Competitive Strengths in a New International Economy.* Armonk, NY: M. E. Sharpe, 2005.

Chan, Steve, and Cal Clark. *Flexibility, Foresight and Fortuna in Taiwan's Development.* London: Routledge, Chapman and Hall, 1992.

Chang, C. Y., et al. *Made in Taiwan: Booming in the Information Technology Era.* Singapore: World Scientific, 2001.

Cho, Hui-wan. *Taiwan's Application to GATT: Significance of Multilateralism for an Unrecognized State.* Westport, CT: Greenwood Press, 2001.

Chow, Peter C. Y., et al. *Taiwan in the Global Economy: From an Agrarian Economy to an Exporter of High-Tech Products.* Westport, CT: Greenwood Press, 2002.

Clark, Cal. *Taiwan's Development: Implications for Contending Political Economic Paradigms.* New York: Greenwood Press, 1988.

Fei, John, Gustav Ranis, and Shirley W. Y. Kuo. *Growth with Equity: The Taiwan Case.* New York: Oxford University Press, 1979.

Galenson, Walter, ed. *Economic Growth and Structural Change in Taiwan: The Postwar Experience of the Republic of China.* Ithaca, NY: Cornell University Press, 1979.

Greenhalgh, Susan M., and Edwin A. Winkler. *Approaches to the Political Economy of Taiwan.* Armonk, NY: M. E. Sharpe, 1987.

Ho, Samuel P. *Economic Development of Taiwan, 1860–1970.* New Haven, CT: Yale University Press, 1978.

Jacoby, Neil H. *U.S. Aid to Taiwan: A Study of Foreign Aid, Self Help, and Development.* New York: Praeger, 1966.

Koo, Anthony Y. C. *The Role of Land Reform in Economic Development: A Case Study of Taiwan.* New York: Praeger, 1968.

Kuo, Shirley W. Y. *The Taiwan Economy in Transition.* Boulder, CO: Westview Press, 1983.

Kuo, Shirley W. Y., Gustav Ranis, and John C. H. Fei. *The Taiwan Success Story: Rapid Growth with Improved Distribution in the People's Republic of China, 1952–1979.* Boulder, CO: Westview Press, 1981.

Li, K. T. *The Evolution of Policy Behind Taiwan's Development Success.* 2nd ed. Singapore: World Scientific, 1995.

Mai, Zhaocheng, et al. *Taiwan's Economic Success Since 1980.* London: Edward Elgar, 2001.

Poon, Teresa Shuk-ching. *Competition and Cooperation in Taiwan's Information Technology Industry: Inter-Firm Networks and Industrial Upgrading.* Westport, CT: Greenwood Press, 2002.

Reardon-Anderson, James. *Population, Politics and Foreign Intervention in Taiwan.* Armonk, NY: M. E. Sharpe, 1992.

Schive, Chi. *The Foreign Factor: The Multinational Corporation's Contribution to the Economic Modernization of the Republic of China.* Stanford, CA: Hoover Institution Press, 1990.

Simon, Dennis, and Michael Yin-mao Kao, eds. *Taiwan: Beyond the Economic Miracle.* Armonk, NY: M. E. Sharpe, 1992.

The Taiwan Development Experience and Its Relevance to Other Countries. Taipei: Kwang Hwa Publishing Company, 1988.

Wang, N. T., ed. *Taiwan Enterprises in Global Perspective.* Armonk, NY: M. E. Sharpe, 1992.

Wei, Wou. *Capitalism: A Chinese Version.* Columbus: Ohio State University Press, 1992.

Winkler, Edwin A., and Susan Greenhalgh, eds. *Contending Approaches to the Political Economy of Taiwan.* Armonk, NY: M. E. Sharpe, 1988.

Wu, Yuan-li. *Becoming an Industrialized Nation: ROC's Development on Taiwan.* New York: Praeger, 1985.

Wu, Yuan-li, and Kung-chia Yeh, eds. *Growth, Distribution, and Social Change: Essays on the Economy of the Republic of China.* Baltimore: University of Maryland School of Law, 1978.

Yang, Maysing H., ed. *Taiwan's Expanding Role in the International Arena.* Armonk, NY: M. E. Sharpe, 1997.

Yu Tsong-shian. *The Story of Taiwan: Economy.* Taipei: Government Printing Office, 2001.

Foreign Relations

Barnett, A. Doak. *U.S. Arms Sales: The China-Taiwan Tangle.* Washington, D.C.: Brookings Institution, 1982.

Bereuter, Douglas. *Taiwan, the PRC and the Taiwan Security Enhancement Act.* Collingdale, PA: Diane Publishing Co., 2001.

Bush, Richard C. *At Cross Purposes: U.S.-Taiwan Relations Since 1942.* Armonk, NY: M. E. Sharpe, 2004.

_____. *Untying the Knot: Making Peace in the Taiwan Strait.* Washington, D.C.: Brookings Institution, 2005.

Chang, Cecilia S. T., ed. *U.S.–R.O.C. Relations: From the White Paper to the Taiwan Relations Act.* Jamaica, NY: St. John's University Press, 1984.

Chang, King-yuh. *A Framework for China's Reunification.* Taipei: Kwang Hwa Publishing Company, 1986.

_____. *ROC–US Relations Under the Taiwan Relations Act: Practice and Prospects.* Taipei: Institute of International Relations, 1988.

Chang, Parris, and Martin L. Lasater, eds. *If China Crosses the Taiwan Strait.* Lanham, MD: University Press of America, 1993.

Chase, Michael S. *Taiwan's Security Policy: External Threats and Domestic Politics.* Boulder, CO: Lynn Rienner, 2008.

Cheng, Tun-jen, Chi Huang, and Samuel S. G. Wu, eds. *Inherited Rivalry: Conflict Across the Taiwan Straits.* Boulder, CO: Lynne Rienner, 1995.

Chien, Frederick F. *Faith and Residence: The Republic of China Forges Ahead.* Houston: Kwang Hwa Publishing Company (USA), 1988.

Ching Choeng. *Will Taiwan Break Away: The Rise of Taiwanese Nationalism.* Singapore: World Scientific, 2001.

Chiu, Hungdah. *Koo-Wang Talks and the Prospects of Building Constructive Relations Across the Taiwan Straits.* Baltimore: University of Maryland School of Law, 1993.

Chiu, Hungdah, and Karen Murphy. *The Chinese Connection and Normalization.* Baltimore: University of Maryland School of Law, 1979.

Cline, Ray S., ed. *The Role of the Republic of China in the International Community.* Washington, D.C.: US Global Strategy Council, 1991.

Clough, Ralph N. *Reaching Across the Taiwan Strait: People-to-People Diplomacy.* Boulder, CO: Westview Press, 1993.

Copper, John F. *China Diplomacy: The Washington, Taipei, Beijing Triangle.* Boulder, CO: Westview Press, 1992.

_____. *Playing with Fire: The Looming War with China over Taiwan.* Westport, CT: Praeger, 2006.

_____. *Words Across the Taiwan Strait: A Critique of Beijing's "White Paper" on Taiwan.* Lanham, MD: University Press of America, 1995.

Denise, Donald J., and Diane D. Pikcanas. *Can Two Chinas Become One?* Washington, D.C.: Council for Social and Economic Studies, 1989.

Downen, Robert L. *Of Grave Concern: U.S.–Taiwan Relations on the Threshold of the 1980s.* Washington, D.C.: Center for Strategic and International Studies, 1981.

Finkelstein, David M. *Washington's Taiwan Dilemma: From Abandonment to Salvation.* Fairfax, VA: George Mason University Press, 1993.

Frost, Michael S. *Taiwan's Security and the United States Policy: Executive and Congressional Strategies.* Baltimore: University of Maryland School of Law, 1982.

Gregor, A. James, and Maria Hsia Chang. *The Republic of China and U.S. Policy: A Study in Human Rights.* Washington, D.C.: Ethics and Public Policy Center, Inc., 1983.

Henckaerts, Jean-Marie, ed. *The International Status of Taiwan in the New World Order.* London: Kluwer Law International, 1996.

Hickey, Dennis Van Vranken. *Foreign Policy Making in Taiwan.* London: Routledge, 2007.

_____. *Taiwan's Security in the Changing International System.* Boulder, CO: Lynne Rienner, 1997.

_____. *United States-Taiwan Security Ties: From Cold War to Beyond Containment.* Westport, CT: Praeger, 1994.

Hsieh, Chiao Chiao. *Strategy for Survival: The Foreign Policy and External Relations of the Republic of China on Taiwan, 1959–1979.* London: Sherwood Press, 1985.

Kintner, William, and John F. Copper. *A Matter of Two Chinas*. Philadelphia: Foreign Policy Research Institute, 1979.

Lasater, Martin L. *Security of Taiwan: Unraveling the Dilemma*. Washington, D.C.: University Press of America, 1978.

_____. *The Taiwan Issue in Sino-American Strategic Relations*. Boulder, CO: Westview Press, 1988a.

_____. *Policy and Evolution: The U.S. Role in China's Reunification*. Boulder, CO: Westview Press, 1988b.

_____. *U.S. Interests in the New Taiwan*. Boulder, CO: Westview Press, 1993.

_____. *The Changing of the Guard: President Clinton and the Security of Taiwan*. Boulder, CO: Westview Press, 1995.

Lee, Bernice. *The Security Implications of the New Taiwan*. New York: Oxford University Press, 2000.

Li, Victor H. *Derecognizing Taiwan: The Legal Problems*. Washington, D.C.: Carnegie Endowment for International Peace, 1977.

Lilley, James R., and Chuck Downs, eds. *Crisis in the Taiwan Strait*. Washington, D.C.: National Defense University Press, 1997.

MacFarquhar, Roderick. *Sino-American Relations: 1949–1971*. New York: Praeger, 1972.

Myers, Ramon H. *A Unique Relationship: The United States and the People's Republic of China Under the Taiwan Relations Act*. Stanford, CA: Hoover Institution Press, 1989.

Myers, Ramon H., and Jialin Zhang. *The Struggle Across the Taiwan Strait: The Divided China Problem*. Stanford, CA: Hoover Institution Press, 2006.

Poston, Dudley, et al. *The Chinese Triangle of Mainland China, Taiwan and Hong Kong: Comparative Institutional Analyses*. Westport, CT: Greenwood Press, 2001.

Rawnsley, Gary D. *Taiwan's Informal Diplomacy and Propaganda*. New York: St. Martin's Press, 2000.

Romberg, Alan D. *Rein In at the Brink of the Precipice: American Policy Toward Taiwan and U.S.-PRC Relations*. Washington, D.C.: Henry L. Stimson Center, 2003.

Sheng, Lijun. *China's Dilemma: The Taiwan Issue*. Singapore: Institute of Southeast Asian Studies, 2001.

_____. *China and Taiwan: Cross Strait Relations Under Chen Shui-bian*. London: ZED Books, 2002.

Snyder, Edwin, A., James Gregor, and Maria Hsia Chang. *The Taiwan Relations Act and the Defense of the Republic of China*. Berkeley, CA: Institute of International Studies, 1980.

Stolper, Thomas E. *China, Taiwan and the Offshore Islands*. Armonk, NY: M. E. Sharpe, 1985.

Swaine, Michael D., Andrew N. D. Yang, and Evan S. Medeiros, with Oriana Skylar Mastro, eds. *Assessing the Threat: The Chinese Military and Taiwan's Security*. Washington, D.C.: Carnegie Endowment for International Peace, 2007.

Tan, Alexander C., et al. *Taiwan's National Security: Dilemmas and Opportunities*. London: Ashgate, 2001.

Tkacik, John J. Jr., ed. *Reshaping the Taiwan Strait*. Washington, D.C.: The Heritage Foundation, 2007.

Tsang, Steve, ed. *If China Attacks Taiwan: Military Strategy, Politics and Economics*. London: Routledge, 2006.

Tucker, Nancy Bernkopf, ed. *Dangerous Strait: The U.S.-Taiwan-China Crisis.* New York: Columbia University Press, 2005.

Wang, Mei-ling. *The Dust That Never Settles: The Taiwan Independence Campaign and U.S.-China Relations.* Lanham, MD: University Press of America, 2002.

Wang, Yu San, ed. *Foreign Relations of the Republic of China on Taiwan: An Unorthodox Approach.* New York: Praeger, 1990.

Wheeler, Jimmy W., and Perry L. Wood. *Beyond Recrimination: Perspectives on U.S. Taiwan Trade Tensions.* Indianapolis, IN: The Hudson Institute, 1987.

Wu, Hsin-hsing. *Bridging the Strait: Taiwan, China, and the Prospects for Reunification.* New York: Oxford University Press, 1994.

Zhao, Shisheng, ed. *Across the Taiwan Strait: Mainland China, Taiwan, and the 1995–1996 Crisis.* London: Routledge, 1999.

INDEX